Broken Boy

How I Survived Child Abuse and Bullying

By
Dave Rossi

Warning

This book is a work of non-fiction. Dates are approximate, but the events are exactly as they happened. Names, in some cases, have been substituted. This book contains multiple graphic descriptions of extreme physical abuse, depraved verbal and psychological abuse, and profane language perpetrated on a child by an alcoholic adult. There also are multiple graphic descriptions of peer-to-peer bullying and extreme violence from groups of children perpetrated on a child of similar age, as well as injuries described in graphic detail. This book also describes multiple incidents of suicidal thoughts as well as a suicide attempt by a child. Reader discretion is advised.

Introduction

Everything was black. So black. Everywhere that a streetlight didn't touch was seemingly blacker than usual. That was unusual with a rainstorm going on. Usually, the sky at night was grayer when it rained. Not so this time. Rain tapping at the awning hanging a few feet in the air above me was a reminder of where I was. It was also a reminder of what had happened earlier that night and why I was huddled in the limited shelter of a closed storefront a few blocks from where I lived. I tried with all my might not to focus on it. Instead, I attempted to find solace in the kinds of things that usually brought a little happiness to me.

The inky blackness of the wet asphalt in the glow of the street lamps. The trees are aglow with leaves of wetness. The drops of rain hit puddles and shimmer their surfaces. Some of the raindrops looked like sparkles, especially when they caught the headlight beams of the passing cars driving in the street.

I tried, but it was pointless to attempt to push aside the events that led me to this moment in the rain. It was past 9 o'clock, dark, and I was alone, except for the uninterested stray cat that wandered by and kept going, trying to stay close to the building so as not to get too wet.

A glow of lights paused in front of me, and looking up, I saw that it was a police car. This was the third or fourth time I had seen it drive by. I knew that I needed to look like I had only tried to get under the store awning long enough to stay out of the pouring rain so I wouldn't be completely soaked.

'Look normal. Look like you're just walking home, and nothing's wrong,' I told myself.

I stood up and started walking on, trying to appear like everything was ok, giving what I hoped were occasional non-obvious side glances to see if the police cruiser had moved on. I watched cautiously as the police car drove off up the street, and I took the opportunity to sit at the shelter of another closed storefront. This one had a much larger alcove in front, with an even bigger awning, but there was a homeless person sleeping there on the sidewalk, so I only stayed a moment before continuing on to a stoop with an overhead projection in the doorway. It offered limited coverage from the elements, but it was better than nothing.

Any refuge was welcome at this point, as I couldn't be in that house one more minute.

I rubbed the side of my abdomen, which was hurting considerably and was probably quite bruised, though I didn't lift up my rain-soaked shirt to find out. It wouldn't be easy to see anyway, in the limited light of this nighttime rainstorm away from the street light. I didn't need to see, I could feel it, and all the other injuries, and that was enough. I tried again to focus on the good things, like the fact that right now, this very minute, I wasn't being hurt.

She couldn't do it to me anymore. I had run away. I was free.

I didn't have a plan; I hadn't encountered any internal advance notice that I was going to do this; I just instinctively ran from her. She was a monster, and I had to get away. Getting away was the only thing that mattered.

She had hurt me again and again with a wood yardstick, a curtain rod, and her fists. Anything she could find was a weapon in her hands, and her anger was the greatest weapon of all. Not that I did anything to warrant such attacks, and they were much more frequent, intensely abusive, and hurtful than any typical child-related spanking. I was simply the broken boy, the bane of her existence, I should never have been brought into the world, so she reminded me every chance she had. I was humiliated again and again by her words, which were as merciless as the physical attacks that went along with them. The cuts and bruises healed, but the pain of the words lasted forever.

A crack of lightning lit the sky and the wet pavement. Moments later, a rumble of thunder followed it in quick succession. Even being in a thunderstorm was better than being in the raging storm that was my mother's existence. At least here in the streets, I had a better chance of escaping unscathed for a longer period of time. She wasn't here, and anything else that could get to me wasn't nearly as credible a threat as another bout of her flying fists and cutting words. Here, at least for the moment, I was safe.

With the lightning, a new downpour of greater intensity made it difficult to stay here under this limited shelter. I stood up and looked in front of me, and that same police car was back, this time with its red and blue lights on. Along with the cruiser's headlights, they gave the curtain of rain a bright red, white, and blue hue that looked like a glowing American flag. The cruiser parked at the curb, and an officer got out. I tried again, desperately, to look as if I was ok and pretended to be headed home. I walked on in the rain, and he called to me.

"Hey! Buddy, are you ok?"

My mind was reeling. I started to shiver, not from the cold of my wet clothes that clung to my body, but from fear. The fear of what could happen if HE, this officer, or anyone else knew what went on at home. I already knew that I was never to reveal anything that happened at home and that 'ok' was something I was guaranteed not to be if I did share anything that went on at home. That was 'our business,' as my mother put it. To make sure I remembered to stay silent, she reminded me of what would happen if anyone ever found out. She struck me across the head repeatedly with the yardstick and then punched me in the stomach and the back until I collapsed to the floor. While there, she kicked at me everywhere she could, just so I was sure never to forget that this was what I would receive every minute of the rest of my life if I brought 'them' home, which would be a very short life because she would kill me.

"I can't tell him. I won't tell him," I convinced myself in my head as I got myself in check and stopped shivering.

He came up behind me with a flashlight on and touched my shoulder. I winced, not because it hurt, but because I couldn't stand to be touched by anyone after the years of torment I had already endured.

My soaked, hole-riddled canvas sneakers sloshed a bit at a puddle on the sidewalk as I recoiled from the officer's touch. I looked at the officer's silhouetted outline of the light of his flashlight and nervously replied

"Yeah, I'm fine"

Even though I couldn't see his face clearly in this eclipsed state of light, I knew by his body language that he was disbelieving in my faked, reassuring tone.

'You don't look ok. I have seen you for quite a while tonight out here in this rain'

The red and blue lights of the cruiser cast an eerie glow around the officer, but he had an air of kindness about him. What would I say? How would I get out of this?

'Stay calm, stay calm,' the voice in my head said. Easier said than done when it feels like your heart is beating fast and hard enough to crash through the bones of your chest.

'Make up a story,' the voice continued.

"I…I…I was on my way home from my friend's house, and I left my umbrella at his house," I stammered with obvious un-believability.

The officer lowered his flashlight so I could see him a bit better. He was a big, tall man with broad shoulders and, from what little I could discern in this unnaturally lit environment, a kind face. But how could that be? I was told that people, police in particular, are not kind, and they are people to hate and despise. This is according to my mother, who hated everyone on the planet. Raindrops struck the plastic cover he wore over his policemen's hat, and the ones that fell in front dripped onto his nose and chin. Was he someone to hate? I wasn't sure. Still, I wasn't about to take any chances.

"Yeah… OK….so where do you live?" he asked, firmly planted in the soil of the business at hand.

It was the one question I didn't want to hear because it was the one question I absolutely COULD NOT answer. If I did, he might escort me there and then want to talk to my mother, and that was forbidden. If that happened, it would be my death sentence. I panicked. I could feel the adrenalin building up inside me. I begged

"Please, really, please, I am ok. I just need to get home, please just go away and leave me alone and let me go home!"

And I started to walk away from him, ready to break into a run in any direction that would allow it. His long flashlight came across my chest and held me back from getting away.

"Now look, I told you, I have seen you out here for a while tonight." He said with concern "I need for you to tell me what is wrong. What's your name?"

I didn't respond. After a few seconds, he offered

"Look, it's just a name. Can't hurt to tell me your name."

Except it WOULD hurt if Mother knew I was this close to a police officer who could find out everything.

"What if I tell you my name?" the officer asked. I refused to reply and looked down at my sneakers, which were as wet as if I had jumped into a swimming pool while wearing them.

Undeterred from receiving at least one piece of information, the officer inquired

"Ok, will you at least tell me how old you are?"

"Eight," I sheepishly replied after a couple of moments of consideration as to whether this might also be forbidden information that could bring the end of my life.

"You're really small for eight," he said. Tears welling up in my eyes, I replied

"I know" and started to shiver again. This time, the shiver was accompanied by pain from what had happened at home earlier. The dull ache became a sharp pain the more I tried to move around to keep the cold and wet shirt from touching my chest or back. Another crack of lightning, this one right overhead, and thunder that seemed to roll on forever, quivering the ground beneath our feet. The surprise of this thunderclap's power surprised me a bit, and I whimpered.

"Look, why don't we go and get a hot chocolate or something? You look like you need it." As he let go of me, trusting that I would walk with him to the greasy spoon-type restaurant a few feet away, I said again

'No, Please, I just need to go home. Please, I have to get home,' and the welled-up tears rolled down and blended with the wetness of the rain on my face.

The officer ignored my pleas and guided me up the street to the coffee shop. There were only 2 other customers inside. One was slurping soup and barely looked up when we entered. The other looked like another homeless person trying to get some shelter from the rain.

The shop was a place I knew well, as I had come to it many times with my grandma. She had very little pocket money, but when she did have it, she'd stop in this tiny diner for a coffee and toast or a muffin for her and a bottle of Coke and a donut for me. I had hoped no one who worked there would recognize me, and with my body being as soaked as it was, that was pretty much guaranteed. The only thing discernible regarding my appearance was my bony ribcage, which was quite defined in the striped t-shirt that was stuck to my chest.

A waitress working on picking up coffee cups from another table came over quickly when she saw us enter. Luckily, it was someone I didn't know. Looking aghast at me, she said

"Lord almighty, look at you! Soaked to the bone! What's going on, Mike?"

"Dunno." Said the officer "Trying to find out. Can you please bring me a coffee and a hot chocolate for my friend here?"

"Sure. Got it. Be right back" the waitress said while rushing to the side counter where the coffee pot and hot chocolate machine sat on a shelf by the wall.

I sat down reluctantly on the edge of the chair by the table the officer selected. He removed his hat, shook off the raindrops, and pulled a handkerchief from his pocket, mopping off his wet face. The waitress returned with our drinks and a dry, clean dishtowel and started trying to wipe off my face. The officer saw that I was not happy about her touching me and shook his hands in a 'no' gesture, and she just left the towel by the hot chocolate on the table and walked away, tending to the soup-eating customer a couple of tables away.

I just sat there, not taking a drink. Arms at my side. I watched as Officer Mike slurped his coffee. Realizing there wasn't enough sugar, he pulled a packet out of the condiment organizer on the table, ripped it open, and poured it into his coffee. Looking at me while he did this, he asked

"So, what am I supposed to call you? If you don't tell me your name, I'll just have to make up something. You want to tell me, or should I just call you 'burble-boop' or something?"

The comment might have elicited a chuckle were it not for the fact that this moment, this very interaction I was having, could be the last one I ever had. This conversation was strictly forbidden. I was having a hot chocolate with an officer of the law. Nothing good could come of this, but that was something I could never, ever tell Officer Mike. I didn't know how I was going to get out of this, but I had to find a way.

"Why don't you drink your hot chocolate" Officer Mike said with a note of concern in his voice again. Now he was looking right at me as if he were trying to see INTO me. Could he do that? Would he know the daily pain I suffered just by LOOKING into my eyes? Maybe he would because now, Officer Mike looked sad.

"I...I...Need to go to the bathroom," I stuttered. That wasn't really true; I just wanted to see if there was a window I could crawl out of. I had to end this unfortunate encounter, and fast.

"Ok. Come on, I'll bring you," and Officer Mike escorted me down a narrow hallway to the bathroom. He stood in the open doorway while I went to the urinal. I looked around for a window. There was one, but it was up too high, and I would never be able to get through it successfully with Officer Mike standing right there. My adrenalin rushed again. Pretend pee time finished, I zipped up my pants, huge holes in the knees and frayed at the bottom, I was a destitute sight of a child.

"All done? Ok, wash your hands,' he instructed me. I washed my hands quickly, now realizing that there was an open wound on the palm of my hand that was a defensive wound artifact of the beating I had received from my mother earlier. I winced in pain as the soap washed it clean. I took a paper towel and dried my hands as officer Mike took me by the hand back to the table.

At first, I grimaced, but then I relented. Maybe he's not the enemy. He doesn't seem like one.

'NO! You won't believe him! Don't believe him! He can't help you. No one can; she will kill you

The voice in my head warned me again. I regained what little strength I had left and shored up my firm composure, determined not to share any information or help this officer of the law hasten my doom.

When we sat back down, Officer Mike looked at me with a stern look on his face and ordered

'I don't usually get hot chocolate for anybody, so drink up,' and he then proceeded to drink more of his coffee.

I picked up the mug. It was still very hot. I sipped it carefully, and the sips were small. I never really enjoyed hot drinks. I put the mug back down and frowned, and Officer Mike started again.

"It wouldn't hurt you to tell me your name, right? Just your name. You know my name is Mike, right? What's yours?"

I thought about it, and it seemed logical that I could tell him my first name. There were a lot of other people in the world with my first name, if I told him that, it was ok because he couldn't bring me back to her just knowing my first name. Or I could make up a name. Maybe even tell him only my middle name. No one ever really uses their middle name for anything so I surmised maybe this was a situation it was designed for. He tried to make eye contact with me by placing his big hand under my chin and raising my head up. I cowered away from him as if the chair I was sitting in was against the walls of a corner of the diner, but we were out in the open, and the gesture raised Officer Mike's eyebrows. He withdrew his hand. Still, he was undeterred. He still wanted to know my name.

"How about if I guess it? Would you tell me if I was right if I said your name as a guess? "

I shook my head, letting him know that I was not up for guessing games of any kind, especially involving sharing my personal information that might end my life.

"Well, look, now' Officer Mike said with more sternness than before, "We can't just sit here all night not speaking to each other. "

I looked at him, and as if he could already see my name in my eyes just as clearly as he could see something was wrong, I blurted out, "Dave!"

Officer Mike seemed to breathe a sigh of relief in that by saying my first name, there was progress being made. His demeanor was soft and reassuring again.

"Look, Dave, I want to help you out. You're in some kind of trouble. Nobody would be out in a late-night storm like this without an umbrella, especially an 8-year-old boy unless there's some sort of trouble involved. So tell me, what is it all about? You rob a bank or something?' Officer Mike cracked a bit of a grin after asking the silly question, and I smiled a bit inside, though I didn't show it to Officer Mike.

I again buttoned up my lip, stayed silent, and grimaced.

"You weren't REALLY on your way home, were you?" Mike inquired, and then when I didn't respond and shifted my posture away from facing him head-on, he asked the ultimate question that seemed to be more of a statement, like he instinctively KNEW what I was going to say already. Like he'd seen it all in my eyes as plain as day.

"Pretty bad at home, huh?"

Another adrenalin rush tore through me. I tried to stifle it, but the surprise of his knowing of my bad home situation showed in my body language as it tightened up, and I looked at Officer Mike with surprise and fear in my eyes, betraying the truth of the matter even further. I felt the blood retreat from my face. Out of the corner of my eye, across the room, I saw the waitress show a pique of interest at the sign of my reaction as she straightened a stack of menus to make it appear she wasn't listening.

Now, with Officer Mike knowing my situation, I didn't know what to do next. Inside, I was falling apart; outside, I was trying to be stoic, to not give away any information, and failing miserably.

'Say NOTHING! Do you hear? NOTHING AT ALL,' the inner voice bellowed.

Then Mike continued with

"Must be awful to be in that house"

'He KNOWS already! Don't give him any more information," my inner voice screamed. A single tear came from my left eye and ran down my cheek. That was followed by two larger tears. I tried to play it off by picking up my hot chocolate but the heat of it was too much for me to take a big enough drink in an attempt to hide my tears. I started trembling so forcefully that I had to put the mug down, and Officer Mike saw my tear-soaked cheek and gave me a paper napkin to wipe it off myself. I ignored it and left it on the table.

"Please let me help you. What happened at home? Why are you here tonight?"

"Oh no, please don't. Please don't ask me that. I can't.... I can't..." Now, tears were running down my face uncontrollably.

"You're safe here, with me. I can help you if you let me. You have to trust someone, don't you? Please trust me. I want to help you. That is my job. I'm a police officer. I help people all day long. Let me help you."

"If you want to help me, please just leave me alone, please just leave me alone. No one can know. NO ONE!"

Now Officer Mike's eyebrows furrowed, and a look of deeper concern washed over him.

"Know about what? Know about whom?"

"I can't even tell. She'll kill me, don't you understand? She will kill me"

"Who will kill you? Please tell me."

"NOOOOO! Don't say it! Don't SAY IT!!!" the voice frantically warned. It was too late, though; the emotions of the moment took over. The words came out even as I tried to stop them.

"My mother."

"She'll KILL you?"

"Yes, she will! Oh, please don't let her find out I talked to you! PLEASE!"

At this point, my shirt was soaked a second time, this time from the tears that were pouring out of my eyes. I was desperate. How could I make him understand how bad she was, what a true monster she was? I wanted to tell him everything, all of it, just so he wouldn't take me back there, just so he could KNOW why I had to leave. The 8 years of hell I had already lived, day after day. I NEEDED him to know so that I could be safe. Just so I could be safe, but she must never, ever know that I told. But then I remembered:

Officer Mike already knew. He KNEW instinctively, it seemed, that I was in trouble, in mortal danger and suffering at every turn in that house. He knew. He wouldn't let me go back into that environment KNOWING that. He couldn't, could he?

"Please, she hurts me. Real BAD. She hurts me. ALL the TIME. Please, it's so bad. Help me, please! Help me!" I pleaded

Officer Mike was holding me now. I don't know when he managed to get his big arms around me but he was holding me, telling me he was going to help me that everything was going to be ok. I didn't push him away. I let him hug me. I let myself feel safe.

The waitress came over and asked if she could get us anything.

"Dave, have you eaten tonight? " Officer Mike asked while getting me adjusted back in my diner chair.

I shook my head. I hadn't eaten in the last 2 days. Sometimes, I would go 4 days without eating. It was partially my mother refusing to let me eat, and other times, it was because I couldn't eat. The pain in my body and mind was too much for me to bear, and the last thing I wanted to do was to eat.

"Would you like something to eat?"

"Can I please have a grilled cheese sandwich?" I asked Officer Mike, now finding the courage to trust Officer Mike enough to let him get me something to eat. When my grandmother brought me to this coffee shop before, the scarce times she had a little more money in her purse than usual, I had a grilled cheese sandwich and a coke, and it was wonderful. I rarely ate much, even when I WAS allowed to eat, unless I was at school or with grandma, and she got me something while we were out, which was only once or twice a month.

"Two grilled cheese sandwiches, please," Mike requested of the waitress.

"Comin' up." She replied as she toddled off to the kitchen to give them the order.

I was visibly shaking from this whole event and didn't say any more to Officer Mike while we were waiting and when the sandwiches came, we were focused on eating, so we didn't talk then either. The rain was coming down harder than ever, and many times, the streaking lightning and booming thunder shook the restaurant walls and windows.

After we finished our meal, the waitress brought the bill, which officer Mike paid.

I was just about ready to call Officer Mike, my friend, when he asked the worst, most terrifying thing I could imagine.

"Dave, where do you live?"

The request was so intensely negative that I became nauseous, and I nearly peed in my pants out of fright at the thought of it. Everything started to feel like it was going black again, like when my mother had a particularly gruesome beating session with me and knocked me out. How could I make him understand? How could I make ANYONE understand? Now, I felt like I had made a grave mistake in trusting Officer Mike. I was sure he understood. He had to. His eyes said he understood. I desperately enunciated, "No! I thought you knew, I can't! Don't you SEE? NO! NO! NOOOO! I CAN'T go back there! Please!"

"Look, she isn't going to hurt you. Do you really think she is going to hurt you when you have a police officer as your friend? Please tell me. Where do you live?"

I tried to break into a run, but I crashed into the waitress as I darted for the door, and it gave Officer Mike enough of an opportunity to reach for and grab my shoulder again.

I couldn't say more. I said too much already. I looked at Mike, trying to telepathically transmit the full force of the horrifying incidents that I had endured through the years in that house. Her drunken rage, her unbridled fury at my being alive. Mike looked at me through eyes filled with earnest kindness and when his gaze met mine, I felt like he really did want things to be better for me. In my mind, I created a new possible narrative. I told myself that I was going home to pack the few things I had. I believed wholeheartedly that Officer Mike was going to save me from my mother. He had to; it was his job to help people. He was an officer of the law, after all. She wouldn't DARE oppose a police officer with a gun and a nightstick and the ability to call up more similarly equipped police officers on his radio if he needed them in order to protect me. I had no other choice; I had to trust Officer Mike. I just knew he wasn't going to let me down.

I gave him my address.

I sat in the police cruiser up front with Officer Mike, and he drove for what felt like the longest ride of my life, in spite of the fact that I was not far from where I lived. Just a few blocks away. He had buckled my frail, tiny body to the seat and locked the door to my side of the police cruiser so I wouldn't be as tempted to go anywhere without him in control of it.

The windshield wipers were on full speed, swiping back and forth across a rain-filled window that never seemed to clear. Mike called in on the radio for a second car to accompany him at my house. Soon after the radio call, another car with two more officers was following us close behind. Officer Mike showed me where the switch was to turn on the red and blue lights and asked me to switch it on just before we pulled up in front of my house.

I peered out the window, and although it was hard to see with the continuous sheet of rain obscuring my view, I could discern that lights were on in my apartment. My stomach and all my insides turned into one big, knotted piece of nautical rope. Suddenly, I was wishing I hadn't eaten most of that grilled cheese sandwich. Too late for that now. The other cruiser parked directly behind Officer Mike's, and they too turned on their 'cherries and blueberries,' the slang term officers used for the red and blue lights on their cruisers, Officer Mike informed me on this short journey back to the address of my pitiful existence. When he visited my school, Officer Friendly also said that's what they called them.

We got out of the car and went up the porch stairs. Someone was peeking through the drapes of our window as Officer Mike, and I entered the hallway of my tenement building. When we got to the apartment door, Officer Mike knocked loudly. There was no answer. He knocked again, even louder this time. He was almost ready to knock again when we heard a click of the lock and creak of the hinges, and the door slowly opened.

My mother appeared as if she were surprised to see a police officer at her door, in spite of the fact she was peeking out the drapes a moment before and probably then racing to make herself more presentable and prepare a story for when he knocked. I knew this because she wore a nice blouse, one that she NEVER wore unless she was going out to the bar to get drunk, and if she were going to do that, she would have long since left the house to be well on her way to getting bombed out of her skull by now. No, this blouse was for appearances, to try and convince Officer Mike that she wasn't some sort of monster.

"Good evening, ma'am. Is this your son Dave?" Officer Mike inquired, staring intently.

"Yes, it is, Dave. I have been worried sick! Where have you BEEN!?" and she reached out to grab my arm to pull me closer to her. The fingernails dug a bit deeper into my arm as if to warn me that I better not say anything that would cause any trouble for her. She hugged me with all the feeling of a dead fish. She was good at putting on a performance.

"You mean YOU don't know?" Mike asked as the two other officers fell in behind her.

"Well, yes, I do, of course. He was upset about me asking him to eat his dinner, and he just got mad and refused to eat, and well, you know how children are. He threatened that he was going to run away, and he did just that."

Mother had washed her mouth out with mouthwash, but the scent of alcohol still permeated the air as she spoke.

Mike listened while the other two officers glanced over his shoulders to look into the apartment at whatever they might be able to see. There wasn't anything for them to see except old furniture in a broken-down, roach-infested apartment. If they looked really close, they would see areas of the rug that were discolored from my blood that dripped onto it when she beat me and forced me to clean up with chemicals while proceeding to beat me more for letting my blood get on the rug.

"He is ALWAYS doing things like that, getting mad and running away and coming back a little while later. You know how children are," and with that statement full of lies, she flashed the phoniest smile she could. It was as if her face would crack. In spite of how good she was at it, she HATED putting on a show. The revulsion was in her creaky smile, but the officers didn't seem to see or sense it. She clearly despised that these police officers were standing at her door and that she had to pretend to care and pretend what she was saying was true. She held herself together like a samurai master.

Officer Mike looked at her with eyes that conveyed understanding, and he nodded affirmatively. Inside, I was dying. He was going to believe her. My hopes of being forever free of her were sinking faster than the Titanic.

"No!" I screamed inside as I tried to pull Mike's focus back to me so he could look into my eyes and SEE the truth there again. He had seen it earlier; I was SURE of it. I had to make him see it again. "Look at me! Please! Please don't believe her! She's lying! She's lying!" I screamed in my head and implored with my eyes. The truth was that she was beating me for no reason that night, as usual, and she refused to let me come to the table to eat dinner. I could feel the knot in my stomach growing tighter. I wanted to scream out loud just HOW bad it was. I wanted him to see the things she hit me with. The belts, the sticks, the yardstick, the electrical cord on the iron, the 2 by 4 piece of wood the landlord left behind when he was rebuilding the trash can platform outside. I needed proof to show Officer Mike. I needed him to know my pain.

Where was Grandma? When she saw Officer Mike pull up, Mother must have sent Grandma to her room and threatened her so she wouldn't interfere or cause trouble while the police were there. Grandma loved me and tried to protect me from my mother, and she would say something if she had the opportunity.

Mother turned and faced me toward the inside of the apartment and told me

"Go on now, and get out of those wet clothes before turning back, she widened her eyes to silently tell me she was displeased, but she kept her tone warm while saying
"Tell the nice officers to thank you for bringing you home"

It was the hardest thing I had ever done, but I quietly said, 'Thank you.' Before turning and walking into my mother's bedroom to wait. I knew this was to be where she would want me to be so she could have her revenge on me for what I had done that night. I knew that this wasn't going to be good.

Mother said some more words to Officer Mike, and a few minutes later, he thanked her and apologized for any trouble he had caused her. All the officers left, and I looked out the window but was only able to see the glow of the red and blue lights from this window's angle. Soon, that light was extinguished, and Mother came into the room, insisting

"Go to the living room and get out of those clothes. NOW!" Her tone was colder than when she was talking to Officer Mike, but not as angry as she usually was when out of sight of other people.

I did as I was told. I walked slowly to the living room to strip out of the rain-soaked clothes. I eased off the shirt as best I could. My bruised shoulder and ribs from where she punched me earlier were making it difficult. I pulled off my sneakers and wet socks so I could get my pants off, a difficult affair due to the fact that they were stuck to the long, raw welts on my butt and thighs from where she had struck me repeatedly with a belt and the yardstick. Still, I trudged on.

When I was completely naked, Mother returned. I instinctively held out my hand to accept the new underwear I thought she was bringing, but instead, I was surprised by her grabbing me by the outstretched arm, lifting me up by it, and throwing me across the room, where I crashed into the coffee table, sending the knick-knacks on it in all directions. Tears instantly started, and I winced at the new pain from having hit the coffee table, my arm on fire where it had hit.

"Oh no, oh no, you don't!!!! OH NO, YOU FUCKING DON'T" she screamed, fury causing her forehead veins to bulge and pulse with every word and yelling into my face, "Don't you FUCKING CRY!"

And she grabbed me by the hair, dragging me across the room as she did so. Tears profusely streaming from the force of being dragged by my hair, I clutched at her hand desperately, trying to get her to release her grip, which she did only after she lifted me up fully by my hair and flung me back across the room. When I hit the floor, she continued screaming with liquor-stench-ridden breath, full force, no more mouthwash scent to cover the stink of the drinking she had done tonight.

"How do YOU get to cry when you brought THEM here?!!! You brought the FUCKING POLICE TO MY

GODDAMN HOUSE! You FUCKING BASTARD! You GODDAMN FUCKING USELESS FUCKING BASTARD! Why should you be allowed to LIVE when you CAN'T follow directions?! I said NEVER tell ANYONE, especially the police, about what happens in this house, didn't I?! DIDN'T I??!!!"

And she picked up an ashtray from the end table next to the chair and struck me across the head with it again and again. Laying on the floor, I begged for it to be over, but I didn't know if I was saying it out loud or in my head. I couldn't tell anymore. My vision was blurry from being hit so many times. Lumps were forming all across my scalp. The pain was immeasurably high.

"Think you're such a BIG man, don't you, bringing THE COPS TO MY MOTHERFUCKING HOUSE! What did you tell them, you worthless FUCKING PIECE OF SHIT?!!! What did you TELL THEM?!" she screamed into my face, punching me in the chest and then again with even more force in my belly, causing me to vomit onto my chest. I wasn't able to respond because of the pain radiating from multiple points in my body all at once. There was no time between blows to focus.

My grandmother appeared in the living room and screamed

"Shirley, stop it! That's enough, please, stop!" to which Mother darted across the room with the speed of a leopard, grabbed the yardstick from beside the second chair, and lifted it like a samurai warrior, swiftly bringing it down in front of her and causing it to make the sound it always makes as it cut through the air, approaching my grandma simultaneously.

"You get the FUCK out of here, old lady. You wanna be next? Go ahead, stick around, and I'll put YOU through the wall next. Now GO ON! BEAT IT! Get the fuck to your room and don't come out, bitch!' Mother's eyes were mad and wild with anger, and Grandma went to her room, cowering all the way into her bed against the wall, fully expecting to be hit. With her gone, I was back to being my mother's target, which she hit again and again with the yardstick. Thwack! A strike against the back,

"What did you TELL them, you stupid little FUCK?!!"

Thwack! Another across the thigh.

"Answer me, you piece of SHIT!!!!"

And another smack of the stick across my back as I attempted to retreat. She grabbed me forcefully by the shoulder and spun me around before I could escape her wrath.

"It really doesn't matter because why the hell would they believe anything a STUPID LITTLE FUCKING BASTARD says anyway. "

Thwack! This time across the head, hard. That one really hurt a lot, stinging my cheek.

"You KNOW you're STUPID. All your teachers always say so. Goddamn stupid little ASSHOLE!"

Thwack!Thwack!Thwack! in quick succession across the head and protecting hands. With nothing to protect my hands as I tried to focus on them, she came across with another blow from the stick, striking my neck. I was screaming with each connected hit. It did nothing to stop or slow down a mother from her attack.

Over and over, it went on, and each time I tried to protect my head with my hands, she struck those just as hard as well. Now she demanded

'Get your fucking hands down!" When I refused, she stabbed me hard in the ribcage with the blunt end of the yardstick, causing my hands to instinctively go to my ribs, which left my head exposed. As I turned my head to look at her, this time, she struck me across the face with the yardstick, breaking the tip of the stick.

'GODDAMN FUCKING BRAT! You broke my STICK! Fuck you, you ASSHOLE FUCK YOU!!!!!!

And she took her leather belt off. I crawled away, somehow mouthing the words, pleading

"No more! Please! No more!"

But my pleas only enraged her further. The belt came down again and again, striking me everywhere. She swung over and over, never taking a break. When she became bored with swinging the doubled-up belt, she wrapped it around her hand several times and punched me with it on her closed fist. I never knew where the next punch would land as she continued her onslaught. My nose was pouring blood, and one eye was completely closed over, like a boxer in the ring who has been struck in the same eye too many times. My jaw was swollen, and I couldn't open my mouth anymore, which was bleeding steadily from the teeth burying themselves in the flesh of the inside of my mouth when she punched me again and again in the face. Then suddenly, she stopped, but not because she was finished; now she was back to picking me up and throwing me across the room. One time, she did it by grabbing me by the arm and swinging me by it so hard that my shoulder dislocated. At one point or another, I struck all the furniture in the room, including the metal stereo cart, which my forehead hit very hard.

"Think you're gonna bleed on MY rug, you fucking BRAT! FUCK YOU! FUCK YOU TO HELL! Do you hear me FUCK YOU TO HELL!" She yanked my head back by the hair and told me, 'Lick that blood off the rug! LICK IT NOW! EAT THE RUG YOU FUCK!" I did as I was told. If only she would finally have had enough and stop this torture. But no, she wasn't done.

She started kicking me in the legs, the stomach, and the back, at which time she screamed

"Bring the police to MY house, huh? Think you're so tough, bringing them here, do you? You don't think you're some big tough man now, DO YOU? You worthless FUCK! Just a stupid little dumbass boy!" And she kicked me as hard as she could in my groin. As if once wasn't enough, she did it over and over, grabbing my arms, digging her nails into them, and pulling back as hard as she could when I tried to go into the fetal position and protect my groin with my hands. At one point, she kicked me so hard that I thought one of my testicles ruptured.

Next she went to the kitchen and grabbed the 2 X 4 from next to the back porch door and started using that to add more heft to the injuries. She struck me with it in the abdomen and groin, and one time, as I was trying to get away, she used it to sweep across my leg as I stood, hitting it hard and taking me down, causing me to hit my head on the floor when I fell. On another pass, she used it like a battering ram right into my belly, sending me across the room and crashing into the console TV.

I prayed it was over, but this went on for what felt like an eternity. Finally, exhausted, her fists swollen, her strength gone, she quit. She went to her room and slammed the door. She still had enough rage to slam it again and again until chunks of paint were flying off it and the doorway each time she slammed it. Sometimes, when slamming the door repeatedly, her already full tank of anger somehow filled up even more, and it instigated her to come at me again, but it didn't happen this time.

I was sure I was dying. I couldn't move. Every part of my body, inside and out, throbbed and cried out with pain. Every piece of me had welts, cuts, bumps, and bruises. I swore both my arms were fractured. Bits of broken knick-knacks and a busted glass ashtray were embedded in my knee, foot, and abdomen, and I was laying on top of several more pieces, stabbing at me, but I couldn't move. There was pain like a burning fire in my belly from being punched and struck with the 2x4 repeatedly in the stomach and back. Huge lumps taking up almost all of my head raised up my scalp all around. I was blind in one eye, almost blind in the other. My cheek and the side of my head were swollen and bleeding where the yardstick had struck it. Blood from my nose pooled on the rug in front of me, and though I couldn't see it at this point, my nose was 3 times its normal size and as broken as several of my ribs. I couldn't cry anymore. No tears could come out. I couldn't speak. Not even a whisper. Moving my head was impossible. Moving any part of my body was even less possible. Breathing through my slightly open and swollen mouth was the only effort I could make, and those breaths were extremely shallow due to the pain in my torso.

I knew, though, that Mother was right about one thing: the police were NOT our friend. Officer Mike WAS the enemy, after all. He had proven that. He brought me back to THAT house, and because he did, it was the worst she'd ever been. I tried to convince Officer Mike that she'd kill me, but she did far worse than kill me; she left me wishing I was dead. All those times, Officer Friendly came to my school to talk about how the police were our friends and we could count on them when we needed them most. All lies. For me, there was no escape. There would never be. As I lay on the floor suffering and bleeding and crying inside, I had to face the fact that for me, there was no shelter, and everything was black. So black.

September 1975 - first grade

The clock on the wall of the classroom showed there to only be 3 more minutes before the bell would ring to signal the end of the day dismissal. While I enjoyed reading and art in school at this point, I didn't like anything else, and I certainly wasn't any good at school in general.

In my first grade class Miss DePietro led the class with kindness toward the students, but she also was a stickler for rules and favored the students who followed them. In her class, the two biggest rules were to listen and do the work. She expected a lot of independence from her students, even if they weren't quite capable enough just yet to be able to properly exhibit it. Rather than focus on the children who needed help the most, she gravitated toward those who always completed their work without incident. That label didn't fit my disposition most of the time. I had trouble focusing and difficulty with numbers and how they related to each other. Oh sure, I recognized the numbers and could count easily enough thanks to watching Sesame Street since age 3, but in regards to math, I was at a significant disadvantage compared to my peers.

I was at the chalkboard at this moment with chalk in hand, trying to work out a problem on the board. I wasn't getting anywhere. My classmates took great glee in the times that I was invited to work out problems on the board because it gave them an excuse to make fun of me and call me names. Sometimes, Miss DePietro would chastise the class for their behavior in these instances, but more often, she let it go on. Either way, no punishments were ever given to the children who acted this way.

The hand on the clock had ticked forward one more minute and Miss Dipietro informed the rest of the class that they could put away their materials and line up at the door. I was to wait until the class was dismissed before I could go back to my desk, stash my stuff, and leave. I hated when this happened because that gave the bullies of the class a head start and, therefore, a chance to better position themselves outside to wait for me to pass, which they would have no intention of doing without inflicting pain on me. I was not only labeled as the dumb kid, I was also the smallest kid in class, and by a lot. This meant that all who bullied me had plenty of excuses to do so.

The bell rang, and the children hurriedly filed out the door of the classroom. I was still putting my books and pencil away when Miss DePietro said, "You could have left with them if you had tried to do the problem on the board."

I didn't bother to reply to her statement, didn't bother to tell her yet again that I couldn't do the problem because I didn't understand it. It did no good to try and explain it to her when she didn't care enough to help me to better understand it anyway. All that mattered now was that I could go, and I did just that, running as fast as my feet would take me down the hall toward the door to freedom. That meant I didn't have to deal with school again until tomorrow.

I was mid stride and almost to the door with my arms outstretched to push the bar to open it when Luis Matos, one of the bullies, darted out from the other hallway meeting with this one and tripped me. I fell to the floor, and a bunch of other kids laughed. Luis took off through the exit door and ran to catch up to his friends.

As usual, Mr. Shedruff, our school principal and a tall and perpetually angry-looking man, was stationed outside with his arms crossed as he surveyed the dismissal of the students from the school. He watched as the children were escorted to waiting cars or school buses and others walked home.

I surveyed with Mr Shedruff, but it wasn't his responsibility of the orderly dismissal process I was concerned with; I was focused on where my tormentors might be and whether they would again be grouped and ready to hurl insults and fists my way. I didn't see Luis or the rest of the group anywhere, and Mr.

Shedruff put his hand on my shoulder and pushed me forward, saying

"Well, the day is over. Are you gonna stand here all day looking at people, or are you gonna go home? Go on, get moving."

With trepidation, I obeyed him, moving ahead but slowly to make sure I wasn't going to encounter one of the bullies tripping me again. I got to the edge of the brick wall open gate when I saw Luis Matos. He was flanked by the other Luis and the leader of the bullies, Edgardo, whom everyone called 'Eggy.' I tried to pass them but there was no use in trying to do that because now they just created a wall around me that I couldn't penetrate. One of the other boys in my class had crouched down behind me and gout on his hands and knees. Edgardo then pushed me, and I lost my balance, rolling over the kid behind my legs and falling to the ground, hitting my head on the sidewalk.

"What's the matter, stupid? Can't walk."

Eggy asked sarcastically, eliciting laughter from the bullies and everyone else who saw the scene playing out before them. I couldn't respond as I was in great pain in my head from hitting the concrete. I tried not to cry because I knew that if I did, it would only make their attacks worse, but I couldn't help it in this instance, and I started crying hard. I tried to turn my body toward the gate to see if Mr. Shedruff was watching, but I was stopped by Luis Matos's foot kicking me back to face Eggy.

But Eggy and the rest were already moving away. They didn't want to take a chance that Mr. Shedruff would come and see what the commotion was about. Not that he ever did, or would, since what happened outside the gate of the school was of no business of the school, no matter what.

"You're DEAD if you tell Mr. Shedruff like a little pussy." Luis said as he, too, moved away from the scene, leaving me to clutch my head and the knot that was forming just above my right temple next to my forehead. I slowly got to my feet and glanced in Mr. Shedruff's direction. It seemed as if whenever this happened, and I tried to make eye contact with him, he'd always try to look away as if he didn't see me. Today was no different.

I carefully started walking toward home, and I realized that when I hit the ground, I had landed on my shoulder and busted the sleeve seam of my shirt. Now I had the knot on my forehead plus the torn shirt. That also was a common combination; my clothes in tatters and the injuries I sustained from bullies went hand in hand.

'It's ok,' I thought to myself. 'Grandma will fix it.'

That's what she did every day. Grandma lived with us because we were the poorest of the poor. Our neighborhood was one of the worst ghettos not only in the city but in the entire nation. Grandma took care of all the washing of clothes and keeping the apartment clean and she had the unfortunate job of taking care of my wounds and keeping my ratty clothes mended. There was back-to-school time shopping for clothes and no other time because there wasn't any money for new clothes, only food, rent, and utility bills. Every penny was meticulously accounted for, so Grandma was constantly active with the needle and thread, trying to keep my clothes held together throughout the school year.

Now, as I took a right turn onto my street, I looked cautiously around to be sure that some of the bullies hadn't taken up spots behind trees or other obstacles so they could continue their assault on me free from the prying eyes of anyone, like teachers of the principal. Luckily, I didn't see anyone. All I saw were old cars that were in various states of disrepair and others that people in the neighborhood were working on so as to keep them on the road. My head was throbbing with pain. I carefully stroked the injury and felt that the area had indeed raised up considerably. This was a big lump that wasn't going to reduce in size quickly with ice. That meant doom for me because of my mother.

Within a couple of minutes of walking, I reached the front porch of my apartment tenement and saw that there were two new rat holes near the front left side of the building. You had to keep your eye out for rats here because, unlike most rats, they were known to sometimes be brave enough to come out in the daylight. There didn't seem to be any nearby. I walked up the rickety, rotted wood stairs of the porch, the boards creaking with each step I took. I pushed open the large, heavy hallway door and made my way to the apartment, knocking on the door. Grandma undid the chain and unlocked and opened the door, and immediately when she saw my injury said

'Oh no, not again. Are you ok?' and she bent down and picked me up, bringing me into the kitchen to sit at the table. Two roaches that were on the table scurried away as she sat me down in one of the old chairs that made up our kitchen set.

"Get your shirt off" She said hurriedly as she went to the refrigerator to get ice. She wrapped up the ice in a face cloth and handed it to me as I finished taking my shirt off.

"Keep this ice on your head so maybe the swelling will go down before your mother gets home," Grandma said as she went to get her sewing kit to fix the shirt. She had to drop everything else she was doing when there was a moment like this.
You see, whenever I came home with torn clothes because of a beating I had taken from the bullies at school, my mother used it as an excuse to berate me and beat me even more. Grandma always hoped that if she could get whatever tear or hole was in my clothes fixed before Mother got home, maybe Mother wouldn't notice anything and wouldn't go through with any beatings this time. She tried everything she could to spare me from Mother's wrath, but ultimately, Mother didn't need a reason to beat me; she did it even without any excuse or provocation.

Grandma rustled in her sewing kit box and found a spool of thread that matched, eased it through the eye of the needle and immediately started sewing the seam as quickly as her arthritic fingers would go. The washing machine that was on had just finished its final spin and shut off. She put the shirt down and went to the washer to empty it, saying

"Is the swelling going down?"

aAnd I took the ice off it and gingerly passed my fingers over the area. It was numb now but felt no smaller.

"I don't think so," I told her, and she came over to look at it. The look of concern on her face grew deeper and hardened her soft, matronly features behind her horn-rimmed glasses.

"Well, keep that ice on it, and maybe…"

She didn't finish the sentence; she only went about finishing emptying the washer.

A bit later, she finished the sewing job on my damaged shirt and the seam was good as new. She hadn't seen my shoulder, however. Alongside the bruises on my upper back from my mother's previous day's beating, there was a new bruise on my shoulder, and it was a big one, obviously from the fall.

Now, having seen this injury, Grandma hurried me to get my shirt back on and hide the evidence.

She'll be home soon,' she said to Mother, "and you can't let her know they hurt you again."

I wondered how we would be able to hide the lump on my head, but while grandma was fixing the shirt, I went to the bathroom to look at it in the mirror over the sink and saw that the ice had finally reduced the swelling down somewhat and it wasn't as visible. Maybe Mother wouldn't see it. There was always hope.

Grandma was making chicken drumsticks and wings now, and the kitchen smelled amazing. We didn't have much, but Grandma always tried to do the most she could with what little we did have, and her cooking was really very good. What she could do with highly limited ingredients and a tiny amount of spices was truly amazing.

click of the deadbolt lock on the front door was the sound neither of us wanted to hear, but that's exactly what we heard. Mother was home. I watched as a look of dread took over Grandma's face, and she raised up her eyebrows as if to say, 'Don't let on that anything happened today'. I understood the look.

Mother threw her keys down onto one of the living room end tables and pushed past me, going directly to the pantry to get out some of her liquor. She came out with a bottle of vodka and poured some into a plastic cup on the table. She gulped some down and sarcastically said

"Well, don't everybody talk at once."

randma broke the silence with, "Dr. Sayers called and said he will be able to come by this Saturday."

"Good," Mother replied. "I need more medicine."

The medicine she was referring to was an anti-depressant that she took on a daily basis. Dr. Sayers made house calls to patients who had limited means of transportation, and since we had no car and his office was not on any bus line or close to one, we qualified for the home visits.

"No word from you, huh?" she sneered as she looked in my direction. I just looked down at my pants and sheepishly said

"Hi," as I tried to keep the lump on my head away from her view.

Now she directed her attention to starting a conversation with grandma

"I was talking to that asshole of a boss at the office about getting more hours to do the bookkeeping work, but he refuses to give me the hours. Fucken jerk'

Grandma tried not to look at Mother dead on in the face when she was cooking because if her rage was awakened, it might cause another incident like the time grandma was boiling water for macaroni and cheese and Mother picked up the pan off the burner and threw it across the kitchen, spraying grandma with hot water as the pan hit the wall. She didn't want a repeat occurrence, so all she said was

"Well, what can you do? The boss is the boss, after all. It's his company."

Grandma knew the truth. She knew that Mother had missed a lot of days due to her hangovers and drunkenness. She understood that was the real reason why Mother wasn't going to get any more than part-time hours from him. She didn't dare bring it up, however, with hot chicken and a pan of peas and carrots on the stove.

"Fucken place is gonna go under. Fuck him to hell. He's a motherfucker to work for anyway."

I got up from the table to go play with a toy truck grandma bought for me at Newberry's when she went there a few days before. I kept the side of my face with the bump away from Mother's view in case she locked eyes on me again as I passed. My heart was pounding in my chest out of nervousness that she might catch a glimpse of it. I had succeeded. I was past her and in the living room. Now, I could play safely without fear of what my mother might do. I played there for about 15 minutes when Grandma said, "Ok, time to eat."

And I came to the kitchen and sat down at the table. Grandma sat down at the table in the center position of the long side of the table, which was where Mother usually sat.

"Why are you sitting there?" she asked, squinting her eyes at Grandma as she said it.

"Just felt like it, that's all."

Grandma was trying to protect me. If Mother had to sit at the other end of the table, she'd be farther away from me and less likely to notice the lump on my head.

"Ok, whatever," Mother said as she plopped herself down in the chair at the opposite end of the table to mine, drank the rest of the vodka in her cup, and poured more.

We all started eating the chicken, and after a time, Mother said, "So, you learn anything today" while looking in my direction. I ignored her and instinctively put my hand against the side of my face, trying to hide the lump. My hand accidentally brushed the hair aside a little, making the lump more visible.

"He came home talking about some new words he was writing, right Dave?" Grandma said as she pretended to rustle my hair but was really trying to reposition it so the lump would be hidden again.

"Wait a minute. What's that?" Mother inquired.

"What's what?" Grandma said in a retort, showing nervousness in her expression.

"That on his head," Mother said and got up from the table, moving to my end of the table.

Grandma got up too and tried to get between us but was unsuccessful due to Mother moving too quickly and forcefully. She yanked my hair aside to see the bump. She grabbed my arm to lift me up off the chair and I pushed her with my other hand to try and stop her. She was too strong, and she got right in my face and screamed, "Don't you DARE push me, you little bastard." And instructed me, "Put your hand on the table."

"No, Shirley, please stop," Grandma pleaded.

"And you GET THE FUCK AWAY FROM ME" she screamed at the top of her lungs at Grandma.

"Put your MOTHERFUCKING HAND ON THE TABLE NOW, YOU PIECE OF SHIT!" she yelled directly into my face. I looked to see if Grandma had put out any knives on the table, and luckily, she hadn't. I never knew what to expect from Mother, and I wouldn't doubt that she might use a knife if one was ready and waiting. I shook as I put my hand on the table. She slammed her fist on it as hard as she could, and I retracted it and started crying.

"Put it back!" she demanded.

"Noooo," I whimpered.

She let go of my other arm, yanked my hair back, and punched me in the knot on my head

"PUT YOUR HAND BACK NOW YOU PIECE OF SHIT!" she screamed.

I put it back, and she grabbed my wrist with one hand to keep it there, and she repeatedly punched my hand on the table with the full force of her strength.

"This is what you get when you push your mother. YOU LIKE THIS YOU WORTHLESS BASTARD? HUH?!!! YOU LIKE IT?!"

She let go and then picked me up by one arm like a rag doll, my feet fully off the floor, and she punched me again on the bump on my head.

"What did you do this time to cause THAT? Huh, loser? What are you DOOOOOOOO?!"

"He got beat up by the kids at school again," Grandma yelled and tried to get Mother to let go of me by grabbing at her hand that she was using to grip my arm

"Don't you EVER touch me bitch" she yelled at Grandma, making her grip on my arm too much to bear. I tried and tried to wriggle loose but had no success. I was too small and weak. I was less like a boy of six years and more like four.

"I'll twist this fucker's arm off if you interfere bitch. Don't you even try to interfere, you hear me BITCH? I know the kids at school beat him up. Is it because you're STUPID? Huh, dummy? You STUPID in class again?! Of course, you were. Useless BRAT!"

And she punched me in the head again in the same spot and then let go of my arm. I took advantage of the opportunity and ran out of the kitchen to my grandma's room and hid under her bed. Grandma followed me quickly, slammed the door shut, and locked it.

I saw that Grandma made it to the room and locked the door before Mother could get there, and I scrambled out from under the bed.

Grandma sat on the wood bench where she did a lot of her sewing and reading and tears were running down her cheeks, which only made more tears fall from my own eyes. I crawled up onto her lap and hugged her, and said, "Please don't cry, Grandma. Please, Grandma. I love you,' and we sat there holding each other and crying for the rest of the night until Mother passed out in a drunken stupor on the living room couch.

November 1975 - First grade

The end-of-the-day school bell echoed throughout the hallways of the school, and you couldn't find a time when there was a group of happier kids than this time of the day. Everyone poured into the halls with the vigor of an Olympian, realizing they won the gold medal.

I looked to stay close to my best friend, John, who was one of only 2 kids I actually called 'friend.' Bullies picked on John from time to time, too, but much less frequently. John did well enough in his subjects where he didn't seem like the dunce that I was. He wasn't as easy a target, even though, like me, he was small for his age. The difference with John was that he didn't wear the same clothes quite so often, and he wasn't as skinny and frail as I was, with my bony stature and non-existent musculature. Anyone looking at me thought I was from some third-world country where they didn't have enough food to eat, which actually was closer to the truth with our poverty-stricken household.

Other than my grandma, John was one of the only people I counted as an asset in my young life. Where everyone else seemed to be against me, John was someone I felt I could count on.

So here we were, with everyone else in the hallway moving toward the exit door with its tube push bar. I reached it first, and since the door was one that tended to stick, it was difficult for me to open. John lent a hand before the kids behind us protested and got the door open.

On more than one occasion, especially when the bullies from the class were directly behind when I wasn't able to push the door open, they pushed me into the bar in an effort to get through the door, which, like everything else they subjected me to, led to injuries.

Today, the bullies had gone first through the door and were already outside and shouting obscenities and insults my way, but I ignored them and kept moving with John. Today I was going to his house. The bullies had expected me to take my usual right toward my house, and so they were waiting for me on the right, and it threw them off when I went in the opposite direction toward John's house.

He had some new Legos to play with, and he wanted to show them to me. His father had surprised him with the Legos the previous weekend, and it wasn't even John's birthday, Christmas, or some other special occasion or holiday. John's parents bought him things whenever they felt like it, and that wasn't any kind of luxury I enjoyed.

John's parents weren't rich, but their mom worked in an office, and his dad worked for one of the insurance carriers. John didn't have a babysitter, but the next-door neighbor kind of peeked in on him from time to time, as was common for what was termed latchkey kids in the 1970s.

We ran up the street, crunching the acorn tops that littered the sidewalks. We always moved quickly to John's house because there were lots of things to do, and I never stayed long. If I did, mother got upset. If I wasn't home when she arrived from her afternoon bar trips or from working the part-time jobs that never lasted for her, she punished me even more severely than usual.

We got to John's house, and he offered me an apple like always. John's mom loved apples, and she always kept them on the table for the family and their guests.

I declined the apple this time, and we ran to John's room. John pulled out his new Lego box, and we rummaged around through the box, pulling out different sizes, both of us building spaceships.

We spent a lot of time building with the Legos, and as it neared the time that John's parents got home, I started to become nervous. I looked at the clock on his night table by the bed. John noticed I wasn't as into building as I had been before, and since this was a common trend every time I went to his house, John sat up a bit straighter and, while clicking another Lego in place on his spaceship's right wing, he asked, "What's wrong?"

I just looked up at him like I didn't know what he was talking about.

"You always want to leave right when we are having fun."

"I have to. When it gets to be dinner time, Mom wants me to be home."

"Well, you know, you can eat here. Want to stay for dinner?"

Even though I really wanted to, I couldn't, and there wasn't any way I could explain it to John. I couldn't tell him of the beating I would get if I weren't home. Anyone finding out what went on at home was forbidden and worthy of Mother's ultimate wrath.

"I can't. I have to be home soon."

"Why?"

"I just have to, that's all."

The door downstairs opened, and John's mom shouted upstairs

"Hey Johnny! I'm home."

"Hey, Mom. Dave's here."

"Ok. Is he staying for dinner?"

John looked at me as I shook my head and turned his head to shout back out to Mom, "Naw, he's going home soon."

"Ok, well, too bad. We are having chicken casserole tonight."

That was one of John's favorites. He turned to me and licked his lips at the thought of his mom's delicious casserole. I felt bad for making John feel sad that I wasn't staying to play with him again, so I told him, "I guess I will go home now."

"Now?! Dinner's not for another hour?!"

"Yeah, I just remembered we are having chicken casserole, too."

Which was a lie. We were having pork chops, which I detested even more than the terrible frozen fish sticks we ate, but they were cheap, so we had them once or twice a week. Plus, there weren't any other options to eat. If I didn't eat what was served that night, I just plain wouldn't eat, and I would get a beating from Mother just before bed so that my pain would keep me awake alongside my empty stomach. Of course, when it was pork chops or fish sticks, I frequently didn't finish everything on my plate and would get beaten just as badly as if I hadn't eaten at all.

We walked out to the living room, and John's dad walked in from work, messed up his hair, and gave him a half hug.

John's parents were always doing stuff like that. I was convinced that was only a show for when visitors were in the house. I surmised that John's parents didn't really love him like they tried to make it appear. I just assumed that based on my own home life situation, every other kid's life was the same, and every child was regularly berated, called names, and beaten severely by their parents. How would I know any different? After all, this was the only experience I had at a young age.

John looked up at Dad as if to say, 'Stop embarrassing me in front of my friend,' and said, "Ok, see you tomorrow."

John's dad said as he did every time I visited, "Dave, you should stay and have supper with us some night."

And I responded with my usual reply, "I will. Just not tonight. Gotta get home."

I grabbed my jacket, which I had tossed on the floor by the hinged side of the front door when I arrived.

I ran as fast as my feet would take me. The streetlights had already come on, and it was starting to get dark. I knew that by now, Mother was almost certainly home. John only lived 3 blocks away from the school, but that meant I had to go those three blocks plus the block and a half from the school to my street and then past 4 houses on my street before I got to mine.

When I reached the porch, I slowed down just enough to still be almost running into the hall to my apartment door. I turned the doorknob, but the deadbolt lock was locked. I knocked. My grandmother went to the door and started to unlock it when mother yelled

"No! Don't open it. He knows the rules and how he needs to be home after school. He can stay out there in that hall and rot. Little fucking troublemaking twerp."

I may have been in the hall, but I could hear the slur in all of Mother's words. She was already well on her way to a drunken stupor.

I knocked and knocked, to no avail. The next-door neighbor thought someone was knocking on their door, so they opened their door, and the lady my mother referred to as 'Fang Face' peeked out. Since she hated everyone, Mother always had nasty nicknames for them.

"Please let me in!" I pleaded again and again. Nothing.

After an hour of sitting in the hallway, finally, the door opened. Grandma had opened it after Mother had passed out on the couch from all the booze.

"Come on. Don't make any noise. You know what will happen if she wakes up."

Grandma reminded.

I went to the kitchen as quietly as I could. Grandma was warming up my dinner in a little pizza oven one of Mother's former coworkers had given her for Christmas one year. I sat down at the table, and the sugar bowl top rattled a bit.

Within seconds, Mother was awake, and she came to the kitchen to see what the noise was. When she saw me at the table waiting for dinner to be warmed up, she moved toward me, and I instinctively brought my hands up to my head in protection mode. She just decided to punch me in the back, where I wasn't guarding. Then, she grabbed one of my hands, twisted it, and flung me out of the chair at the same time. I fell to the floor and tried to scamper away into the pantry. I didn't make it there because she grabbed my left foot and dragged me across the living room carpet, giving me rug burns on my arms and hands. When we got close to the door, she grabbed me by the hair to stand me up. I squealed and screamed with pain from her pulling my hair hard enough for some of it to be left in her hands.

"Open the door!" she demanded. When all I could do was cry with the pain, she kicked me in the ribs and screamed, "I said open the FUCKING DOOR!"

Now, I was bent over and wailing from the kick to my ribs. She grabbed me by the hair and slammed my head into the door.

"Open the FUCKING DOOR YOU FUCKING BASTARD! NOW! Do it, GODDAMNIT!!!"

Now dizzy and tears flowing like a river, to the point I couldn't see, I tried to comply with her demands. I turned the deadbolt and opened the door.

"Get OUT!" She yelled.

I was shaking my head when, before I knew it, one of her feet was coming at me again, and it made contact with my hip. The force of her thrust lurched me forward out into the hall, and I hit the floor with a thud. She slammed the door and went back to the kitchen, where she unplugged the pizza oven and brought it to the door. She opened the door and threw the oven with my dinner into the hall, where my pork chops, peas, and carrots flew out of the oven and crashed against the hallway floor.

I cried over and over for the next 3 hours until my grandma finally came to me after Mother passed out again on the couch. Grandma picked up the pizza oven, which now was severely dented on one of its front corners, and brought it back into the house. She tried to get me to come inside, but I refused. I didn't want more of the same treatment for coming back inside again, and she woke up. I stayed there all night in the hallway and watched as the roaches feasted on what was supposed to be my dinner.

October, 1976, second grade

The schoolyard always bustles with activity in the morning, and this day was no exception. Children played games of tag, others played wall ball, and still others hung on the monkey bars and the climbing rocket ship in the playground area. Unlike play places of modern times, there are no soft edges, no cushy foam, and no thought for safety of any kind. The equipment is anchored to the asphalt and the children swing precipitously over it and inevitably fall upon it.

Mr. Shedruff is standing by the door to the school with his usual stern expression. Teachers mill about, keeping a watchful eye, but only when they know the principal is watching them. Now, Mr. Shedruff turns and walks inside the school building. Instantly, the few teachers on the playground relax their guard and pay less attention to the students and more attention to having conversations with each other.

The bullies know about the teachers' waning attention as the principal leaves, and they take full advantage of it.

I was on the rocket ship climber about 3/4ths of the way to the top when Edgardo and his buddies decided to start in with their usual tactics of intimidation and abuse.

"Hey dummy, watch out now, don't fall," Edgardo yelled up, getting the attention of the other kids on the structure started to climb down to get out of the path of the bullies' behavior.

I stayed where I was, transfixed to my spot on the narrow steel tubing that made up the rocket ship structure. I knew that if I climbed down, I would only be leaving myself open to whatever they had in store. If I climbed to the top, I might lose my grip and fall. Staying where I was clearly ruled as the only choice for me.

Luis started climbing and he made his way to me quickly where he climbed around me so he could get above me. Once there, he edged himself over, standing on the same bar that I was holding with my hands. I tried to move to the side but couldn't do so fast enough and Luis stepped on my left hand.

Now I grabbed onto the vertical tube next to me, where one of the other bullies was already moving up. Now Luis and the other bully were kicking and punching at me so that I would fall. Edgardo just stood pointing and laughing, waiting for me to fall at his feet in front of him.

Luis used the heel of his sneaker to stomp on my shoulders. The pain is tremendous both from the place where he is kicking and in my armpit and upper arm that is clutching the iron bar to try and stay on. I start to scream and cry, and Edgardo warns me

"Hey, shut the fuck up, or we are gonna kill you after school today!"

But I couldn't stop screaming. The pain was too much. Luis was destroying me with his feet. He stomped and kicked relentlessly as I tried to maintain my grip on the structure, which I nearly failed to do on numerous attempts, only evading a fall by re-grasping a bar at the last possible millisecond. The other bullies were now on either side of me, punching me and clutching at me, trying to fling me off the rocket ship to the asphalt below.

"What's wrong, stupid? Too dumb to hold on?!" Edgardo taunted from below.

Then it happened. Luis got in a great kick to my arm, making me let go, and then he kicked me across the forehead, and I fell to the ground, but not before striking my arm on one of the rocket ship bars as I fell.

The pain was instantaneous and searing. I screamed.

Edgardo got down next to me and punched me in the ribs, telling me

"If the teacher comes, we're gonna kill you after school. You hear me? Wanna die, dummy? Huh? Do you?"

He could have been sharing the cure to cancer and plans for definitively achieving world peace; it wouldn't have mattered. I wasn't hearing Edgardo, only my own screams from the pain in my arm and my bleeding knee and elbow that had hit the asphalt.

Now, hearing what was going on, a teacher from another classroom came over, walking slowly, since my screams had interrupted their conversation with colleagues, and they were annoyed by it.

"Move aside," the teacher instructed the onlookers. Edgardo and his cronies had already dispersed when they saw her walking over.

Tears drenched my face and chest while huddled in a sort of modified fetal position; I alternated between holding my left forearm and my right elbow and knee.

The teacher looked me over, hoisted me into a standing position, brushed me off, and ushered me forward, informing me

"We're going to the nurse's office. Come on, let's go."

And she shook her head and made hand gestures toward the other teachers, denoting her displeasure that I was ruining her morning by needing medical attention.

The information came with zero effect or note of concern, just matter-of-fact delivery. I was just another kid who was causing trouble for the school staff attending to supervising the playground. There was no attempt to find out why it happened, who might have been involved, and therefore, no consequences for the bullies who perpetuated the event.

It was excruciating for me to walk, my knee pain causing me to wince and more tears to flow with every step I took. The arm that struck the bar was already swollen and starting to bruise noticeably.

After what felt like a lifetime, I finally arrived at Nurse Booth's office. She was a middle-aged lady with horn-rimmed glasses similar to my grandmother's glasses; a kind demeanor always seemed to be generated from her.

"Oh my, what happened to him?" She asked the teacher.

"Fell off the rocket ship." The teacher replied with all the effect of a prison guard speaking to an inmate.

"Well, let's see what's wrong here," Nurse Booth continued as the teacher left, never looking back.

"First, let's see about this knee," She said as she moved the now torn knee patch that grandma used to cover up a hole that occurred a couple of weeks before from another altercation with the same bullies.

"Ok, those pants are going to have to come off" She insisted, and helped me by removing my shoes. I then stood up and slowly took off the pants to reveal a knee that was badly scraped from the asphalt, dirt still in the wound, and a scrawled blood trail down my shin.

She cleaned around the wound first with some cool water on a white, soft cloth. As she got close with some of her passes of the cloth, I flinched, afraid she was going to touch the wound.

"Now I am going to have to clean this scrape," she said, to which I shook my head vigorously, eyes wide, screaming, "NO! NO! NOOOO!!"

She put her hand on my shoulder reassuringly and softly said

"It's ok. There's no medicine on the cloth, just water. We are just cleaning it. It won't hurt, I promise."

After giving a protesting scowl and shifting my leg away from her, I eventually timidly accepted her words as fact as she tried again and again to reassure me I wouldn't feel it and let her continue.

She gently and gingerly touched the wound with the cloth, going back to the sink to rinse it and returning with a newly wet and clean cloth to finish the job.

After finishing, she got a bandage roll and put some medicine on a gauze pad. She told me

"Now, I need you to be a big boy. You might feel a little bit of pain as I put this bandage on, but I promise I will try not to hurt you as I put it on, ok?"

I was afraid, but I was feeling a bit more trusting of her since she hadn't hurt me when she cleaned the knee. She was just as careful and attentive to not causing me pain as she applied the bandage, wrapping it around my knee and finishing with some tape to hold the end in place. Now, she focused her attention to other areas of my body, noticing that I had a knot forming on my forehead where Luis had kicked me.

She went to the refrigerator, pulled out some ice, and placed it in an ice bag she retrieved from the nearby shelf.

"Here, hold this on your head while I look you over. How many fingers do you see?" She asked while holding up 3 fingers.

"Three," I quickly replied.

She looked at my arm and saw the swelling there, and with great concern in her voice, she said, "I am going to have to get a better look at that arm and to do that, I am going to have to touch it. I know it hurts, but I have to make sure it's not broken. Will you let me touch it? I will try really, really hard to make it so I don't hurt it even more than it already does, ok?"

I nodded so she knew it was ok and I timidly held up my arm for her to have a better look at.

She carefully checked and re-checked and sometimes touched the area ever so gently.

She got more ice and another ice bag and told me

Hold this bag on your arm while I look at your elbow. Luckily, that only required some cleaning and a Band-Aid, though it was one of the big Band-Aids usually used for large knee wounds.

"I will be right back," she said as she left the room to go into the office next door. When she returned, she said the words that destroyed my mood far worse than the injuries ever could hope to:

"I have to call your mom."

lurched up out of my seat, dropping the ice bags to the floor, tripping over my pants on the floor as I lunged for the phone receiver in her hand, pleading, "No! Please don't! Please don't call her!"

Nurse Booth looked through and above her glasses with surprise, saying, "It's ok, you will just get to go home early; you get a day off from school."

I vigorously shook my head. 'No,' and she took her glasses off, placed them on the desk, and put her hands on my shoulders. I cringed as I did whenever anyone touched me. She quietly said

"David, I HAVE to call your mom. When a child gets hurt at school, mommies and daddies need to know about it. If you are afraid of missing a day of school and being in trouble, don't worry. Mom will be ok with it because you are hurt."

I thought about what she had said. I had been hurt plenty of times at school, and my mother was never contacted. Sometimes, it was just because teachers were too busy to be bothered; other times, I had done all that I could to try and hide whatever happened from Mother. I hoped that if she didn't find out, I would be spared from another beating. More often than not, it didn't work. She nearly always found out, and I was subsequently on the floor pleading for her to stop hitting me or being comforted by Grandma afterward.

And mom would most certainly NOT be ok with me missing school because I was hurt. If anything, it just meant that now there would be more hours spent at home where she could torment me between her daily neighborhood bar visits and booze drinking at home.

Plus, there was the torn knee patch that was now flapping wide open and the blood staining the knee area. These were beige-colored khaki pants that would be impossible to get free of blood stains.

Ignoring my protests, Nurse Booth went to the office next door, retrieved my file, and then dialed my number on the black rotary dial telephone, and I was deflated. I went back to the chair, sat down, put my pants and shoes back on, and placed the ice bags back where they belonged on my injuries so they could be numbed for the moment. One thing was certain: no amount of ice bags would be enough to numb my body after the beating from my mother I was certainly going to receive today. I shook and shivered at the prospect of the terrible day that now lay ahead for me.

After a couple of rings, someone answered. Nurse Booth spoke to the mother about the various injuries involved in this incident and agreed on a time about a half hour from now for her to come pick me up from school.

During the time I waited, Nurse Booth attended to me several times as she checked the temperatures of other children who entered the office, claiming to feel ill. Most were just kids who didn't want to be at school and they were claiming to be ill so they could go back home. During her passes back and forth between the children trying to bamboozle their way out of a school day, she checked to see if the swelling and bruising on my arm and head were getting any worse. My knee was feeling less pained now, but I was sure that once I started walking around, it would begin to hurt again. Maybe I would be able to stay at school. I would gladly take the place of one of the kids trying to go home. They would eventually be found not to be sick, and they'd have to stay at school. That would be better than my fate at my mother's abusive hands that I would have to endure for ruining her drinking binge.

After sitting there with Nurse Booth for about 45 minutes, Mother walked in the door. She glanced at me with eyes that were both a warning of what was to come and a show of fury at the fact that I had done something negative that required her to show up and deal with the people at school. Mother being forced to interact with anyone was a strict no-no, so I was now just as sure as ever that I was really going to get it bad when we reached home.

"Ok, so is there anything I have to sign to take him home' was all she mustered, saying, mostly to the air and not to Nurse Booth, who was attending to a sick girl sitting in another chair across from mine.

Nurse Booth, clearly alarmed at mother's blurted outburst upon entering, responded with

"Ma'am, who ARE you?"

Mother looked at the nurse with a smirk of disdain and said, "I'm HIS mother," and pointed to me as if I was some sort of family reject that shouldn't be seen in daylight, which, unironically, was the way Mother felt about me.

"Well, if you'll give me a moment, I will get the paper for you to sign, and I would like to go over a couple of things."

"Well, hurry up, lady; you know people don't have all day."

Nurse Booth glanced back in mother's direction and gave a look of disdain all her own.

Mother instructed me to take off the ice packs and get ready to go home. I was beyond ready NOT to go home, but there wasn't going to be any choice in the matter.

Nurse Booth handed Mother a clipboard with an early dismissal form, and Mother signed it, turning toward the door to leave when the nurse said, "Now, I don't think the knee is too bad, but that arm needs to be looked at, and his head probably should be too."

"Oh, don't worry, his arm and head will be 'looked at,' "Mother retorted sarcastically, shaking her head as she left and then forcefully grabbing me by the hand, voicing with actions her level of displeasure for this misadventure that now threatened to interrupt her daily drunken escapades.

I knew that the only 'looking 'that would take place at my arm, was going to be done by me. I knew in my heart that I wouldn't be going to any doctor or the emergency room where I would be headed with any sort of parents who loved me.

As we turned the corner to my street, instead of continuing to walk straight ahead on the route that would take us toward the hospital, I knew my fate was sealed: No doctors would look me over to be sure I was ok.

We reached the stairs to the house, and I resisted, saying, "I thought we were going to the hospital."

, "Well, you thought wrong, dipshit" You're not going to any hospital. Now GET INSIDE!" and she yanked my arm hard, throwing me toward the stairs to our tenement building.

e got inside the apartment, and Mother told me, "Get out of those pants so Gramma can sew them AGAIN." I took off my sneakers and eased out of the pants, leaving them on the couch. Mother picked up one of my shoes and smacked me across the head with it repeatedly.

"Little fucking troublemaking loser!" Can't even get INTO the school before fucking things up now! Have to start the day in trouble. WHY?"

AShe hit me in the head 3 more times with the shoe; my hands went up to my head to protect me, but she grabbed my swollen, bruised arm directly on the injury, squeezed it hard, and threw it aside. I screamed with new agony, and she told me through clenched teeth and a crazed look in her eyes

Shut up! Shut the FUCK up! Does it hurt? Does it HURT you fucking pussy?! Does it REALLY?" as she continuously hit it with the shoe. Now, she told me to take the bandage off my knee. I kept pleading with her, screaming, "NO!! NO!!! NOOOO! PLEASE DON'T!"

But when I didn't move fast enough, she lifted me by my ankle with one hand and unwound the bandage with the other hand. Now free to the air, the injury was fully exposed. She grabbed the yardstick and struck the knee wound repeatedly. I tried again and again to get free and move away, only to have her grab me and throw me back down to the floor in front of her so she could continue her assault. She struck the knee wound again and again, and whenever I tried to block her attempts, she struck my swollen arm with the yardstick or her fist, too.

After 20 minutes of this, she relented to my and my grandma's pleas and left the room in a huff, slamming the door to her bedroom. Before entering, she demanded

"And don't YOU try and help him by getting ice. The little troublemaker needs to learn a lesson."

I wondered what lesson I was supposed to be learning from this circumstance that was never my fault in the first place. Grandma did as she was instructed thought, and even though she held me and comforted me while Mother was in her room, Grandma didn't dare get any ice for me.

When mother emerged a few minutes later, she was dressed to go out to the bar, but she would have a long wait because the bar didn't open for another 5 hours. No matter. She used the time to cut into a six-pack of beer and some gin. By the time she was ready to leave for the bar, she was already wasted, and I was still trying to recover from the increased pain of my injuries. Finally, after she left the house, grandma applied face cloths filled with ice to my injuries, and I wept again and again, not from the pain, but from the sorrow of knowing that I was nothing but a worthless troublemaker to my mother, in spite of the fact that I didn't cause the troubles I always seemed to be in.

My injuries screamed with pain, but I didn't even care. I just wanted one thing: to be dead.

Officer Mike – Part 2 – October 1979

Light poured into the living room window, although I couldn't appreciate it. I could barely see it. I was still in the exact same position that I had been left in the night before when I had received the near-death experience of a beating after Officer Mike left. All I could do was smell the scent of the rug, and with the state of my destroyed nose, barely even do that.

My body was reporting in from every station that things were not good. Even if I decided to move, I wouldn't be able to do so effectively or in any manner that resembled normalcy.

I thought about what it would take to die. How could I still be alive after what had happened? I couldn't imagine how much worse mother's attacks would have to get before death finally released me from them. What would it take? Just how much more would she have to do?

My breaths were still shallow due to the damage she inflicted on my ribs. There was a certainty that multiple ribs had to have been broken. I instinctively knew that. She had punched, kicked, and used objects to hurt that area of my body on numerous other occasions, but the results were never this intense.

I couldn't be sure, but it felt like I would be unable to move from my spot. I felt trapped there somehow, frozen, as if I were paralyzed. Was I? Had she hurt me so badly that I was now unable to ever walk again? I didn't know, couldn't know for sure. It was possible due to the extreme level of her attack.

Maybe in all the horror of it, she had broken my back permanently beyond repair. I thought that perhaps that would be the wake-up call that she needed, that if I were a paraplegic, she wouldn't hurt me anymore, that finally I would be free of her anger, and maybe that she might even be locked up for what she did.

Then I thought about Officer Mike and how he had completely let me down. If he couldn't have been counted on to save me from the terror that was my mother, surely the rest of the officers and representatives of the law would be no better. No, I had to accept that there wasn't going to be any reprieve to come from anyone related to law enforcement. This was simply my fate, even if I were in a wheelchair. Mother would probably use that as an excuse to hurt me even more anyway. I would be a sitting duck, unable to escape whatever she wanted to do to me if I were confined to a wheelchair for the rest of my life.

If I were a cripple, would I have to go to school? I didn't know. I had never seen any disabled kids at my school. If not, I would at least be free of the bullies. Life is certainly an interesting prospect when being permanently paralyzed is the one thing you can hope for to improve your situation even a little bit.

Could I even talk? I tried to say something. Nothing would come out. I wasn't able to breathe enough to make a sound without the effort, bringing about searing pain from multiple points in my body.

Then, I heard a noise that made me tense a bit. The involuntary and instinctive response from my brain caused a ripple of pain to rise across most of my body. Multiple areas and injuries all join together to sing a chorus of agony.

I heard sounds again and recognized them as the squeaks of the mattress springs of Grandma's bed. That meant she was getting up. At least there was a tiny amount of good news. If she were up, maybe I could get her to confirm whether my body was damaged beyond repair, was too wrecked for me to ever be able to walk again.

Now, Grandma had opened her door and padded quietly to the living room in the cheap slippers she had bought from Bradlees. She glanced over in my direction, and a look of horror came upon her face as she saw me in that destroyed state, lying face down on the living room rug.

I tried to say something but couldn't manage the words, couldn't get them out. She understood. She came over and knelt by my side and tried to lift me up off the rug. I tried to tell her no, that it would be too painful, but I couldn't speak. I started to understand some of the nature of why I seemingly couldn't move. Blood from my nose and a cut on my face had congealed and dried around my face on the rug, and it was stuck to the rug, as were my stomach and one of my legs due to cuts that also bled profusely and cemented me to the rug.

As Grandma tried to release my face from the blood that had become an adhesive, it felt like the two sides of Velcro were tearing apart, except that it also hurt immensely.

"NOOO," was all I could get out, and it took every effort and all the strength I could muster to do it, and the result was another wave of resounding pain.

"Ok, Ok. I know, I Know. I will be right back." Grandma assured me. She went to the kitchen, took a dry dishcloth from a cabinet drawer, and poured hot water over it, returning quickly to my side.

She applied the cloth to my face, pushing the wet cloth against the dried blood that was keeping me immobile. Slowly, a bit at a time, her work paid off, and my face was free. She went to work on the other areas of my body that were adhered to the carpet in the same manner. Each one was eventually freed the same way. All of the effort, though, was wreaking havoc on my broken body.

"Ok, let's try and get you to sit up. Ok?"

"No. Please, No," I weakly said, tasting the remnants of blood in my mouth from my mother's violent activity. I desperately tried to stop her from getting me into a seated position, but I eventually relented, though I wished that I hadn't because now my body was protesting any movement at all, initiating searing, heated waves of pain and begging for a motion to stop.

Somehow, I was now in a seated position with my grandma hugging me across the shoulders and upper back. Under normal circumstances, I would have given anything for one of grandma's hugs, as they were consistently the one thing that could get me through even the worst aftermath of attacks from mother, but this time, I was in too bad of a circumstance, and I couldn't stand being touched at all, I used whatever effort I had left and pleaded

"Please, no, Grandma, please don't touch meee," and the tears of agony poured down my face onto my chest, blending with congealed blood there and running down my torso.

Now I begged, "Please make it stop! Please!!!! It h-h-h-hurts. It h-h-hurts s-s-s-soooo much!"

"I know, baby, I know… Grandma will stop the pain. Where does it hurt the most?" Grandma said while letting go of me. I couldn't answer; my sobs were coming too strong, and I was almost hyperventilating while crying, the result of which was causing my ribs to sing with as a result of their damage even more.

"Ok, ok, don't worry… we are going to make it stop. We will. Grandma is here. Grandma will make it stop. Calm down. Calm down."

She reassured me while gently stroking my chin and cheek, two of the only safe places where injuries were non-existent on my whole body.

Now she got up and went back to the kitchen. She returned quickly with two washcloths filled with ice, put one in each of my hands, and gently raised my hands to my face where the ice could do its work, numbing the area and hopefully reducing swelling. Each ice pack found an eye. That was good since the left was sealed shut like a prize fighter after a particularly punishing bout, and the other was nearly shut completely as well.

She picked up the washcloth that she had used to free my stuck body from the rug and cleaned around a deep cut on my arm. Grandma worked gingerly and carefully, with great precision and focus on trying not to induce more pain from the welts, lumps, and bruises that populated my arm. A medical professional could do no better.

She then gently pulled a piece of broken glass from my stomach next to my belly button. The wound wept with blood, but given the severity of the rest of the elements making up this circumstance, not so much to cause major concern.

Next, she focused her attention on my right leg, where there was another piece of broken glass protruding from the skin on the side of the calf muscle. Unlike the piece of glass she had just removed from my stomach, this piece had penetrated deeper and because the blood had dried around it, trapped it, preventing it from being removed. She could have used the washcloth to free the glass as she had done to get me freed from immobilization on the rug, but since this piece seemed deeper embedded, she didn't want to take a chance that this wound would bleed a lot when the glass was removed.

"Look, I am going to have to go to the store to get some things to help you." She told me as I winced and tensed up every couple of seconds as a response to the extreme level of pain that I was in.

If she left, that would mean I would need to stay here with Mother, who might wake up at any time and do God knows what to me since my blood was now staining the living room rug.

"NOOOOOO! Please don't leave me! PLEEEASE don't! Take me with youuuuuu!" I pleaded with the determination of a prisoner of war, begging to obtain their freedom as they watched one of their fellow soldiers escape. That analogy is accurate, too, because, in that house, there was a war every day with Mother around.

"I can't take you with me. We don't even know how bad the injuries are. I will be back quickly and I will have more things to help you then." Grandma reassured me. She stood up slowly and walked to her room, where she got out of her bathrobe, slippers, and nightgown and into a dress and outdoor shoes. She returned wearing her raincoat that served as her light spring and summer coat as well and said, "Now don't you move, you hear? You stay put right here until I get back. Don't you move an inch?"

I wanted to tell her that I wouldn't move, but I think she understood that I felt that I couldn't move anyway, as it would elicit pain from too many places if I did.

I stayed still as an icicle and didn't move a muscle except to breathe, which was and would continue to be shallow.

After a few moments I heard the distinct stirrings of mother. It sounded like she was trying to get out of bed and to her feet. My stomach clenched, and I bit my swollen upper lip and hoped against hope that she wouldn't enter the living room until Grandma returned with whatever she was getting from the store to help my situation. My hopes were short, however, as Mother opened the bedroom door and dragged her feet laboriously through the living room on her way to the bathroom. That reminded me that I needed to pee. I would have to wait until it was safe to move again.

A few moments later, Mother repeated her labored gait through the living room, past me, as if she hadn't even seen me, and she shut her bedroom door. By the sounds coming from her room, the squeals of the ancient mattress and box spring were an indication that she had gone back to bed.

Thank goodness.

Maybe I could count on being safe until Grandma got back. I hoped her return would be quick, both because of my mother's sudden activity and the horrendous pain I was experiencing.

What seemed like forever but was really only a short while later, according to the clock on top of the TV, Grandma returned with bags of stuff. She had taken the two-wheeled grocery cart that we used to lug all our supplies home from the store. In it were brown bags filled with three bags of ice, bandages, gauze roll, tape, adhesive butterfly closures, and St Joseph's chewable aspirin for children. There also was a splint kit and ace bandage.

"It won't be long now. You'll be feeling better soon," she said while looking at me with that knowing look of concern she had when she was worried about whether or not the words that were coming out of her mouth were true.

She gave me a chewable aspirin from the bottle after she had removed the cotton, put away her coat, and took the bags of ice to the bathroom, where she poured them into the tub along with cold water. After a few minutes, she turned off the water.

"Look, we have to get you into the tub to get all the swelling all over your body to go down so I can better see how bad the injuries are. It won't hurt; it will just be very, very cold. It will be good because it will stop a lot of the pain, too. Ok?"

Nodded carefully up and down to the affirmative so as not to induce too much pain with my own motions. She came over to me, knelt down, and instructed, "Now grab onto the back of my neck with your left arm, not your right, and I am going to lift you up to take you to the tub."

I did as I was instructed, my arm singing with agony anyway. She scooped me up carefully and brought me to the tub, placing me gently in it. The cold was jarring, but I dared not move too much. When I was submerged, I stayed as still as possible.

"Now, wait here until I get back. Don't lean to the side on the leg with the piece of glass." And she went back to her room to take off her outdoor shoes and get back into her slippers.

As I lay there in the tub, waiting for what was to come next, I thought about what the rest of my life would be like if I were, in fact, crippled. Would grandma have to tend to me this way, putting me into a bath and to bed and in and out of a wheelchair every day until the day she died? Mother certainly wouldn't do it, so my guess was yes.

Grandma returned a few minutes later with two towels. She laid one out on the bathroom floor for me to sit on. I put my hand out to grasp her neck again, and she reached down into the bath to put her arm under my legs and lift me out of the water.

She placed me carefully on the towel on the floor, once again in the seated position. She dried off my hair carefully and patted my face and body as gently as she could, getting most of the water off me. Now, she took the opportunity to check my wounds and injuries. She pressed areas with as little pressure as possible.

She said matter of factly, "This arm may be fractured." While moving on to other areas.

Then she arrived at my ribs on both sides, I winced and withdrew from her touch, indicating to her a concern that she had voiced, "…and you probably have several broken ribs."

She then focused on the piece of glass in my leg. She got a butterfly closure, square bandage, and gauze roll ready before pulling the glass out. After being in the water, the glass now was easily removed. She had been right to wait until now to take the glass out. The wound started bleeding profusely. She wiped the area with a wet facecloth, dried it with another and then pinched the wound closed and placed the butterfly closure over it. She placed the bandage over that and wrapped it with the gauze roll.

Everything was hurting but nowhere near as much as it would have if she hadn't submerged me in the water earlier. Grandma knew, though, that this numbing cold situation wasn't going to last long, so she worked quickly.

Next, she focused on the right arm. She placed the two pieces of rigid wood in place and wrapped my arm with the ace bandage. My arm was small and the wood pieces were long and came down to my hand and went past my elbow, but it was going to have to do because there was no possibility of going to the hospital. Mother would never allow it, and if Grandma tried to take me, Mother would either make Grandma's life a living hell afterward, beat her too, lock her out of the apartment, or all three.

"Your other arm might be fractured too, but I didn't have enough money to get two splints," Grandma stated with sadness, causing tears to well up in her eyes. She had been saving that little bit of pocket money she had in her wallet for a trip to the diner and the S and A store that weekend so that she could buy me a small toy. Now, it had to be spent on these first aid supplies instead. How I hated Mother for taking what little joy Grandma had in this world. It meant the world to her to take me out for a soda and a toy, and it really meant so much to me, too, because it was the only time I could be free to enjoy my time with Grandma without the fear of what mother might do because she was in the next room or due to arrive home soon.

Grandma had almost nothing but what she had she always shared with me. There was little money left over from her social security check that she used to help her mother pay the rent and bills. Usually less than $10. She tried so hard to make things better for me, and she loved me far beyond the pity she felt due to my mother's abusive nature.

She examined my back and looked at my eyes again. The swelling that had closed my eyes wasn't going down, and that was bad news because that meant the injuries could be more severe. My nose was three times its normal size as well, and there was little doubt it, too, was broken.

"She may have broken bones in your face too, I don't know. We'll just have to pray that you'll heal up ok. It's going to take time, though. Probably a lot of time." She said with concern in her tone. Now she focused on all the welts and bruises, checking to see if there might be any more broken bones.

If the healing was going to take a while, that meant I would probably not be going to school. Not because Mother would be concerned about my injuries but because she would be more concerned about what people might think of the way the injuries were sustained. It might bring questions from teachers or school officials or, worse yet, the authorities, and she wouldn't have that. I would be out of school for an extended period of time with some excuse that she would dream up, like the flu or pneumonia or bronchitis, that would warrant a longer stay at home. Being home, at least, would keep me from having to endure beatings from the bullies at school, so at least there was that tiny silver lining in this cloud of doom.

Now Grandma went to the medicine cabinet to get the Band-Aids out to put on the rest of my open wounds, and I cried silent tears as she finished her work. The numbness of the ice water was wearing off, and I was beginning to intensely hurt at all points in my body again.

'Ok, I think we can maybe get you up and walking," Grandma stated with some level of certainty. I wasn't so sure, so I emphatically said

'Nooo, please, not yet. I don't want to yet!'

"Ok, Ok, we won't try walking yet. How about getting some clothes on? Maybe then you'll feel better," Grandma said as she went and retrieved some clothes for me to put on. I don't think she believed her own words, she was just trying to make me feel better at the suggestion of it.

Although the attempt was excruciating, with Grandma's help, I got a pair of underwear, pants, and a T-shirt on.

"Ok, ready to stand up?" she inquired, knowing full well I wasn't, but I decided to try anyway. I reached up for her hand to steady and guide me to my feet and was able to stand. She let go of my hand almost completely, and without her stability to rely on, I fell to the floor. The pain was just too much. Now, I was bawling out loud because when I fell, my splinted arm hit the bathroom floor, sending waves of pain up and down my arm.

"It's OK, I've got you. I've got you now, and I promise I won't let go again," and she knelt down to lift me up to a standing position while she hugged me.

The crying had brought Mother out of her room, however, and now she was standing sternly by the bathroom with her arms angrily crossed, veins popping out on her forehead.

"What's all this FUCKING NOISE going on?' she screamed as grandma stood up with me in her arms and brushed past mother while continuing to repeat, 'It's ok, I've got you, I've got you,' and while giving Mother the most intense scowl of contempt that she could, she brought me to her bedroom, laid me on the bed and went back to the bedroom door, which she slammed and locked as mother was now approaching it.

April 1977, second grade

For most of the kids in my class, a joyous time was about to take place. No, it wasn't recess; it was gym. Anytime gym class would come up; it was a time for fun and joy for those who found it to be a welcome release from the burdens of having to sit in class. In my case, it was yet another reason for the rest of the boys in the class to point out just how much different I was from them. It wasn't enough that I was small for my age and had difficulty in the classroom; I also had to be blessed with being a boy who had no skills in sports.

Most boys are at least somewhat athletically inclined, but that was not true in my case. I hated nearly all team sports because I was no good at them. Soccer and indoor hockey were the only games I was even remotely adept at playing with bare minimum proficiency, but of course, those were the two games that were played the least. The rest of the time, I had to endure kickball, baseball, softball, basketball, and, worst of all, football.

As I was thinking about and dreading the fact that I was going to have to be part of gym class, in my mind, I heard the taunts and chants from the other boys, calling me derogatory names for my inability to play their beloved sports games that they had obviously taken more seriously than anything else in their lives. They acted as if sports were the end all be all of existence, as if time itself would cease to exist and the universe would collapse in on itself if their game went poorly or if they were unable to play.

The bell loudly rang, and everyone grabbed their rolled-up towel and gym uniform and shuffled out the door with the teacher as lead at the front of the line and the assistant teacher at the rear, escorting us to the two locker room doors in the hall outside the gym.

"You ready, faggot?"

Edgardo, who stood behind me in line, chirped while jabbing his finger in my shoulder quietly, already taking the opportunity to insult me with the favorite one used by boys who could play sports to describe the boys who couldn't. There was apparently some unwritten but male-agreed rule that said if sports simply wasn't your thing, you couldn't be a true male, and being a homosexual was the go-to derogatory statement for anyone not thought to be a real man. Actually, being labeled gay was the way that kids described any behavior, actions, or out-of-the-ordinary traits. It didn't matter if the fact was that you weren't gay, or even whether you could understand what the label meant, your actions were simply labeled as such, and by virtue of your actions, you automatically were thought to be gay. 'Gay' or other similarly associated words were simply the substitute words for 'abnormal.'

A couple of chuckles from two other boys followed Eggy's insult and made me remember my humiliating experience of not being able to hit the ball the last time gym took place and what an absolute fool I must have looked like as I tried to execute the play with the posture and stance Mr. Quage coached me to use to be successful.

Miss Lloyd, the second-grade teacher, didn't chastise Eggy for his remark other than to elicit the 'Shhhhhhh' quiet sound, reminding us to walk quietly while in the hall. It was always more important for teachers to make sure we weren't too noisy in the hall rather than dealing with derogatory remarks and taunts.

Mr. Quage was the physical education teacher for the boys and he knew all the ins and outs of the strategies and mode of operation for every game. He tried his best to teach me anything he could each time it was my turn to do something or to correct my actions when I did something wrong, but no matter what ways he tried to help me succeed in any sport, it was to no avail. I simply never was able to make my body do the things that were required to make plays or do whatever needed to take place in the games.

There were times I envied the other kids for their ability to excel in sports, if only because their ability to do so made them appear normal in the eyes of everyone else around them. I didn't care that they were actually good at the games for the game's sake, as I never enjoyed even being a spectator of most sports except hockey. It all seemed so silly and pointless, even watching others do all of these required actions that seemed foolish or ridiculous in the overall scheme of things. I just never understood why anyone found any of it interesting in the slightest. Apparently, though, liking sports in any capacity was normal, as most everyone did, or at least seemed to, so, of course, I was abnormal.

Coach Quage opened the door to the locker room and allowed us to file inside.

As we changed into our gym shirts and shorts, Mr Quage told us, "Today, boys, we are going to play baseball again."

My feeling of dread came back ever stronger as Luis Matos called out, "Maybe the faggot will hit the ball today."

And his comment was rewarded with laughter from the rest of the boys, the sound of it echoing off the walls and hanging heavily in the air.

After finishing changing, Mr Quage told us to line up at the door by standing near the door to tell us that was where he wanted us. He was a man of only necessary words and descriptive phrases that helped the kids to do well in their games, but not much else. Sports was more than an activity for Mr. Quage; it was his way of life, and everything else took a secondary focus or back seat, at least to the children he taught.

Mr. Quage was ALL man if using sports as the barometer of what makes a man was the measure of choice to prove it. In his office were the many trophies, certificates, and awards he received for winning championships in a variety of sports. His walls were populated with his team photos going back to his time as a youth.

Now we were all lined up, so Mr. Quage opened the door, and we all ran to the baseball field of the schoolyard, or at least what qualified as the baseball field. Mr. Quage had placed bases on the grass that the other kids recognized as first, second, and third base and home plate. While I recognized home plate, I didn't know first from third and wouldn't know the direction to run even if I did somehow suddenly gain sports ability and magically hit the ball.

My only chance at some reprieve from the foolishness of the activity was if my best friend John were named as one of the captains of the team. That was rare, of course, because Mr. Quage frequently named other, more adept players as captains. John wasn't bad at sports; he was just adequate, so he wasn't an obvious first choice to be captain. Plus, John had been recently named captain, so it wasn't likely that it would happen again today, and it didn't.

Edgardo and Luis Matos were the choices to be captain, so humiliation was going to start right away because neither one of them wanted me on their team, so I was simply the last kid who got assigned to whichever team had the final pick. Frequently, in these circumstances, the captain wouldn't even name me, just walk away as they picked the second to last kid while I sheepishly looked down at my shoes, trying not to look in their direction, not because I was sad that they weren't choosing me, but because I wasn't good enough to make them want to pick me. I didn't like sports, but it would be nice to at least be adequate, so I didn't seem to be as abnormal as I obviously was.

I was on Eggy's team this time, and we started out in the field while Luis's team was up at bat. I was always assigned to the outfield where I would have the least amount of expectations to be forced upon me. Rarely did any of the boys hit the ball hard enough to come as far as the outfield. That was good, because I wouldn't be able to throw the ball hard enough to whichever teammate guarding whichever plate I was supposed to get it to.

We didn't ever play a full set of regulation innings, just as many innings as could fit into the timeframe of the gym class. Still, that meant I had at least a couple of instances in the field and a couple at bat, plenty of time to showcase my lack of skills and prowess as the male of the species, and plenty of time to be reminded of the fact by all the boys in class.

Now it was my team's turn at bat, so we exchanged places with the other team that was on the bench waiting for their next turn to swing moments before. My heart raced with anticipation, not in a good, anticipatory way like most boys had when they knew it would soon be their time to swing the bat over home plate, but with fear and anxiety because this was the thing that I did worst and would be ridiculed for relentlessly by the boys on both teams. Plus, making it worse was the fact that I was on Eggy's team today. If I did something that caused his team to lose the game, it would make the after-school beating all the more brutal today and the rest of the week.

'I'm going to hit the ball today.'

I told myself.

"I'm going to get a run today."

I tried to convince myself in my mind, though every fiber of my being knew that this was just a fantasy and a highly unrealistic one at that.

John was the third person on my team at bat. He got two strikes before hitting the ball, but it was caught by the third baseman, and he was out.

At least he had hit the ball. Eggy said, "Good try, good try. Ok, come on, Antonio, let's get a hit!'

aAs Antonio took up the next turn at bat

I was about to be up to bat after the next kid. Anticipation had my heart feeling like it was pounding so hard it might escape the confines of my ribcage.

Finally, it was my turn. My stance at bat was completely wrong. Mr. Quage came over and adjusted my footing and arm positioning, and picked up the bat to show me how to swing my hips in an attempt to hit the ball.

"Look here, over the plate, and only swing at it if you are sure that you are within the means to hit it."

He told me as if I was supposed to somehow gain instinct as to when I was within 'means' to hit the ball.

The ball came toward me and I thought I was within the means to hit it, but I swung the wooden bat and missed, looking ridiculous as I mistimed how and when to shift my weight into the swing as Mr. Quage had told me. Laughter and insults became a cacophony on the field, and Mr. Quage made a quiet motion with his hands and came back to my side at home plate.

'You swung when the ball wasn't in the zone. It wasn't a pitch you should have swung at. Only swing when it's a good pitch."

Ok, sure, that sounded like good advice, but how exactly would I KNOW if a ball was in the Zone or not? What was a good pitch? What made it good? What made it different from a bad one? I guess all of this was just more of that sports instinct that I didn't possess.

Mr. Quage positioned my legs and arms again for the next pitch and went back over to the bench to try and get my teammates to cheer me on positively instead of negatively.

I just was looking forward to my turn at bat being over with, and I could go back to the outfield where I could just stand and do nothing.

The pitch came in slow, and I swung and made a hit, but it was a weak hit, and it went off to the side of home plate.

'That's not a strike, it's a ball.'

Mr Quage said.

"That's good. You saw that it was in the zone, and you hit it. Now try and only hit the ball if it's in the zone and its moving fast enough."

This was more of that sports knowledge that was foreign to me. The ball coming toward me was the ball coming toward me. I wasn't able to decipher whether it was moving fast enough to hit it. How would anyone be able to tell that?

Mr. Quage did all his work to get me in the right position once again, and a few seconds later, the ball was coming at me and it was moving fast, so I swung, and it was way too early before the ball got even close to the home plate box, and I completely missed.

"That was a good swing, but it wasn't at the right time." Remember, your timing is important too. Swing at the ball at the right time, swing only at balls moving at the right speed and swing only at balls in the zone

Mr. Quage told me as he repositioned me again, this time seeming a bit annoyed.

This was so much to remember, so much to know how to do. How did the other boys do it? I had no idea, but right now, I didn't care. All I cared about was hoping that this would be the last time I'd have to swing this stupid bat at this stupid ball in this stupid game.

The ball was coming in fast, was in the zone, and I swung at just the right moment, but my swing was way off, and I missed. That was my third strike

"Sit down faggot, and let someone get up there that can hit the ball, loser!' Eggy shouted to me.

One more time in the field and at bat had come and gone, and now we were all headed back into the locker room to take a shower. We were required to shower after gym class so that we didn't go back to class stinking it up.

This was always the worst time for me because it was a time for the rest of the boys to ridicule me even more for my terrible performance in gym class.

'He's just a baby who can't play baseball. He'd rather be sucking his thumb. Are you gonna suck your thumb? Huh, little baby? Luis Matos sneered while the other boys laughed.

"He's a faggot baby. He wants to suck something else. Hey faggot baby, you wanna suck something else?" Eggy chimed in while moving his naked hips around and making all the other boys except John and Juan, my two only friends, laugh continuously.

"That's enough of that. Get to the showers," Mr. Quage told the boys, and he positioned himself at the edge of the doorway to the showers where he always stood and handed out the soap from a metal pail containing them.

The school provided these small bars of soap that got reused over and over until they were gone, and today, we had a lot of new bars. That was bad because Eggy and the rest of the bullies liked to throw the soap bars at me, and when the bars were new, the sharper edges and corners hurt more when they hit me. Every time Mr. Quage turned his head, one of the boys took the opportunity to throw their soap at me. One of the other boys would kick the soap back over to the kid who threw it before Mr. Quage could regain his focus on the shower room. Today was no different. This time, 3 boys simultaneously threw their soap bars at me. One hit my chest, another hit my head, and the third hit my groin.

As the boys finished their shower, they exited, dried off with their towels, and went back to the lockers to re-dress themselves for class. If Eggy finished quickly, he took the opportunity to do something to my clothes. Today, he threw my shirt up on top of the lockers.

When I was getting dressed, I always put my briefs and pants or shorts on first, then my shirt, so I was standing there in my pants and looking for my shirt. John knew that they had thrown my shirt on top of the lockers, and he climbed up on a bench to try and get it down for me, but he couldn't reach it. Mr. Quage saw him and said

"What the hell are you doing? Get off that bench before you fall and get hurt."

"Dave's shirt is up there," John told him.

"What? Again? Didn't I tell you boys to stop throwing clothes on top of the lockers?!" and he stood upon the bench himself to get the shirt down. He handed it to me, and it was covered in dust and a large dead beetle. I tried as best I could to get the dirt off my shirt as well as the beetle. I brushed at the dirt with my clean hand, getting it dirtier than when I entered the shower a few minutes earlier.

Eggy waited until Mr. Quage went over toward his office door close to the locker room exit to pick up the beetle off the floor where I had left it.

"Get his hands."

He told Luis Matos, who put me in a half nelson, pinning my arms and preventing me from being able to use them or my hands effectively.

"Open your mouth faggot baby," I refused as he tried to stuff the dead beetle in my mouth.

"Come on, open up," Eggy demanded while the other kids stood and laughed. When I tried to turn my head away, one of the other boys held my head in place while he tried shoving it between my lips in into my mouth. One of the beetle's legs broke off and fell to my chest.

"I SAID OPEN UP!" Eggy yelled and stomped on my foot. I cried out in pain, and the moment my mouth was open, in went the beetle, and the boy who was holding my head was now using his hands to keep my jaw shut.

"Chew, bitch!"

Luis Matos said between yowls of laughter. I refused.

"You boys need to finish getting dressed and get to the door to line up, or you're gonna be late for class."

Mr. Quage said while walking in the general direction of the lockers where the bullies were tormenting me. As his voice got closer, the boys relented their attack, and I was able to spit out the beetle. The idea that it was in my mouth was enough to make me nauseous enough to throw up. I pushed past boys who were laughing and trying to block my path, and as soon as I got past them, I ran as quickly as I could to the toilet and vomited.

When I washed my face and hands afterward, I found all the other boys had finished getting dressed and were waiting in line to go back to class. Mr. Quage was standing in the middle of the locker room with his arms crossed; a look of disdain was on his face.

"Why do you always have to be the last one dressed? Come on David lets go."

And he helped me get my shirt on and then told me, "Now, get your shoes and socks on."

I did as he said, rolled up my gym clothes in my towel, and got to the line at the end.

"Yum yum," said one of the boys, prompting spontaneous laughter from the rest of the boys who had seen what happened.

"QUIET!" Mr. Quage said loudly, "You're going back into the hall to walk back to class quietly."

The two teachers were waiting for us in the hallway, and they walked us back to class, ending another wonderful, joyous, fun-filled time in gym class. All that was left to do was wish I were dead, as usual.

Later, the school day was over, and even the bell seemed to be excited about the prospect. It seemed to ring more energetically than usual, signaling the time of day that most kids looked forward to with the enthusiasm of the most positive person on the planet. For me, as always, it was a mixed blessing. Sure, I was happy not to have to sit in that classroom anymore for the day, but it also meant I would have the brutality of the bullies and mother to look forward to, today even more so.

During recess after lunch, I was playing tag with my friends John and Juan when Eggy decided to start trouble as usual, mocking my running and yelling', "Look at the dumb baby run," making flamboyant and exaggerated gestures, mocking the way I ran while catching up to me and shoving me with his hands, interrupting our game. The other children laughed, some making silly, mocking running gestures of their own. Juan got tired of their daily attacks on me, and today, he decided he was going to do something about it.

'"Leave him alone, Eggy." He demanded and moved quickly toward Eggy and pushed him hard. Eggy lost his footing and went to one knee for a brief couple of seconds. Juan was not big, certainly not as big as Eggy or Luis, but he was strong. His arms were short, but they were thickly muscled.

"You wanna fight' Eggy said as he got back up and moved face to face close to Juan.

"Let's go," Juan said with arms open wide, welcoming the opportunity for Eggy to throw the first punch so he would have a reason to hit back. Juan was smart. He knew that with witnesses who would see Eggy throw the first punch, Eggy would be suspended.

But Eggy was smart, too. He glanced at a teacher a few feet away, now looking in this general direction.

"Naw, that's ok. Later. We'll do it later." Eggy told him, edging away from Juan and never blinking his eyes as he cautiously watched both the teacher and Juan simultaneously.

The rest of the day unfolded with Eggy taking every opportunity to pick on me even more, especially when he knew that Juan was watching, just so that he could try and appear superior and challenge Juan into doing something before it was a good time.

One time, we were walking to art, and Eggy got behind me and put his foot on my butt, and thrust me forward into Juan, who was in front of me. Eggy and his friends laughed as he said

'Baby's still learning to walk; AWW poor baby fall down and go boom.'

When Juan looked at him in anger for what he had done and said, Eggy just used a similar motion to Juan's with his arms outstretched as if to say, 'Come on, I dare you to hit me.'

"What's going on back there? Stop fooling around, and let's get to the art room."

The teacher called out in an attempt to stop the commotion.

During art, Eggy got up to sharpen his pencil, and on his way back to his table, he jabbed me in the side with the sharp tip while I was drawing with my own pencil. I jumped and scrawled a mark across my drawing when he surprised me.

"Awww, poor baby can't even hold a pencil," he said with mock glee as his friends giggled along. Juan, who was sitting across from me at the same table, was only able to give a disparaging look in his direction and try to ignore Eggy's pleas to start a fight.

The day unfolded in much the same way as Eggy tried again and again to get Juan to throw the first punch.

Now, with the bell ringing and signaling that the students could leave the building until tomorrow, the moment of truth had arrived. John and I waited in the hallway for Juan, and after a few minutes of not seeing him, we decided to leave. It was possible that Juan's mother had brought him to the cafeteria where she worked as one of the lunch ladies. She sometimes picked him up at dismissal and had him wait with her in the cafeteria while she finished the end-of-the-day duties in the kitchen.

decided that today, I wouldn't go home, and I asked John, "Hey, can I come over today?"

"Sure," John said, "I've been working on a new starship with the Legos'.

I couldn't be happier because I knew that meant I was home free to be able to avert a beating after school today, and it meant another afternoon of building with Legos alongside my best friend, something I absolutely loved to do.

We took a left outside the gate of the school and avoided Eggy and his crew, who were off to the right and obscured by the crowd of children moving through the gate.

John's mom and dad had arrived home at separate times, and his Mom went right to work in the kitchen.

"Will you be able to stay this time?"

John's mom asked me.

"We are having macaroni and cheese casserole, John's favorite." It served not only as John's favorite but mine as well. I said, "Sure."

The word flowed effortlessly from my lips. John's mother seemed surprised as I usually always said 'no' to her invitations. Not this time.

I didn't even care what my mother would do to me for being late, had barely given it even a first thought, let alone a second, until John's mother reminded me

"Well, just make sure to call home to make sure it's okay for you to stay for dinner. Your mother might have something she's working hard to make for you. "

'Mother? Make something nice for dinner? For anyone?!'

I thought to myself. Oh, if she only knew how ridiculous a prospect that was. Mother was probably stumbling drunk already and well into her journey toward passing out drunk by now. Cooking was never even the third priority she could think to do, cooking was grandma's department. I had called home earlier and pretended to talk to mother, holding my finger over the receiver button and talking to no one, telling John and his parents afterward that she said it was ok for me to stay. If I had actually talked to her, she'd have told me no and that I'd better get home quick, or the beating would be even worse. There was no hope of Grandma answering the phone either, as Mother forbade Grandma from touching the phone, ever, unless she was the only one home.

After thanking John and his parents, I put on my jacket and headed for home. I wasn't even running this time. It was fully dark, and I didn't care. I had a good night, and I wanted it to go on a little bit longer.

Suddenly, something came at my face and struck me dead in the right eye, knocking me down. I saw stars flowing again and again.

Someone had stepped out from the bushes of the front yard of a house. As I was on the ground, someone else came up to my left grabbed me by the coat, and pulled me up, punching me in the stomach before I could fully get to my feet.

A third person behind me struck me with something long and hard that might have been a tree branch or a baseball bat. It was dark here, with the streetlight blown out. I couldn't see anything clearly; all I knew was that people were hurting me.

Another punch landed dead center of my face, and my nose instantly started spraying blood down my mouth and chin finally landing on my shirt.

"Where's your bodyguard now, huh, dumb baby?" Eggy's distinctly mean voice asked in the chilly night air as another punch to the gut and another hit to the back happened at the same time.

Now another fist to my left eye and I was back down on the ground again, when they lifted me again because they weren't finished.

"I don't see Juan anywhere, do you, dumb baby?"

And now, an even harder punch to the stomach followed by a kick to the groin. I crumpled to the ground for the last time as I heard the boys running away.

Someone walking by saw me on the ground and picked me up

"Oh my god! Come on, let's get you home."

I just waved the person off and said

"No, no… leave me alone; I'm ok."

I hadn't realized just how bad things were and the fact that I couldn't see out of either eye very well as they were both closing over from the swelling caused by the punches. Not seeing or sensing it, I walked off the side of the curb, nearly into a car driving by, when this bystander pulled me away from the traffic.

She said, "I will walk you home because I don't think you're in any shape to do so on your own." I surmised that she was probably right, so I let this unnamed stranger walk me home. We got to the next house over from mine, and through the small slits between the swelling of my eyelids and lower eye areas, I could see the light in my apartment.

I told the bystander, "That's my house right there. The one on the first floor with the blue flowered drapes." I informed her as I pointed.

"Ok. You sure you can get there alright?" she inquired, still seemingly unsure of whether or not I was able to get there under my own motivation and ability.

"Yeah, thank you."

I said with as much reassurance in my voice as I could feign.

I walked up the stairs slowly as my Good Samaritan buddy turned and walked back in the direction of her own home.

When I got into the house, I was lucky enough to find that Mother had gone out to the bar tonight, so she wasn't there to make my agony worse. She would inevitably see it the next day, however and surely that would initiate her wrath. I was just happy that I wouldn't be getting any more suffering right now. Thank goodness for small mercies.

Grandma did her usual good job with ice and wet facecloths to clean me up. She put my blood-soaked shirt into the dish pan she used when washing dishes and sprinkled a liberal dose of powdered Tide detergent over it. She knew this time; there was so much blood, my shirt would have to get this pre-wash of sorts overnight if there was to be any chance of saving it.

The ice had done its job of reducing the swelling of my eyes and nose, although they did remain slightly puffier than usual.

My back, on the other hand, had large bruises and was extremely sore and sensitive to the touch. Whatever that object was, it had done a number on me with the help of the bully who was wielding it.

I sat on the couch, afraid to sit with the back of the couch supporting me, as the pain would surely be severe if I put weight against my injuries.

"Is it broken?" I asked grandma

"Your nose? Probably," she replied matter of factly.

"No, my back."

No, I don't think so," she said as she gently reached across my shoulder, inspecting the severity of the bruised areas.

I decided to lie down on my side. Grandma stayed beside me for the next two hours. As I lay there, tears started to fall from my eyes. I wondered, as usual, if dying could be much worse than my sad excuse for an existence.

The next morning, I was still on the couch in the same position. I hadn't slept, and I was in the same position I had put myself into the night before. Mother had come home after 2:30 in the morning.

Now it was 7:00 am, and Grandma was up and pouring cereal and making toast for breakfast.

"Come on. Come and eat," she said as she guided me to my feet. The whole right side of my body was asleep from being in the same position for too long a time. I had to wiggle my arm and leg to get it to wake up, and this motion served as a reminder that I had injuries to my back, which now sang a song of pain from my motions, trying to get my body back to normal. Now I had the pins and needles sensation in my arm and leg.

I walked to the table and plopped into the chair, causing me to wince from another pain jolt.

Mother heard the noise and came to the kitchen to see what was going on. Her breath hung in the air like a lead weight, the air thick with the stench of alcohol and cigarette smoke from all the bar patrons and their bad habits.

Mother poured herself some tomato juice but, this time, decided to forego the usual vodka that went with it to make her bloody mary wake-up beverage.

She sat down at the table and glanced in my direction.

"What the fuck happened to you?" she asked with furrowed eyebrows, the anger lines in her forehead above her nose creasing.

"Now, don't start, Shirley. He got jumped by those bullies on his way home."

"Good. That's what he gets for coming home late. What time did he even get in?"

"6 o'clock," Grandma lied. It was closer to eight, but Grandma didn't want it to seem even worse than it was. Mother had left at around 5:30 to take her tour of the bars nearby.

"So you got home over 2 hours late," and she got up and moved to my side of the table. I put up my hands instinctively to defend myself. She took the opportunity to grab my arm that I was using as a defense and twist it. Then she grabbed one of my fingers and bent it backward with force

"Maybe we should just break off one finger for each hour you were late."

My finger almost past the breaking point of the joint, I frantically tried to free myself from her grip, screaming, "NOOOOOOO! PLEEEEEASE! Let GO!!!!!!!"

And finally, she relented. She then punched me quickly, twice in the jaw. I instantly tasted blood, and tears rolled silently down my cheeks.

"Get out of my sight. Go and get dressed so you can get to school. Move it."

Even though my face was swelling up, I did as I was told. I didn't want to be here any longer than I had to. I left my cereal and toast at the table and went to put on fresh clothes. As I pulled on an old pair of ratty jeans, I wondered if this was the way any other child had to start their day and thought about whether dying could be any worse than my sad excuse for an existence.

I surmised that it couldn't.

May 1977 - Second Grade

I sat alone near the edge of the stairs that led down the east side of the school toward the street behind the school. I didn't want to be seen by anyone. I wasn't sure just what else I wanted at that moment, but not being seen was definitely at the top of the list.

As I sat there, I saw Juan and his mother approaching. He lived on this street behind the school, and he came this way to school every morning. Other children weren't allowed to use this stairway into the grounds of the school, but since his mother worked in the cafeteria, he was able to not come through the main gate with everyone else.

"Hey," Juan said as he came closer. Then, when he was within a few feet of me, and he saw my face, he asked me what had happened.

I went to John's house after school; they were waiting for me when I went home.

"Oh no, that's it…"

Juan balled up his fists, and his mother grabbed him, speaking to him in Spanish, probably about not getting involved and getting himself into trouble. She talked a mile a minute, pointing into his face the whole time. He finally put his head down and nodded. Now calmer, he turned his attention to the location I was in.

"Come on, you're gonna get in trouble with Mr. Shedruff if he catches you here."

"I don't care. I don't care about anything right now." I told Juan, turning my body away from him. It was true; I really didn't care about anything. Why would I? What reason did I have?

It didn't matter what I did or didn't do. I was always in trouble, always had some sort of problem no matter what.

Now John was approaching from the top side of the playground

"Hey, come on, here comes Mr. Shedruff!" John warned.

"Come on," Juan said again, holding his hand out to help me up

"No, please, just leave me alone."

Both Juan and John went up to get closer to the school where the kids were allowed to be when they were on school grounds outside.

Mr. Shedruff walked over toward me and said, "Hey, get back with the rest of the kids. That staircase is not safe. It's too steep and old. You could get hurt."

I ignored his warning. When he saw that I wasn't moving, he came closer to see why I wasn't listening.

"Hey, did you hear what I said? Let's go. Away from the stairs."

I still didn't respond and he moved closer still, reaching out a hand for me to take so he could walk me back over to where he felt I needed to be.

I still showed no recognition of his efforts.

"Ok then. See me after school. Maybe a detention will do you good." and he pivoted to walk away.

"NO! " I shouted, "No detention, please!"

And I got up and started walking back toward the playground. He tried to put his hand on my back to guide me, but I recoiled away from his touch and broke into a run to get there without his urging. There was no way I was going to stay after school and get a detention. That would require the mother to get a detention notice that she would have to sign, and that would spell even more than the usual amount of doom for me.

I almost ran directly into Luis Matos and the other Luis on my way there.

They both took the opportunity to bother me, as usual, "Your bodyguard gonna protect you today, little baby?" Luis Matos asked in a sing-song voice, prompting Eggy, who was on the monkey bars, to let go of the bars mid-stride and run to his cohorts' side.

"Hey, little baby, where you are going?" the other Luis called out.

"Feeling chicken, I guess."

Suddenly, Eggy was on the ground. He had been pushed by Jose, a boy from another class one year ahead of mine and someone who was the same height as Eggy.

"Why don't you pick on someone your own size, asshole," said Jose.

Upon seeing this scene play out, the two Luis went toward Jose, and before long, fists were flying in all directions. Eggy was in the middle of it, too, as he had gotten back to his feet and joined the fray.

Mr. Shedruff came over hurriedly and broke up the fight.

"Get to my office! Right now! All of you!"

He yelled sternly and through an angry red face. He walked behind the quartet, and as Danny passed me, I saw that he had what surely was about to become a black eye and a busted lip that was bleeding.

The ruckus called an abrupt end to the morning arrival playtime. Teachers started lining up their classes early.

Juan got in line behind me and informed me, "I told Jose about what happened. " Jose and Juan were friends because they lived next door to each other so they had a good relationship in spite of the fact that Jose was older.

"He already knew about Eggy and his friends, but after what they did to you last night, he wanted to do something. Something to fix them. When they started with you again just now he decided it was the perfect opportunity, I guess."

"Juan, please, I know you want to help, but please don't do anything else, ok? That's what got me beat down last night on the way home yesterday. It was because you tried to help me yesterday when you pushed Eggy. That's what they keep saying now. "Where's your bodyguard?' and stuff like that.

John, who was a couple of spots back in line, piped up and said, "They got what they deserved."

I couldn't argue the point, John was right about that. They did deserve what they got and so much more, but what would I now have to deal with because of it? How much worse would things be? There was no doubt that it was me who would be blamed, and it would be me who would have to face Eggy and his minions.

Then I thought about them in Mr Shedruff's office. Would they get the paddle? It was on Mr. Shedruff's office wall, and it was rumored that when any kid did something bad that required them to see him, he paddled them. I wouldn't doubt it. I had never been paddled by him but heard about kids crying like they never had before after they left his office.

I didn't have to think about it for very long, just 3 days, because that's how long Danny's suspension was. Eggy and the 2 Luises got a week each. When Danny came back to school, I got to talk to him about what happened after the fight. John and I were on the playground together on the morning Jose came back to school and we approached him as he came through the gate.

"What happened in Mr. Shedruff's office? Did he spank you? I asked Jose as we all made our way over to the playground.

"No, not me, but I think he spanked Eggy and the two Luises. I went in to talk to him first. Then he had me wait with the lady at the desk while she called my parents to come pick me up. They were still in his office when I was leaving with my dad."

As I was talking to Jose, our conversation was interrupted by a deeper-voiced older boy calling my name. I looked behind me and saw a very tall, very muscular boy who looked at us and said

"After school today, out front. You're dead."

And with that, the boy walked off the playground and out the gate, where we could see Eggy and the two Luises waiting for him.

The end of the day came, and that boy, along with the usual band of bullies, were all waiting outside the gate of the school.

"Look, we don't have to go out that gate."

John said as if it were a true statement.

"You KNOW we will never get off the school grounds using that staircase on the side of the school, not with all the teachers watching to make sure we are going out the front gate."

"Come on."

John said, and he walked quickly back toward the main door to the school on the playground side.

"Excuse me, we forgot our math books, and we need them for homework. Can we go back in and get them?" John asked a teacher by the door

"Yes, but hurry up; we are going to be closing and locking the doors soon."

We went inside.

"What are you doing?" I asked John with exasperation.

"We'll wait here for the teachers to go inside the building after dismissal; then, we will be free to leave and go whichever way we want off the schoolyard."

It was crazy, but it was plausible that it could, in fact, work.

We did exactly as John suggested. We pretended to be getting our books in the classroom, but we were really standing at the classroom doorway to see when all the teachers were inside.

When we felt all was clear, we took off out the exit nearest to that concrete side stairway of the school.

We took off at top speed so that our legs would safely carry us down the stairs of the side entrance. We ran into Juan and his mother at the bottom, and we tagged along with them on their walk home. We knew the bullies wouldn't mess with us if we were in the company of an adult, especially one who worked at the school. After saying goodbye to Juan for the day, we went back in the direction that we came, and I hung out with John for a while. I went a longer way around the school to get home so as to avoid the bullies if they were out there again, and this time, I was able to thwart their attacks.

I ran up the rickety old wood stairs of my porch, proud that we had evaded the attacks of the bullies and whoever that tall kid was for today at least. I knocked on the door to get Grandma to open it. I was greeted instead by my mother, who instantly grabbed me by the arm and flung me across the room.

What the FUCK did you do THIS time, you useless FUCK?! Huh? WHAT?!!!

I couldn't fathom what was going on now. I hadn't done anything that would warrant such an interrogation. What on earth could she be referring to? Before I had any chance of finding out, Mother was coming at me with the doubled-up belt and swinging it, hitting me anywhere she could connect with.

I got a call from that fuckhead principal at your school saying that the other day, you were named in some incident other kids had because of YOU!

More than likely, they had been calling for the past two days as well, but Mother simply wasn't answering the phone, which was business as usual for her as she hated talking to anyone at all. She apparently answered the phone today, though.

"Why did that ASSHOLE PRINCIPAL call me? Huh, you FUCK? Why were those other boys fighting? What did you have to do with it?!"

She yelled as she continued swinging the belt.

I couldn't answer. I was wracked with pain from the belt already and was bawling loudly and hyperventilating.

"TELL ME! She creamed directly into my face as she swung hard and fast again, striking my previous injuries from the attacks of the bullies when they used a bat or branch days before; wounds that still were in the healing process. I wailed in misery when she struck this still highly sore area of my body.

"Strip, asshole"

"NO Please, Please…"

"I SAID STRIP! NOOWWWW!"

And she grabbed the shirt hard at the back of my neck, choking me as she lifted me up by it and tried getting the shirt off of me. It tore at several seams, but it finally was free of my body. I took off my shoes slowly and surveyed her, standing there, wild-eyed with rage, breathing heavily and ready to grab me if I attempted to run. I took off my pants and underwear, and she held me by the shoulder with one hand and swung as hard as she could with the other hand holding the belt. It hit me hard on the side of my butt. Then another lash across the back, then the back of my thighs, then back up to the butt again. She continued her assault over and over, hitting me everywhere and never relinquishing any power in her swings, each just as powerful as the ones that preceded.

The more I pleaded for it to be over, the longer it lasted. My legs, arms, torso, and back were red with so many welts it was hard to see where one welt ended and another began. It was the strikes that crossed over previous strikes that hurt the most, and there were several of them.

"Now get the fuck out of my sight. Go ON! I don't want to have to see your ugly face."

And with one more swipe of the belt, she struck my face. After painfully putting my clothes back on over my now massively inflamed body, I sought out Grandma to see where she was so she could help me. She was nowhere to be seen. After looking throughout the house, I went to the back porch door. It was locked, and Grandma was out there, locked out. Mother had locked her out of the house when, just before I had arrived home, she went to take in the clothes that were drying on the clothesline. Grandma told me that Mother did it to keep her from interfering with   this   beating.

I helped Grandma carry some of the clothes inside as Mother was at the kitchen table, pouring a large glass of vodka for herself. The rage was still there in her eyes. I dared not look in her direction long; I just retreated from the area with grandma as quickly as possible, helping her fold the laundry; both of us were quiet except for the occasional whimper from one or both of us as tears fell and hit the clean clothes while we folded them.

June 1977 - Second Grade

Today would be a truly happy day for me. The RIF program, short for Reading Is Fundamental, was set up in the library. Miss Day, the librarian, was smiling as she oversaw the classes as they came through the library, students looking to add new books to their collections. RIF was a non-profit organization who traveled from school to school to give books to children in an attempt both to increase love of learning and reading proficiency. It was a simple premise, really: every child gets to look at all the books offered on the different tables and then choose one to bring home and keep forever. Books that I didn't have to return were the best part of RIF. I loved that part because I enjoyed taking books out of the school library, but I hated returning them.

As I looked at all the tables, I saw so many books I wanted to take. I was having trouble deciding. Which book was going to be the one that I would add to the very few books I already had, all of which I had gotten from RIF before? I finally narrowed it down to three. Two were Charlie Brown cartoon books, of which I already had a couple. The other was Charlie and the Chocolate Factory.

As I came to the end of the table by the door where the rest of my class was lining up, Miss Lloyd, my second-grade teacher, impatiently informed me, "Put two of them back and take just one. We are about to leave and get back to class."

One of the RIF program attendants heard Miss Lloyd's statement and came over to the table where I was standing and staring at these three books that I knew would bring me joy.

She bent down to get on my level and said, "Wow! You've got three great books there. You know, I love Charlie and the Chocolate Factory. But I love Snoopy, too. Happiness is a warm puppy is my favorite of all time.

"Really?!"

I exclaimed, unable to contain my excitement over the fact that I may have been holding one of the best books ever. My 7-year-old mind reeled in anticipation of what lay between the pages of that book that made it so good. But I wanted to know about this kid Charlie and what he had to do with a chocolate factory. The cover art had lured me in, begging me to find out more about this kid. Surely it must be a great adventure if a chocolate factory is involved.

I loved chocolate more than almost anything else in the world. Sometimes, instead of getting a soda at the diner, I'd beg grandma to buy me a Hershey bar or a Nestle Crunch bar because it was SO delicious. I always ate every morsel of the bar, searching the foil wrapping for any remnants of leftover bliss that I may have missed.

"Yes, Really. I'll tell you what… You can put one of the three books back and take two, but don't tell the other kids, ok?"

The attendant whispered to me. I nodded my head up and down and tried to contain my excitement over being able to take more than one book. I didn't want to give it away and get her or myself into trouble. Then she led me back to the table at the back of the library where I could put one of the peanuts books back. She then told me

"Stick the Snoopy book under your shirt. Tuck it into your pants with the shirt. No one will know."

With my back toward the class I did as she said. Now carrying Charlie and the Chocolate Factory in my hand, I thanked this kind attendant and walked quickly back to the line, getting into it and saying nothing.

When we arrived back at class, I took every chance I could to read about Charlie and the Chocolate Factory. When it was time for reading, I placed the book inside my reading textbook that had stories that didn't match my advanced reading level, and I found it boring. At recess, I lounged by the school building, away from the other kids, reading about the incredible sights the children in the story were experiencing. During spelling, I kept the book on my lap while I did my spelling workbook exercises. I always finished my spelling and vocabulary work quickly, so it left me with plenty of time to get another chapter or two in. I was mesmerized by Charlie, Grandpa, and the other children visiting the factory.

When the end of the day came, I walked with John out the door of the school and through the gate before finally taking the Snoopy book out from my shirt and telling him

"Look, I got two books!" John looked at my selections and said

"Aw man, you're lucky! Did you just take an extra one?"

"No, the lady said I could."

"Oh. Ok." That was all he said. I knew I could trust John. He wouldn't tattletale that I had two books.

I was so excited about my books that I didn't initially see Eggy and his gang hanging out to the left of the entrance today instead of the right until it was nearly too late. When they saw John and I, they immediately took notice and started approaching. We booked it, no pun intended, as quickly as we could up the street toward John's house. Eggy and his friends only ran a short distance to catch us and then decided to give up.

When we arrived at John's house, it was a less exciting visit. John had chosen the other peanuts book I had been interested in, and we both spent the rest of the afternoon reading, pausing only once to get a game of Battleship in.

It got late fast and I had lost track of the time due to being so engrossed in the story. When John's dad walked in the house, I knew it had to be close to dinnertime as that's usually always when he gets home. I looked up at the clock on John's living room wall and bolted toward the door, where I put on my jacket and said

"See you tomorrow." And John responded

"Yup. See ya!"

And I ran top speed all the way home, clutching my new books tightly as I ran. I was like a marathon runner all the way until I got to my front porch, where my mother was walking up the stairs. She was just arriving home from work. She had found another secretarial job that she likely wouldn't be able to keep for more than a month due to her drunken binges. She already had been drinking on her way home. She had stopped by one of the bars on the way for a belt or three.

"Why are you getting home so late?" she inquired as we met on the porch and made our way inside to the hall.

"What's this?"

She inquired while pointing at the books with one hand and trying to grab them with the other. I instinctively held them even tighter and turned my body away from her.

"They're books I got for free from RIF," I told her.

"Oh, more books for the dumb bookworm. I see," she said mockingly.

After tossing her keys to the end table by one of the living room chairs, she turned to me and said, "Wait… why do you have two books? I thought RIF only let every child only get one book at a time?"

I panicked. I knew I had to tell her the truth. If I lied, she would surely punish me severely.

"The RIF lady, she let me have two."

Mother looked at me, furrowing her eyebrows.

"Well, why do you think she did that?" she calmly asked

I started to get nervous, stammering

'I-I-I don't Kn-n-now... I guess she knew I wanted both."

"Oh... You WANTED both."

"Y-y-yeah"

"You know they have a rule for a reason, right?"

Now, my heart was beginning to pound. I tried to ignore it. I focused on holding my precious books. My hands were beginning to sweat, making it more difficult to hold the books as tightly, the skin of my hands slipping on the glossy paperback book covers.

"Making it so that every child only gets one makes it fair for everyone. You understand that, right?"

"Y-y-y-y-yes," I stuttered.

"You know what I think? I think you just wanted two books, and you took them. She didn't just LET you have a second one. Why would she break the rule only for you?"

The beat of my heart was now faster and harder than it ever should be, even running at top speed.

"N-N-NOOO! I didn't take it! She did give it to me! She did! I swear!"

"Did your teacher see her give it to you?" She inquired. Mrs. Lloyd didn't see it. Nobody did. It was a secret between the RIF attendant and I. There was no way to prove my innocence.

"N-N-Nobody saw her give it to me. She didn't want me to get in trouble." I told her, but she wasn't listening.

"So now, you're going to have to destroy one of the books. Which one?" Mother demanded.

I looked at her, aghast that she would dare to suggest such a cruel thing

"NOOO! Please! NOOOO! She GAVE me the other book, I SWEAR! PLEEEEASE don't rip it!"

"Oh no, I'm not going to rip it; YOU'RE going to do it. You took the extra book, so YOU have to destroy it. Now if you don't want to destroy them both, you need to pick one right now. This is your last chance. If you don't tell me which one, then you'll have to destroy both."

Tears were streaming down my cheeks. I dropped the Snoopy book. I hadn't read that one yet and the attendant said it was her favorite. One of the best books ever, so I had to keep that one to find out.
"Ok, start tearing the pages out of the book and when you are done tearing the page from the book, then tear the page in half."

I did as she said, repeatedly pulling pages from the book and ripping them before dropping the pieces onto the rug. I cried harder and harder as I continued to ruin the Charlie and the Chocolate Factory book beyond repair. When I finished, she instructed

"Now, get your clothes off."

"NOOOO! Please!!!"

"Shirley, please don't. It was punishment enough for him to have to tear the book," Grandma said from the kitchen doorway.

"He's a LIAR and a THIEF! Do you think that's ok? Huh, DO YOU? Maybe YOU need some yardstick time too, huh bitch?"

"I'm not a liar! She GAVE me the book! I didn't STEAL IT! PLEEEEASE, believe me! Call John He'll tell you!"

"What? Your friend, who will lie to you? He probably stole a book too," Mother retorted.

"NOOOO! He didn't! PLEEEASE believe me."

"I SAID STRIP!"

I did as she demanded as she pushed her way past Grandma, going to the pantry to get the yardstick.

"WHAP! Across the back. She wasted no time. I was still trying to get my pants off when she started wailing at me with the yardstick.

"Pick up the pieces of the pages."

I did as instructed, carefully picking up a couple of pieces.

Now, bring them to the trash basket in the kitchen. I tried to walk but couldn't because my pants were still caught around my ankles. Mother became violent, striking me hard and making me cry out loudly from the instant agony. I finally got my pants free of my ankles as she continued swinging the stick. Whap! Whap! Whap! Every attempt made hits its target and brings a swollen welt to the skin's surface.

"You better clean up my rug and do it QUICK, you little lying THIEF! Get MOVING!!!" she bellowed, swinging again and again, making me drop the pieces as I picked them up and tried to get to the kitchen trash bin. I went back and forth again and again. Mother hit me over and over with the stick, never reducing the power of her lashes.

I wailed and begged for an end to the torment, and it finally came when I threw the last of the torn book pages into the trash.

"Now, give me that other book."

"NOOO! Please! You said only one!" I desperately tried to remind her. She just swung the stick at me 5 more times, one of the attempts making contact with the side of my face and ear, making the cartilage of my ear cry out with pain.

"I said, GIVE ME THE OTHER BOOK!"

I picked it up off the floor and handed it to her, almost flinching as I expected her to swing the stick again. She didn't. Instead, she opened the book to a random page and started reading out loud.

"Happiness is a pile of leaves," she read. Then she struck me with the stick again.

"Happiness is three friends in a sandbox with no fighting." Whap! Another hit.

"Happiness is a smooth sidewalk" Whap!

"Happiness is climbing a tree" Whap!

"Happiness is knowing all the answers. Well, I guess that's one you don't have to be happy about, huh, dumbfuck? You don't have any answers. Fucken moron" WHAP!

"Now get dressed."

And she walked back to the pantry to put away the yardstick. Then she went to her bedroom and opened the top drawer of the tall dresser and put the Peanuts book in it. I wondered what she was going to do with the book or if I'd ever see it again, but I didn't dare ask. I was in enough pain from this beating without bringing more of it.

I sat down wordlessly at the kitchen table after I got my pants and shirt back on. No one spoke all throughout dinner. The only sound at the meal was the clinking of forks against the plates. After dinner, Mother said.

"I want you to write an apology letter to the school right now for stealing the book. You'll read the story to your class."

"NOOO! I didn't steal it, please! Don't make me do that! Eggy and all his friends will beat me up so bad if you make me do it!" and without warning, she slapped me hard across the face and then wrenched my arm and lifted me up by my armpit to meet her face to mine.

"Do you want me to get the stick again? DO YOU! I'll beat you all night if I have to! You will write an apology letter, and you will READ IT TO THE CLASS! I will be calling the school, and if you don't read the letter to your class, you won't have any skin left on your body because I'll beat you until it's gone! Do you UNDERSTAND ME?! Now get to writing and bring it to me when you're done!"

And she threw me to the floor.

I wrote the apology letter as best as I could with my body being in absolute agony. I brought it to her, tears in my eyes, anticipating what she might do to me next.

She read it aloud, slurring her words from the alcohol she drank earlier and the new batch she had started drinking after dinner.

"Dear class, I am very sorry for stealing a book at the RIF book fair. I will never do it again. Good. Now get to bed."

I went to bed, pulling the covers over my head, and I cried all night.

The next morning, Mother pulled back my covers and said, "You get no breakfast. You have to talk to your teacher before class about what you did, so I want you to get on your way right away. Now get up and get dressed. Move it."

I didn't have the energy to argue. I just obeyed her wishes. When fully dressed, I was about to walk out the door, letter in hand, when she brought me the Happiness is a Warm Puppy book.

"Because you stole an extra book, you'll get to keep no book at all. You'll take this book and give it back."

"B-B-But the RIF fair is over. It's only one day."

Now, mother's mood was becoming inflamed with anger.

"Then you'll donate it to your school library. Now go on. Get out of here."

And she unlocked and opened the door and then kicked at me to get me out of the apartment.

I left the building and walked slowly, thinking about how unfair it was that even when I told the truth, I was punished. When I arrived at school I went and sat against the wall of the entrance. Tears were flowing silently down my cheeks. My teacher saw me and came over.

"What's with you? You just got here. What do you have to cry about already? I pondered whether I should tell her everything, the extent to which Mother had punished me for nothing. I decided to show her the letter and tell her what Mother wanted me to do.

Miss Lloyd read the letter and said, "Ok, you stole a book."

"NO, I didn't! The RIF lady said I could take two because she saw that I really, really wanted more than one. Please believe me. Please. I didn't steal it. Honest! I swear!" Now, tears were coming down in a steady stream. Miss Lloyd put her arm around my shoulder to comfort me.

"Please don't make me read that to the class! That's what my mother wants me to do. She's gonna call you to make sure I did it. Please just tell her I read it. If I do read it, the kids are gonna make fun of me and hurt me. She wants me to return the other book too."

Miss Lloyd gave me a concerned look and then replied to my ramblings.

"Ok, Ok, it's ok now. Don't cry. I believe you. I believe you didn't steal the book. It won't be the first time someone from RIF lets a child take more than one book. They do that often. You don't have to read this letter to the class and if your mother calls I will make her understand about what happened. Ok? And you can keep the other book too. You don't have to turn it in."

"How? How can I keep it?" I asked through sobs

"Well, you have a desk in the classroom, don't you? You can just keep it here at school, ok?"

I nodded, indicating that I did understand.

"Ok, now go and play," she told me, and she re-focused her efforts on supervising the children on the playground.

I ignored her encouragement to go play and instead stayed where I was to think. Maybe she wouldn't even call. That was a highly likely scenario because she hated talking to anyone, most notably anyone at my school.

When we all went inside to start the day, and I got to my desk, I hid the book under all my textbooks and pieces of completed art. I thought about the book and the few passages Mother had read out loud regarding happiness. I wondered what true happiness was and whether I would ever be able to experience any of my own.

At the end of the day, I had already read the entire Peanuts book over and over. I tucked it back underneath all my books on the desk for safekeeping until Monday rolled around. It was Friday, and I couldn't decide if I was happy or sad about the prospect of the weekend being upon me. It was hard to be happy or sad about it since no matter where I was; it was always a miserable time for me.

I wondered, too, about whether or not my mother had called my teacher. I know Miss Lloyd had accepted a call early in the morning on the black rotary dial classroom telephone on her desk, but the call was brief. She had written the caller's phone number down and promised to get back to them later.

John and I walked out the main door, and being still sore from my beating the day before, I wasn't feeling up to going over to John's house today, even though he had invited me. Luckily, today, the bullies were nowhere to be seen because Eggy had gotten into trouble for shooting spitballs at people in the class and was sent to detention. That meant his followers just dispersed and went their own way right after the bell rang, making their way home like everyone else. I went straight home as well, walking quickly.

When I arrived at my door, I was greeted by a sign that read, "Gone to the store to get milk. Wait here." It was in my grandmother's writing. I went back to sit on the porch stairs and wait for her. After a few minutes, instead of seeing Grandma walking up the street toward home, it was the angry face of my mother. I knew that look, and it meant that my day was about to get a whole lot worse.

She got to the porch and lifted me up by my arm, wordless, as she dragged me through the hallway to the apartment door. Before putting the key in the lock, she flung me toward the door of the apartment next door. I hit it with a thud, causing the neighbor to open the door to see what was going on. The neighbor looked down at me, then at my mother, saying, "Everything ok?"

To which Mother smiled her fakest, most plastic smile and replied, "Oh sure, everything's just peachy."

And then looked down at me, telling me sternly, "Get up, klutz!" As if to blame me for crashing into the neighbor's door. I stood up and walked into the apartment. Mother slammed the door as hard as she could, paint chips flying from the door and doorway. Then she reared up on me, backhanding me across the face and sending me to the floor once again.

"You little MOTHERFUCKER! You are no good lying, little FUCKING BASTARD!" she screamed. All I could think was why is this happening? This can't be a continuation of the previous night. Miss Lloyd believed me and said that she would straighten it out with my mother.
She started taking off her belt while she went on raving

"I called your teacher today. You know what that bitch cunt said? She said you told her the same phony story you tried to tell me. The thing is, she believed you. She said that the RIF people sometimes let kids have more than one book. She said that YOU told HER that I made you write the apology letter and read it to the class. You know what she said then?" She screamed.

Whap! The belt struck my stomach.

"He doesn't have to."

Whap! The belt hit my chest

"Read it!"

Whap! Now it hit my shoulder

"To the class!"

Whap! Whap! Whap! Three direct hits across the face.

"You know what I said to that? Huh fucker?"

Whap! Whap! Whap! Now, she was holding me down by the throat with one hand while hitting me with the doubled-up belt with the other.

"I said that's FINE. I said if he didn't have to read his apology letter to the class, we'd find some other way of taking care of the situation. She said in her mind, the situation was already taken care of. I said ok, and I hung up on the bitch."

"So then, now we are going to take care of the situation. You tried to make me look like a FOOL!"

And with the word fool, she dropped the belt and punched me in the back.

"Who's the fool now, huh? Who?" and she punched me in the thigh, "Who is it? Who?"

And another punch, this time to the groin.

"WHO IS THE FOOL NOW, YOU LYING PIECE OF SHIT, NO GOOD THIEF?! WHO?!"

I was crawling to try and escape; my lip was bloodied from her backhand slap. Mother was having none of that. She grabbed me by the foot, flinging off my shoe as she tried to grab me.

"Get back here fucker!"

She screamed, her reddened eyes full of terror. She finally got a good grip on me and pulled me back to her, and she lifted me up by my arm, twisting it behind my back. She got right next to my ear and said, "You're going to read that letter Monday. Say it." I was screaming and crying, tears dripping onto the rug, and I couldn't speak.

"I will break this arm and twist it off," and she twisted my arm so hard the two bones in my forearm felt at the breaking point, as did my shoulder joint.

"SAY IT ASSHOLE!"

"I-I-I w-w-w-will Read the l-l-l-letter M-M-M-Monday"

"To everyone in my class," she continued, not letting up the pressure on my arm

"T-t-to e-e-everyone in my c-c-c-c-class"

"And I will apologize for making my mother look like a fool"

"Aaand apppologggize for mmmaking mmmy mother lllooook like a f-f-foooool"

And with the completion of the statement, she let go of my arm and threw me to the floor just as Grandma was coming back in from the store. She put down the brown bag containing the milk she went to the Dairy Mart convenience store to buy and came instantly to my aid

"What the hell is happening now?" she yelled to my mother while trying to pick me up to comfort me.

"THAT little bastard, your precious grandson, got out of everything. He told that teacher he didn't steal the extra book from the RIF thing. She said he didn't have to read the apology note because she didn't think he was guilty."

"Well," Grandma said, her eyes furrowing. "Did you ever stop to think that maybe, just maybe, he DIDN'T steal it? Oh no, you just automatically have to believe the worst about him and assume he's a thief."

At this comment, Mother's fury and rage came back in full force, and now she moved toward Grandma, getting right in her face and screaming.

"I THINK the worst because he IS the worst. Nothing but a goddamn little motherfucking troublemaker from the day he was born. I never should have HAD him. Worst fucking decision I ever made bringing him into this world. And who does that bitch cunt teacher think she is, undermining me. I'm his mother, and I will decide what he should or shouldn't do. I said I wanted him to read the apology letter to the class, and I meant it. And if YOU don't like it, go and pack YOUR FUCKING BAGS and get the FUCK out."

With that final declaration, my mother kicked my grandmother in the shin and then spun around and went to the kitchen to pull a can of beer from the refrigerator. She pulled the top and chugged it like it was Coca-Cola.

Grandma helped me over to the couch, where she took my shirt off to see if there was any serious damage since she hadn't witnessed all that took place while she had been on the milk-buying errand.

"What did she do? Did she hit you only with the belt?" Grandma asked.

"N-n-n-no, she s-s-s-lapped me and p-p-p-punched me too."

"It's all over now; she's not going to hurt you anymore"

"N-n-n-not n-n-n-now, but w-w-w-what about later?" I said, reminding Grandma that there would always be later or tomorrow or the next day or the day after that for Mother to come at me again. Grandma held me gently, and feeling powerless, all she could think to tell me was

"It's all over. For now"

The next morning, my mother violently shook me awake.

"Wake up, dummy."

She didn't have to shake me, as I was already awake and dreading the day, as was the common feeling most mornings for me.

"I'm walking you to school today"

'Oh NO!' I thought. I couldn't imagine what she was up to this time. SHE was walking ME to school?! My mind started racing. She hadn't done that since the second week of kindergarten, at which time it was deemed unnecessary for her to accompany me any longer, and I was independent enough to get to school on my own. One thing I was certain of, however, was that this couldn't be good and surely wouldn't end well for me.

After making sure that I was awake and sitting up, she wordlessly padded back to her bedroom in her worn-out slippers.

When she left her room, she saw that I was just sitting there and hadn't yet started to get dressed; she came back to the side of my bed, slapped my head, and loudly said, "Wake up, you fucken dreamer. Get dressed. Let's go."

Her slap snapped me out of the thoughts I was buried in, trying to figure out what plot or scheme she was trying to lay out by escorting me to school today.

I sat with my mother and grandma quietly at the table.

"I'm bringing HIM to school this morning"

Mother said out loud with enough disdain in her voice to let any listener know just how little she thought of me as she said the word 'him'. It was the kind of intonation of the word that indicated that she put me in the category of the lowest slug on earth.

Grandma didn't question her motives, just continued eating her piece of toast she had warmed up in our very old toaster and buttered moments before. It was best not to entertain Mother when it seemed obvious she was trying to initiate a negative conversation. Mother hated this when Grandma wouldn't take the bait, and doing so meant she wouldn't be able to deride me again and work up her rage.

Mother sighed and took a sip of coffee.

"Alright, come on. Finish up. We need to go."

"Are you going to work early?" I asked, thinking that perhaps because of needing to get to work early at her secretarial job, her journey would take her past the school earlier, so she could walk with me and drop me off.

"No, I am not going to work early," she said in a mocking tone, making fun of me and my question as if it were the dumbest thing I could ask her.

"It's none of your fucking business anyway," she said while lifting her coffee cup and finishing it.

"Now, let's go."

I left my bowl of Cocoa Puffs on the table and put on my jacket, my heart now racing with fear over what Mother might do right now.

"What is she up to?" I thought again. I couldn't fathom whatever it could be. Surely she wasn't going to talk to my teacher. That would be something she would try to avoid at all costs as she despised all interactions, especially against anyone at school.

I decided to forget about whatever she could be planning or had already planned and to just go along with her actions of taking me to school. I wouldn't question her anymore, lest I invoke her wrath at this early hour of the morning, mother's most hated time of the day, as she was usually seriously hung over from all the alcohol she drank the night before. As close to the edge of insanity as Mother was at all other points of the day, she was especially twitchy when she was experiencing the negative side of drinking and its aftermath.

I walked out of the apartment building with her and saw the people going to work and other parents walking their kids to school, happily talking to them with smiles on their faces. In contrast, the mother just stared ahead with the scowl of a person who was angry to be put upon to pay attention to a child they had never wanted.

When someone looked in her direction, she furrowed her eyebrows and stared back in their direction as if to say, 'What the fuck are you looking at? Mind your business and stop looking at me.' It was her go-to way of dealing with the world. As if she was about to do something that she hated and she despised anyone looking at her as she went about doing it. As I was about to find out, that was closer to the truth than usual.

We arrived at school, and she silently motioned for me to go play. I didn't. I just stood there to see her turn around and leave out of the gate she had just walked in, except she didn't. Instead, she made a beeline toward Mr. Shedruff. I moved to where I could better hear what was being said, but it looked like I was blended in with some girls playing double dutch and some other boys playing with their spinning tops.

"I want to talk to you about David's teacher." She said while pointing in my teacher's direction where she stood, surveying and supervising the children as they played. All of the teachers took turns, 2 or 3 at a time, to accompany Mr. Shedruff on the playground, and today was her day.

Mother proceeded to explain the situation about the extra book at the RIF event and how she was not happy about Miss Lloyd's proposed outcome.

"I had told David that he would have to read his apology letter to the class and she said it wouldn't be necessary because she didn't think he stole the book."

"Well, to be honest, ma'am, I'm not so sure he did either. RIF loves it when a child is showing signs that they LOVE books, that they LOVE to read. That's what their program is about to encourage a love of reading. They often let a child take more than one book."

"That is NOT the point. The point is that Miss Lloyd undermined my authority when she said that he didn't need to read the letter. That was MY decision as his mother and wasn't for her to question; you follow me? I don't appreciate being made a fool of, and that is what that teacher did. Now, I am going to explain what is going to happen. David is going to read his apology letter to the class. He is going to apologize on his teacher's behalf for taking part in making me look bad, and if you refuse to make this happen, you will both be out of a job because I will see to it. I guarantee it. Do you understand me?"

"Perfectly, ma'am. Have a good morning," Mr. Shedruff replied.

"I mean it," she said as if to really drive home her point.

"Thank you, Ma'am," Mr. Shedruff reiterated more sternly "Good morning"

He held his arm in a gesture toward the gate of the school, encouraging Mother to leave the premises now that she had said what she had wanted to say.

With that, Mother pushed her way past some children playing, nearly knocking one of them down, and she marched off the playground area and out the front gate without looking back, focusing her gaze forward as the idea of seeing anyone here any longer would bring the sickness of some deadly disease upon her.

Mr. Shedruff signaled for Miss Lloyd to come over. I walked away, out of their sight as best I could, to the edge of the concrete staircase on the side of the building where I could sit and ponder my fate of having to read that apology letter to the class. I was innocent; that's what made it so bad, and Eggy and the gang would use it as an excuse to pummel me again after school; that's what made it even worse.

I considered playing hooky, just going down these stairs right now, leaving school behind for the day, and not caring whether one or more teachers or even Mr. Shedruff saw me do it. That would bring phone calls from the school to my mother, though, and that would most certainly worsen my fate, adding yet another beating from my mother to the mix.

I glanced over at Mr Shedruff and Miss Lloyd talking. Miss Lloyd was more animated than I remember ever having seen her. Her arms were moving wildly as a show of how upset she had been made by the situation. I felt bad for her but knew that she had as yet, gotten off easy. In spite of having a negative phone conversation and now this altercation, Mother had been kind to her compared with the hell she put me through on a daily basis.

Mr. Shedruff instructed the teachers with a hand signal that it was time to line up. Miss Lloyd, looking visibly upset, called my class to line up. We were the first to go inside today, and our pace was quicker than usual.

I put my jacket on the back of my chair as Miss Lloyd glanced in my direction and tried to avoid making eye contact, turning away and looking somewhere else each time it nearly happened. We recited the pledge of allegiance to the flag as was customary each day and then she quieted the class down as they started talking after finishing the pledge.

"I want to make an announcement. There are times when we must come clean with something we did; we have to talk about what we did."

'Oh NO! Here it comes!' my inner voice cried out at the prospect of my having to apologize to the class. How would I do it? What would I say? I didn't even practice, and I no longer had the letter. Miss Lloyd tore it up and threw it away when it was determined that she believed I was innocent and wouldn't have to read it to the class.

My heart was slamming into my ribcage and trying to break through the ribs, the fear of what I was going to have to do right now making my heart beg for escape.

"But there are other times when we have to be strong, times that we have to use our courage to stand up for ourselves when what someone special in our lives believes is wrong about what they think of us when they don't believe us when we have been accused of something that we didn't do. This is one of those times. There is someone in our class who has been accused of doing something that they didn't do, and they were brave enough to come forward and tell me about it. They could have kept it in the dark and never talked about it, but they didn't do that. They were innocent and they did not want to be made to apologize for something they didn't do. And they shouldn't have to. They won't. Not in my class. If I believe someone is innocent, then they are just that, and I am not going to change my mind simply because someone, anyone, says so, no matter who they are and no matter what power they believe they have over me. It's wrong to accuse someone of something that they didn't do, and it's right to come forward and say so."

I glanced at the open door to our classroom where Mr. Shedruff stood and nodded his head in agreement.

"Ok, let's get out our math books and turn to page 135."

I was amazed. I couldn't believe what was happening. Miss Lloyd and Mr. Shedruff were standing up for me, standing up for what was right. I wasn't going to have to read the apology letter. They defied my mother, fought against her negativity, against her belief that I was lower than the lowest life forms on the planet, and, more importantly, they were going to be able to do it and survive, or at least not care what mother would do if or when she found out they didn't abide by her demands. Maybe, just maybe, there was hope for me to eventually be able to do the same.

Maybe.

July, 1977 - Summer Break

It was the best time of year to be a kid. It was summer. Summer on our street meant that it was noisier than usual, with the sounds of the children playing games, riding their bikes and big wheels, and just plain having all the fun that they couldn't have when they were in school for the whole day, every day during the school year.

For me, summer was at least a little bit of a reprieve from some of the daily violence I was subjected to, as there was no school for over 2 glorious months. That meant I didn't have to deal with the wrath of the bullies.

I spent a large quantity of the days outside playing games of tag and street hockey with friends and digging in the dirt with my tonka bulldozer and dump truck. I loved those Tonka trucks because they were made of heavy gauge steel, almost as thick as what was found on real cars of the time. That meant Mother couldn't destroy them, or she would at least have a very difficult time trying.

Often, I would bring one of my trucks with me to John's house as he had a much larger space in his yard than I had in mine, but this particular day, John brought over his Tonka steamroller so we could dig and create cities and make perfectly flat roads with the steamroller.

One of the best parts of summer was the daily visits from the Good Humor and Mister Softee ice cream trucks. The good humor truck usually rolled through in the morning and Mister Softee in the late afternoon.

After a full day in the blazing sun, we always looked forward to enjoying a vanilla or chocolate cone. The telltale ding of the bell on the truck could be heard while the truck was on the next street, giving all of the kids on my street the chance to get change from our parents so we'd be ready when they arrived and parked. In my case, my mother wasn't home, so I'd have to get money from grandma. She always had loose change in the bottom of her purse for such occasions.

"Grandma! Grandma! Quick! Get your purse! The ice cream man is here!" I excitedly exclaimed after rushing into the house.

I asked John if he had money.

"Yeah, I do. Let's go," and with that, we were off running up the street three houses away, where Mr. Softee's truck was waiting with some kids already in line.

Our impatience grew and grew, and with each child who was handed a tall cone, swirls and swirls of ice cream stacked on top, the mouths of all the other children waiting watered with anticipation.

"Vanilla or chocolate?" the ice cream man asked me.

"Vanilla."

"Oh, ok, being adventurous today huh? You usually get chocolate."

"Yeah, I know," I told him. "My best friend came over today. He's getting chocolate so we are gonna eat some of each other's cones." And I pointed at John behind me in the line.

"Ok, makes sense."

I handed him the money, and he went to work making my cone. I watched in amazement as the star-shaped ribbon of ice cream oozed from the spout as he turned the lever. Around and around, the ice cream star-shaped tube piled upon itself as he moved his hand holding the cone, ending in an icy pointed spike. It was a joy for any child on a hot summer day such as this to behold. Like an edible work of art that all of us couldn't wait to devour once ours was completed.

"You want chocolate sauce?"

"Yes, please."

And with that, he spooned some chocolate sauce and poured it on. It would be messy, but I didn't care. It was worth it.

After the ice cream man finished making John's cone, which was also coated in extra chocolate, we proceeded to eat our ice cream. When we ate all the ice cream on top and got down to the top of the cone where the only ice cream left was inside of it, we traded cones so we could see what each other's cones tasted like. John found out that he liked vanilla this way a couple summers back and we had been trading cones like this ever since.

Now, after eating our cones, we were a complete mess with chocolate and some melted ice cream all over our hands and faces, so we went to my house to wash our hands. I was surprised to see a mother sitting in the living room chair. I could tell she was drunk. She had spent the afternoon at the bar and it was evident in the way that she was bobbing her head while sitting there. John looked at her, too, as if trying to figure out what was wrong with her.

I didn't want some sort of a typical mother scene to get initiated in front of John, so I said, "Come on, let's wash our hands; we have to finish making our city."

To take his attention off my bombed-out-of-her-skull mother.

We took turns at the sink in the kitchen and got our hands and arms clean. Then we ran back outside to finish our city. We had buildings to create and roads to pave, and we wanted to be through by the time the streetlights came on.

When dinnertime rolled around, Mother took the box fan out of the window where it was perched and shouted out to us in the front yard, "Hey, is John staying for dinner? It's macaroni and cheese with hot dogs."

Grandma usually always cooked light in the summer and she always made something that she figured John would like on the few occasions he stayed over to eat dinner.

"Is it ok with your mom and dad to stay?"

"Sure, they are always ok with it"

"Yeah. He can stay."

"OK, dinner in ten minutes. K?"

"Yup. Ok"

"Your grandma is really cool," John said. I wasn't sure, but I thought he might be trying to say my mother wasn't and what was wrong with her in this polite way. But I just said, "Yeah, grandma is the best," in reply.

When dinner was ready, Grandma came back to the window to call us inside.

We wasted no time and came running, going straight for the sink to wash up again.

When we finished, we sat down at the table and started eating right away. We had only eaten the ice cream and had a couple of glasses of grandma's lemonade all afternoon, so we were super hungry by this time.

While we were scooping up spoonfuls of macaroni, Mother got up from her chair in the living room and drunkenly weaved her way to her bedroom, slamming the door when she got inside.

John, startled, dropped his fork onto the plate and looked at me, concerned. Nervously, I tried to cover up the interruption by saying, "I guess Mom's sick. Oh well! More macaroni and hot dogs for us!"

And I grabbed the spoon and scooped out a bunch more for Jahn before heaping even more on my plate. And then gave grandma more as well.

After dinner, John and I helped Grandma do the dishes even though she said she didn't want any help.

"You two get back outside while there's still time."

"No, grandma, you do a lot. I'll help."

And I picked up the dishcloth from the suds-filled pan in the sink and washed a plate. John washed his plate, fork, and glass. We dried off our hands on the dish towel and bolted for the door. We continued building our town until the streetlight came on.

"Ok, I gotta get home," John said, picking up his steamroller and holding up his hand for a high five.

We slapped hands, and I said, "Hey, come back tomorrow. Steve might have his day off tomorrow and open the hydrant for us."

Steve was one of the neighbors in my building. He worked for the fire house as a firefighter so he worked a few days in a row and then had some off. He was due to have some off, and all of the kids in the neighborhood looked forward to that because we knew he had the special wrench to open the fire hydrant so we could get cool. We would knock on his door and beg him to come open the hydrant, which he always did if it was a hot enough day.

"Ok, I'll bring my bathing suit."

"If he doesn't have the day off, maybe we can go to Juan's house and hang out there. He got an air conditioner this summer, so it's like winter in his house right now."

"Wow! Yeah. Ok. See you tomorrow."

Having an air conditioner was rare for the people of our neighborhood. That was a luxury very few could afford, and even if they did have one, they had to save up for a whole year before having enough money to afford it. Anyone who did have one seemed rich to us.

After making several trips to bring my large, heavy Tonka trucks and smaller plastic trucks I had brought outside, I went immediately to the bathroom to take a cold shower. I wasn't doing it to get the dirt and sweat off my body; I was primarily interested in cooling off. Today's temperature was 95, and the humidity made it feel like it was over 100.

After I got out of the tub and dried off, I went to my room to get some underwear to put on. Tonight would be too hot to wear pajamas.

When I got to my room, I was surprised to see Mother standing there.

"What the fuck do you think you're doing, just inviting John over without asking me?"

"Y-y-you weren't home… grandma s-s-s-said it was ok."

"So you think just because I'm not here, I don't have any say over what happens? I heard you telling him to come over tomorrow, too. I suppose 'grandma' is ok with that too?"

She said with a mocking tone in her voice when she said 'Grandma.'

Now, I had been over John's house many, many times and had stayed over for dinner more than once. I certainly owed him, but more than that, it was nice to have him there, if, at least, to help prevent me from getting violent treatment from her as she dared not try anything with the company around. But Mother hated people, all people, so naturally, that included John, especially since he was my friend. She hated the fact that I at least had John and Juan as friends.

"You think we are made of money? You know the food he eats while he's here costs money, and you know every meal is planned out for the three of us."

I could have reminded her that tonight, there was more than enough to go around since she was too drunk to join us, but I didn't want to incite her anger any more than it was already inflamed.

"B-B-But I can just eat less when he's here; I don't mind..."

"YOU don't mind?!" Mother yelled, anger tinting her cheeks a deeper shade of red than they already had turned from the alcohol.

"Who the FUCK are YOU?! This is MY house? You hear me?!" Whap! A slap across the head.

"It's MY house, and if I don't want someone here, then they won't BE here? Do you hear me?!"

"Y-Y-Yes," I said

"Now you'll tell him he is NOT coming over here tomorrow, you got it? Or do I have to explain it again to you because you're so stupid?"

"I u-u-understand. It's ok. We'll just go to Juan's house. He's got an air conditioner, so it will be cool there."

And with that statement, Mother brought her leg back and kicked me as hard as she could in the back. She was still wearing her shoes so it hurt even more because of that.

"Well, la de da! He's got an AIR CONDITIONER. Isn't that NIIICE" You know someone with an air conditioner? FUCK YOU! You hear me FUCK YOU and your rich 'air conditioner' friend too. Fuck you and everybody else all to hell. Fuck you all! And she grabbed me by the shoulder with one hand and repeatedly punched me in the ribcage with the other.

When she finished, she slurred.

"Remember, I don't want to see him here again tomorrow. If I do, you won't be sleeping here tomorrow night. You can go sleep on the street or his house or your rich air conditioner friend's house. I don't care where. Fuck you. And him. All of you," and she stumbled her way back to her bedroom, passing out for the night.

The next day, Steve wasn't home. I was actually kind of glad because if he was home and he opened the fire hydrant, I would be shirtless and might have to explain to John why I was so bruised on my ribs and back. During the school year, when we took showers together in gym class, it could be explained away easily because of the bullies who tormented me every day and left marks on me. In the summer, it would be more difficult to explain.

At about 11:30 in the morning, I was out front looking at what we had built the day before, and I saw John walking up the street toward my house, already wearing his bathing suit and carrying a towel.

"Steve's not home. He's working again."

"Aww. Too bad." John said.

"Come on, let's go see what Juan's doing," I said as I saw Mother peeking through the drapes to make sure I was not going to let John in the house today.

We walked to Juan's house while Mother watched us go as she now spread the drapes further apart to get a better view out of them, scowling at us and swearing under her breath at us the whole time.

August 1977 - Back to School Shopping, Third Grade

Back-to-school shopping was a mixed blessing. It was one of the only times of the year that I was able to go to Bradlees, the department store within walking distance from my house. It was next door to Stop and Shop, the grocery store where we got almost all our food. It was also a reminder of just how poor we were. Mother only bought the cheapest of the cheapest clothes and sneakers for me, and never enough of them.

"You're lucky to be getting any clothes at all," she would tell me if I protested that I should have more clothes than the couple outfits she was getting me.

"You're going to bitch and complain about not getting enough clothes when I had to put off paying the light bill just to be able to afford to get you the few things I can?!"

There was always some bill hanging over us that we had to forego paying in order to be able to afford something else that was needed. It was a way of life when you were as poor as we were. It was considered a major feat of brilliance if we were ever able to be caught up on bills, something that only happened once or twice during my entire childhood, and only for a month as there was always some need or emergency that would always come up to spoil the success and put us back into debt.

"You wouldn't need to get any clothes at all if you would stop being a useless fucking sissy and getting beat up by the kids in your class."

She was at least partially right about that. Unlike other kids who were growing at great speed and outgrowing their clothes on a regular basis, I was barely growing at all. I was not much bigger at age 7 than I was at age 5. I still fit into pants and shirts from two years before that I had to use for play clothes at home since they were now too tattered and threadbare to be worn for school. Even grandma, master of the sewing thread that she was, could not save my clothes when they had been washed so many times you could see through the fabric when you held it up to the light.

The clothes from the past year, however, were still fair game to be worn since they still fit and weren't yet candidates for window screen substitutes or cleaning rags.

The sneakers, however, were something else entirely. Even though they still fit, they had to go because they were far too short to be repaired. Numerous times, grandma tried to fix the separating soles with glue, to try and glue fabric patches over the holes, to sew torn seams in the canvas, but there was no more that could be done to keep them on my feet any longer. Mother had me sit on the bench while she forced a new sneaker that I didn't like onto my foot, checking its size. Same as last year, but they looked a far sight better, being that they were new.

"Can I have those?" I asked about a pair that I liked better.

"No, you can't have THOSE because THOSE cost $14, and these cost $8 because they are on sale. If I get you the $14 ones I won't be able to buy you some new socks, which you need. Besides, there's no reason why those shoes are so much more expensive than these. Sneakers are sneakers."

There were no Nikes or any other big-name brand shoes for me; it was always store-branded shoes costing the least amount of money possible.

We got to the racks with the pants and shirts in the boy's section, and Mother went to work putting outfits together. A brown and orange striped shirt and some burnt orange pants, both Garanimals brand, the most embarrassing brand of clothes kids in my neighborhood could possibly wear. I had gotten some the year before, and I was ridiculed mercilessly by the rest of the class on my first day of school. Garanimals were seen as 'baby clothes' in spite of the fact that they came in sizes to fit children of all ages.

But, as with the shoes, the Garanimals were all on sale this week, so that was what Mother bought. She grabbed a pair of jeans in my size, threw those into the plastic store cart, and wheeled it over toward the fitting room.

My heart leaped up to my throat as I saw Luis Matos in front of one of the fitting room doors with his mother, checking the fit of his new jeans, the same brand as the ones I was about to add to my collection. I darted behind one of the underwear display cabinets so as not to be seen.

I quietly said to my mother, "Don't forget, I need underwear."

"Oh. Right."

She pulled the shopping cart over out of the way of some other moms measuring shirts against their children's torsos and leafed through the facings of the Fruit of the Loom underwear, searching for my size. I did, in fact, need new underwear as the elastic had worn out from many washings, and Grandma had stitched numerous holes in several pairs, but as with the rest of the clothes, I would have to be ok with only getting 3 new pairs. I would still have to wear the least worn of the worn-out pairs until we could afford to buy more, which wouldn't be until next school year's back-to-school shopping trip.

I watched cautiously to see when Luis left the fitting room and hoped that when he left the area, he went in a different direction than the underwear section. I saw underwear in his cart, so it was a safe bet that they would go somewhere else when he was finished trying on the choices his mother had made for him.

"Ok, come on, let's go try stuff on."

Mother said as she tossed a 3 pack of my size underwear into the cart. I panicked, seeing that Luis was back in his own old clothes but still standing by the fitting room talking to his mother.

"NO!" I said nervously, "I need a new winter coat," I informed her.

"A new winter coat? Are you out of your mind? The one you have is only a year old."

"Yeah, but…but….but the inside is falling apart' I said, inventing a reason that did, in fact, exist, but was still within the means and knowhow of grandma to fix with her sewing needle.

I hid behind the rack of children's coats at the edge of the boy's department but parted some of them so I could see through them in the direction of the fitting rooms.

"I swear, you go through clothes like water. There's not gonna be enough money to pay the phone bill either if I have to get you a coat too, or we're already two months behind on the phone bill."

Mother said loudly and without any care for anyone else around us, knowing just how poor we were. Finally, Luis and his mother left the fitting room area and started walking toward the front registers.

Mother had me try on an Arctic Eskimo-type winter jacket that was popular at that time, surmising

"Looks good, but it's too expensive. It won't be winter for a while. Maybe it will go on sale before then. Take it off and we'll go to the fitting room to try the rest of this mess on."

I did as she instructed. Place the coat on the hanger and back on the rack. We went to the fitting room, where the attendant gave us a number 5 for the 5 items I was to try on.

Like most children. I hated trying on clothes at the store. Unlike most other children, however, I had more of a reason to hate it. Clothing manufacturers always made their pants so that if they fit me in the waist, which for me was very tiny, they were far too long, dragging the floor or worse yet, being so long that they covered the bottom of my feet and I could walk on them. I hated that. It made me look too small for the kid I was. Today would be no different.

I exited the fitting room with the garanimals outfit on. I looked like an absolute clown with pants that, based on the length, looked like they were three sizes too big, a fact made worse by the fact that they were also the flared style of pants that were super popular at the time. I looked like a two-year-old playing dress-up and trying to wear my dad's pants.

"Oh well," Mother said as I stood in front of the dressing room door to show her, "Grandma will fix them. OK, try on the jeans and one of the 2 shirts. We aren't going to get both of those other two shirts, just one, so we'll pick the one that looks like it fits better."

'Fits better' in this case meant that mother would pick the one that was obviously too big so that in case I DID suddenly have a growth spurt, I would still fit into the shirt and be able to finish the school year wearing it, and maybe even get another year out of it too.

The jeans were a case of the same thing, although not quite as bad, and one of the shirts did indeed have a larger cut, and that was the one mother chose to go with the jeans.

"I don't want the orange pants," I told Mother after getting re-dressed in my old clothes and returning to her side at the cart as she tossed a 6 pack of socks into it. Mother grabbed my ear and tugged it hard upward while she bent at the waist to better meet my face and sneered, "Well, guess what? Too fucken bad because you're getting them. It's all I can afford. Now, come on, we're leaving. "

and she let go of my ear and pushed the shopping cart toward the registers. The whole way home, tears silently dripped from my eyes and onto the ground in front of me as I looked forward to the teasing and violence I would be subjected to when I got back to school, and the kids saw me in these awful clothes.

Grandma had done her usual good job with having me put on the garanimals polyester pants and pinning them up so she knew how much to take off the bottom. She stitched them like a pro who did alterations for a living in a high-end clothing shop. The jeans looked almost as good as Levi's when she finished making those a proper fit for me as well.

The morning of the first day back to school, I was to wear the orange outfit because my mother insisted upon it. I reluctantly put on the outfit and looked at myself in the mirror. It didn't look nearly as horrendous as it had before Grandma's great alteration job, but it still looked bad enough that I knew I was in for it when the kids saw me.

I ate breakfast as slowly as I could to delay the inevitable time when I'd have to leave the house to confront the kids and their laughter and jeers.

"Don't mess your new clothes up."

Mother warned me with a look in her eye that said all that needed to be said about what would happen to me if I did. I wanted to tell her that I wasn't going to mess up the clothes but that the clothes were going to get me messed up, but it would be a fruitless argument that would start more trouble with her I was in no mood to take on my first day back to school, my most hated day of the entire year.

When I got to the entrance to the school, I met up with John, who was walking in at the same time. He looked at me, and while he didn't say anything about my clothes, it was clear that even he knew the amount of laughter that was about to ensue. We weren't disappointed, as while John stood there in his respectable maroon, tan, and white plaid button-down shirt, jeans, and white Asics runners, I stuck out like a sore thumb in my burnt orange pants and pumpkin shirt and cheap black canvas and white rubber knock off brand converse all stars.

The laughter was coming from all sides, now with all my favorite bullies kicking at me and pushing me. I was up and down over and over. As soon as I'd stand up, someone would push me down.

"Where'd you get those clothes?! A clown at the circus?!" one of the bullies said, "He got them from the baby store!"

Luis Matos shouted, eliciting another wave of raucous laughter from everyone else. How I wanted to tell him and all of them that I saw Luis at the very same store buying the jeans he had on right now. He'd just call me a liar and keep right on picking on me.

I got more of the same treatment at recess and at the end of the day. By that time, I had a hole in one of the knees of my pants, and they, along with my too-orange shirt, were filthy from my being pushed to the ground so many times.

I inched my way home slowly, readying myself mentally for the beating I was about to receive. Mother told me not to mess up my new clothes, but my clothes were far beyond messed up, as the bullies were worse than ever with their cruelty when they witnessed how ridiculous I looked.

Blood from my nose where one of the bullies had punched me stained the top of the shirt, and a dirty footprint of one of the bullies' new shoes emblazoned the right side of the lower part of the shirt from when Eggy had purposely stepped on me, calling the shirt an orange rug.

After Grandma opened the door and saw the state I was in, she helped me get out of the clothes and into my play clothes, and she went to work trying to fix the pants and shirt. The shirt went into the wash that she was already in the middle of doing, the Whirlpool washer making its' trademark sloshing sounds.

Mother wasn't home yet, but she would be soon. I tried to forget about the day by watching TV. The RCA console was already on, grandma keeping it blazing the room with its glow while she did the various household chores.

After Grandma had started making the dinner, Mother walked in the door. She wasted no time, walking straight over to me, seeing my nose all swollen again, dirt on my face and arms.

"What the fuck happened to you, and don't you even tell me your new clothes are messed up."

"Th-Th-The kids made fun of me; they said I was wearing baby clothes."

SLAP! One hit across the left cheek.

"Didn't I tell you not to mess up those new clothes?"

"It's ok. There was only a small hole in the knee. I have it almost fixed. When they go in the wash, they'll be ok,' Grandma said in an effort to get Mother off my back.

"I don't care. I told him not to mess them up. Where are they?'

"The pants are there. "

she said as she pointed to the arm of the living room chair where she was sitting earlier while she mended them.

"The shirt is in the washer."

Mother walked over and grabbed the pants from the chair. She stuck her finger underneath the portion of the rip that

Grandma hadn't yet finished, and she yanked hard at the material. It tore. She grabbed at the now huge hole with both hands, tearing in opposite directions.

"Is THIS what you want? Huh, fucker? Do you WANT to wear clothes that look like this? Huh!"

Now she grabbed the scissors from the sewing kit grandma left on the footstool in front of the chair. She cut slit after slit in the pants. Then she turned to grandma and bellowed, "Bring me the shirt."

"I can't," Grandma replied, "it's on the spin cycle."

"I SAID BRING ME THE MOTHERFUCKING SHIRT!!!!!!"

Grandma held her arm up to prevent Mother from hitting her in the face, which she was completely prepared for as Mother had balled up her fist while issuing the demand.

Grandma opened the lid, and the machine slowed to a stop. When it finally came to a halt, she fished around for the shirt. Finding it, she handed it to her mother, who tore it at the collar and then used the scissors to cut it in numerous locations.

"Is this BETTER? Huh, you worthless bastard? YOU LIKE THIS BETTER!"

She yelled while swinging the destroyed shirt in my face.

All I could do was copy my grandma's action of trying to put my arm up to deflect a hit to the face or torso, but my mother was too smart for that. She wouldn't hit me when my hand was up in defensive mode. She waited until I lowered it, started walking away, and then, with my relaxed stance, she punched me hard in the chest. Then she dragged me off the couch and screamed, "Get your play clothes off NOWWWW!"

I sheepishly did as she said, but when I moved too slowly, she kicked me in my thigh to remind me to move faster. When I was down to my underwear, she said

"Underwear, too."

I took off my briefs as well and sat there naked, waiting for my next instruction.

She unlocked the living room door and opened it

"If you can't keep your clothes in good shape, you don't get to have any. Now get out."

"Shirley! What are you DOING? He can't go out there naked."

"Shut up, you hear me! SHUT THE FUCK UP! He most certainly can, and he WILL. Gonna make me waste my money on new clothes! Can't even keep them in good shape the first day he wears them?! FUCK HIM. That's what he says to me when he comes home with clothes looking like this. He says 'fuck you'. He's got to learn."

Now she reared up on me again.

"Get OUT"

She said while grabbing my arm and leading me to the door. I pulled back in the opposite direction, trying to prevent her from throwing me into the hallway of the apartment building where anyone who lived in the building, coming or going, would see me naked.

Ultimately, I lost my battle, and her strength won out over my puny, frail frame.

When I hit the floor in the hallway, she shut the door and locked it.

Grandma came to the door and tried to unlock it, saying she was going to call the police if Mother didn't let me back in. I heard a scuffle between mother and grandma. It sounded like Mother had slapped or punched her more than once. I balled up my fists and started banging on the door

"Grandma!!! NOOOOO! Please don't hurt her! Don't hurt grandma!!!!"

Finally, fearing what the neighbors would think was going on, hearing the commotion of me screaming and banging on the door, she opened the door. I saw Grandma on the floor, crying, her glasses far away from her on the other side of the living room.

When I saw this, I slammed the door, found courage I didn't know I had, and screamed

"Leave her alone! GET AWAY from her and LEAVE HER ALONE!!!!" while trying to put myself between her and grandma.

Mother, rage causing all the veins in her face to pop out, reached for me and grabbed at me, but missed getting a good hold on me as I ducked and darted to the side to try and evade her grasp. I took the opportunity to go to the phone, grabbing the receiver and screaming

"I'll call the police!"

Mother advanced on me like some kind of mentally deranged prize fighter, punched me full force in the chest, snatched the receiver from my hand, and struck me across the head and back with it numerous times. Then she wrapped the coiled receiver cord around my neck and started choking me. I desperately tried to get free, but each attempt was met with the cord tightening its grip and further restricting the airflow to my lungs.

Grandma got to her knees and came over to Mother, trying to knock her down to loosen her grip on the phone cord.

"Stop it! Please STOP IT! They're only CLOTHES! Please STOP!" and Grandma managed to get Mother's grip loose enough that I could squirm my way out from the phone cord. I was free of it, and I somehow managed to wrench the receiver loose from Mother's grip while she focused on trying to get Grandma away from her by kicking and punching her with her other free hand.

I dialed the operator in an attempt to get her to connect me to the police. My mother saw me doing it, and she pulled the phone cord, connecting the phone to the wired wall outlet. It let go. She picked up the phone and threw it across the room. It crashed into the coffee table, making a mark on it and tumbling to the floor. She stood up, exhausted. The aftermath of the rage-induced adrenalin rush caused her to shake now as she calmed down. After a couple of minutes of slow, deep breaths, we waited for what was to come next. Mother finally told me.

"Get to the shower. You're filthy. Like your clothes were."

Grandma, aware that the tirade was finished, stood up and walked over to where her glasses lay on the floor. She picked them up, put them back on, and escorted me to the bathroom, turned on the water, and sat down on the toilet seat, wracked with exhaustion from the episode herself, shaking all over.

I got into the shower, the hot water both hurting the areas she struck me with the phone and helping them to feel better at the same time. My neck was red and hurting where she had wrapped the cord around my neck, tiny pain pricks issuing from the area as the steady shower water hit it. Outside the shower curtain, Grandma sobbed, full on. I listened and heard the front door open and shut. Mother left, off for a night of drinking at the bar.

We were safe.

For now.

November, 1977 - Third Grade

Nurse Booth was sitting at her desk with the chair angled toward me. In one hand, she held the phone receiver and used her other hand to rub my back in an attempt to comfort me. My third-grade teacher, Miss ManWarren, was sitting across from me. My face was a bloody mess, and the bleeding still wasn't finished. It poured from my mouth in what seemed to be jets. I was holding a white cloth against my mouth that Nurse Booth had handed me moments before.

'Why is there so much blood?'

My inner voice asked as I lifted the pressure from the cloth a bit, and the red flow coming from my mouth was allowed to burst loose of the cloth dam against my lips, dripping more blood onto my shirt.

Miss ManWarren told me to keep the cloth tight against my mouth and not to move.

I wasn't about to argue with her suggestion after seeing more blood come out of my mouth and fall upon my already-soaked shirt.

The pain, which had not registered as much before, was now beginning to register in my mind.

"We are going to have to call an ambulance if we can't get ahold of his mother soon."

Miss Booth said, holding her hand over the talking end of the receiver she still held in her hand, the signal of a constantly ringing phone emanating from the other end against her ear.

I cried harder than before at the prospect of my mother coming to the school to see me in this condition. I shuddered and shook with fear at the prospect of what violent course she would pursue if she had to pick me up and take me home while looking like this.

The day played out much the same as any other day in class. We were working on cursive handwriting when Miss Manwarren came to my desk, and upon seeing that, I obviously hadn't been paying attention when she showed the class how to make a capital letter G on the board; she tried helping me.

"Try it like this," She said, taking me by the hand and guiding me through the motions between the blue guidelines on the paper with my pencil. When she let go and I tried to do it on my own, I failed miserably, and she just said what she usually said.

"I'm going to need you to take out your other notebook and write 100 times 'I will pay attention in class.'"

I did as I was told, as Eggy said, "Little baby can't write. Needs the teacher to hold his hand!" to which Luis and 3 other boys all laughed.

A single tear came from my eye as I got out my notebook to repeatedly print what Miss Manwarren asked for. I worked hard to try and make my printing as legible as possible so that she wouldn't tell me to do it over as she had done before.

My right hand worked feverishly, trying to get all 100 sentences as identically neat as possible. I was certain I would get a blister on my fingers from all the writing, but after the 40th time, she came to my desk to see how I had done so far.

She had already told the rest of the class to put away their handwriting work and get out their spelling books but told me I should keep working. She was intent, it seemed, that I finish my task that she apparently hoped would get me to better focus on what she was saying at the front of the class in the future.

I had completed this task numerous times, but no matter how many times I had done so, things hadn't changed for me. Schoolwork was just a struggle for me and no amount of punitive repetitive sentence writing was going to do anything to positively alter that fact.

"Ok, that's enough for now. You can get out your spelling book. You'll finish writing those sentences in detention."

"NOOO!" I exclaimed, "Not detention!"

One of the boys mocked me, saying, "NOOOOOO."

In an exaggerated tone, making fun of my voice. Laughter poured across the classroom. Miss ManWarren turned her gaze in the direction where the first boy's voice had originated.

"Carlos, for that outburst, you'll join him. Anybody else wants to join them?"

Silence now took over the room.

Carlos's face turned from mocking glee to an angry expression and at the news he would keep me company in detention, he hit his fist against his other hand while looking directly at me. Carlos was another one of Eggy's favorite people as, like the two Luises, he followed Eggy's example and stuck to him like a shadow.

I now focused again on Miss ManWarren's words as she said, "Yes, detention." I will give you the detention notice later that you'll have to bring home for your mother to sign and return to me tomorrow when you come to school. Understand?"

"Y-Y-Yes"

I understood completely. I understood that I was going to get pummeled after school again today by Eggy, Carlos, and whoever else decided to stick around after detention ended. It was a replay of events that had previously unfolded on various occasions. Miss ManWarren was well known for keeping order in the classroom by liberally handing out detentions to troublemakers.

For me, that was bad news because while most children only had to deal with minimum punishments like getting dessert or TV time taken away for getting detention, I had to endure the wrath of my mother.

At the end of the day, when the bell rang, and we all lined up at the door, Miss Manwarren had Carlos, and I wait while the rest of the class left the classroom at a great velocity in their quest to free themselves of the school building for the day.

Now, I want you two to walk to Mr. Shedruff's office and sit there. David, you'll finish writing your sentences from earlier. Carlos, you'll write 'I will not make noise in class' 100 times.

We did as we were told, with Carlos telling me, "You're dead meat" on our way to our destination.

After spending more than a half-hour writing, Mr. Shedruff stood up from his desk and said

"Ok, you two walk. Don't run back to class and apologize to your teacher."

We did as instructed as Mr. Shedruff posted himself as a sentry in the hall to be sure we did so without incident.

When we reached the classroom, we saw that Miss ManWarren was writing grades into her grading log book she had used to keep track of assignments.

Before we could say our apologies, Miss Manwarren said, "Ok, you two go home."

Without even looking up from her log book and handing us the detention notices.

We both took off at top speed down the hall, myself in the lead, Carlos following. Carlos, however, caught up quickly, and he used all the strength in his body to push me down while I was in mind stride. My body lurched forward; I lost my balance and fell face first to the tiled hallway floor below, hitting it hard, my two front teeth burying themselves into the inside portion of my lip, slicing deeply into it as they did so. The force of the impact sent a wave of stars across my vision, and immediately, I =started crying. All of my front teeth were deeply stuck into the flesh of my mouth, and Carlos had already darted through the exit door a few feet away and was on his way home.

I screamed as blood poured from my mouth onto the floor. I shook with pain and fear.

In a moment of this, Nurse Booth came from her office nearby, as did Mr Shedruff, who called out, "Miss ManWarren!" Who came running from the open door of her classroom?

Nurse Booth and Mr. Shedruff got me to my feet, but the extent of my body shaking with such force didn't allow me to allow my feet to find the floor and walk, so My Shedruff picked me up and carried me to Nurse Booth's office, sitting me in the student sized wooden chair next to her desk.

I felt cold as ice even though none had yet been applied, and I was sweating profusely. Nurse Booth went to a cabinet to get a blanket and came back and put it around me while placing a cold, wet cloth against my mouth. Then she returned to the other side of her office, this time to the refrigerator, to take an ice pack from the freezer.

She returned to my side and placed the pack over my mouth, telling me to hold it in place.

"NOOO!" I screamed through my wall of tears that were joining with the continuous flow of blood and meeting on my shirt below. I couldn't bear any pressure on my mouth. The pain was excruciating.

"Now, after Mr. Shedruff returned with my file, Nurse Booth looked at my number on the contact sheet and dialed the rotary phone as quickly as the dial would allow.

There was no answer. This went on for some time.

'Where is grandma?'

I wondered. If Mother wasn't home, Grandma always was, unless, of course, she had to go to the store for milk or bread or some other item we needed that had run out.

Back in the present time, after which many attempts had been made to contact my mother, Grandma finally answered.

Nurse Booth informed her of the situation, and that someone needed to pick me up immediately to get me to the hospital.

"It's ok, it's ok," Nurse Booth tried to reassure me.

"Grandma is coming. Grandma is coming."

That was at least some relief; I wouldn't have to see mother quite yet. I knew that when I did see her, there would be hell to pay for this. I would be blamed and would get the usual beating.

About 15 minutes later, mother arrived. My heart sank as she walked into Nurse Booth's office.

I got home just after grandma had answered the call, mother informed us, speaking to the air and making eye contact with no one, slurring her words as she made her declaration. It was more likely that she was passed out drunk at home while grandma had gone to the store for an errand when the calls from Nurse Booth were made.

Now, Mother finally made eye contact, and it was my direction she had decided to cast her gaze.

"What's all this?" she asked, waving her hand up and down in front of me."

"It seems he was leaving and had been running down the hall and tripped.

"NOOO!" I tried to tell them, "It was Carlos. He pushed me.

Mr. Shedruff put his head in his hand, knowing that now things would get even more complicated since someone else had caused this situation to occur. Adding to that, it was someone Mr. Shedruff had known all too well. Carlos was a frequent visitor to his office, and not because of good class conduct.

Mother told me, "Get that cloth out of the way, and lemme see." I did as I was told and was surprised by the severity of the injury; Mother said, "Holy shit!" as more blood poured from my mouth.

"Alright, come on, put the cloth back, and let's go."

"We'll have forms for you to sign when he comes back to school," Mr Shedruff almost sheepishly said

"Yeah, I bet you will." Let's go, Mother said, jerking me by the hand to get me off the chair and walking quickly toward the exit door.

Mother was silent the whole walk to the bus stop for the bus that would take us to the hospital. After a few moments, the bus arrived. Mother still remained silent on the bus ride.

It was only when we arrived at the hospital that she started to talk, and that was to the attendant at the emergency room desk.

"Well, you certainly have a nice red design on that shirt, haven't you?" the attendant joked about the amount of blood that had soaked into my shirt and adhered it to my chest. We both ignored the attempt at humor.

"Would it be ok if I could maybe see under that cloth?" The attendant asked me in that annoying, childish voice many adults use around young children.

"I carefully let my grip on the cloth lessen so I could bring it down a bit, and the attendant said, "Ok, that's enough. Got it." And she wrote something down, then informed us

"You can have a seat in the waiting area, and you'll hear when your name is called."

"Come on," Mother said with an annoyed tone in her voice. We sat across from a man with a bad cough and another woman crying and saying her stomach hurt over and over. Before long, the waiting area, which originally had about ten people waiting, had swelled its' population to almost thirty.

After over an hour had passed, finally, my name was called by a nurse.

We followed her to a room in the emergency room, and I sat down in a chair opposite the examining table.

I looked around the room. I saw a glass-doored cabinet that had bandage rolls, gauze, Band-Aids, and many other things you'd expect to see in a hospital emergency exam room.

A couple of minutes later, a man entered and introduced himself simply as 'the doctor.'

"So let's see what we have here. Go ahead and drop the cloth. You won't need it anymore. He was right. The blood had either stopped or was now very little. I still tasted it though, bitter and nasty each time I swallowed.

The doctor washed his hands and then put on rubber gloves. He then wheeled a small table with some instruments and bandages on it. One of the nurses had obviously prepared it before we came into the room.

There was a clean, dry, medical-grade white cloth on the table. The doctor took it and gently wiped at the area to clean up some of the blood so he could get a better look at the injured area and make a determination of what he needed to do.

After looking at the wound, he said, "Well, there's no doubt you're going to need stitches."

At the prospect of stitches, I panicked and said, "NOOO!" to which mother sternly said, "Yes, stitches. Now stop it. Let the doctor do his job."

Mother had all the positive bedside manner of a dead fish. Her lack of concern was breathtaking. All she was worried about was getting this over with as quickly as possible so she could be back in our shabby apartment where she could continue her drinking binge.

One of my teeth was still embedded in the wound it had made when my face struck the floor, and the doctor gently maneuvered the tooth out of the flesh.

Next, the doctor picked up a syringe filled with lidocaine and stuck the needle into the top of the bottle.

"W-w-what is that f-f-f-f-for?"

I asked, wrenching my mother's grip on my wrist that she had applied to make sure I stayed where I was and didn't move.

"I am just going to give you a little medicine so that when I stitch your wound, it won't hurt, ok? I promise it will just be a little stick, and then your lip will start to feel cold, and then you won't feel it at all. Ok?"

And he bent down and lifted me up with his hands under my armpits, sitting me on the table.

"Ok, lie back and stay still, ok?"

Apparently, 'ok' was his favorite word. No, it was not ok. A needle was about to go in my lip, and then another kind of needle was going to stitch my lip. 'Ok' was the last word I would use to describe this terrible situation. I was scared, and my heart was racing, and all this doctor could do was keep saying, 'ok.'

Now, he washed the wound with some sterile water in a bowl that had been poured earlier. It ran out of the wound and down my cheek and onto the table where I lay.

Mother held my head still while he stuck the needle into my lip in one area, and then he changed position and stuck it in another location, and then a third. I was squirming, trying to get free. He lied. The needle hurt, and the lidocaine burned before it got cold. I hated this, and all I wanted to do was get free and run away. Mother struggled to keep my head still, and a nurse who had been walking by the examining room came in to hold my legs so that I could be more still.

"All done. Now we'll just wait until it's numb, and then we'll do the stitches." The doctor informed me and dropped the syringe into a box mounted on the wall. At least he didn't say 'ok' again.

After a few minutes, the doctor tapped at the area with his finger.

"Can you feel me doing this?" He asked

"No," I replied.

"Ok then, time for the stitches."

He tore open a suture pack that was waiting for him on the rolling table and went to work. The black thread went in and out of the wound, and within a few minutes, he was finished.

After he was done, he said

"OK, champ, I don't want to hear any stories about you eating a bunch of potato chips any time soon, ok?"

I didn't understand at the time that he meant there was so much salt in potato chips that they'd really sting if salt got in the wound, but I tried my best to smile anyway, failing because I couldn't smile accurately while still being numb from the lidocaine.

"7 stitches. Now, he will have to come back to have them removed, or you can go to his primary pediatrician, who can do it. You should also pay a visit to his dentist because his two front teeth are pushed in and loose. They aren't likely to come out, but those are his permanent teeth, so you should definitely have the dentist take a look at everything just to be sure everything is going to heal alright. If he has pain afterward, which he likely will, children's aspirin is fine."

"Ok, so are we done?"

Mother asked coldly, leaving being her only concern.

The doctor looked at her as if surprised this was all she could think of to say and replied, "Yes. You're done. In a few minutes, the nurse will bring his discharge papers, and you can go.

"Ok"

Mother said. It seemed even more sarcastic than usual for her since it was the doctor's favorite word.

The entire trip home on the bus and then the walk from the bus stop took place in just as heavy silence as the journey to the hospital. The air was thick with what wasn't said. The doom that lay ahead for me. I was going to get it bad this time. Mother had to not only make herself available to go to my school but also to the hospital. Two big public appearances in one day, plus two trips on public transit. This wouldn't end well for me.

I steeled myself for what was to come as Mother unlocked the apartment door, and Grandma rushed to my side to see what had happened. My lip was swollen, and the lidocaine had largely worn off now.

"Come on, come and eat. I saved your mac and cheese. I'll warm it up for you."

Grandma said while Mother just gazed upon her with a look of contempt. Mother hung up her coat and went to the refrigerator, retrieving a can of beer and popping its top open, chugging it while I waited at the table for Grandma to finish stirring the warmed-up macaroni and cheese on the stove.

It was uncharacteristic for Mother to be this silent for this long. I started to wonder what she was up to. Surely, she was working on some sort of an angle involving torment for me. The anticipation of what she might do was often worse than when she was actually executing her plans. Plus, the fear of what she might do was often eclipsed by the actions she would take in reality.

Mother walked into the living room as mother scooped macaroni onto my plate.

"Do you want yours too, Shirley?"

Now, Mother returned to the kitchen.

"Oh sure, now ask me. Ask me after you took the time to FALL all over the fucking KLUTZ here FIRST." Mother sneered through beer-drenched breath.

"No, I don't want any of it. Give it all to the klutz who can't even walk without causing a bunch of problems."

"NOOO! It was Carlos. He pushed me." I tried to correct her. Bad move. She came over to me and grabbed the fork, picked up some of the macaroni with it, and shoved it into my mouth forcefully, the fork scraping against the wound and almost pulling out one of my stitches.

"Eat your dinner that your precious grandma saved just for you, you bastard, and don't try any bullshit lies about someone pushing you. You did this to yourself."

And with that, mother retreated to her room with her beer can back in her hand, slamming the door once she got there. I didn't have an opportunity to defend myself regarding the truth of what had happened, and it didn't matter because my mother wouldn't believe it, no matter how much I tried to make her believe it.

The rest of the evening went without incident.

"Be careful brushing your teeth, "Grandma told me before bedtime. When I finished brushing my teeth, Grandma read me a story as she had when I was younger. Now, she only did it when there was some terrible injury that hurt or was more severe than usual. I welcomed it though, her holding me while she read.

At around 2 am, I heard my door open. Then, I saw a shadowy figure coming toward the bed. I instantly froze up as I recognized the silhouette as the one that belonged to Mother.

A fist came down hard on my chest, then another to my abdomen.

Mother continued the assault silently for more than five minutes. This wasn't out of the ordinary, as Mother often came to my room in the middle of the night to beat me for no reason other than the fact that I existed.

These beatings were especially terrifying for me because, in the absolute darkness, I had little to no indication of where mother's fists would strike me next and I had no way of protecting myself defensively in hopes of softening or eliminating being hurt by the blows. She didn't even allow me to leave the bed while she did it, holding me down with one hand while doing her damage with the other.

I screamed again and again as the assault continued.

When she was satisfied that she had done enough to me, she retreated to her room.

Now, I heard another door open, as I frequently did during these incidents. It was Grandma this time. Unlike Mother, she turned on the light. When she did, she saw my lip bleeding profusely. Mother had landed one punch to my mouth, and it had busted one of the stitches the doctor had given me earlier. As best she could, she tried to hold the wound closed to get it to stop bleeding.

When the bleeding finally subsided, Grandma returned to her position of holding me while she read a story to me to get me to calm down. She stayed with me the rest of the night, crying herself and me to sleep.

Officer Mike - Part 3

As before, on the living room floor, Grandma attempted to lift me up into a sitting position, this time against the headboard on her bed. She put her hands beneath my armpits and hoisted me up there.

A loud bang on the door followed my mother's voice.

"There you go again, babying the brat."

Mother always hated Grandma's attempts to help me in the situation aftermath of what she had actually caused.

"He's a worthless fucking troublemaker. When are you gonna wise up and understand that? I guess never since you're worthless,   too."

"You've gone much too far this time, Shirley. He's got serious injuries." Grandma responded through the door. The truth was that mother always went too far. This time, however, as Grandma said, she REALLY had done so.

There was a louder bang on the door, and Grandma recoiled, stepping back a couple of steps away from the door.

"You Think so? You really think so?" Mother replied, a sarcastic tone strong in her voice.

"If that little fucker is still alive, it isn't far enough. He brought the cops here last night. Do you hear me? He deserves even more than he got." Mother continued, her voice getting louder and the sarcasm transforming to anger.

"He needs to come out here and clean up his mess," Mother demanded.

"What mess?" grandma inquired

"You KNOW what mess, you dumb bitch. The blood on the living room rug. THAT mess"

"He can't. Not now. He can't even stand up on his own, thanks to what you did to him."

"He doesn't NEED to stand to clean the rug. Get him out here NOW!"

"No. I will clean it up later. Leave him alone. Please…"

"No, it is HIS goddamn mess. HE will clean it and he will do it right now. Get him out here now, or I will break this door down."

A few seconds passed with Grandma not responding, and then

CRASH!

Mother used her fists against the door so hard it seemed a miracle she hadn't punched a hole in it.

"You get out here and clean this mess, you BASTARD!"

"Please stop; please just leave him be! He can clean it when he is feeling better. Please just go away!" Grandma yelled through the door.

CRASH! This time, she hit it even harder, and splinters of paint flew off the door.

Grandma came to sit on the bed with me. Frequently, in moments like this, she wished there were a telephone extension here in her room, but there was no money for that. Extra phones were an extravagant luxury when you were as poor as we were. For many months, the phone bill for the lone phone we did have wouldn't even be paid due to lack of funds, usually because Mother had spent even more on her booze during that month.

The only thing they could both do now was to stay in here and hope that the door would hold up and that mother would either give up her attack or get too tired to continue with it.

CRASH!

And more paint sailed to the air.

CRASH! And this time, the door bowed in a bit.

The deadbolt of the ancient lock held strong but it wouldn't be able to do so indefinitely with continued attacks upon it. Eventually, it would tear through the door jamb if her behavior continued.

I thought about the possibility of getting out through the window, but in my injured condition, that would be almost impossible, not to mention grandma's arthritis, which would make her escape impossible as well.

A couple of minutes passed, and it was silent. It seemed as if Mother had given up. I hear her moving about in the kitchen, opening the refrigerator door. Then the sound of the electric can opener, a cheap model that rarely worked properly and was the only 'luxury' appliance we owned. The sound of that device this early in the morning meant only one thing: Mother was opening a can of tomato juice to make a Bloody Mary. She was going to start this day the way she started most, well on her way to drunkenness.

A few moments later, she returned to the door to converse with us again.

"You're both going to be sorry if you don't open this door and come out right now. "She sneered between sips of her alcoholic concoction.

CRASH!

This one was much harder. Now, she was resorting to using her feet. A large crack formed in one of the middle section wood panels.

When there was no response, mother retreated. We listened and heard a rustling in kitchen drawers. What was she looking for? A couple of minutes later, she returned.

This time, we heard a crunch. It was the distinct sound of plastic breaking. Then he heard the sound again. What was she doing? Then we heard it again. This time, it sounded as if she had sent pieces of something flying because, after the crunch, we heard the telltale sounds of plastic pieces hitting the wall.

"What are you doing?" Grandma asked after getting up and moving closer to the door one more time.

"I'm breaking all the toys you bought him. I used the hammer to smash the new truck you got for him the last time you went out. He doesn't deserve any of those toys anyway. He deserves nothing. You hear me bitch?! NOTHING!"

Grandma let out a sob, and I tried desperately to get to my feet but couldn't do it, the pain being too much to bear. I fell to the floor with a thud. Grandma came to my side to help me back up   onto   the   bed.

"If you don't come out NOW, I am going to break another toy, and I will keep breaking them until there are none left.

"Please NOOOOOO! I pleaded and tried to get up again, but Grandma stopped me and held me in place on the bed.

"No, we can't go out there. You know how she is. You know what she'll do," Grandma told me with exasperation.

"No, I'll just clean the blood, and everything will be ok, and she'll stop, please Grandma, let me go out there," I pleaded, "No, I may not be able to fix what she does to you this time if you go out there. Do you understand? We have to stay here."

More crunching sounds were happening outside the door, and another of my toys was meeting its fate and would never be played with again. A few seconds passed after that toy was fully destroyed. This behavior continued with two more toys and the mother saying

"Ok, fine, I'll just smash them all, no problem," and I heard the sound of more and more breaking plastic. I cried full-on while Grandma held me.

Then, Mother became bored with destroying my toys and went to work with the claw of the hammer on the door. She wedged it between the door and the jamb, attempting to make enough space between the door and the claw of the hammer so she could get the claw behind the lock bolt and then push the door open. After a few tries at this, she was successful, and the door flew open. Grandma jumped up off the bed and attempted to use her body as a barricade between her and me, but Mother just pushed Grandma aside, and she fell to the floor.

"Get OUT there NOW!" Mother screamed as she grabbed me by my splinted arm and swung me off the bed and to the floor, kicking me hard in the thigh and ribs, trying to maneuver me out the door to the living room.

"No, please don't, Shirley, Please! He's hurt so bad already! Please leave him be! Grandma got to her feet and again tried to get between us. The moment she did this, Mother seized the opportunity to grab Grandma by the neck and held her by the throat against the door jamb, screaming, "He's got to clean up his mess you hear me BITCH?!!"

And she dug her fingernails into Grandma's throat. I somehow got partially up and was on my knees, pulling at the top of Mother's pants with my un-splinted hand.

"Noooo, please don't hurt her; I'll go, I'm going! Let go! Please! Let goooo!" I yelled as I tried to make my way out to the blood-stained rug.

Mother let go of Grandma's throat and re-focused her attention squarely on me.

"Well, if you're going, the GO!" and she slapped my head while going back to kicking me to get me where she wanted me. Then, when I was close to the stains, she went to the kitchen to get out cleaners from under the sink. She brought me a bottle of Fantastik cleaner and told me

"Now, get those stains out of my rug"

She provided no sos pads or clothes or anything else to clean the satins with, so I asked her, "How? You only gave me this," and I held up the bottle she had brought a moment before.

She grabbed the bottle, slapped my face with it, and shouted, "With your HANDS, you worthless IDIOT?! What else?"

I had no choice but to do as she said. I sprayed the stains, and they were considerably large this time and used my knuckles to rub at the soaked blood. Over and over, I tried to work the cleaner deep into the stiff fibers of the tightly woven berber-style carpet with my hands and balled-up fists, grinding them against the stiff rug. At times, I tried using the wood splint to help get the stains out, to which my mother responded by slapping my head or kicking me, reminding me that I had to use my hands. It was the only acceptable method for her.

"You'll stay there and scrub as long as it takes to get the stains out of my rug. You hear me, dummy?"

She asked while urging me again with a kick to my broken ribs. I dared not let on that doing this sent stabbing pain through me and made breathing even harder, not that I really wanted to since all I could smell was this toxic chemical she was forcing me to use. If I showed any signs that I was hurting or started to cry, the attacks would only get much worse, which I knew from heavy experience.

The more I rubbed at the stains, the more raw my knuckles became until they started adding more blood to the Fantastic cleaner-soaked rug, making my efforts even more fruitless. The pain of the cleaner in my raw knuckles became stronger and stronger with the continued effort, and grandma just sat on the floor where mother had left her after she choked her, quiet sobs eliciting from her as she watched me try and fail at cleaning the stains on the rug.

I stayed there for the better part of the next hour while Mother watched me try and do her bidding. When she wasn't satisfied with the results, she had me use other cleaners in this same manner, which went on for another hour.

When she felt that I had suffered enough, she relented.

"Go get one of the old rags from under the sink and finish the job."

"I-I-I can't. " I told her

"Why the fuck can't you?"

"He can't stand up and walk," Grandma reminded her, "That's not my problem. He brought the cops here. Can't stand up and walk?! No, but he can bring the fucking asshole cops to my house though, can't he? Oh sure, he can do that just fine"

And she kicked me hard in the ribs again.

"I don't give a fuck if you have to crawl, I don't give a fuck if it takes you till next week to get there but get the old rag and clean my fucking rug!"

She yelled into my face, the stench of her bloody mary and all the liquor from the night before still strong on her breath.

I did as I was told and somehow made it to the kitchen on my hands and knees, getting an old rag out from under the sink and then returning to the scene of the stains the same way as I came to the kitchen.

After another hour of nearly non-existent positive results, the mother said, "Ok, that's enough," and proceeded to grab me by the hair and position my face so that it was square with hers. I quickly was unable to see anything, however, as the tears obscured my vision.

"This is what you get when you bring the police to my house. You got that? Huh stupid? You got that?"

I was trying to get her to release her grip on my hair by using my bloodied hands to grab her wrist to get me loose, but she was too strong for me.

"Answer me, you FUCK! Is this getting through to you, you FUCK?! Answer me, or I'll pull your fucking scalp off!!!"

"YEEESSSSSS!" I yowled through my agony.

With my response, she let go, and I plopped back down on the rug and splinted my arm, hitting the floor hard and sending another shockwave of pain through me. She took one more opportunity to kick me in the ribs as she walked off toward the kitchen, where she poured herself a large portion of straight vodka and drank it down as if it were Kool-Aid.

Grandma and I watched as she made her way to the TV, turned it on, and walked to the couch to lie down on it.

"Get out of here, both of you. Just get the fuck out of my sight. I don't want to have to look at either one of you."

Grandma got to her feet and moved over toward me. She gently lifted me up and then took me by the hand.

"Try and walk," she urged. She just wanted to get both of us away from Mother before she decided to inflict more sorrow upon us. I slowly and carefully tried taking a step. I was able, but not without a great deal of protest coming from my aching body.

Eventually, we made it to the bathroom, where Grandma positioned me in front of the sink and turned on the water.

'Ok, come on, we have to wash those hands.'

And she guided my hands under the running water. Instantly, my wounds from scrubbing the rug sent forth a new wave of a different kind of pain, even stronger than just that of the cleaning chemicals in the open wounds on my knuckles. It subsided after a moment, but I was crying full-on and loudly.

"Shut that brat up!"

Mother shouted from her position on the couch. Grandma made the quiet hand sign with her finger to her lips. I tried controlling my sobs to a quieter whimper, but it was difficult to maintain through this ordeal.

Now grandma went to the medicine cabinet and got out the tube of Johnson and Johnson first aid cream. She applied it liberally to the wounds on my hands and then wrapped them with the small amount of gauze that was left from the day before.

Grandma and I spent the rest of the day together as she tried to glue two of my smashed toys back together and then mended a pair of my pants while I listened to music on her very old clock radio.

Later that day, I wanted to read but couldn't because it wasn't possible for me to hold the book open with my bandaged hands, so Grandma read the story of Charlie and the Chocolate Factory to me while we both, on occasion, allowed some tears to quietly fall.

February 1978, Third Grade

Today, Miss ManWarren seemed especially cheerful as we arrived at class. I wasn't sure of the reason, but I was happy to see it. John and I were trading Wacky Packages cards at our desks when she called for the day to start by saying, "Ok, everyone, please stand."

Which always initiated the recitation of the Pledge of Allegiance to the flag.

After we finished and sat back down, she passed out stacks of paper to the first desk of each row.

"Please pass them back," she instructed the first-row children.

"We are going to be having a class spelling bee this week so we can see who is going to represent us in the school-wide spelling bee this year."

Well, this was new. I had never heard of this event happening before, but apparently, I wouldn't have known about it before because she continued with, "Third through sixth grade participates each year. The winners of our school spelling be go on to the district championship and compete against all the other schools in the district participating in the spelling bee."

Finally, we were doing something that was up MY alley. A spelling bee would be awesome for me because I was a champion speller. I rarely ever spelled any words wrong on my spelling tests, and usually, if I was marked as being wrong, it was because the teacher had difficulty reading my messy handwriting and mistook one letter as another. When I brought it to their attention, they'd correct the grade.

"This afternoon after recess, we will have a practice round with words you may get in the actual spelling bee." She told us and then asked, "Anyone have any questions?"

Luis Matos raised his hand, and Miss ManWarren called on him.

"Do we have to do it?"

"Yes, we want everyone to participate in this first part in the classroom, but you won't have to participate in the school spelling bee if you don't want to."

"Good," Eggy called out, which elicited a chuckle from the other Luis, Carlos, and a couple of Eggy's other followers.

"One more outburst without being called on, and you will start losing recess time, Edgardo."

Eggy and everyone else got silent quickly. Of course, he didn't want to participate in the spelling bee. That would be seen as 'uncool' and might reduce his status as king of the class hill in the minds of his minions and he wasn't going to allow that. Eggy thrived on being the center of attention, even if the way he attained the title was because of his negative and destructive behavior.

Meanwhile, I looked at the list of words I might be asked. There were some easy ones that we saw in the units of our spelling book, but there were other harder words on the list, too, which were more advanced.

I was ready for the challenge, however, and I hadn't yet met a word that I couldn't figure out how to spell. I knew all the tricks of how some words sounded one way but were spelled another and the exceptions to the rules that made the English language a very convoluted and confusing language to understand, at least as far as spelling.

When it was time for us to practice, Miss Manwarren called on us and had us say the word, spell it, and say it again, just as we would have to do in the actual spelling bee.

John got called on.

Miss Manwarren looked at her list and decided on a word.

'Expression'

John thought for a second and said

"Expression. E-x-p-r-e-s-s-i-o-n. Expression"

"Good, you remembered that sometimes words with the 'tion' sound are spelled with an 's' instead of a 't' " Miss ManWarren said, repeating rules of spelling as they came up with the word selections so we would remember them and not get tripped up during the spelling bee.

"Edgardo, spell 'away' "

"Away. A-w-y. Away"

We all laughed.

"No, that is not correct. Rosalinda, please spell 'away'."

"Away. A-w-A-y. Away." She enunciated the 'a' that Eggy missed with a more vocal expression so as to call attention to his mistake, which also got a chuckle from the class. I wasn't so sure he didn't know how to spell the word. It seemed as if he did it on purpose so he wouldn't have to be called on again to spell any more words since his error meant he was disqualified from continuing in the contest.

"David. Spell 'repetitive'"

"Oh good, it's an easy one"

I thought.

"Repetitive. R-e-p-e-t-i-t-i-v-e. Repetitive"

"Yes, that's good. Lots of repeating 'I's and 't's in there to remember."

As the spelling bee went on, Rosalinda and I were the last two participants, and it was a fierce battle. We were going back and forth spelling word after word until Rosalinda finally got a word that she had trouble with.

"Rosalinda, spell 'generalization'"

"Generalization.   G=e-n-e-r-a-l-i-z-a-s-i-o-n. Generalization."

"No, that is not correct. David, please spell it"

"Generalization.   G-e-n-e-r-a-l-i-z-a-t-i-o-n. Generalization."

"Yes! Correct. You won the practice round of the spelling bee. Everyone congratulate David"

The class all politely clapped except for Eggy, who, as soon as Miss ManWarren's gaze went to a different part of the room, flipped me the bird, and the other bullies followed suit. I didn't care about them. I was focused on the fact that I had finally been able to do something in front of the whole class that didn't make me look like a complete idiot. I was competent at something, and now I was confident to go on to the school wide spelling bee.

We practiced every day for the school-wide spelling bee for the next two and a half weeks. Every day, instead of doing our usual spelling exercises in our books, we created another mock spelling bee, which I won every single time.

Miss ManWarren had been using the third-grade words but also injecting some harder 4th through 6th-grade words in the mix as well. I aced them all, much to the surprise of even Miss ManWarren, who was aware that I was a good speller of words of my grade level but now had proven to be a great speller of even the most difficult 6th-grade words.

The day of the school-wide spelling bee arrived, and the top 10 representatives from each of the 3rd through 6th-grade classes sat on the stage of the auditorium while the rest of the 3rd through 6th-grade classes sat in the audience to cheer us on.

I at least had John and Juan on stage with me to ease some of the butterflies I was feeling in my stomach from having to be on stage with the kids from the older classes.

Mr. Shedruff announced the rules of the spelling bee to everyone as we began.

"Each grade will compete with their classmates, and the winners of those contests will go on to compete against the winners of each of the other grades."

'Ok, this is going to be fun and easy, 'I told myself.

Third grade was up first. 4 other kids were called before they finally came to me.

"David, spell 'preposterous'"

Mr. Shedruff instructed.

"Preposturous. P-r-e-p-o-s-t-u-r-o-u-s. Preposturous"

"Yes, correct."

Applause from the audience.

'It's preposterous they asked me such an easy word,' I thought to myself, making me grin.

Luis Matos was in the audience with the rest of the class and saw me grin and made fun of my grin by exaggerating one of his own, eliciting laughter from the other kids and prompting Miss ManWarren to give him a warning look while shaking her head as a reminder that he should be exercising proper manners.

As the spelling bee went on, more and more children in my class were being eliminated until it was just me and John left.

"John, spell 'uncertainty'"

"Uncertainty. U-n-c-e-r-t-a-n-t-y. Uncertainty"

"No, that is not correct. David, if you can correctly spell uncertainty, you will be your classroom's champion, and you will go on to compete against the winners of the 4th, 5th, and 6th-grade classes after they finish their turns."

After a couple of seconds of thinking, I confidently said

"Uncertainty. U-n-c-e-r-t-a-i-n-t-y. Uncertainty."

"Correct! David, you are your class champion."

Raucous applause initiated by the teachers and continued by the students resounded through the auditorium.

Now, it would be a waiting game while the other classes went through their spelling bee turns.

Upon completion, it was down to 4 of us, the winners for each of our classrooms.

I was first up.

"David, spell 'accommodate' "

"Accommodate. A-c-c-o-m-m-o-d-a-t-e. Accommodate."

"Correct." Mr. Shedruff stated.

'Piece of cake. Easy word.' I thought to myself. I started to think I might actually win this whole thing. Was that possible? Me? Of all people?! It was beginning to look like it might just happen.

"Ayala, spell 'camouflage'"

Ayala was in the 4th grade, and he gave her an easy one. I was sure she would get it.

"Camouflage. C-a-m-o-f-l-a-g-e. Camouflage."

"No, I'm sorry, that's incorrect."

"Paul, spell 'camouflage'"

Paul was a fifth grader. Surely, he knew how to spell this easy word. He took a couple of seconds to ponder it in his mind and then stated

"Camouflage. C-a-m-o-u-f-l-a-g-e. Camouflage."

Generous applause from the audience.

"Yes. Correct."

"Ok, Xavion, spell 'deceive'"

"Deceive. D-e-c-e-i-v-e. Deceive."

"Yes. Right."

"David, spell 'descendent'"

'Really?' I thought. "He's not going to make this hard?'

"Descendent. D-e-s-c-e-n-d-e-n-t. Descendent."

"Correct."

Applause again.

"Paul, spell 'cautious'"

"Cautious. C-a-u-t-i-o-u-s. Cautious."

"That's it, yes!"

"Xavion, spell 'confectionery' "

Xavion didn't even blink an eye.

"Confectionery.   C-o-n-f-e-c-t-i-o-n-e-r-y. Confectionery."

"Yes, correct."

Now it was my turn again, and Mr. Shedruff got a different sheet of words from the table nearby.

"David, spell 'oblique'"

"Oblique. O-b-l-i-q-u-e. Oblique"

"Yes, you are right."

"Paul, spell 'vaccine'"

"Vaccine. V-a-c-s-i-n-e. Vaccine"

"No I'm sorry, that is not correct. Can you spell 'vaccine,' Xavion?"

"Vaccine. V-a-c-c-i-n-e. Vaccine"

"Correct"

'David, spell 'parentheses''"

'Still giving out the easy ones,' I thought

"Parentheses. P-a-r-e-n-t-h-e-s-e-s. Parentheses."

"Yes. Very good."

"Xavion, spell 'extraordinary'"

'Ooh, this one might get him,' I thought. Mr Shedruff had pronounced the word the way most people do, not sounding out the 'a' and acting as if it didn't exist. My heart started beating faster.

"Extraordinary. E-x-t-r-o-r-d-i-n-a-r-y. Extraordinary"

"Yes! He got it wrong! He skipped the 'a'!" I celebrated in my head. Wait, why was I celebrating, now it would come down to ME to spell it right. Oh wow! This couldn't be happening to ME! I was about to win this whole thing!

'Stay calm, stay calm.' My inner voice said reassuringly.

"No, that was not correct, Xavion. David, if you can spell the word extraordinary, you will be our school's spelling bee champion. Everyone, please be absolutely quiet"

I concentrated on looking out into the audience. I saw Miss Manwarren chewing on a fingernail out of anxiousness and John and Juan were both on the edges of their auditorium seats and bouncing up and down already. They knew I knew it because when I was studying the words with them, they had both given me that word at two different points in our practicing.

"Extraordinary."

I paused for a moment to get the clearest picture of the word in my mind. I looked at the letters with my mind's eye and started naming the letters.

"E-x-t-r-a-"

'Don't screw it up,' said the voice in my head

"o-r-d-"

'Keep calm and keep going,' the voice said reassuringly

"i-n-a-r-y. Extraordinary"

Mr. Shedruff smiled. It was the first time I had ever seen him do it. He was actually SMILING as he said.

"Congratulations, David, you are our school spelling bee champion."

John, Juan, and Miss Manwarren leaped to their feet, clapping and cheering.

"Let's get all the class winners up here so we can properly congratulate them too, because next month, they will be going to the District spelling bee championship to represent our school! Come on up, winners!

The other three class winners for 4th, 5th, and 6th grade all came back on stage, and we stood next to each other on the stage while the audience cheered.

"Ok, take a bow," Mr. Shedruff told us.

We did our bows again and again as kids from our class and the others were still cheering and whistling. I started crying. Nothing this amazing had ever happened to me.

"Later, we will be bringing your certificates to your classes. Again, Congratulations! Let's hear it, everyone!"

and the applause became even stronger, and the cheers echoed even louder in the auditorium. We took our bows one more time and then stepped down the staircase on the left of the stage.

John and Juan ran over to me, ran up to me, and gave me high fives, and Juan lifted me up on his shoulders while the rest of the class, minus Eggy and his gang, all continued cheering as they surrounded me. After a couple more minutes, they put me down, and Miss ManWarren came to me and gave me a big hug.

"That was extraordinary, to borrow the word that won you the title of school spelling bee champ! I couldn't be prouder. You spelled sixth-grade words with NO PROBLEM! You are an incredible speller!"

I couldn't believe it was real.

"Is this a dream? I asked John and Juan"

"If it is" don't wake up John said, "Naw, it's not a dream! You DID that." Juan reminded me, "You really are the school spelling bee champion!"

I had to let the words sink in for a moment. I had not only done something right, I did something better than everyone in my school. I was a champion. ME! A CHAMPION!

I cried the whole way back to class, and for a change, they weren't tears of sadness; they were tears of joy.

I was extraordinary.

February 1978, third grade

At the end of the day, just before dismissal, one of the office secretaries came to my classroom to deliver the certificates stating that I was the class spelling bee champion and another stating I was the school spelling bee champion. TWO certificates with my name on them!

Miss ManWarren beamed again when they were delivered and led the class on another run of applause when she handed the certificates to me. John and Juan cheered the loudest. Eggy and his friends made mocking, sarcastic gestures.

To keep my certificates safe, I put them inside my spelling book with the permission slip that my mother would have to sign regarding the trip to another school for the district spelling championship.

It FINALLY happened! I had done something that Mother would be proud of! I asked if I could bring my grandma too, and Miss ManWarren assured me that I could. I don't know if I was more excited about today's wins in the school spelling bee or the prospect of representing our school against all the other elementary schools in the district. Then, the realization hit me.

'What if I WIN that spelling bee too?!' my inner voice excitedly asked.

I could win. It was possible. I had won this one, a feat I never in a million years would have thought could happen to dumb, stupid me. But things were different now. I wasn't as stupid as I and everyone else had thought I was.

"You're gonna beat everybody at the next one, "John reassured me when I shared what my inner voice had pondered.

"Yeah, you know spelling words so well; no one knows how to spell like you do." Juan agreed.

Now we were lined up at the door, ready to leave, and Miss ManWarren reminded me, "Remember to get that permission slip back to me tomorrow. It's important. All of you must get those permission slips in tomorrow because our whole class is going to the district spelling bee to cheer David on to victory."

'Victory," the voice repeated in my head 'Even Miss ManWarren thinks I could win. This is incredible!'

The bell rang, and I was happier than I had ever been about going home. I was even happy about seeing Mother. I couldn't wait to see the reaction on her face when she learned that I did something great for a change at school.

Clutching my spelling book with my certificates and the permission slip, I ran out the door as quickly as my legs would take me.

"John! Juan! Come on," I called out to them, "I want you to come with me!"

They both did as I asked, and all 3 of us ran past Eggy and his gang before they could even station themselves in their usual spot to try and torment me.

We took turns being first in line as we ran to the porch of my house. All three of us booked it up the stairs, through the open hallway door, and to my apartment door. I knocked with more intent than usual, excitement causing my fist to knock harder and faster.

Grandma opened the door. We all barreled in. John was last in, so he closed the door.

"Grandma! Grandma! Guess what happened?! Guess?! "

"Well, I don't know, but you've got me really curious. What? What happened?"

"The school spelling bee today… I WON it! I'm the class champion AND the school champion!"

"Really?" Grandma said with almost as much excitement at the prospect as I had just used knocking on the door.

John and Juan both nodded up and down.

John said, "Yeah, he's the champ."

And Juan continued with, "He beat EVERYBODY, even the sixth graders!"

"OMIGOSH! That is incredible!!!" And Grandma picked me up, spinning around while she hugged me tighter than she ever had before. When she eased her grip, and I could breathe again, I said, "I want you and Mom to be there for the next one."

"Next one? There's gonna be another one?"

"Yeah, the next one, he's gotta go against the winners from ALL the schools in the city and even further!" John said with pride

Grandma put me down and I opened up my spelling book to show her the permission slip.

She looked concerned, but she tried to keep her energy level high

"Well, isn't this great!" She said.

"Yeah, our whole class is going to see him win, too. I think the 4th, 5th, and 6th grade classes will be there too."

Juan told Grandma.

"Yeah, it will be a big event for sure," Grandma said, calmness in her voice replacing the excitement.

"Look at these."

I said, showing Grandma the certificates.

"Wow! That is sooooo great!"

Grandma exclaimed while bending to hug me again.

"Well, we are going to have to celebrate. Come on, we are going to have to get a cake at the bakery. And we will have to stop at the gift shop to get some frames for these certificates."

Grandma was so happy that she forgot she was wearing slippers and, when she realized it, said, "Oh wait, I'll need shoes."

John said.

"Hey, congrats again," and held up his hand for a high five as Juan did the same, and both walked out the door saying, "See you tomorrow."

"Thanks! See ya!"

I said.

Grandma returned with shoes on a couple of minutes later and put on her coat.

"Come on, spelling bee champ; we are going to get the best cake we can buy. And bring those certificates. We'll use them to measure the frames to make sure we get the right size."

Grandma secretly kept a little money hidden away in a compartment of her purse for emergencies. This may not qualify as an emergency, but I wasn't about to question her wanting to buy me a cake at the bakery when it wasn't even my birthday.

We arrived at the bakery, and the display case was filled with the most delicious, sweet, baked treats you could imagine. Cupcakes of all varieties, Danishes, cookies of every description, and, of course, cakes lined the shelves, beckoning everyone to buy something not only due to their incredible appearance but also their mouth-watering scents. I loved being in the bakery just for the smell alone. It was as if you could taste the air with every breath you'd take.

Grandma was a good cook, but when it came to baking, she preferred to leave it to the experts.

"They do it professionally for a living."

She'd say if anyone asked her why she didn't bake, referring to bakers.

"So they can do it a lot better than I can. Might as well buy theirs since they're so much better."

"Which one are we gonna get?" I asked her

"Well, you're the spelling be champ. You decide"

I pointed to a chocolate frosted cake and said

"May I have that one, please?'

To the attendant.

"Sure can, little man. Is it your birthday?" The attendant inquired.

"No, he won the school spelling bee. Show her the certificates."

I opened my spelling books to show off my certificates.

"What? Champion speller of the whole school?! And so YOUNG, too? That's pretty cool."

The attendant beamed. Now, customers in the bakery congratulated me, too.

"Gotta be super smart to be able to spell words that even the older kids can't spell. Congratulations, young man."

Said an elderly lady about grandma's age holding a box of treats she had just bought.

The attendant put the cake I had chosen into a white box and tied it to the box closed with string.

On top of the box, she wrote 'For David, the spelling bee champ' with a marker.

After a few minutes of talking with the bakery patrons and staff, where Grandma told them she knew I was smart because I could read when I was just 3 years old, we walked up the street to the gift shop to get frames.

After measuring the frames we bought them and had a similar situation where we got to talking to the cashier and customers of the gift shop. Grandma was always proud of me, talking with people everywhere she went about me even when I hadn't done anything as momentous as winning the school spelling bee; so today, she REALLY had a lot to beam about, and she wasn't wasting the opportunity. We even stopped by Rexall Drugs to get an ice cream soda at the soda counter, where she REALLY had the time to be able to show me off to the public. She made everyone listen to my spelling bee exploits and I was being enthusiastically congratulated by more complete strangers than people I actually knew.

Due to the spelling bee, I had become a bit of a minor celebrity thanks to Grandma being my publicity agent.

When we arrived home, Mother still wasn't there, which meant she had gone straight to the bar after work.

Grandma made macaroni and hot dogs for dinner because this was MY day, or at least that's what she declared it to be. Mother's portion of the meal stayed in the pot on the stovetop covered with a plate until well after 10 o'clock that night.

I had eaten two helpings of macaroni and cheese and a huge slab of chocolate cake and was still on the living room couch watching TV, though half asleep, when the door opened, and Mother stumbled through the doorway.

I immediately woke up fully and showed Mother the two framed certificates on the wall. After dinner, Grandma had put the certificates into the frames and hung them on the living room wall.

"I'm going to the district spelling bee! Isn't that great? I want you and Grandma to come!"

Mother didn't exhibit the same cheerfulness or excitement at the idea that I had done something special as everyone else had shown me.

"So you won a fucking spelling bee. So what. And what do you mean you want me to come? Come to what?"

Mother said with all the feeling of a corpse ready to be buried in the graveyard.

"The district spelling bee. He is going to compete against the winners from the other schools in the area," Grandma said.

"Oh, he's gotta do it again? Well, I can't go. I have to work. Where is it?" and she looked at the address of the school.

"Wow, that's far," She slurred. "Grandma will have to take the bus and transfer twice. She can't go."

"Why? Why can't she go?" I whined, tears welling up in my eyes at the prospect of no one being there to cheer me on.

"Because buses cost money, for one thing, and we don't have extra money."

Now I was not only sad but angry. There wasn't money for Grandma to go, and Mother couldn't go because she had to work, but it was perfectly ok for her not to go to work when she had drunk too much the night before, and there was always plenty of money for her booze.

"And do you think it's fair to ask your grandma to go all the way across the city just to watch you spell words? Come on, use your head, kid. What the fuck is wrong with you? You don't need her to be there."

I stood there dumbfounded. I wanted to hit her. I wanted it with every fiber of my being. I wanted to hit her with all my might.

"I WANT her to be there," I shouted.

'OH, you WANT her to be there. She said sarcastically. Well, I want a million dollars, but that ain't happening, so neither is this. Now, get to bed. It's late."

"You have to sign the permission slip for the trip."

I told her, retrieving it from my spelling book that was sitting on the hassock.

"I told you, we aren't going. I am not signing anything."

"You have to sign it because his whole class is going on the bus. It's a field trip form," Grandma informed Mother.

"Oh, that's ok then. As long as it doesn't say anything about us having to be there," she read it over carefully, her head bobbing back and forth from all the alcohol she drank at the bar.

She scrawled her signature over the form and I placed it back into the spelling book for safekeeping. Upset at the prospect of not having any family to represent me at the event, I retreated from the living room and went to my own room, where I took off my play clothes and put on my pajamas for bed.

I sat on the edge of the bed, thinking about how unfathomable it was that strangers were more supportive of my spelling bee win than my own mother. It was obvious that I would never do anything that would make me worthy of any respect from Mother.

I got into bed, and Grandma came to tuck me in.

"I am proud of you. So proud. What you did IS incredible no matter what she says, "Grandma said, referring to Mother.

Something sailed across my room, crashing into my old dresser where my clothes were kept. The object made a loud sound of breaking glass. It was followed by a second object, which also crashed and sent glass pieces flying.

"Those certificates don't belong on the living room wall," Mother said. I jumped out of bed past Grandma to see that Mother had thrown the certificates into my room, and the glass shattered to pieces upon impact with the dresser.

"Be careful! Grandma warned me! Get away from the broken glass!"

And she went to the kitchen to get the broom and dustpan. It was too late, though, as a piece of glass had penetrated my foot and was still lodged there.

I picked up the certificates and brushed off the broken glass, tears streaming down my face.

I was furious at her beyond any anger I had felt before. I couldn't keep it bottled up. Not this time. Before I even had the time for any second thoughts about confronting Mother, I walked out to the living room, not even caring that blood was pouring from the glass wound on my foot. I stood tall, lifting myself to tiptoes as I let the rage come out of me at full force toward Mother.

"I HATE YOU! Do you hear me? I FUCKING HATE you, I HATE YOU, I HATE YOU, I HATE YOU!!!! "I screamed at Mother.

She lifted up a leg to kick me, and it landed on my hip, sending me across the room.

"The feeling is mutual, you STUPID fuck!" Mother shouted.

"Think you're so great because you won a spelling bee? Fuck you. You can spell words. Well, la-de-fucking dah and whoop te do for you. What the fuck good does winning a spelling bee do you when you can't do anything else in class because you're TOO STUPID?! HUH, fucker?"

She yelled directly into my face and then picked me up by the ear, forcing me to get to my feet. She forcefully guided me back to my bedroom doorway, planting her foot against my back and thrusting me into the room, where I landed in the middle of the glass Grandma was sweeping up.

I cried and shook uncontrollably with the mix of emotions I was feeling right then. Now, even though there wasn't previously any question of it, with this event, I REALLY understood my true worth in my mother's eyes, and it was less than zero. Even when I had accomplished something to be proud of, it meant nothing in Mother's eyes.

I was, indeed, extraordinary.

March, 1978 - Third Grade

It was the day of the district spelling bee championship, and we would be leaving the school at 10:30 to get across town to the other school where the event would be held. Our schedule had changed, and since we would miss gym class later in the day, the time was moved up to the first period. After changing into our gym shirts and shorts, we went out to the gym to find the hockey nets were set up. That was at least some reprieve because at least I could do a bit better with a hockey stick than a ball.

I still wasn't any captain's first choice, but I held my own in the game, and today was no exception. Indoor hockey was the game I wished we played the most, but in fact, it was the game we played the least.

I need to go to the bathroom Eggy informed Mr. Quage during a break in the action before another face off.

"Go ahead," Mr. Quage said, and Eggy ran to the locker room to use the bathroom there.

We went on about the game, and I was on the end of the bench waiting to be called back into the game to play when Eggy returned, and he whispered something to one of the other boys on the bench who were also waiting for their turn to play. The boy laughed out loud. And looked directly at me while he did so.

I wondered what Eggy was up to now but didn't have time to think about it since Mr. Quage was calling me to hop back in the game, taking the place of one of the other boys who was sweating profusely and tired from some rigorous plays that had just taken place.

Gym time was over a few moments later, and we all retreated to shower as usual after the game.

Eggy was doing his usual pranks on people, cracking his towel at the other boys and, on occasion, taking a moment to whisper something to those who were most loyal to his whims, which initiated more laughter. God, how I hated them. I tried to put them out of my mind as we would all be leaving soon to go to the spelling bee championship.

After my shower was completed, I grabbed my towel, dried off, and put on my underwear and pants. All around me I was noticing the boys were starting to giggle. I paid them no mind as I then put on my socks and shoes. It was then that I noticed my shirt didn't seem to be in the locker where I had stored the rest of my clothes that day.

"Did you throw it on top of the lockers again?" I asked as I turned to face Eggy. Now overwhelming waves of laughter came from the boys who Eggy had whispered the secret and some of the other boys who had also found out from others who were told.

"NOOOOO, it's not on top of the lockers. You walk around, and I'll tell you when you're getting close to it," Eggy said.

"Come on, I don't have time for games. Just tell me where it is. What did you do with it?"

Eggy just laughed and, through his evil laughter, said

"Well, I guess you don't need your shirt, and you can just go be on stage in the spelling bee half-naked." And that got the other boys laughing

"Ok, Ok, I'll walk around." I walked to the other row of lockers, and Eggy said, "Cold."

So I changed my trajectory and walked toward the box of soap bars we used for the shower, and Eggy said, "Still cold."

Now, I walked toward Mr. Quage's office, where he was standing in the doorway, completing the attendance for today's class.

"Nope. Cold as ice."

Where else was there? All that was left was the bathroom. I walked toward the bathroom.

"Now you're getting warmer."

I walked close enough to get to the doorway.

"Now you're HOT! On FIRE!"

Eggy and numerous boys came over closer to the bathroom as I stared at the first urinal. There was my shirt, in the urinal, in a puddle of yellow pee, soaked in it. When Eggy left the game to go to the bathroom, that was when he had pulled this disgusting prank, I realized. That's the secret he had been whispering to the other boys from the moment he got back from his bathroom trip.

I spun to face Eggy, only to instead face all of the boys except John and Juan, laughing at me.

"Come on," John said. "Leave it."

I did as he said, returned to the locker, and put my sweaty gym shirt back on.

"No, here, wear this," and John handed me his button-down plaid shirt. He still had his Fruit of the Loom white undershirt to wear, so he didn't feel he would miss his plaid shirt. John was only slightly bigger in stature than me, so the shirt, though it wasn't a perfect fit, was close enough not to look too big.

"You need it more than I do, being on stage for the spelling bee." He said.

When someone does something like this for you in a moment of need, you recognize just how important having true friends really is, and I appreciated John more in that moment than I ever had before. If we weren't here in the locker room in front of all the other boys, I would have hugged him to say thank you.

"Would you boys hurry up and finish putting your clothes on?! The buses are here to take you to the spelling bee."

We all rushed to finish up and got in line.

Mr. Quage led us to the hallway where our teacher, Miss ManWarren, was waiting for us.

"OK, come on, everyone. The buses are here." We walked up the hallway past the office where all the office personnel, including Mr Shedruff, stood applauding as we passed.

"Good luck!" Mr. Shedruff said with a wide smile.

'My goodness,' I thought, 'smiling again? His face might crack.'

Juan, not missing a beat, was standing behind me in line and, as if reading my mind, said, "Mr Shedruff is smiling again. Look out, his face is gonna break."

I half turned around in line and high-fived him for saying what I was already thinking.

Outside, we saw 3 long yellow school buses waiting for us. This was an extreme rarity for me, as I didn't ride the school bus except on field trips with the class. I kind of liked the school bus and couldn't understand why so many kids didn't. I guess I liked it because it was more of a novelty for me.

Miss ManWarren handed me a stack of paper with words on it.

"You can study on the trip," she said.

"Thank you," I replied, putting the papers on my lap but not bothering to look at them. I knew the words already, instinctively. I chose the time to talk to John, who was on the bench seat sitting next to me, and Juan, who was in the aisle-facing seat on the bench behind ours.

We all talked and played games like 'I Spy' on the ride to the other school. When we arrived, we saw a school that looked to be twice the size of our own.

We shuffled inside to the cafeteria, where we ate a lunch of pizza, French fries, milk, and brownies, all prepared by the lunch ladies. Then, we were escorted out of the cafeteria to take a bathroom trip. We all went six at a time to each of the two bathrooms in the hallway. Due to the line order, I had somehow been relegated to the batch with Eggy and a couple of his minions.

We went to the urinals to pee, and midstream, Eggy turned for a split second, his stream of pee grazing across my jeans.

"Whoops," he said as he returned his stream to face the urinal. Luis Matos, who was at the urinal on the other side of mine, repeated Eggy's actions.

"What the FUCK is wrong with you! I said. And both boys stopped peeing and pushed me, and Eggy said, "Come on, do something stupid, baby. Do something" while zipping his pants back up. We stared at each other intently for a moment. They knew I wouldn't do anything to them under regular circumstances, let alone on a trip to another school. It was an empty dare.

Luckily, it was only a few drops from both of them, and I was wearing dark blue jeans, so the wetness didn't show. I wiped and blotted at my jeans, nonetheless, with paper towels at the sink after I had finished washing my hands.

I went back to the line to get ready to go to the auditorium, and Eggy and Luis were already telling the other boys who weren't in the bathroom when it had happened about what they had just done. Now, the other boys teased me, saying, "Hey, Dave," and when I turned, they pretended to hold their penises and made the sound, "SSSSSSSSSSS."

As if to signify they were pissing on me, and then everyone except my friends roared out with laughter.

A few moments later, we arrived in the auditorium, which was much larger than ours, accommodating a much larger potential audience.

I wondered if Grandma was going to brave the 3 buses she would have to take to be there to see me compete.

I didn't have long as the principal of this school, a man who looked a lot like Mr. Shedruff, only with more hair, explained the rules to us. The four winners from each school were to compete with each other again to represent our school in the finals against all the other schools.

We sat while row after row of students, teachers, parents, and other relatives filed in to fill up the auditorium, and by the time they were through, the auditorium was indeed very full. There were rows of people standing behind the last row of seats and also taking up an upper balcony area.

'Where is grandma?'

I wondered, but the moment was fleeting as we were about to get started, which was signified by the lights being dimmed, lights on the front of the stage being lit, and a spotlight shining upon us. I still didn't see Grandma, but it would be difficult to do so anyway, what with the glare of these lights and the dimmed lights making everyone in the audience look like dark silhouettes. Unlike the previous spelling bee, where we didn't dim the lights or use the stage or spotlights, this was going to be a more serious professional event.

The competition started.

A woman who was the moderator used the microphone to tell us over the booming sound system in the theater that she would be acting as the moderator who delivers the words and that all the words selected would be from the official National Spelling Bee lists, as this is the first of the 3 steps in that competition. She welcomed all of us and got started. As champions of the different schools, we were always to take the lead, spelling the first word for each step in today's event. After 2 other school champions took their turns, I was up next.

"David, spell 'improvement'"

"Improvement. I-m-p-r-o-v-e-m-e-n-t. Improvement."

"Yes, very good."

This went on throughout the first part of the competition, where the champion from each school had their turns, and then a second member represented the best of their grade level until it was down to me and one other champion from my school.

"Paul, spell 'importance'"

"Importance. I-m-p-o-r-t-e-n-c-e. Importance"

"Not correct. David, please spell 'Importance'"

"Importance. I-m-p-o-r-t-a-n-c-e. Importance"

"Correct. Once again, David, you have won for your school."

"Oh my GOD! I did it! I'm still the champ of my school."

The voice in my head excitedly called out

But that was only the first part of the competition. Next, the champions from all the other schools in the district would have to compete. I was ready for it. A few moments later, the second portion started. After 4 other school champions took their turns, I was called to the microphone on the stage.

"David, spell 'constitution'"

"Constitution. C-o-n-s-t-i-t-u-t-i-o-n. Constitution."

"Yes. Well done!"

Time went on, and the contest was winding down to just 3 of us. I was becoming more and more nervous with each person who was eliminated from the contest.

"Michael, spell 'milquetoast'"

"Milquetoast. M-i-l-k-t-o-a-s-t. Milquetoast."

"Incorrect. David, spell Milquetoast"

"Milquetoast. M-i-l-q-u-e-t-o-a-s-t. Milquetoast."

"That is right. Layla, spell 'cologne' "

"Cologne. C-o-l-o-g-n-e. Cologne"

"Yes. David, spell 'originality'"

"Originality. O-r-i-g-i-n-a-l-i-t-y. Originality"

"Correct. Layla, spell 'quantitative'"

"Quantitative. Q-u-a-n-t-i-t-a-t-i-v-e. Quantitative."

"That is correct. David, spell 'Interference'"

"Interference. I-n-t-e-r-f-e-r-e-n-c-e. Interference."

"Yes. Ladies and gentlemen, as we pause to ready another word list, let's take a moment to recognize the wonderful effort these young people have put into their spelling proficiency."

And she initiated applause that rang out through the theater, echoing loudly.

"Ok, we are now ready to resume."

The moderator said as she took a new word list in hand. Layla and I were on stage for what felt like forever, spelling word after word correctly. After about 50 words, the moderator paused a moment while she got another page of words ready in hand.

"Layla, spell 'pneumonia'"

I am not sure how I knew, but I realized this was it. Miss Manwarren had warned us of words with silent letters and to remember that you don't always hear all the letters pronounced when a word is verbalized. There had been some examples of words like this in the contest so far, but this one, at least to a 3rd or 4th grader, which defined us, was a bit obscure. Although the word was used in everyday life frequently, it was rare to see the word in print. I was counting on that fact and that maybe Layla had never seen the word. I listened as intently as I could above the pounding of my heart in my chest as she said, "Pneumonia. Newmonia. Pneumonia"

Incorrect. David. If you can spell Pneumonia, you will be the winner of the district-wide elementary school portion of the national spelling bee. I need complete silence from everyone in the audience. Please, do not make a sound now." The moderator paused while the auditorium became so completely silent the only thing you could hear was the combined breaths of anticipation of whether I would be able to spell the word, and then she stated

"David. Please take a deep breath, relax, and spell 'pneumonia' when you are ready."

I was more than ready. In spite of my readiness, the cold beads of sweat still formed on my forehead, dripping into my eyes as the stage spotlight on me seemed to glow even brighter as I calmly said, "Pneumonia, P-n-e-u-m-o-n-i-a. Pneumonia."

Louder applause than I had ever heard in my entire life emanated from the auditorium and nearly completely drowned out the moderator, who loudly said into the microphone, "Congratulations, David, You are our new district spelling bee champion!"

My class and the other classes from my school were all stomping their feet and screaming and cheering louder than anyone else in the theater. It was deafening as the moderator came up on the stage and said, "OK, everyone, please settle down, settle down. "After a couple of minutes more cheering and a reminder from the teachers, the auditorium grew quiet once again.
The moderator said, "On behalf of the national spelling bee, we wish to honor you with this trophy."

And someone else who had joined the moderator on stage handed her a giant trophy, which she then handed to me. It was heavier than I had considered, as it had pieces of marble incorporated into the multi-tiered design.

"We also are giving you this golden edition of the Doubleday dictionary."

I put the trophy down as she handed the dictionary to me. It was beautiful. The pages were edged in gold, and the "Doubleday Dictionary' printing on the hardcover was done in gold as well.

Again, the audience erupted in applause, and my class stormed the stage. John and Juan lifted me onto their shoulders while everyone else in the theater continued their applause for what seemed like forever. I saw the flashbulbs of many cameras blasting as well, and news crews were present with their cameras beside them.

After they put me down, Miss ManWarren led the class off the stage, minus myself, as I had duties to perform. As district spelling bee champion, I had to do interviews for the press.

The tears were still streaming down my face as I was barely able to comprehend that I was the champion speller of the district.

One of the TV news reporters aimed a microphone toward my face and asked me how I knew to spell so many words, many of which were beyond my grade level; I looked at her and said, "I don't know. I just have always been able to read and spell. I love it. I love it."

The reporter continued by surmising that I could probably spell 'supercalifragilisticexpialadocious'

I didn't miss a beat and just started spelling it

"S-u-p-e" and the reporter cut me off, laughing and telling me that the spelling bee was over and I didn't need to spell any more words today.

"Ok, do you have anything else you want to say?"

"Hi, grandma. I love you!" I said as I waved to the camera lens a couple of feet away.

And I heard.

"I love you too," and realized she was standing next to me. In the hectic nature of this amazing moment, I had no idea she had come onto the stage. I turned to her, and she lifted me up and hugged the stuffing out of me as the cameras were still rolling. I cried hard with the most and the largest tears of joy I had ever experienced. This was an even bigger moment than winning my school spelling bee.

"I didn't see you! The lights on the stage were so bright! I didn't know you were here!"

"I was here the whole time. I was in the second row."

"Thank You! Thank you for coming. I love you so much!" and I hugged her with as much force as she hugged me.

After a while, I was able to finish brief interviews for all 3 major local network TV stations and PBS, as well as two local newspapers.

"Can Grandma come with us on the bus? Please?"

I asked my teacher when I finished the interviews.

"No, I'm afraid not. There's no room, remember. The buses are all completely full. You can see her at home later."

I was disappointed but understood.

"Ok, I'll see you later on at home, Grandma."

"Yes. See you then. I love you."

She said, lifting me for another huge hug and a kiss on the cheek.

We came back on the bus and were celebrating and really whooping it up, repeating and spelling words from the competition again and again. When we arrived again at my school, I was greeted by Mr. Shedruff who had already heard the news and asked if I wanted to temporarily donate the trophy to the school's trophy case. I said, 'Sure.'

And he put it inside, the first academic activity-related trophy next to all the sports championship-related trophies for the many sports the children who attended the school played throughout the years.

I wasn't donating my dictionary, though; that was much too precious to me.

My friends and I walked to my house, each of them taking turns to hoist me up onto their shoulders. If there was a cloud nine, I was definitely on it right now. I wasn't stupid. I was a champion. A champion of the entire district. My picture would be in the newspaper, and I was slated to be on the six o'clock and the 11 o'clock news on all the local TV stations. My life could never and would never get any better than this. I was sure of it.

March 1978, third grade

When I arrived home, Grandma wasn't there yet, as it took a while to get home, having to ride three buses to be able to do it. Mother was home, however.

It was almost time for the news at 6, and I excitedly showed Mother my new dictionary.

"I did it! I really did! I WON the spelling bee! I am the district champion!" I waved my beautiful new dictionary in front of Mother as she sat back down in the living room chair across from the TV.

"Yeah, yeah, ok, so you won. Get that fucking book out of my face and go sit someplace and calm the fuck down. "

I couldn't calm down; I continued telling her the story

"After I spelled the last word 'pneumonia,' people from the TV news had microphones, and they talked to me about the spelling bee. I'm gonna be on TV!!! I'm gonna be in the paper, too!"

Mother, unimpressed, said nothing and just picked up the plastic cup on the end table next to her and took a long swig of whatever alcohol she had put into it earlier.

Partially deflated due to Mother not showing a single emotion beyond annoyance, I sat down on the rug in front of the TV, waiting for the news to start. Grandma hurriedly walked in a couple of minutes later.

"Did I miss it? Were you on yet?" she asked, referring to my TV appearance.

"No, not yet! The news isn't on yet."

Grandma looked at Mother with disdain over the fact that she didn't even seem to be the slightest bit happy about my having done something as momentous as winning the district spelling bee. Moments such as this, where a child my age could be in the spotlight, were few and far between, and Mother just sat, expressionless and more concerned with drinking her usual amount of alcohol as if it were just another day where nothing of consequence had happened. Grandma hung up her coat and sat in the other living room chair, gazing at the TV.

As usual, human interest stories were saved for later in the broadcast after the weather forecast was finished. As they were going into the commercial segment following the weather, the anchorman said

"Up next, a momentous day as a new district spelling bee champion is declared."

The footage of my interview was played without sound; music played instead.

"There I am!"

"There you are!" Grandma and I shouted simultaneously.

I turned to see what mother's reaction was. Her head was resting against her hand and she was looking down at the TV guide in her lap, reading an article.

After the commercial, the anchorman said

"a special day for a young man who can really, really spell. He is the youngest winner of the first step of the National Spelling Bee in recent history. 8-year-old David Rossi became the district spelling bee champion this afternoon after spelling the word 'pneumonia' correctly, a feat his final older competitor could not do."

The footage of my interview played next.

"It's easy to see how happy he is. The tears of joy say it all," the anchorman said.

"Yeah, and I like the fact that it was grandma that he called out at the end of the interview, not 'mom' like most kids do when they know they are going to be on TV," the co-anchor replied

"Yes, that was really heartwarming to see. Well, congratulations to David and, of course, Grandma, too." The anchor said with a smile, and the two anchors chuckled before introducing the sports commentator.

I looked over at Grandma; she was crying tears of joy. She got up from her chair and came over to me, lifting me up and hugging me.

Now the phone was ringing. Grandma put me down, and I ran to the phone and picked up the receiver

"Hello."

"Hey, I just saw you on the news! That was so great!" It was John.

"Which channel?"

"I had ABC on."

"Really?! Wow! I had CBS on. I wonder if I was on NBC too."

"I changed the station, and I have it on now. Yes! Turn it on! You're on there!"

I was. And this time I got to see grandma hugging me on stage.

"This is sooooo incredible!!!" I exclaimed into the receiver. Hey, my dad wants to talk to you. Here he is! "

John's dad's deep voice came on the line

"David?"

"Yes!" I said with joy in my voice.

"I just wanted to congratulate you. We are all so proud of you."

"Thank you, sir. John helped me study the words. I might not have won if he didn't help me. "

"Well, that's kind of you to say. John's mom wants to talk to you, too."

And now John's mom was on the line.

"David, like John's dad said, we are so proud. Listen, we are going to have a special dinner tomorrow just for you. Can you come? Will it be ok with your parents?"

"I think I can."

"Ok, what would you like to eat?"

"Can we have macaroni and cheese with cut-up hot dogs in it?"

"Yes, of course you can." John's mother said with a bit of levity in her voice, not surprised in the least that I would want such a kid-centric meal but amused by the fact nonetheless.

"Ok, we'll see you tomorrow, then after school."

"Ok, bye."

And I hung up.

"John's parents want me to come over for a celebration dinner. Like a party, I guess.
"I said, apparently to the air since Mother still hadn't looked up from reading her TV Guide article. It didn't matter, because she wouldn't have time to respond anyway, as the phone was ringing again.

"That will be Juan," I said knowingly

"Hello"

"David, why has your line been busy so long?!" Juan asked impatiently.

"John called me to tell me he saw me on TV, on the news.

"Yeah, that's why I'm calling you. I saw you on CBS. And then I saw you on NBC."

"Yeah, I know; John saw me on ABC at the same time as I was on CBS."

"This is so great! You're FAMOUS!"

"I know! I can't even believe it. I still can't believe it's real."

"Hey. Mom wants you to come over tomorrow. She said she's gonna make the chicken and rice that you love and eat so much of when you're here."

"I can't tomorrow. I told John I would go to his house because they want to do a party or something too."

Juan talked to his mom in Spanish and then came back on the line to tell me

"She said its ok and she will make the chicken and rice the next day. Will you come?"

I didn't even bother to look at or ask my mother. She obviously didn't care, and she wouldn't be home anyway, as she would probably be at the bar after work, as she had done nearly every other day.

"Your mom's Spanish rice and chicken? You KNOW I will be there."

"Ok, good. Hey see you tomorrow in school, Mr. Famous."

"Ok, bye," I said through a laugh at 'Mr. Famous'

Grandma had retreated to the kitchen to warm up some frozen Ellio's pizza since it was getting late and Mother hadn't started preparing anything for dinner, in spite of her knowing that Grandma wasn't home yet. She had priorities, and they began and ended with whatever bottle of alcohol she favored that night.

Mother got up and walked toward the TV.

"Is it ok to turn it off, or are you going to be on some other news show where people are falling all over you and worshipping your greatness?"

Mother sarcastically asked

I just ignored her and went to the kitchen table to wait for the pizza to be ready.

As I sat down, Mother came closer to the kitchen doorway.

"Hey, king speller, get back in here."

I nervously got up from the table and sheepishly went back to the living room.

"Where did you get that shirt?"

So much had happened since gym class that morning that I had forgotten I was still wearing John's shirt that he had loaned me.

"I-I-it's John's"

"John's? Why are you wearing John's shirt?"

Mother asked, moving closer to me.

"Eggy was mean to me and messed up my shirt."

I said, leaving out the fact that he had urinated on it. That information was embarrassing.

"Oh really? How did he have time to mess up your shirt when you went to the spelling bee today?"

Mother was furrowing her eyebrows and beginning to get that look that told me I better be ready to dodge a fist or foot soon.

"W-W-We had gym before we left to go to the spelling bee," I told her, already in flinch preparation mode

"What did he do to your shirt?" Mother asked, fury clearly rising in her booze-bloodshot eyes. I didn't say anything.

Mother slapped my face.

"Shirley! Stop it! It doesn't matter what happened to the shirt. Can't we PLEASE just have one normal day? Please? He had such a great day; can't you just be happy for him?"

Grandma courageously shouted to the living room from the kitchen, where she was monitoring the pizza.

"The fucker isn't wearing his own shirt, and YOU don't care or have questions?! Well, I DO! So butt out, bitch."

Now she grabbed me by the ear, wrenching it hard and twisting it.

"I SAID WHAT DID HE DO TO YOUR SHIRT?!"

Tears flowed from my eyes. I tried to grab my dictionary from off the phone table where I had left it earlier and run from the room, but Mother was too quick for me. She yanked the dictionary from my hand and hit me across the head with the spine edge, knocking me down.

Mother knelt against my legs, preventing me from running away, punching me in the ribs twice.

"Tell me WHAT HE DID to YOUR GODDAMN SHIRT YOU PIECE OF SHIT!"

I knew it was fruitless. I had to tell her, so I did.

"He pissed on it. He put it in the urinal in the bathroom in the gym locker room, and he PISSED ON IT!"

I yelled, trying to get Mother off me at the same time

Mother took a moment to consider the story, and then she countered with, "You have GOT to be kidding me. You have got to be kidding. Where the fuck was the gym teacher while all this was happening?!"

"He was with us in the gym. Eggy told Mr. Quage he had to go to the bathroom, and that's when he did it.

"But what about when you found the shirt? Where was he then? Why didn't he see it?"

Mr. Quage had given the students privacy, largely, when they were showering; he didn't stand where he could stare at us while we showered, and he did the same while we were getting dressed, letting us change privately amongst each other and he didn't inspect the bathroom on a regular basis, at least not in our presence. We were guys, and this was part of the 'guy' code and considered good practice for a gym teacher supervising children who were naked or changing.

I didn't explain this to mother, I just said.

"He was in his office by the locker room exit door waiting for us to finish getting dressed and line up."

"That is one hell of a fucking story." Mother sneered almost jokingly and clearly disbelieving of what I had told her.

"Story or not, ENOUGH. It probably DID happen just the way he said. You KNOW how mean those kids are to him. Now, leave him alone. It's time to eat. Come on, David, let's eat." Grandma said, standing up for me for the second time tonight, determined not to let Mother get to me tonight.

Mother pushed past me, went to the kitchen window, opened it, and then the storm window, and walked back to the table where the plates of pizza were sitting with heated steam rising from the cheese. She picked up all the plates and threw them out the window, where they hit the ground below.

"Yeah, go ahead, go eat, ungrateful bastard. Your own shirt that I bought you is not good enough for your big spelling bee. Fucking lying asshole. Get the fuck out of my sight, both of you."

She went back to the window, forcefully shutting the storm window, which cracked, and then slamming the main window shut and locking it, surprisingly, not cracking it too from the force she used when closing it.

We both left the kitchen, Grandma leading me to her room so she could put on her shoes and then leading me back to the living room, saying

"Get your jacket on. Tonight, we are going OUT to eat, just you and me."

"Where the FUCK do you think you're going?" Mother said while standing by the living room door to the hallway.

"Get out of our way. We are going OUT to eat since you threw our dinner out the window. Now move aside," Grandma said

"Oh, you're going out to eat, huh? Well, aren't you SPECIAL!"

Mother belted out, still not moving. Grandma and I walked quickly to the kitchen back door, and before she could get in our way to stop us, we went through it and outside. We were surely going to be in for it when we returned because Mother was not going to let us have the upper hand in any situation and would punish us for trying, but for the moment, we had the edge, and we were free from her negativity at least for a little while.

We went to the diner nearby, where Grandma told the story of my big win in the district spelling bee. There was a TV in the diner behind the counter where people ate their meals sitting on the stools that lined it.

One of the waitresses said

"Yes! I saw you just a little while ago! You said you love grandma."

"Yeah. I do too," I told her as I smiled.

"Well, since today is your special day, you get to have whatever you want, and it's on me." The waitress informed us.

"Really? Even chocolate cake?" I asked, ecstatic at the prospect.

"Yes. Even chocolate cake."

"How about a bottle of coke?" I asked.

"Coming up, and yes, that's free for you too."

A couple of minutes later, she returned with the coke in her hand, taking the cap off with a bottle opener.

We stayed there and ate a meal of cheeseburgers and French fries and I enjoyed every last morsel of it, and we finished up with double chocolate cake. When it was time to go home, we started to get more and more nervous, walking slower and slower to delay our doom with Mother, but we were surprised to find that she had left the house to go drinking again.

At least she was out of the house, and we wouldn't have to deal with her tonight. We both took the opportunity to watch

TV and enjoy what we were watching without the threat of what awful event Mother would suddenly decide to subject me or both of us to, as she did so frequently when she was home.

Mother came home so drunk she could hardly walk. She left the living room as quickly as she had entered and passed out on her bed, never to be heard from until morning.

The next day when I showed up to school, I was greeted by many kids I didn't know, who were all interested in what had happened at the spelling bee. I had to tell the story over and over, but I didn't mind. It was nice to be getting some positive attention for a change.

Unlike the way things were normally, my class was the last to leave the playground to start the day. John and Juan, and some of the other kids were not here yet and I wondered why they hadn't arrived yet. I wouldn't have to wait long, as when we arrived at the classroom, John, Juan and the other kids who I thought hadn't arrived yet were there in the classroom with Miss ManWarren and Mr. Shedruff.

"SURPRISE!" They all yelled as we entered.
The classroom was decorated with streamers and on one of the blackboards, 'Congratulations David' was written in multi-colored chalk.

John and Juan led me over to my desk to see that there was candy, a cupcake, potato chips, popcorn, and a bunch of small cards that the kids all signed. Miss ManWarren had the kids secretly sign the cards on the way back from the spelling bee. She had faith that after what she had seen at the school spelling bee, I would become the district champ, and she came prepared with the cards and markers without my knowing. She must have put them into her large purse to keep them hidden from view.

We spent the whole first period re-living the incredible events from the day before as the children from the other classrooms all came to visit with their teachers to congratulate me as well. I ate so much candy and had so many snacks I thought I'd burst. Each time I thought there was no more, one of the teachers from the other classes would bring even more.

When my congratulations party ended, it was time to get back to the business of school as usual, in more ways than one.

During recess after lunch, I had to go to the bathroom and I asked the teacher on duty watching the playground if I could go to the bathroom, and she waved me inside.

While midstream at the urinal, Eggy and Luis Matos walked in. I finished my business and zipped up my pants, headed toward the sink to wash my hands. Luis stopped me by blocking my way and pushing me toward Eggy, who said

"Remember yesterday in the bathroom at the other school? You wanted to start something. Go ahead, start something now, stupid baby."

POW! A fist to my chest, knocking the wind out of me and sending me backward.

Now Luis moved to my side, kicking me in the stomach and ribs again and again

"Come on, baby, get up. Do something"

Eggy taunted while Luis continued kicking me.

When an older boy came into the bathroom, Luis and Eggy pretended to zip up their pants as if they had just used the bathroom and walked out past this other boy. Seeing me lying there on the floor, he came over to me and asked me

"Are you ok?"

And tried to help me get to my feet.

I assured him I was ok, tears streaming down my cheeks and betraying the truth.

As I left the bathroom, I thought about the contrast of this whirlwind of the past two days where so many people had seen me as a hero, congratulating my performance in the spelling bee and making me feel like less of a nobody, as if I had worth after all. How lucky for me that I had people like my mother, Eggy, and his friends to show me I was still the same stupid, worthless loser as ever.

May, 1978, third grade

Aside from reading and spelling, art was my favorite school activity and the one thing I enjoyed doing more than any other at home. From the time I was able to hold a pencil in my hand, I was using it or a crayon or marker to draw things with. Grandma would buy me doodle pads, which were more precious than gold to me, and I would spend hours drawing cartoons and pictures of houses, cars, and trees.

Mr. DiFiore was my art teacher, and since he was consistently impressed with my work he always encouraged me in my artistic pursuits. He taught me to see things as they are and to draw what I saw one line at a time, never allowing myself to feel overwhelmed by the completed picture. He made art not only fun but easy as well.

Today, however, we weren't drawing. We were creating something for our mothers for Mother's Day, which was coming up that weekend.

"Today, we are going to do something that will take two days to do, so we will do the first part today and the second part on Thursday."

He informed us.

"Now, you remember a couple of months ago, I asked the class who had baby brothers and sisters at home to bring in their baby food jars for a project we would do soon. Well, today, we are going to use those jars."

And from within a box, he passed out the jars, one to each student. Finished, he then went to his desk and picked up a larger jar that he had done. It had transparent colors that he applied in blocks to the jar, making it look like stained glass.

"Today, you'll be using a special paint to make boxes of color on your jars. We have six colors, and you can use them all, but you must remember to wash out your brush in a jar of water before you change to another color. Remember, you can make some squares of rectangles larger than others and some smaller. It will make a nice effect."

I picked up a brush and thought about what color my grandma would like, since I would be giving it to her since she would appreciate it more. She was the one who always encouraged me and was genuinely interested in my art. She deserved this jar more than Mother.

I carefully and slowly applied different blocks of color to my jar and watched as my classmates did not do the same, applying colors haphazardly and not being attentive to their details, creating misshapen blobs rather than neatly defined squares or rectangles.

When we were finished applying our colors, Mr. DiFiore told us to place them on a shelf on the wall to dry, and for the remainder of the art class, we had time to free draw anything we wanted to. I chose to make a card for Grandma to go with the jar when I would give it to her on Sunday. I drew a scene with trees and flowers, using many colors of crayons for the flowers because flowers were something she loved. Any time we were out walking, Grandma would point out flowers in people's yards. She knew the names of many of the different types of flowers, too, and she always shared them with me. She taught me to appreciate the beauty in nature because, unlike so many things in this world, nature didn't cost anything to partake in; it was simply all around you and free for you to enjoy. Now, being in the city, I didn't get to see a whole lot of nature in its purest form, but she took advantage of any opportunity, calling attention to examples of it, no matter how small, even just some greenery in people's yards, or the shapes of the trees that grew seeking the light of the sun.

On Thursday, we returned to art class, and Mr. Difiore had placed cups of a black liquid on our tables and gave us our jars back. He had written our names on a piece of masking tape he had applied to the bottom so he could better discern who each jar belonged to.

"Today, you're going to use your paintbrush to apply this black paint as a border around each color square you made."

He held up his jar as an example, which now had black lines defining each color box on it.

"Remember to paint carefully and not to smudge it. To make it easier, I am passing out pieces of cardboard so you can use a piece of rolled-up masking tape on the bottom of your jar, making the jar stick to the cardboard. Now, instead of moving the jar around and possibly smudging the black paint, you move the cardboard instead, so you don't have to touch the jar when you need to go to a new area to paint the black lines."

Mr. DiFiore was always thinking of procedures to make things better and easier for us to create our art. It made for a more appealing-looking final product.

I carefully painted thin lines around each color, being careful not to cover too much of the colors. As before, other students in the class didn't exercise nearly as much care, making the lines way too thick in some areas and too thin in others. No matter, mine would be neat and that's what counted. I focused on making mine look as perfect as possible as if a professional artist had made it and it was worthy of being sold in a store.

At the end of the day on Friday, I went to the art room to get my now dry jar alongside the rest of the class, who also came to get the jars on the way to class that morning, and all I could think about for the rest of the day was the jar and how excited grandma would be when she received it. I would take the jar from inside my desk where I was keeping it and hold it up to light so that I could see the beautiful prism of color illuminate my desk. I couldn't wait for the day to end so I could get it home to Grandma. I wasn't going to wait until Sunday; I wouldn't be able to do so. It was too beautiful an item to keep secret for days at a time. She would simply have to see it right away.

When the end of the day came, I decided I wasn't going to allow Eggy and his gang to have the chance to torment me after school today, so a few minutes before dismissal, as we were lining up, I asked Miss ManWarren if I could deliver her attendance sheet to the office. She usually asked one of the girls to do this, so it wouldn't be surprising if I just walked out the door to the school right after getting to the office as the girls had done when they delivered it, the end-of-day bell ringing right after they got through the door. That would be all the advantage I would need to avoid the bullies, leaving before they had a chance to set up their bully barricade, preventing me from passing.

Now, as I was on my way home, I decided to go a longer way, too. I thought about how much grandma loved flowers, and I was going to find some to put in this tiny jar to make my gift even more special than it already would be. I went down a side street next to mine.

I saw some beautiful purple flowers as well as some large yellow-petaled ones. While I wasn't sure of the variety of flowers either of them held, I knew one thing, and that was the fact that Grandma was sure to love them both. The problem was that they were in a gated front yard.

They were not wildflowers either; these were flowers that had been planted and cultivated by the owner of the house; the garden displayed other types of flowers in small segmented groupings as well, with space between each one defining them.

I nervously looked around to see if there was anyone around who would try to stop me from picking their flowers. When I saw no one, I cautiously and quietly opened the gate so as not to call attention to the fact that I was in their yard, about to pick some of their flowers.

First, I focused on the purple flowers, picking one of those. Then I pulled at the yellow flower. It was harder to break the stem, but I was finally able to. I tucked each stem into my jar, noting that they were too long and wouldn't allow the flowers to stay in the jars. I broke off the stems lower and tried placing them into the jar again. Now, they would stay.

I decided to get one more purple flower, but I had to wait for a bumblebee collecting nectar to fly away before picking it. I didn't want to get stung. That would ruin the moment of giving grandma the jar, having to tend to a bee sting before being able to enjoy it. The bee flew off to find other flowers and I picked the third flower, placing it with the other two in the jar.

Now, I left the yard quickly and closed the gate so as not to be caught and have my plan of surprising Grandma ruined by the house owner taking back my flowers. I marveled at how beautiful the three flowers looked sticking up from the mouth of the jar. I walked as quickly as my legs would allow me to do so safely without dropping the jar.

When I got home, I knocked at the door, and Grandma opened it.

I held out the jar of flowers toward her and said

"This is for you."

A single tear came from Grandma's eye as she said.

"Look at this JAR?! This is BEAUTIFUL! Did you make this?"

"Yeah, I did." And I reached out my arms to hug Grandma. She knelt down and hugged me with one arm while holding the jar in her other hand.

"Well, we are going to have to get some water into these flowers too. Where did you get the flowers?"

"I found them on my way home." This was technically true; although they were in somebody's yard, I had passed on my long way home.

Grandma put water into the jar and placed it with the flowers in it on the window sill of one of the two windows in the kitchen.

Then I realized I had forgotten something.

"Oh NO!" I exclaimed.

"What? What is it?"

"I forgot the card. I need to get the card. I have to go. I'll be right back."

I ran out the door, down the porch stairs, and up the street at top speed. I had to get back to school to get the card.

When I got closer to the school, I saw Eggy and his friends were STILL stationed in their spot on the sidewalk near the school entrance. I would have to go around the block and use the side entrance to the school if I was going to have any chance of getting back into the school before they had locked it up for the weekend.

I ran as fast as my legs would go around the block. Luckily, when I got all the way up the stairs and into the yard, I saw one of the school janitors in the open door to the playground, bringing the doormats out so he could wash the floor and buff it.

I ran past him into the building, and he stopped me by putting a hand on my shoulder.

"Whoa, whoa, whoa, now where do you think you're going?" He asked.

"I forgot something in my desk; I have to get it," I told him, trying to get free of his grip. He let go and said, "You better hurry up; almost all the teachers have already gone."

I ran up the hallway and saw Miss ManWarren stepping into the hallway, about to lock the door.

"Wait!" I called out.

"I   forgot   something!

"David, what are you still doing here?"

And I ran past her and into the classroom over to my desk. I looked under some textbooks and found the card I had drawn 2 days before.

"Ok. Got it. Bye!"

"Bye," Miss Manwarren said, puzzled, "Have a good weekend."

I made my way back past the janitor, who was getting ready to start mopping the hallway floor. I went back to the side stairwell to go home. As I was running down the stairs, a teacher getting into their car in the parking lot called out

"Hey! You're not supposed to use those stairs!"

I ignored the voice and kept right on running home.

When I arrived, I saw Mother walking up the street from the other direction.

I got inside and handed Grandma the card. She looked at the picture on the cover and beamed. Wow! I think this is the best artwork you've ever done so far. Then she looked at the message inside. I had scrawled "I love you grandma' in my messy handwriting. She didn't care what the handwriting looked like; She just loved the message and, of course, me for making the card.

"Thank   you!   I   love   you   too."

and she bent to hug me. We were mid-hug when the lock clicked, and Mother walked in.

"Well what's all this, and what were you doing coming home from the opposite end of the street, away from the school?"

Mother inquired.

"Oh… well, I forgot this card I made at school, and I had to go back for it. When I left, I went the other way home. That's all."

"Oh, that's all, huh? Why were you in somebody's yard on a different street, picking flowers?"

My heart went up to my throat.

'What?' The voice in my head called out in surprise. 'How did she know?!'

"I watched you today. I wanted to see what it is you do after school and why you always come home beat up. Well, I guess I got my answer."

"No!" I tried to explain, "Today was different!"

"Yeah, it sure was different. You broke into someone's yard to steal flowers, and the kid or kids who live there didn't catch you and beat you up today."

"NOOOOO! Listen…"

I desperately tried to explain.

"No, now YOU listen. Where are the flowers?"

"They're over there" and I walked to the kitchen doorway and pointed to the jar on the window sill.

"Ok, get them."

I walked over to the window sill and picked them up.

"Now let's go. Outside. Move it"

Mother insisted, leading me to the back door.

Once outside, she led me to a large rock by the garbage cans.

"Smash it"

"What?! I said, panicking. "Why?!"

"Because you stole flowers."

"B-B-But I MADE this jar for grandma."

Mother, not caring who might see what was going on, slapped me hard across the face."

"I SAID SMASH IT. NOWWWW!"
I did as she demanded through tears of sadness and confusion. Pieces of the jar flew in different directions, and the flowers lay among the remains of broken glass that managed to stay on the rock.

"Inside. Move it."

I did as I was told. Looking back at her to see if she was showing any signs that she was going to beat me." I got my answer when we arrived back in the kitchen as she went to the pantry to get the yard stick.

"Clothes off. Now! "

She commanded.

I slowly took off my shirt, and before I could get any further, she swung the yardstick over and over, hitting my back and chest.

"What the FUCK is the MATTER with you?!!!" She screamed.

"No good fucking troublemaker!"

And she swung again and again. I couldn't even finish taking my clothes off, as I was too busy trying not to get hit, or at least not as hard. Of course, as usual, that just meant my arms and hands were injured, too, as I used them to try and defend the rest of my body from suffering damage.

Now, she stopped a moment.

"You will go to that house after school tomorrow to apologize for stealing their flowers. Do you hear me?!" she bellowed and then swung the stick to strike my shoulder, nearly hitting my face instead.

"If they want you to plant more flowers in their garden as punishment, too, you'll do it. Understand?"

And while I tried to nod, the stick came across my left side, making a deep welt. I screamed out because the stinging nature was so much stronger with that hit.

"Now, get your pants off." I did, and before I could get the underwear off, she continued her assault for over 5 minutes, the stick a blur through the air repeatedly. She struck me so hard that the welts bled, and you could see the lines of blood seeping through, across my white briefs, crisscrossing back and forth.

"No dinner for you, and I don't want to see you. Get to your room. And don't come out unless you have to pee or shit."

I went to my room and shut the door. Laying down on my bed, trying to find a position that didn't hurt as much as others.

Now she started in on grandma

"And YOU?! Where is your fucking common sense? Oh wait, you don't have any!"

"It was just some flowers, Shirley. I am sure they have plenty more. You didn't have to go THAT far"

Oh yes, yes, I did have to go that far. He's lucky I didn't go a lot farther. It's all clear now. Now we know why he gets beat up."

"No, you don't know that. Those boys are just MEAN and vicious and cruel just as YOU are to him."

Their argument went on for over a half hour as I just lay there on my bed, motionless and in agony, wanting so badly to die.

September 1978 - Fourth Grade

The new school year, as usual, meant a new teacher, and my new fourth-grade teacher's name was Mrs. Apostoledis. Unlike my former teachers who got by with stationary, regular chairs at her desk, Mrs. Apstoledis had an old wheeled gray wheeled office chair that she seemed to favor above all else in her classroom, as she rarely left the chair except to write things on the chalkboard or to hand out ditto sheets. That was her other favorite thing, ditto sheets. She handed them out constantly, the odor of their blue ink permeating the room so heavily that it was just the signature scent of her classroom.

Other things were changing this year as well. The number of latchkey kids, children who were to look after themselves after school without adults present in their homes, had gone up significantly in recent years, and schools were starting after-school programs. My school was no exception and Mrs. Apostoledis passed out a ditto regarding our school's new option. This year, we would have an after school program to go to. If the children's parents signed us up for it, we could stay after school and play games and do activities. I had seen the new air hockey table and a pool table in the basement at lunch while we were in line for lunch outside the cafeteria, and I was interested in trying out the after-school program. Mr. Difiore, the art teacher was slated to lead it as well, so that piqued my interest. He was one of the few teachers I liked, mainly due to our shared love of art.

"I want to play that!"

I told John as I stared at the air hockey table from a distance in the lunch line.

"Me too." John agreed.

"I'm gonna bring the permission slip home so I can come down here after school."

"Yeah, I am too." John said.

"My uncle has an air hockey table. It's so fun," Juan chimed in.

"You coming after school?" John asked Juan

"Yeah," Juan replied.

After a day where Mrs. Apostoledis established herself as a teacher who didn't really do much as far as actually teaching anything of value to the class or even doing any teaching at all, We lined up for dismissal.

"Now, those of you who are interested in staying for the new after-school program, line up on this side, and the rest who are going home, line up here on this side."

The bell rang, and Mrs. Apostoedis opened the classroom door, telling the kids who would stay for the after-school program.

"Now, all of you go down the same staircase we used to go to lunch." She told us as if we didn't already know since she had already covered how the after-school program was going to work in class earlier in the day.

Mr. Difiore was in the center of the room, ready for our arrival. There were several tables set up with activities on them, and the air hockey and pool tables had been moved out away from the wall where we had seen them parked when we were in line for lunch and waiting to enter the cafeteria.

In my excitement to get down to see the new after school program and play air hockey on the new table, I had failed to notice that Eggy and his friends had also chosen to join this new venture as well.

"Ok, we have a variety of games on the tables. Sign your name on the sheet at each table for the things you want to do and your name will be called when it's your turn. The signup sheets for pool and air hockey are taped to the wall next to them. If you want to do art, come to one of these two tables over here."

And he pointed to two tables where there was a variety of arts and crafts materials laid out.

There were two other teachers here in the room, one that I didn't recognize. The air hockey and pool tables had the longest lists of students wanting to try them out. John and I had wasted no time signing up, having done so before he had finished his first sentence about signing up for areas in which we had an interest.

"Remember, today is your free pass to check out the after-school fun program. Tomorrow, you will need to bring us your permission slip signed by your parents to enter the room, or you won't be able to attend." One of the other teachers supervising the room informed us.

"If you don't have a permission slip before you go home, pick one up at the art tables."

I instantly fell in love with the game, beating John by 3 points during our game and going on to play a boy from one of the upper classes. We of course, had re-written our names on the list so we could play again once it was our turn to do so.

The time in the room went quickly, and before too long, we were up again. Somehow, my turn came at a time when I would have to play Eggy. I declined, and he called me chicken, and the other boys in his gang made similar derogatory comments. Mr. Difiore stood up from his spot at the art table and looking in the direction of the air hockey table and directly at Eggy, he loudly said, "Hey! I will not have that kind of behavior here. If you can't be kind, you will be told to leave, and you will not come back tomorrow or any other day."

Now I liked Mr. DiFiore even more. He wasn't going to tolerate any nastiness from anyone just because it was the after-school program and we weren't in our classes.

We also saw Juan's mother finishing her work in the cafeteria. Just before she left, she called Juan, John, and me over to the cafeteria doorway and handed each of us something wrapped up in foil.

"Now, don't tell anyone else. SHH!"

She told us, making the quiet signal with her finger over her lips. I unwrapped the foil on mine a bit to see it was a sloppy joe sandwich that was apparently left over from lunch. Juan's mom was always doing things like that, sharing extra food with Juan and his friends, and she always reminded me not to tell anyone else she did so. We put our sandwiches in the pockets of our jackets and said nothing.

We went back to playing, and John's name was called. The boy who had won the previous game said he didn't want to play, and John's name was next on the list, so we got to play again together. This game lasted longer, and John finally won by one point. We shook hands on a well-played game, and next, a few moments later, while drawing at one of the art tables, we heard our names call for a game of pool. I didn't enjoy the pool as much because I had trouble controlling the stick in order to hit the cue ball with enough force to knock one of the other balls hard enough to go into a pocket. With practice, I got better at it, but I still enjoyed air hockey a lot more than pool.

At the end of the day, many children had already left to go home. The program would be set up as a drop-in program, meaning that any child could leave to go home when they wanted, but once they had signed out for the day, it was assumed that they were going home and they couldn't return.

I had decided to go home when John was leaving too, at around 4:25. Eggy and his friends had already gone a half hour before. We ate our sloppy joe sandwiches as we walked away from the school, then as we finished, John said, "Let's go get candy!"

I agreed, and we went to Dairy Mart, where they had a spectacular assortment of every kind of candy conceivable. I had a quarter in my pocket left over from lunch. That was also new. This year, even if you had received free lunch before, you had to pay fifteen cents for your carton of milk. I told the lunch lady I didn't have the money and she let me have the milk anyway for free, so I got to keep the quarter grandma had given me that morning. John had done the same thing with his money for milk so he would have money for candy.

I had grabbed a Whatchamacallit bar, which was brand new at the time and John got a Nestle Crunch bar. We broke each of our bars in half and shared the half with each other.

"Wow," John said with a mouthful of whatchamacallit, "I'm gonna get that next time."

I had already eaten Nestle crunch bars on other occasions, usually while out with grandma, so I knew how delicious it was, but I still said

"Crunch is great too."

Since we were pre-occupied with paying attention to our candy bars, we had missed the fact that Eggy and his friends were outside the store as we left.

"Hey, look, it's the chicken who's afraid to play air hockey against me."

Eggy said as the others laughed. We ignored them, crossing the street and walking toward John's house. We looked back a couple of times to see if they were following, but they were more interested in whatever they were doing than to continue making fun of me. I didn't mind. It would have been embarrassing if they started doing more than verbally insulting me in front of John, even though John knew full well just how much of a target Eggy and his gang considered me to be.

After John went inside his house, I made my way to mine since it was getting late.

When I arrived at the corner of my street, I saw that Eggy and his friends had decided to station themselves there, so I decided to go around the block the long way around to get to my house by coming from the other direction.

When I got to my porch, I saw Eggy and his friends walking in my house's direction, so I got inside quickly, hoping they hadn't seen me, and decided to come and start trouble.

They had seen me. They started throwing rocks from the driveway at our windows. One of the larger rocks broke the glass on the window, and the boys scattered in all directions, away from our house.

Mother, who was in the kitchen with grandma had come into the living room to see what was happening as I was knocking on the door to get in, following their breaking of one of our apartment windows.

"What the FUCK is going on?" Mother yelled as she unlocked and opened the door, dragging me inside by yanking my arm hard and slamming the door shut.

"Look at this. Glass all over the floor. And it's gonna be cold tonight. The landlord won't be able to fix that tonight. "

Now she focused her attention on me fully, screaming

"You worthless FUCK! It's bad enough you make them beat you up at school; now you're bringing them HERE to MY motherfucking HOUSE! Now CLEAN THIS UP!!!" she smacked me across the head, left the room, and got the dustpan and brush from the pantry, throwing them at me when she arrived back in the living room.

"You better get ALL the pieces of glass too. If you miss any and I step on them, you can sleep outside tonight."

After I cleaned up the glass, Mother started in on me again.

"Why the fuck are you so late?" she asked.

"T-T-There's a new thing after school. We can play games and do art. I stayed to see it…I want to go every day; you'll have to sign this."

And I pulled the folded-up permission slip from my pocket. Mother wrenched it from my hand and unfolded it, read it, then tore it to shreds.

"No. If this is the result of it, if you pissed these asshole kids you go to school with so that they came here to do THIS," she said angrily while pointing at the busted window," then you're not doing it."

"B-B-B-ut I didn't! They just hate me."

"SHUT UP! Now strip."

"W-W-Why?!"

"Are you STUPID as well as blind, you FUCK?! You brought THEM here, and they did THIS!! LOOK at it! You know we are going to have to pay for that. The landlord isn't just going to replace the glass for free. Now get your clothes off."

And she started removing her belt, doubling it up when she finished taking it off.

She swung again and again, furiously, making my behind and back raw with welt after welt.

"Now get to your room. Put pajamas on and go to bed. No supper for you."

I didn't care. Luckily, I had eaten the sloppy joe Juan's mother had given me and candy for dessert. I didn't obey her about putting my pajamas on, though; I was in too much pain. I just lay down on the bed without any clothes and cried about not being able to go back to the after-school program with John, Juan, and Mr. Difiore. I hated my life so much.

The next day, we had music class where our music teacher, Mr. Sam, had a special announcement.

"This year, we are starting a glee club for the 4th, 5th and 6th graders. We will be meeting after school 2 days a week on Tuesday and Thursday. If you like singing and want to be part of the club, turn in the permission form to me tomorrow. Our first after-school practice will be on Thursday. In December, we will sing 3 songs on stage at the Christmas show."

I enjoyed singing enough to want to be part of the club, and I asked John if he was going to join. He said yes. Juan would do it too, he told us.

Then I remembered that my mother didn't want me to do after-school activities. I would simply have to not tell her about it and have Grandma sign the permission slip instead.

At the end of the day, I raced past Eggy and his bullies before they could place themselves in my path home outside the school and made a beeline to my house.

Grandma read the permission slip.

"Please sign it. I really want to do this. John and Juan and a bunch of kids from my class and 5th and 6th grade are doing it too. We are gonna put on a Christmas show!"

I blurted out with excitement, barely taking time to breathe before getting all the words out.

"Calm down, calm down. It's ok with me, but you will have to get permission from your mother."

My heart started sinking. I pointed at the broken window that now had a piece of cardboard taped in place until the landlord could replace the pane and said, "NOOO! Remember, she doesn't want me to stay after school. She will say no. Please, please, PLEASE sign it."

Grandma, seeing how intent I was on being part of the glee club, signed my permission slip.

"Alright, here. Now hide that in the pocket of the pants you'll wear tomorrow."

Grandma instructed so that we wouldn't get caught in the act of not telling her about this.

On Thursday, the newly formed glee club members assembled in the music room after school, and we practiced a couple of songs that didn't have ties to Christmas. Mr. Sam was just testing to see where our voices were and trying to get everyone on key and singing in their vocal range. Luckily, Eggy and his friends were nowhere to be seen, having left school at the end of the day as normal.

When glee club practice was finished. Mr. Sam gave us ditto pages of lyrics for 'The First Noel,' 'Silver Bells,' and 'The Little Drummer Boy' and told us these were the songs we would sing in the show.

"Don't forget to practice. The more you practice, the better you'll remember the words to the songs in addition to getting better at singing them." He reminded us.

John, Juan, and I all left school, taking off for Juan's house to walk him home first before John walked me home and took off on his own to get to his house.

When I got inside, I asked Grandma if Mother was home yet.

"No, not yet."

Thank goodness for that. I took the folded up song sheets out of my pocket and hid them in an old sock that was too threadbare to wear anymore and tucked the sock under the other good pairs I wore each day, themselves not in much better shape. I closed the drawer, took off my school clothes, and put on my play clothes.

A loud crash and something coming straight from my face interrupted me as I was about to leave my room to go to the kitchen and help Grandma set the table.

"What was THAT?!" Grandma exclaimed and ran to my room. I was on the floor, having just been hit by a rock that had come through my bedroom window. Grandma looked out the window. The rock had hit my cheek, which was now bleeding.

"Come on, let's go to the bathroom and get that cut cleaned up," Grandma instructed. I was shaking from the suddenness of what had just happened, the surprise of it.

Grandma was washing the cut-off with sprays of bactine and dabbing at it with a face cloth when we heard the click of the lock unlocking and Mother walking in the front door.

She ambled over to the bathroom and, upon seeing the cut on my face being worked on by Grandma, immediately went into fury mode.

"What the FUCK happened now?" she slurred through alcohol-thick verbiage.

"Someone threw a rock through another window, this time his bedroom. The rock hit him in the face." Grandma, matter of fact, told Mother.

What? You've gotta be kidding me?!" Now there's TWO busted windows. Come here, you little bastard," and she grabbed my hair, dragging me out of the bathroom while I tried desperately. To get her to release her grip. She let go when I was back in the living room and backhanded me across the face.

"You brought them here AGAIN. Didn't YOU?!" she screamed, the rage in her eyes distorting their shape as her anger twisted her features.

Now she picked me up by the armpit with one hand and punched me in the chest with the other.

"Answer me, you FUCK! You brought them here again, didn't you? And she released her grip on my armpit, allowing me to fall to the floor, where she kicked me in the chest and back as I tried to crawl away.

"What did you do to make them mad and bring them here?! Huh?!" she demanded to know

"N-N-NOTHING! I swear! I cried out, still trying to get away from her. She was having none of it, though, and she grabbed me by the waist of my pants and threw me across the room. I hit the leg of the coffee table, sending the knick-knacks that were on it flying in different directions. Grandma came out of the bathroom to try and defend me and Mother immediately shifted focus to her, warning her, "You better not start trying to defend him. Now make yourself useful and go cook dinner, or I'll put your face through the wall."

Then she resumed interrogating me.

"Now, are you gonna tell the truth? What did you do that made those fucking assholes in your class break another one of my windows?"

When I didn't respond, she punched me in the thigh repeatedly.

"Ok, if you're not gonna tell me, you can just go clean up the glass and stay in your room the rest of the night. No supper, got it?"

I nodded my head as best as I could, still shaking all over from everything that had happened.

I got the dustpan and brush and went to my room and swept up the broken shards of glass and smaller pieces carefully and went back to the kitchen to throw the pieces in the trash. I returned the broom and dustpan to the pantry and padded off to my room while Mother took a long gulp of vodka she had just poured into a plastic cup.

When Grandma finished making dinner, she put a plate on the table for Mother and walked out of the kitchen.

"Where the hell are you going?" Mother angrily slurred

"To fix the cut on David's face from the rock. I have to finish."

"Oh, sure, that's great" Mother sneered, and reared up on Grandma.

"Go and tend to the baby troublemaker. Always gotta baby him. It's no wonder he's a fucking little sissy who can't fight or defend himself. "

Grandma ignored Mother's comments and went to the bathroom to get the first aid cream and a Band-Aid to put on my cheek. When she got to my room, she slammed the door. This made mother even angrier, "Oh, you think you're so high and mighty, slamming doors, huh bitch? She yelled through the door and then opened my door and slammed it. Then again. And again. And again. Paint chips were flying in all directions as she bellowed.

"Think you're so high and mighty? I can slam doors too bitch so FUCK you FUCK YOU AND THAT FUCKING BRAT TO HELL. You HEAR ME?"

Then she slammed the door one more time before going back to the kitchen, pouring herself another cup of vodka, storming off to her room, and slamming her own door.

Grandma finished tending to my facial wound, then said

"Come on. Let's go eat."

"NOOO! Mother said No! I can't! I can't!"

and I cried with anxiety out of fear of what she'd do if she came back to the kitchen to find me at the table eating my supper.

Grandma left my room and then returned a few moments later with two plates of dinner. She put them down on my bed and then closed my door gently. We sat there on my bed, eating hot dogs silently as Mother continued on her drinking binge in her room a few feet away.

Not long after dinner, I went to the bathroom to brush my teeth to go to bed and found it difficult and very painful to walk due to Mother punching me so hard in the thigh repeatedly. I hoped that with rest, the pain would subside, but I knew all too well that tomorrow would be another difficult day filled with the pain of the injuries caused by Mother the night before.

So, what else was new?

October, 1978 - Fourth Grade

It was the beginning of the month, and Mother and I stood in line at the bank, waiting for our turn to collect our food stamps and to cash our government welfare check as well as grandma's social security check. On these days, twice a month, I was frequently called upon to go with Mother to help her bring home the groceries from our twice-monthly trips to buy the majority of our meals and staples needed to get us through each month.

We were on welfare more often than not due to Mother's inability to hold a job, thanks in large part to her drinking. If drinking wasn't the cause of her becoming unemployed, it was her loud mouth and attitude that would get her into trouble, and any clerical office job employer would become tired of her antics and fire her. Other times, she would work as a waitress in bars, which would be a wash financially, with all the money she was paid by the bar owners and the tips she'd get from customers getting sunk back into that bar or others to keep her drunken habit afloat.

As we slowly made our way closer to the counter, past all of the other people from the neighborhood getting their welfare benefits paid out, I thought about the next step that would be in store for me that day: helping Mother to carry the groceries home. We had a granny cart that Mother had parked at the inside entrance to the bank, but it would hold just 4 paper bags. We usually filled 6, and that meant I was carrying 2 of them. How I hated carrying those bags. I was a tiny, frail little nothing in stature, so what little muscles I had in my arms ached for two days after our grocery store runs.

Grandma almost never came on these runs because her arthritis prevented her from doing much lifting. For her, lifting the laundry basket and putting the clothes into the washer was a painful enough ordeal.

We finally reached the teller counter after over 45 minutes of waiting in a very long line. It didn't matter when you would arrive at the bank on these days; there were so many people in our neighborhood receiving welfare benefits that you were bound to experience a long line.

The teller, in spite of the fact that she knew my mother from when she had worked there in the bookkeeping department but got fired for poor attendance, always had to get special permission from the bank manager to cash grandma's social security check. Mother had special permission to cash it due to grandma's arthritic condition that kept her mainly at home except for brief jaunts to the convenience store or to get a coffee at the coffee shop or pharmacy.

After the teller had given Mother her books of food stamps and cashed the checks, we were on our way. As we left the bank, Mother grabbed the grocery cart by the push bar and pulled it behind her, the wheels creaking and squeaking as we walked. In a few minutes of walking, we made it to the shopping plaza where Stop and Shop, Medi Mart, and Bradlees resided.

Today, it wasn't to be the grocery store that would be the first of our stops, it would be Bradlees. We had clothes on layaway, and Mother needed to make a payment. There was rarely any leftover money to pay for extra things above and beyond the back-to-school runs, so other times, Mother would put things that were needed, like clothes or things for the house, on layaway so we could pay a few dollars at a time until it was paid in full and we could take the items home.

The batch that was waiting for us right now was a set of dishcloths, some bath towels, a coat for Mother, and one for myself. I hadn't received the coat I wanted last year as I was able to still fit into it and the lining, though falling apart, was still intact enough to get one more season out of it. At least, that's what mother had reasoned. I was, of course, teased relentlessly by Eggy and his friends for wearing clothes well past their shelf life, and that coat was no exception.

The coat I would get this year was a puffy one that hopefully would last me a few years. It certainly was big enough to do so. While it did fit better than my previous coat, it was, in fact, almost a size too big, as the sleeves went well past my wrists and down to the first knuckle of my hand. The body of the coat wasn't snug against my torso and waist either, which would allow the winter cold to float up and make it feel like I wasn't even wearing a coat. No doubt, the teasing would continue as now my coat would be new, but it wouldn't fit properly.

But today wouldn't be the day to pick up our new treasures. We had to make one more payment after this one for that to happen. That would place the acquisition perilously close to the time when I would need to wear a winter coat as the influence of Jack Frost would begin the need for a switch from fall clothes to winter ones.

The time schedule didn't matter; however, what mattered was whether or not the money was there to be able to buy the coat before the weather would deem it necessary to wear it, and the answer to that was no. Since the store wasn't going to allow us to take the coat out of the goodness of their heart, I would have to make due until Mother could finish paying the layaway, even if that meant wearing my old coat again if we experienced an early cold snap or winter snow or ice storm, which was a common occurrence. The weather today was almost cold enough for a winter coat, for example, and it was still clearly fall and had only been so for a couple of weeks.

After paying our next layaway payment, the cashier inserted the receipt that kept track of the payments into a printer slot on the receipt printer and then stapled the receipt back on the bag, placing it back in its bin where it would stay until next month when we would make the final payment and finally own the items.

With our Bradlees errand out of the way, it was time to head to Stop and Shop to do our grocery shopping. Mother put the granny cart into the slot behind the push bar of the store grocery cart, and we walked on the pressure pad that opened the door automatically. I really loved that. I always wondered what it was that made the door able to do that.

We went up and down the store aisles, and Mother reminded me again and again.

"Don't try to sneak anything into the cart. You know what will happen if you do."

The threat of what mother would do was clear enough. She wouldn't dare put me through the torment she did at home in a public place like a supermarket, but this was a time when parents would be commonly seen slapping their children when they acted out in the store. Corporal punishment was a normal, everyday occurrence for the children of that time, and no one would have batted an eye about it or called social services if they saw someone doing it.

I did as I was told and didn't put any extra items in the cart, but when we got to the cereal section, I begged Mother for a box of Cap'n Crunch. She looked at the price and riffled through her coupon organizer to see if she had a coupon to bring the price down to that of the less expensive and less appealing tasting cereals, and she deemed that we could afford it, so she took it from my grasp and threw it in the cart.

Money was tight, and every meal cost was calculated down to the last penny. She counted the meals as she put their ingredients in the cart. There would be no margin for anything extra. I did try, though. I couldn't walk past the Hostess section without asking for a box of Suzy Qs or Big Wheels. As usual, Mother said, "We can't afford a whole box" which caused another customer to look over at her with a look of pity on her face.

"Get the pack of 2. Get two packs of them."

Mother said as if to ease some of the public indications of how poor we were.

I was ecstatic. I had a pack of big wheels and a pack of Suzy Qs. There was little else that could make a kid any happier than knowing they were going to have a special dessert after dinner for the next four days.

"Hey there!"

Someone from the next aisle opening called over to us as Mother was placing two loaves of bread in the cart.

It was the mother of someone I went to school with. She worked at the store, and she was using her pricing gun to put a price on some items before placing them on the shelf.

"Hello?"

Mother answered, unsure of who it was exactly that she was talking to.

"My daughter is in the same school as your son. She's in 5th grade this year. Last year they were in the spelling bee together."

"Oh, I see."

Mother said, anxious already to end this conversation so she could get out of the store and back home to her alcohol haven as quickly as possible.

"Yeah, that was quite a contest. Your son can REALLY spell words. It's amazing really, how he knows so many words beyond what he should for his age. You must be so proud. "

Now, Mother put on her greatest fake smile, the one that made it seem like her face might crack from the amount of effort she was putting into trying to make it seem believable.

"Oh yes, so proud, so very proud."

"Are you going to compete again this year?" she asked me.

I glanced at Mother before answering.

"Yes. I can't wait. I am in the glee club to this year." And immediately after the words came out of my mouth, I had recognized the mistake I made. Mother wasn't supposed to know about me being in the glee club. Would she put two and two together and figure out that I had been staying after school to practice in the glee club for the upcoming performance in the Christmas show? I hoped not.

"Yes, that's nice. My daughter Ayala is in the glee club, too. She comes home from her after school practice on Tuesday and Thursday so excited and singing the songs they are working on for the big Christmas show. I'm really looking forward to being there to see them all perform on stage."

Well, there it was; the cat was fully out of the bag now. I watched as Mother's smile went away and her facial tone turned white as a ghost; then redness took over her cheeks as though she were blushing.

"Well, it was nice talking to you, but we have to get going. Lots of perishable items, you know…"

And she pointed at the milk and packages of pork chops in the cart.

"Yes, nice talking to you too. See you at the next spelling bee," She told me.

"Yup. See you."

I said. Mother didn't utter a word the rest of the time we spent in the store at the register having our items rung up and packed into our cart.

Today, we had six bags, and the majority were relatively heavy, so Mother precariously placed the 6th bag on top of the other 4 in the cart and had me carry just a single bag with the bread, the box of Capn Crunch, and the hostess cakes.

The whole way home was silent, too, except for her to give her usual vocal commands on trips home from the grocery store.

"Come on, weakling, you're walking too slowly. Step it up, sissy," as I struggled to keep a grip on my bag and slowed my pace as the walk home was uphill, making it even more difficult than it would be if it were downhill or level.

When we finally arrived home with the groceries in the kitchen, Mother didn't stop to put away the groceries before the interrogation started while I hung up my coat.

"So, I just heard something about David being in the glee club. Did YOU know anything about this?"

Mother inquired about Grandma, who was smoking a cigarette near the sink. She turned her body away from Mother so that all she could see was the wall above the sink before taking a long drag on her cigarette.

"I'll take that as a yes. Ok, so you knew about it, and I didn't. Was the reason I didn't know about it because glee club meetings are after school?

Grandma still didn't respond. Now, her fingers holding the cigarette started trembling. The smoke from the end of the cigarette made jagged patterns in the air as her hand shook with the fear of what surely was to come next.

"I'll take that as a yes as well. Since he had to have a permission form to be able to take part in the new after-school club, I'll bet he had to have a form signed for the glee club, too."

Finished puffing on it, grandma put out her cigarette by pouring some water on it from the sink faucet, still trembling as she did so. She maintained her stance, saying nothing in reply to her mother's inquiries.

I tried walking out of the kitchen quietly, but Mother said, "Don't you DARE move, fucker."

Grandma saw the trouble that was looming and started to say something.

"Look…"

"No, YOU look. If he needed a signature for permission, how did he get it? Answer me that. Either he forged my name, or it's more likely YOU helped him by signing the slip. Did you sign it? Yes or no?"

Grandma paused a moment before turning slightly to face mother before finally admitting

"Well, yes, I signed it…"

"Ok, that's it. Pack your things and get out," Mother said to Grandma

"NOOO! Stop! Don't make her LEAVE!!"

I yelled.

Whap! A slap across my mouth.

"Shut up. You hear me? Just shut the fuck up! You're just as guilty as she is. You probably begged her to do it."

"NOOO! It wasn't like that!" I tried to reason.

Whap! Another slap across the face.

"Go on, go pack your things. I don't want you in this house anymore. Get the FUCK out"

Mother insisted on Grandma and went to the living room closet, pulling out a very old suitcase and throwing it toward Grandma's bedroom door.

"Shirley, I CAN'T leave. You have my money from my social security check."

Mother went to her purse and pulled out the money from her check that was supposed to pay part of the rent and the bills for the month.

"Here! Take. It! Take it!" and she threw the money at Grandma, bills of different denominations flying through the air and floating down to the carpet.

"Now GET OUT! Do it NOWWW" she demanded.

"NOOOOOO!!!!" I screamed out loud.

Now, Mother turned her attention back to me, picking me up by the arm and punching me in the abdomen and groin as hard as she could.

"You STAY OUT OF THIS, FUCKER! Stay OUT of it!! Go on! Get out of here! Out of my sight!"

"Where will I go?"

Grandma asked through tears

"I've got nowhere to go," she continued a note of pleading strongly present in her voice.

"That's not my problem, it's yours. Now pack your things and get the FUCK out. I don't give a fuck WHERE you go. Just go. Go on, get out."

"NOOOOO, she can't leave! She CAN'T!!!" I yelled.

Mother picked me up forcibly and threw me into my room. I hit the dresser hard with my head and saw stars. A knot immediately began forming in the spot where my head had hit the dresser.

Next, she went to grandma's room, picking up the suitcase as she entered the doorway. She haphazardly opened bureau drawers and stuffed underwear and other items of clothing inside the suitcase, then went to her closet and pulled out a random number of dresses and packed them inside the case with the other clothes. She shut the case, stomped angrily to the front door, opened it, and threw the suitcase into the hallway, where it almost hit the next-door neighbor who was leaving to go somewhere.

"Now, get OUT!" Mother yelled as she pushed Grandma to the doorway and then out of it into the hallway. She slammed the door shut, locked it, and connected the chain from the door jamb to the door.

I came out of my room to try and help Grandma get back inside, but Mother was too quick for me, and she backhanded me across the head. I went to the floor. She picked me up by my foot, dragging me across the carpet and giving me carpet burns on my arms. She then flung me back into my room, where she hoisted me up to the window.

"You wanna go through it? You wanna go through this window? Leave this room and see if I don't put you through it. Go ahead. Leave the room and see what happens, fucker."

And she threw me back to the floor and walked out of my room, going to the refrigerator to retrieve a beer. Hours and many beers and cups of alcohol later, Mother went to her room and succumbed to the blackness that overtook her from drinking so much alcohol. She would be out for many hours. I took it as an opportunity to go outside to get Grandma if she was still there.

I unlocked the door, took the chain off, and then opened the door to the hallway. I didn't see her, so I went outside, and there she was, sitting on the edge of the top stair of the porch, looking sad and forlorn. Her eyes were very red from all the crying she had done that day.

I sat with her and tried to comfort her for a while before persuading her to come back inside the apartment. We put away the groceries, and Grandma then went to her room and put on her shoes as she was still wearing her slippers.

She got both our coats, telling me to put mine on.

"Come on. We're leaving."

I was surprised and astonished at this statement.

"B-But where are we going to go?!" I asked, perplexed as to where we would end up.

"I dunno. The Y, I guess."

I put on my coat and we walked out of our apartment building and up the street, grandma with her suitcase in hand and my hands empty. We walked for a couple of streets until we came to a bus stop.

We waited a few moments, and then the bus arrived. The driver looked at Grandma as she deposited our fares and tore a paper transfer from the pad in front of the fare box.

We sat down in a seat and went a long way on this bus before transferring to another that took us nearly as far.

As we approached our destination, Grandma said

"Ok, stand up on the seat and pull the cord."

I pulled the cord, and a buzzer sounded, indicating we wanted to get off at the next stop.

After departing the bus, we walked a block and found ourselves in front of the YWCA.

What's this place?" I asked Grandma as we turned to walk up the sidewalk to the door.

"The YWCA. It's a place people go when they haven't got another place to go."

We walked inside and up to the front desk, where a middle-aged lady who sat at the desk asked

"How may I help you?"

"I would like a room please," Grandma stated.

"All right. We have just one more available. You'll need to fill out this form. No food or eating of food in the room, in by 9 PM or you will forfeit the room, and your young visitor will need to leave by 9 PM as well."

"Oh no, I will be staying with Grandma," I stated with purpose.

"Not here, you won't. Women only. No men and no children."

"But he has no other place to go."

"Then you'll need to bring him to the shelter or contact the proper authorities so they can get him where he can stay, but he can't stay here."

Grandma, looking deflated and unsure of how to proceed next, said.

"Ok. Thank you, Ma'am," and turned to walk away.

"Look, I don't know your situation, but if you do still have a place to go, why don't you go back there and work out whatever problems you've got."

"Easier said than done," Grandma said. "Thank you"

Hey, the kid's got a pretty big knot on his head.

And we walked back out the door and across the street where we found the bus stop for the bus going the opposite way we came.

Tears were silently streaming down Grandma's cheeks, and that started me crying, too. I couldn't stand to see Grandma cry, and when she did, it inevitably led to me doing the same.

We boarded the bus that took us to the second bus and then arrived at the bus stop across from the one that started our journey. Neither of us cared much about looking out the window or playing traveling games as we traversed the city as we knew that we were going back to the one place we longed with every fiber of our beings to forever detach ourselves from.

Defeated and without answers, we walked back up the rickety porch stairs and into our apartment. We silently went to our rooms and closed the doors, crying ourselves to sleep.

December 1978 - Fourth Grade

As bad as team sports were in my mind, nothing was as bad as dodgeball. This wasn't just because I was the kid that Eggy and his friends would team up to specifically target to brutalize, but because it was one time when the girls would be able to see what was happening too. If you think that girls aren't capable of cruelty, you clearly haven't spent any time with them in a school setting. They could be even more sharp-tongued in terms of their verbal abuse than the boys could ever hope to be.

Unlike many gyms that had a mobile accordion panel style wall that could be slid into place to split the gym into two halves, our school gym had no such feature. The girls would be on one side of the gym playing badminton, volleyball, or some other game designed for the girls, while the boys would be on the other side of the gym playing dodgeball, both sides in full view of each other. This wide-open field of view meant plenty of opportunities for ridicule at my expense, which the gym teachers did little or nothing in the way of preventing or dealing with when it happened.

Even when Mr Quage warned them not to 'gang up' to get specific players out, Eggy and his friends didn't listen and played exactly in that fashion as if to purposely defy him.

As usual, Edgardo got to be one of the team captains. That always seemed to be the case when it was dodgeball day. Luckily, Juan had been chosen as the other team captain and had called me and of course, John, as one of his chosen team players today. He also messed up their advantage by calling Carlos and the second Luis to his team's side.

Even with their side at a disadvantage, they still had some of the bigger, more muscular boys on their team and so, would be highly capable of doing a great deal of damage in terms of getting players on the other team out very quickly.

The game started, and I was able to stay out of the path of numerous balls, some thrown simultaneously toward me, but after a few moments, I was hit by two balls at once, one in the stomach and the other in my left leg. I was out.

It was a rarity for Eggy to be caught. He could avoid the ball as though he were a magician disappearing and reappearing in place. He was always the last one standing.

After all the boys on my team were out of the game, we started a new game. This one ended the way the previous one had, but in the third game, something awesome happened.

Somehow, someone had taken out Eggy, and now it was time for everyone on our team to cheer against him, although Carlos and Luis, his friends who were on our team today, didn't dare to take any negative action his way.

Eggy looked positively furious when he had taken the hit, forced into the walk of shame to join the rest of his teammates on the sidelines who had also been struck and declared out of the game.

I laughed right along with everyone else on my team, though I didn't point and call him negative names like my teammates did. I knew if I did, he would seek me out for an especially violent serving of vengeance later on.

When he re-entered the game for game four, he relentlessly targeted me the entire game, balls coming my way at a furious pace and slamming into the cinderblock wall behind as hard as he could while he and his teammates tried to make me the target of his rage.

Then, it finally happened. Eggy threw the red ball he was holding with as much force as he could get out of his arm. The ball hit me square in the face and caused me to buckle over and hit the floor, my shoulder taking the brunt of the impact. I lay motionless on the floor, crying and tasting blood. The ball had struck me almost dead center of the face, as Mr. Quage and everyone else discovered when he ran to my side and turned me over.

Laughter and cheers were coming from everywhere as Eggy's team celebrated their devastating hit, bringing the girls from the other side of the gym over to add their own cruel taunts to the cacophony of activity going on.

Mr. Quage told the girls' gym teacher

"I'm gonna get him an ice pack out of the fridge in my office."

"Ok. I'll keep an eye on your boys."

Mr. Quage led me through the boy's locker room to his office, retrieved an ice bag, and handed it to me.

"Don't put it on yet," he instructed as he left the office and ran to the bathroom to get some paper towels. He wet two of them and returned to my side in the office. He cleaned up the blood on my face with both the wet and dry paper towels and then said it was ok to put the ice bag on my face.

A couple of minutes later, gym class was finished, and the boys filed through the locker room door and past Mr. Quage's office, where Eggy and his teammates laughed and made motions like a ball being thrown and yelling 'POW" and then laughing uncontrollably.

"All right, that's enough. Now stop it and hit the showers. Move it along!"

And he then got out a form and started filling it out. It was a form to tell parents what had happened.

Finished, he said, "You'll need to bring this paper home and have one of your parents sign it and bring it back to school tomorrow and give it to me."

"Oh no…no…why?"

"Because your parents have to know what happened. You know that. Any time someone gets injured we have to fill one of these forms out."

That may have been true, but I recalled several occasions, especially in gym class, where something happened and caused an injury of a noticeable degree, and no note home was issued.

"Ok."

I sheepishly said.

"Now go shower up, and if it's still bleeding when you get out of the shower, put the ice bag back on it."

I walked over to my locker, stripped naked, and, before going to the shower, stopped at the bathroom mirror. My face had a red circle where the ball had hit.

As I entered the shower, one of the other boys shouted

"Look out! POW!"

Eliciting the laughter of the mean boys and causing Eggy to call out.

"Yeah, look out for flying balls, pussy!"

And even louder, raucous laughter echoed off the shower walls.

"All right, all right, that's enough. If you're done showering, get out and get dressed now," Mr. Quage called from the doorway to the shower room.

The class started exiting the shower and walking over to the lockers after getting their towels and starting to dry off. When I reached the lockers, a bunch of the boys surrounded me after taking my ice bag and tossing it amongst themselves, playing a game of 'keep away.'

"Give it BACK"!

I   yelled.

"I NEED it!"

And those weren't just words; I really did need it because my nose had started bleeding again.

Now, instead of giving me the ice bag back, Eggy tossed it into one of the empty open lockers. When I went to retrieve it, Luis Matos pushed me inside the locker and closed the door.

These being old-fashioned lockers, they didn't allow for a person inside to easily slide a knob up to escape; you had to put your finger into a rectangular slot and pull straight up. The lockers, being old, didn't allow for this to easily take place. The locker was stuck.

I tried again and again to get it open, but wasn't able to do it. I banged hard and loudly on the door, which resounded and practically deafened me inside the locker. I could hear the mean boys outside laughing and carrying on. A few minutes went by that seemed like an eternity, as any amount of time would when you are trapped in such a confined space.

Eventually, Mr. Quage had come over to help at John and Juan's urging.

"Eggy put him into one of the lockers, and he can't get out, and they won't let us open the door."

John told Mr. Quage.

"Now move aside. All of you. MOVE!"

He pulled the handle up and opened the door to the locker.

"That is VERY dangerous. I don't want to see ANY of you doing that ever again. Edgardo, you will stay after school for detention with me today. And all of YOU are lucky I don't keep YOU after school with him."

He said while pointing to the two Luises and Carlos, who had formed a barricade around the locker, preventing anyone from opening the door to free me.

Now free of the confines of the locker, I picked up the ice bag, which was now on the floor, and applied it to my nose again.

"No, not yet. You have to get dressed first. You're going to be late back to class."

Mr. Quage told me.

I put on my clothes as quickly as I could, trying to avoid getting blood from my nose on my clothes. It was bad enough that my gym shirt would probably now be permanently stained, and there was no way my mother would spring for the money to pay for a new one.

At the end of the day, we were lined up to go home, and after school, I went to John's house. He had some idea that I was going to get it bad for messing up my gym shirt with blood, as I had told him mother would probably blame me for it, so as the dinner hour approached, he asked his parents

"Can I walk Dave home?"

His mother, looking concerned, said

"Yes, but be careful, especially on the walk back when you're alone."

"Ok, I will."

John said.

I picked up my gym suit of the t-shirt and shorts rolled up in the towel, and the incident report mother would have to sign and walked with John up the street and toward mine.

"I'll tell your mom what I saw, how it happened."

John told me in an effort to comfort me.

"No, it's ok…"

I said back. I appreciated his effort and ability to be a friend, but I knew that any effort he could make wouldn't cause Mother to change her mind about the fact that it, like everything else, was my fault. She didn't understand the minds of bullies and the fact that they did things to certain people simply because they could, because it brought them a sense of power, not because they were urged into it by something the target did to make them angry. This, combined with her hatred of me, had sealed my fate long ago, and little to nothing would be able to change it.

We arrived at my house, where Mother was sitting in one of the living room chairs, smoking a cigarette, when Grandma opened the door for us.

"Hello."

John said. Grandma, recognizing John, said, "Well, this is a nice surprise. Come in, come in, John," she jovially said, opening the door wider for John to come in.

"I just wanted to walk Dave home so I could tell you about what happened at school today. In gym class, he got hit in the face when we were playing dodgeball. It wasn't his fault; that's just what Eggy and his friends do. They gang up on him until they get him out."

"So why are you telling us this?"

Mother inquired, not even rising from her chair.

"Well, his nose bled. A lot. And some got on his gym shirt."

"Let me see it," Mother said, furrowing her eyebrows. I unrolled the towel, revealing the bunched-up shirt inside. I held it up. Mother snatched it from my grasp and stretched it out by the sleeves so she could see all of it.

"Yeah, that's not gonna come out." She said, shaking her head, her cheeks beginning to redden.

"Oh, I don't know; I think I can get it out with some extra tide and maybe a little bleach. The shirt is white, after all. I don't think the bleach will affect the lettering of the school name... Now, are YOU alright?" Grandma asked, inspecting my nose, which had long since stopped bleeding.

"Yeah. I'm ok."

I replied. I knew in my heart that soon I wouldn't be ok, however, as mother's face was rapidly tinting itself dark red.

"Is there anything else?" Mother wanted to know. Actually, what she really wanted was John out of the house, since she hated everyone.

"Well... yeah...they locked him in a locker too. But I told Mr. Quage, and he got him out."

"Well, thank you, John. We are going to have dinner now."

Mother said, trying more vigorously to get rid of him

"Yes, we are. Can you stay?"

Grandma inquired, making Mother's face become even angrier.

"No, I better go. My mom and dad are waiting for me to start eating our dinner."

John said disconcertedly after looking over at Mother and seeing the rage rising on her face.

"See you at school tomorrow."

I said to John as he opened the door to leave.

"Yup. See ya."

He replied while Grandma shut the door behind him.

Mother got up, looked out the window, waiting for John to be further up the street, and then moved toward me with my gym shirt, now balled up in her fist.

"Open!" she yelled as she brought the shirt close to my mouth. Scared, I did as I was told, and she shoved the blood-stained shirt in my mouth.

"Taste good? Huh, you BASTARD? Does it?!"

"Shirley, it wasn't his fault. You heard what John said."

"Of course, it's his fault. It's ALWAYS his fault. He's a fucking sissy who can't fight back. A baby. Besides, John is his friend, so how can you trust him? He'll stand up for the baby sissy no matter what."

Whap! A slap across the head, "That stain is NEVER coming out of that shirt."

She exclaimed as she yanked the shirt free from my mouth.

"And I have no money to buy you another one. I wouldn't give it to you even if I HAD it, you fucking no good goddamn troublemaker! Imagine locking him in a locker! What a fucking pansy!"

And she left the room to get the yardstick from the pantry. I took it as an opportunity to go to my room and shut the door. I wasn't going to take another beating that wasn't justified. Not tonight, especially after John had come to tell her what had happened.

The latch on my door was broken as a result of Mother jamming a screwdriver into the doorjamb and bending the striker plate out of shape so it wouldn't allow the lock to penetrate the square hole. I pushed at the door furiously to try and keep the door shut. Mother wasn't having that, though, and she rammed the door with her body, knocking me down in the process. Now that she was fully inside my room, the stick came down again and again on my body. Welts were rising up everywhere.

"Now you get up and go to the kitchen. You get out the tide and scrub that fucking shirt until it's clean. You don't stop until you don't see a stain. You hear me, you FUCK? You won't EAT or SLEEP until that fucking stain is gone."

She ordered as she pointed toward the kitchen.

I did as she said, getting the tide and pouring some of the powder on the stain. I got an old dish rag that grandma didn't use anymore to wash the dishes, and after wetting it under the sink faucet, I worked at the blood over and over, using my knuckles to drive the cloth into the Tide-soaked fabric. After working on the stain for nearly a half hour, the shirt material was becoming threadbare, but the stain was almost gone, only a slight ghost remained.

Grandma looked at it and said, "Ok, the rest should come out in the wash."

Mother walked over to the sink with a beer in one hand, looked the shirt over, and said, "Ok, put it in the laundry basket with the rest of the clothes. If the rest doesn't come out in the wash, you'll need to scrub it some more."

I tossed it in the laundry basket, and the rest of the evening was uneventful.

The next morning, as I arrived at school, I saw John sitting on the steps to the school entrance on the playground side of the school. I knew something had to be wrong because the only time someone was on that stoop was if they had done something wrong or they were tired and didn't feel like playing. As I got closer, I saw that John had a split lip and a black eye.

"What happened?!" I exclaimed.

Eggy Luis, Luis, and Carlos were all waiting for me a block away from school last night after I left your house. They waited, hiding behind the bushes in the front yard of one of the houses.

"Oh NO!"

I said, "Oh yeah. My mom and dad weren't happy either. They are coming to the school today to talk to Mr. Shedruff. I told them not to bother because he wouldn't be able to do anything if it didn't happen on the school grounds."

"Yeah, that's right. Plus, they'll just beat you up more if they get in trouble."

"Yeah."

"I'm sorry that happened to you. But thank you for trying to explain what happened in the gym to my mom."

"It's ok; what are friends for?"

Now, having just arrived, Juan walked over to us, forcing John to tell the story again. Juan looked over to where Eggy and his friends were all hanging together and talking and flipped the bird with both hands. Eggy and the gang just returned the gesture, yelling, "Fuck you too!"

When one of the teachers monitoring the playground heard them, she looked in their direction, and they immediately quieted themselves and tried to make it look like they were playing a game. They would get away with their behavior, untouched or bothered by yet another teacher who just couldn't care less. John, Juan, and I just shook our heads as the teacher shifted the direction of her gaze elsewhere, toward the US, as if to imply that we were the cause of their cussing, and while this time, that was partially true due to what Juan had done, it wasn't as if his gesture was unwarranted in the light of the attacks on myself and John the day before.

The simple fact was that nothing would ever change for us as we were constantly treated as the problem rather than Eggy and his gang.

December, 1978 - Fourth Grade

The Christmas season, no matter how terrible the rest of the year is on anyone, is a welcome change to the daily routines of the rest of the year. This was definitely so for me. It was still no picnic in the park, but there was something about that time of year that made my life at least somewhat bearable.

Maybe it was the Christmas tree with all its' lights, ornaments, and garland. Or maybe it was the animated Christmas specials that aired each year during this time. Maybe it was the Sears wish book and the Toys R Us big toy book. Maybe it was the toy commercials that, like the seasonal catalogs, provided children with an ample amount of items we would write on our lists to Santa Claus.

Whatever the reason, I was happier at this time of year than any other. Mother put up the tree on Thanksgiving, as had been a tradition for her when she was growing up. She hated the chore of putting up the tree, though. She only did it because Grandma insisted. Our tree was artificial and older than me, a 4-foot one that had seen many, many years of rotation, and it was showing its age, but strategically placed ornaments and garland and facing the bad side of the tree toward the wall took care of most of the tree's shortcomings. To boost the tree up, it was perched on an old rickety table used only for that purpose. The open table area underneath left room for some of the presents that would appear under it on Christmas morning.

The lights glowed brightly against the tree's dark green coloring, and the smell of burning plastic always seemed to be present whenever the tree was plugged into the now overloaded extension cord. We never could figure out if the smell was because of one light being too close to a branch tip, a bad light socket, or the insulation on the extension cord reaching its' heat limit due to overload. No matter, we always got through the season without any fires, so we counted that as a seasonal success.

The season was fully underway now, and I was circling items in the Bradlees, Caldors, and Kmart circulars that appeared in the Sunday paper. I was on the phone with John as I was going to town with the black crayon in my hand. Since we were all very poor, we coordinated with each other as to what to ask for so that we would each have a different batch of toys on Christmas morning and be able to share with one another. There was no way we would get every item on our lists, but that was ok because we knew if one of us didn't get something, someone else would.

There were exceptions to the rule, of course, as previously, all of us each got a Six Million Dollar Man action figure and an Evel Knievel stunt cycle, but most of the time, we all got different items. This was most especially true about expensive toys like our Tonka trucks. We each always asked for a different one. That was why John had the steam roller, Juan had the crane, and I had the bulldozer with backhoe.

While most kids sent their lists off to Santa Claus or presented the lists to him in person at a store, we always had to show the lists to our parents first. Juan only did the latter. His parents worked hard and wanted him to know that the toys on Christmas morning came from them. Juan's mother, as discussed before, was a lunch lady in the school cafeteria, and his dad was in construction, so they were not shy about sharing with Juan their ethics regarding hard work and the things it would allow them to afford from time to time. They may not have had much, but what they did have, they were proud of, and they were proud to have worked for it. The construction jobs, of course, were few and far between during the winter months for Juan's father, however, and they had to rely on their savings, pinching every penny with just as much force as my mother and grandmother did.

John's mother was a secretary, and his father worked in one of the insurance offices, and while they were nowhere near as poor as my family, they were doing barely better than living paycheck to paycheck. Still, they always saved up their excess few dollars here and there to be sure they had enough money to provide a terrific Christmas for John.

"I'm gonna ask for the 'Operation' game," I told John on the other end of the phone line when I saw it and a pile of other board games in the Caldor circular.

"Yeah, ok, I'm getting 'Mouse Trap,'" John replied.

"Did you see the Hot Wheels Criss Cross Crash set?"

"Oh yeah! We should BOTH get that so we can put the parts together and make the track for it even BIGGER!"

"YEAHHHHH! Let's do THAT!"

We spent hours on the phone this way every Sunday from Thanksgiving to Christmas, plotting and planning our proposed toy haul. There's no way we'd get it all, asking for so much, but we knew we'd get some of it, and that's all that mattered.

Aside from the few cheap cars, trucks, and other toys grandma would buy for me at the five and dime types of stores occasionally throughout the year, birthdays and Christmases were the only times I ever saw more expensive and better quality toys, and I wasn't about to waste any effort on asking for and hopefully getting the best ones I could.

Today, I would have to cut my conversation with John short, however, because we had to go to Bradlees to get some replacement bulbs for some blown-out tree lights. That was great news for me, as I would get to see the expanded toy section of the store and fuel my dreams of a Christmas morning legendary loot batch. Grandma loved this time of year, too, and the reason, of course, was me. She had been saving up whatever little amount of extra money we had for the big day. She hadn't been to the diner or anywhere else since August, choosing instead to save the money from those few lost excursions for toys for me.

A friend of the family, Frank, whose kids mother had babysat when she was a teenager, also came around the house to give mother money for Christmas because grandma insisted on giving me a good day at least once a year. She, of course, spent some of the money he gave her on toys for me but invested the rest in the many bottles that she loved to get sick from. Frank helped Mother because he felt sorry for her, being so poor, and Mother had no problem playing the 'pity' card from her deck of destitution, and she played on his sympathies like a fiddle. She always put on her best act of being a victim when even Frank knew that she was a victim of her own making. Still, he gave her some money to make my Christmas a little better than what it would be without his help.

Now at Bradlee's, while mother went to trim a tree section, I sat with Grandma in the café where she sipped a coffee, and I drank a coke. I was about ready to explode from anticipation as from where I sat in the café, I had a perfect view of the toy department, and its treasures pouring out into the drive aisle in front of it. I saw boxes containing new Hot Cycles in front of the bike aisle and numerous brightly colored new bicycles of every size hanging from the ceiling overhead.

"Are you almost done?" I asked Grandma after taking the last sip of my coke.

Grandma took a final gulp of her coffee and said, "All done," and threw her cup into the trash bin a few feet away. I threw mine in, too, and ran top speed to the toy aisle. I saw Stretch Armstrong, Legos, Play-Doh sets, and enough Hot Wheels and Matchbox cars for a whole city. I was overjoyed beyond reason.

"Grandma! LOOK at all these TOYS!"

I exclaimed as she walked slowly and caught up.

There were home pinball machines, board games, air hockey tables, and train and slot car racing sets as far as my young eyes could see. I wanted all of it. I had to calm myself and remember some of the items I was seeing here in person that I hadn't yet seen in the circulars or the wish books and add them to my already long list.

Mother had arrived beside us and instantly became impatient with the joy I was experiencing in the toy section.

"Come on, let's go. I got the bulbs."

"Just a couple more minutes, PLEEEASE!"

I begged. Mother became irritated and grabbed me by the hand and squeezed it hard

"I SAID we are LEAVING. Let's go. NOW!"

And she started walking in the direction of the front register that would end our trip.

February, 1979 - Fourth Grade

There was so much blood.

I had never seen quite so much blood since the time that Carlos had pushed me, and I had to get stitches in my lip. This time, it was more blood. It had to be. The area of it was large, lying there amongst the ants running around.

I was panicking.

My heart pounded with the force of a sledgehammer against the ribs of my chest. Screaming and crying, I sat there looking at all the blood on the sidewalk. That couldn't have all come out of me, could it?

Knowing the answer, that it HAD indeed come out of me, was fueling my level of shock. Though I couldn't see it at this moment for myself, I would learn from John and Juan afterward that I was pale as a ghost and hyperventilating through the agony-based tears that were flowing heavily from my eyes.

So much blood.

I was scared. Scared that I would be left here for all the blood to pour onto the sidewalk and curb, joining the amount that had already done so. If all the blood poured out of my body, surely I would die, right? I surmised, then frightened beyond imagining and frantic, I looked around for John and Juan. I couldn't see them among the curious onlookers' faces gazing at this spectacle.

"J-J-J-JOHN!!! JUAN!!!"

I screamed. They were nowhere to be found. They had gone to get help. In my upset, confused condition, I had forgotten they'd left. There were just people, so many people around me.

None were doing anything, just staring at the results of the event that had just occurred.

A couple of moments later, Mr. Shedruff was pushing his way through the crowd of people around me.

"I looked up at him and because of the other people surrounding him, with the sunlight behind him, a halo kind of effect had caused the rest of his upper body to appear dark, like a silhouette. For a split second, I thought he was one of the bullies who had returned to hurt me even more than they already had. I put up my arms in a defensive gesture

"NOOO! PLEASE! Don't hurt me anymore! Don't hurt me anymore! PLEEEEASE!!"

I bawled.

"It's ok, you're going to be ok." And Mr. Shedruff knelt down beside me and carefully picked me up, carrying me back inside the school building to Nurse Booth's office. John and Juan, who had both gone to get help, were now back beside me the whole way inside.

"Oh no! What in the world happened?!"

She exclaimed when she saw my condition.

"I have no idea. Perhaps you two can explain it."

Mr. Shedruff said, concern washing over his face.

"It was Eggy and Carlos and Luis Matos." John said quickly.

"Yeah, they were picking on him like always. We were walking with Dave, and they tried to start stuff with all three of us." Juan added.

"Ok, and what happened next?"

Mr. Shedruff said as Nurse Booth was doing the best she could to get me calmed down so she could tend to my wound. I was still alternating between screaming and crying, fueled both by the shock and the pain that now ruled my body.

"They called him names. Baby. Stupid baby. Baby dummy. Stuff like that. And they hit him and kicked him. Luis held me so I couldn't move." John continued.

"Yeah, and Eggy kept pushing me away from Dave when I tried to help him," Juan added.

"Then Carlos pushed Dave really hard, and he went down on the curb, and that's when THAT happened."

John said while pointing at my bloodied knee where a large gash lay wide open over the kneecap, blood still oozing out.

I had hit the sharp edge of the new curb that had recently been installed outside the school as I went down when Carlos pushed me.

"Ok, we need to get these pants off. I have to lift your legs so we can pull them down."

Nurse Booth said while trying to maneuver my body on the exam table so she could get my pants off to take care of the wound. She pulled my sneakers off which both hit the floor with a light thud. And I flinched at the sound, tears intensifying again out of flashbacks of what had just happened.

"Is he going to have to go to the hospital?" Juan asked.

"Yes. But that will be up to his parents. I am going to call his mother now," Mr. Shedruff said as he left the office to retrieve my file so he could get my phone number and inform my mother of what had happened. It was a replay of the previous year when

Carlos had pushed me down in the hallway, and I had to get stitches in my lip. My front teeth were never quite right after that happened, still pushed in, to this day. What would happen to my knee? Would I be able to walk? I didn't know. There was no way of knowing the extent of the damage to the knee just yet. All I knew was there was pain. An astronomical amount of pain. It echoed through my kneecap bone and tore through me like a sword, driving through it and tearing it to pieces again and again.

John looked at the wound and recoiled in horror. He took a few steps back to Juan and whispered, "You can see the bone…"

Juan, now curious, stepped forward and looked while Nurse Booth got two rolls of bandages and two large gauze pads. He, too, looked aghast as he rejoined John a few steps away.

"Now Mr. Shedruff returned to see how things were going and to tell me

"Your mom wasn't home. I spoke to your grandma and told her the situation. She said she doesn't drive, and neither does your mother. Grandma is coming so she can be with you in the ambulance. You're going to have to get to the hospital, and you can't walk on that leg with the condition it's in; the knee may be broken, so you have to go in an ambulance. "

Mr Shedruff said in the most comforting voice I'd ever heard him use with anyone.

"Can we go with him?" John asked, referring to himself and Juan.

"If his grandma says it's ok. But you should call your parents to let them know and get their permission first. He may be in the hospital for a while."

"Ok." Juan and John said together. Juan went with Mr. Shedruff to call his mom, and John stayed in Nurse Booth's office to call his mom at her job since she wouldn't be home yet.

"I can stay with him," John said after putting the phone receiver back on its cradle. "My mom will drive us home afterward."

"My mom said I can stay too," Juan informed us.

As Nurse Booth finished wrapping the last of the gauze bandage roll around the large square bandages on top of my knee and applied tape to hold it in place, Grandma arrived, looking out of breath, having clearly gone at the top speed her body would allow to get here when she heard I had suffered a serious injury.

"What happened?"

She exclaimed as John and Juan then repeated the story of what had happened again.

Moments later, the ambulance arrived, and I was strapped to a stretcher, being wheeled by two attendants toward the waiting ambulance parked at the curb just a few feet from where the injury had occurred.

Grandma got in next, and once inside, she held her hands out for John and Juan, helping them get aboard the ambulance. The attendant who would sit in the back with us got aboard, and the other attendant hopped in the driver's seat and drove away.

After wrapping me in a thick blanket, the attendant who was with us was asking me questions about whether I felt cold or hot and asked me if I knew what day it was. Then he took my blood pressure and temperature.

"His blood pressure is very high, which is understandable after such an incident. His temperature is just a couple tenths of a point above normal."

Grandma acted as if she hadn't even heard his words. She just kept stroking my forehead and face, telling me, "It's going to be ok. You'll be alright." As the tears still somehow flowed from my eyes, though now I wasn't screaming anymore. I couldn't fathom how I still had any tears left after having been crying for so long and with so much force. My stomach ached and I just wanted to be home in my bed. I wanted to be told that this wasn't real, that none of my life was real and that I had dreamt it all, that I was like other kids who didn't get bullied, other kids who had mothers who loved them.

Soon, we arrived at the hospital, where they wheeled me directly into an exam room. A nurse escorted Grandma to the front desk outside the emergency room where she could take my information down.

Juan and John sat with me in the room to comfort me.

Moments later, a man entered the room

"Well, hello there, I'm Dr. Branson," he said to me and then looked over at my friends.

"And who are these people over here? Brothers?"

"No, sir. We are his friends."

"I know, I know, was just kidding. I heard that you both came with him on the ambulance ride. That's being true friends. Thank you for doing that for him. I've got lollipops for both of you later. Remind me to give them to you before you leave."

Juan smiled and said, "We will."

"Well then, let's see this knee here."

And the doctor unwound Nurse Booth's bandage roll and square bandages as Grandma returned to the room.

"Oh, hmm… ok…" He said as he considered the severity of the injury. He then turned to Grandma and said, "He will need to get X-rayed so we can see if anything is broken before we can proceed with anything else. You can stay here with his friends and wait till he returns. It won't be long. I'll get someone to take him. "

"Thank you, Doctor," Grandma replied as the doctor retreated to get an attendant. While waiting, Grandma said to no one in particular.

"Why? Why? Why do these things have to happen? Keep happening?"

"Because Eggy and Carlos and the rest of his friends are really mean," Juan said.

"Yeah, they never leave him alone. They're always being mean to him. Us too because we're his friends"

"I know, I know,"

Grandma said, defeat in her voice.

"But why do some people have to go through so much?"

A single tear rolled down her cheek, and then two more.

No one said a thing for the next few minutes. You could only hear the hustle and bustle of the other things happening outside our room in the rest of the emergency department.

Then, the attendant arrived.

"Ok, buddy, we have to get you to X-ray. Let's get you off the bed and over here," he said, carefully lifting me a few inches from the bed to a wheeled gurney. He then placed a sheet over me.

I was whisked off for an X-ray. A little while later I was back in the emergency exam room with grandma and my friends.

The doctor soon returned, putting the X-rays on a lighted board mounted on the wall across from us.

"He has a fracture of the patella, the kneecap. It's only a hairline fracture. He was lucky. He will have to be in a special device that he will have to wear for a few weeks while it heals. He can take it off for showers and baths, but he must wear it any time he walks."

"Ok, that's fine. " Grandma said as the doctor continued.

"He's got a lot of fluid built up in the knee that we are going to have to drain too."

"When are you going to do that?" Grandma asked

"We're going to do that next. Are you ok to be here with him when we do that? I am going to have to use a needle to remove the fluid. "

"Yes, I can be here. I can't look at the needle when you do it though."

"That's fine; you can just look at Dave's face, hold his hand, and help him to be calm. I'm afraid you boys won't be able to be here for the next part. You'll have to go to the waiting room."

Now, hearing all of this, my heart started racing, and I became scared. In desperation, I yelled

"NO!!! Don't send them away! Please!"

And I started hyperventilating and crying hard again.

"Now, just calm down, calm down. They will be just a few feet away…"

"NOOOOO! I want them HERE! Please! Let them STAY! Please!
"

"Ok, ok, ok, they can stay. But only if you ask them"

"I'll stay," John said, taking my left hand in his.

"Me too," Juan said, placing his hand on John and my hands.

"Ok. That's great. Brave, true friends, for sure. Alright now, David, I am going to have to use a needle on your knee. To take some fluid out of it. First, I am going to use a different, smaller needle to make it so you won't feel the big one, OK?

The doctor went over to some drawers by a sink in the room, washed his hands, put on rubber gloves, and took out a syringe, a bottle of lidocaine, and a much larger syringe for the second part.

He injected the small syringe into the bottle of lidocaine, drew some out, and said

"I need you to stay very still. You may feel a bit of cold, like water is pouring into your knee."

And he stuck the needle in. As before, with my lip injury, the lidocaine burned for a couple of minutes, and it was all I could do not to flex my knee to try and get it away from him. I squeezed John and Juan's hands tightly with my left hand and my grandma's hand with my right. The doctor held my leg still with one hand as he stuck the needle into various places in the knee with the other.

"It's ok, it's ok. He's almost done. He's almost done," Grandma said reassuringly.

Now finished with the pain-killing part of the procedure, the doctor said

"We'll just wait a few minutes to make sure the whole area is numb, and then we'll drain the fluid, and we can get you stitched up and ready to go home."

I let up my grip on grandma and my friends' hands.

Moments later, the doctor said

"Ok, I am going to take the fluid out of your knee now. I want you to tell me if you can feel any pain when I do this. If you do, I will stop, ok?"

Grandma looked at my face and tried to put on her best brave face but she wasn't convincing. She really hated needles.

He inserted the needle and, a moment later, announced.

"Ok, all done," and he tossed the used syringes into a box on the wall.

"Now we can get this knee back the way it ought to be."

And he proceeded to stitch my knee. I held tight to Grandma and my friends' hands even though I couldn't feel him stitching the wound closed thanks to the lidocaine.

"Ok, Now I'm going to get the special device you will have to wear, and then I'm going to get the nurse to show him how he is going to get around for the first week or two with crutches. Be right back."

Moments later, he put the device on my knee, being careful to show Grandma how to put it on and take it off.

Then the nurse came in and got me up off the bed with crutches under my arms and showed me how to use them. I thanked her afterward, and soon it was time to leave.

The doctor returned and said

"He'll need to see his pediatrician in a week, and he will be able to decide if David can walk on it without the crutches or if he should keep using them for a longer time. If there is extreme pain beyond the help of the painkiller, I am going to prescribe, or if the knee swells, you need to bring him back here to the emergency room right away. Sometimes, fluid builds up again in the knee after a few hours. Hopefully, that won't happen for him."

"Ok, thank you so much for everything."

"You're very welcome. He should be able to get back to normal in no time."

"Doctor, I need to call my mom so she can come get us."

John piped up.

"Yes, you can come to the desk out in the hallway. I have to get my lollipops from there for you anyway. Come on."

"Be right back," Juan said as he followed John out the exam room door. Grandma grabbed my hand again, holding it tightly and looking like she was trying to hold back more tears from falling. A moment later, they returned with their lollipops and one for me.

About 20 minutes passed, John's mother arrived, and we made our way to her Datsun 510 wagon parked in the hospital parking lot.

"What a terrible thing to happen. Terrible and so unnecessary. And all because of those awful boys." John's mom said after he and Juan recounted the story again on the drive home.

She stopped at my house first to drop Grandma and me off.

Grandma and I got out of the car and we said our thank yous to my friends and John's mom, and mounted my crutches, taking care to go slow. When we got to the porch stairs. Grandma took the crutches and, instead, helped me up the stairs by supporting me under my armpit and taking all the weight off that leg as we made our way inside.

The lights were all still off, so Mother wasn't home.

That was at least some comfort, as the last thing I wanted to deal with right now was more of Mother's angry antics.

As I lay down flat on my back, I realized that the lidocaine was wearing off, and the pain of the injury was making itself apparent once again.

Grandma made macaroni and cheese for me without even asking if I wanted any. In all of the excitement, I had forgotten or hadn't even realized I was hungry.

"What time is it?" I called out to grandma in the kitchen

"It's 6:30"

Somehow, over 3 hours had gone by. I wondered how that was possible. There is such a different sense of time any time you have to go to the hospital.

After eating my dinner, Grandma helped me get to the couch in the living room where I could watch TV. Before bed, she took the knee immobilizer off, helped me get into my pajamas for bed, and helped me put the immobilizer back on. Mother never came home that night before I had finally drifted off to sleep.

Today, bad as it was, turned out to be a good day after all.

A very good day.

July, 1978 - Summer Break

The car was huge. Frank's 1975 white Chrysler New Yorker was one of the biggest cars I had ever seen. It had a maroon vinyl roof and a matching maroon interior made of leather. The seats were plusher and more comfortable than a living room couch and the ride was exquisite. It was like riding on a cloud.

Frank, Mother, and I were on our way to an amusement park that was about an hour and a half away from our house, the closest amusement park to us. Grandma stayed at home because walking around the park for hours would be too much for her.

Frank had divorced his wife years ago after all his children had become adults. Since that time, Mother had tapped Frank for money every chance she got, the frequency of which was increasing with the passing years as her alcohol usage and dependency had steadily increased. The more she drank, the more she spent on bars and alcohol at home, and the less she was able to steadily work, making her short of cash to meet the bills and rent. Frank always came through, falling for her stories about how things were just getting more and more expensive and how hard it was for a woman to raise a son on her own.

Those statements were true of course, but if she were able to get off the sauce, she would be able to meet her obligations far easier than she could with a drink constantly in her hand.

Now, in more recent years, Frank had suggested that maybe they should combine forces, and Mother, Grandma, and I could live together at his house since he would retire soon, and his pension from the post office plus his social security checks would allow him to afford a comfortable retirement. He already owned his large house now had many empty rooms since the kids had grown up and moved out on their own. Mother always manipulated Frank, saying that maybe she would do it and that she'd think about it, but never actually followed through, and each time she needed money from Frank, she'd dangle the 'maybe I'm ready to move in with you' carrot in front of him, only to never actually do it.

This time it was a trip to the amusement park that she wanted. She convinced Frank to take us and promised that she would talk with him about moving in together, something she still had zero intention of doing. She was just using Frank, as usual, to get something she wanted. In his absence, she had nothing but derogatory things to say about him, as she did about everyone. Now, she was putting on her best fake persona, pretending to be happy on our trip and putting false hopes into Frank's mind, playing up his loneliness.

The truth of the matter was that Mother liked rollercoasters, and she had just wanted to ride one again since it had been so long since she had last been on one. She cared nothing about the 'Frank' part of the equation; he was just a means to an end who could make it happen for her. She didn't care that this was my first trip to an amusement park either. In fact, even the idea of bringing me wasn't hers; it was Frank's. But nonetheless, no matter whose idea it was that I should be along, I was excited. I have seen the commercials for this park on TV many times. It reminded me of Disney World when I had also seen that on TV.

Now, it was a reality. We were on our way there. I alternated between sitting and lying down in the back seat of this incredible car. I marveled at the gorgeous details. It was nicer than the Cadillacs of the time. Frank wasn't rich, but he seemed to be when he drove this beautiful machine. He had bought it when it was only two years old and he said it was the best car he had ever owned, and now, having a ride in it, I could certainly agree with that assessment.

Now, after our long trip, we were approaching the park. It was the kind of day that you would label as 'perfect' for visiting an amusement park. The sky was rich with beautiful blue color and white fluffy clouds that looked like wads of cotton floating through the sky. It was just over 70 degrees and the sun felt great, with little humidity in the air to spoil your enjoyment of the warm temperature.

We waited in the line of cars to get in, and even from back here, I could see the rollercoaster that Mother wanted to ride, climbing the lift hill and then going over the hump, causing riders to scream and shout. With each car length that we inched up toward our turn to greet the parking lot attendant, my anticipation grew from being able to see other glimpses of the park to the left and right. I saw the swinger ride and the pirate, both rides I couldn't wait to get on.

We finally were able to get into the lot and park, far enough away that we waited for the tram to bring us from the parking lot to the front gate.

We rode the tram with other families that had already been to the park in the past. We heard them recount stories of the last time they were here and the tales of the rides they had experienced. My anticipation grew stronger as we exited the tram and got in line behind the other people who were just arriving as well. I was going to have the best day of my life; I just knew it.

It was now our turn. Frank paid our admission fees and we got our hands stamped with a blue ink symbol of the park's logo that was always on the TV commercials.

"So, what should we do first?" Frank asked

"Let's go on THAT!" I yelled, pointing at the swinger. It was swinging people round and round in a circle, high in the air.

"Ok," Frank said, and we made our way over to it. Frank pointed out a girl with cotton candy.

"Want some of that?" He asked.

"YEAH!" I had never eaten cotton candy, but it looked delicious, and that was enough to convince me that I wanted it.

"Ok, we'll get some after we ride this," Frank told me.

As we stood in the line for the swinger, I smelled so many delicious things in the air. I had no idea what any of them were, but I wanted to try them all.

When it was our turn to board the ride, the ride operator stopped us and had me stand against a post with a paint mark on it. The mark was above my head.

"Sorry, he can't ride this ride. He isn't tall enough." The ride operator said.

"There is a smaller version of this ride on the other side of the park, though. He should be able to ride that one."

"Ok," Mother said.

"Thank you!" Frank said.

"Ok, what now?"

"That one over there!" I exclaimed upon seeing the slingshot ride.

But when we arrived there, it was the same story. Too short to ride. The pirate's ride operator didn't change the tune either. I was too small for that one, too.

Frank, seeing disappointment taking over my face and overall mood, had a suggestion.

"Hey, you know what I want to do? I want to ride the monorail. It goes WAYYY up in the air, so you can see the whole park. Let's do THAT!"

That was something else I had always wanted to do. On The Wonderful World of Disney, I had seen the monorail at Walt

Disney World and always wanted to ride it. Riding a train in the sky seemed like it would be a great adventure, and one I wanted to be on.

When we got on, I pretended to be Captain Kirk on a planet, using his communicator to tell the ship he was on the planet's skyway train. Mother was not amused. Frank laughed and encouraged me, pretending to be one of my crew members and using an invisible tricorder to record our findings.

As we glided through the park, we saw all the different rides, the log flume ride, places to eat and everything else the park had to offer I pointed to all the things I wanted to do. Lastly, we saw the rollercoaster as we came closer to our destination stop. Mother, looking like someone had shot her dog, beamed a bit when we got closer to the rollercoaster.

"We exited the monorail, and Mother said, 'Come on, let's get on THIS."

"YEAAAAH!!!" I shouted with glee, though my enthusiasm was doused like a fire being extinguished by a bucket of water when a man at the coaster entrance measured me and found I was too short for this ride, too. I started to cry and Mother rolled her eyes and said

"Oh great, here we go. The baby's gonna cry."

"Go ahead Shirley, you go ride it. I'll stay with him and get him some cotton candy. We'll be right over there when you get off."

Frank told her, pointing to an area set up with picnic tables for people to sit and eat their treats.

We walked over to the cotton candy stand, and I watched in awe as Frank lifted me up so I could see the girl turning the paper cone and twirling it around, weaving the candy onto it from the metal drum that was transforming the candy syrup to cotton.

It was the coolest thing I had ever seen. My tears were now gone as Frank paid the girl, and I received my cotton candy.

I thanked Frank, then took a bite and it was the most delicious thing I had ever tasted to that point.

We sat down at a picnic table, waiting for Mother to get back from her rollercoaster ride. I smelled something else delicious in the air, and I asked Frank, "What's THAT smell?"

He sniffed the air and said.

"Oh, that's fried dough. We'll have to get some of that before we leave today."

Now, Mother walked to the table and joined us, seeming to be in a better mood.

"Was it good?"

Frank asked her, referring to the coaster

"Oh yeah, it was great."

Now I started to feel sad again. I wanted to ride it.

"I hear there's another coaster here that YOU can ride," Frank said, looking at me.

"REALLY!? There IS!? I want to ride it NOW! Can we? PLEAEEEEAAASE?!"

"We can if you hurry up and finish your cotton candy" Frank said, then getting up and walking to a nearby map of the park to see where that coaster was.

"Ok, it's not too far from here. Short walk. I bet you'll have your cotton candy all finished by the time we get there."

Frank said enthusiastically.

"YEAAAHHH! ALRIGHT! Let's GOOO!"

I yelled as I got up from the table and started walking fast, still taking bites of my cotton candy as I walked. Mother and Frank tried their best to match my pace as they walked behind me.

Frank was right; all that was left of my cotton candy when we arrived at this coaster's entrance was the paper cone. As we neared the front of the line, I saw another boy who was younger than me being denied entry because he was too short. I panicked.

What if I was too short to ride this one too?

Every young child my age experiences some of the bigger kids and adult rides they can't get on but I was still two years or more behind peers my age as far as height, so I was able to ride far less good rides than other kids my age.

We got to the front of the line, and a man there had me back up to the post, and the orange line was right at the top of my head.

"Just made it," he said.

"YEEEEAHHHH! I screamed in celebration.

While this wasn't a coaster like you'd find at the fair, it was a family-friendly coaster that had some nice airtime hills and exciting drops, especially the first one. It was a proper first coaster for me.

When it was our turn to board the train, after about 15 minutes of waiting, Frank and I boarded the front seat, and Mother sat in the second row.

Now we were moving up the lift hill. My stomach was already turning somersaults, my pulse racing, and my heart feeling like it was everywhere in my body all at once, pounding away as the rollercoaster anti-rollback chain dog clanked over the chain gaps. It took a long time, but we finally reached the top and went over the first drop. I screamed as we descended the first drop. Now I understood why people yelled at the first drop of a coaster. It was exhilarating. The tickle in your belly as you drop, the speed of the wind blasting your face. It was the most wonderful thing I had ever felt in my life. I didn't know it yet, but that first ride sealed the deal: I was hooked on rollercoasters.

As the coaster hit the bunny hops and I rose up out of my seat, I exclaimed

"OH MY GOD!" again and again. There was no doubt that I was going to have to ride this coaster again. I had to experience that feeling of being in mid-air, out of my seat again. I couldn't WAIT to tell John and Juan about this!

We exited the coaster, and I immediately said

"OMIGOD, that was soooo incredible. Can we please do it again? PLEASE! PLEASE PLEASE PLEASE PLEEEEEEEEASE???!!!!!"

"Of course, we can."

Frank said, and we actually rode it three more times, and each time, I noticed something different and exciting about the coaster to love. I even got brave, and on the last run, I let go of the bar when I knew the bunny hops were coming so I would be lifted out of my seat even higher. I was, indeed, a coaster fanatic now.

After we finished with the coaster for the time being, we went to get some lunch. I chose a cheeseburger with the works. It was the biggest burger I had ever seen. The bun was gigantic, as was the burger patty, and the ingredients were stacked so high there was no way I could get my mouth to open wide enough to get all of the ingredients into one bite. No matter, I devoured the whole thing in a short time, what with my roller coaster adrenalin rush causing me to become suddenly famished.

Next, we went to some of the intermediate rides that I was tall enough to ride. One, a spinning rocket ship ride that the rider could control the height of, became a favorite. I also got to ride the smaller swinger, and although it didn't go quite as high, it went almost as fast. Then, it was time for the log flume.

We all held on tight when the log arrived at the top of the lift hill and dropped us to the splashdown zone, getting us soaking wet.

To dry off, we decided it was time for two more rides on the rollercoaster that were just as exciting and fun as the first three.

We then went around to the different midway games. I played the water pistol game where you aim at the clown's mouth and make his hat rise off his head. It was a full table of players, but I won on my first try, and I got a stuffed teddy bear for winning. I was so ecstatic I couldn't stop jumping up and down. I usually had to wait to go to the store with grandma and hope that I could get a toy if she had enough money, but here, I was in charge. I wanted that bear, and I won it without any help. It felt great. I loved being there so much.

The end of the day in the park had come, and we had eaten candied apples, fried dough, ice cream, and chocolate cake, but we still somehow had room for dinner. This time, it was pizza, and it was the thickest, stringiest cheese pizza I had ever eaten.

We finished up the day in the arcade, where Frank taught me how to play skeeball. I got pretty good at it for a kid my age, scoring lots of times in the 40 or 50 holes. We had a lot of tickets at the day's end, and I got a small metal car with my winnings, and Frank combined his tickets with Mother's so she could get a small porcelain cat that she would put into the shadow box of other knick-knacks that resided on the living room wall.

After a full day of so much excitement, I was absolutely exhausted and laid down on the New Yorker's pillow, tufted back seat, and fell asleep for most of the trip home. I only woke up after the car's motion from the highway back to the city had initiated it.

When we got home, as mother retreated to the kitchen to get a cup of whatever alcohol she had decided to drink that night, I changed out of my amusement park clothes and into my pajamas and was treated to the James Bond movie "Live and Let Die' being shown for the first time on ABC. Grandma was watching it. I shared all the fun we had with Grandma, leaving out no details. Then I laid down on the couch. After a half hour, I clutched the teddy bear I had won and started to drift off to sleep, realizing that I just had the best day ever. Unlike my usual everyday existence, for a few hours, I experienced joy. I was a normal child, just like every other child at that park.

If only that experience could last...

November, 1978 - Fifth Grade

Today was quite a strange day. It started out as normal, with a morning of math work and gym class. It was at the end of gym class that things began to change. Mr. Quage asked me to stay with him after the rest of my class went back with Mrs. Quinlan, my 5th-grade teacher.

After dismissing the rest of the class, Mr. Quage had me come to his office.

"Have a seat, please, David."

He said, offering me a chair in his office right across from his desk.

He sat in silence for a moment. Then, seemingly having found words to start with after some searching in his mind, he asked me

"David, I need to ask you some questions, and I want you to be honest with me."

"Ok," I said

"Are things ok for you?" he inquired, a look of deeper concern than I usually had seen on his face washed over it.

"At school?" I asked, my defensive guard, readying itself to go up.

"No, not at school. I know you've had some struggles here at school. I'm talking about at home."

'Why is he asking me this?' the voice inside my head frantically wanted to know.

"Well yeah…things are ok," I lied, hoping that my facial expression didn't betray me and give away that I wasn't telling him the whole truth. Things were ok with grandma, she loved me. But mother…That was another story, and one I couldn't tell.

'Remember Officer Mike,' the voice in my head beckoned me to recall. I didn't need the reminder. I had already known all too well what would happen if my mother's behavior toward me was revealed. I had survived the last time; I wouldn't this time. Still, why was he asking me this question? I didn't have to wait to learn the answer.

"There are marks on your back, your chest and legs. I saw them when you got out of the shower to get dressed."

My heart's beat started to become twice as strong and fast. He had seen the results of his mother's latest rage episode that happened the previous night.

"Oh, yeah. That happened after school yesterday. Eggy and his friends beat me up. They do it a lot."
I told him, doing my best not to appear alarmed in any way. This time, it hadn't happened, though. These welts and bruises were all a result of mother's belt and fists.

"Oh. I see. David, I want to ask you again….and remember, you can tell me the truth, and I will help you. Do you want to tell me about anything else that might have happened?"

I tried to summon every ounce of courage to answer him in a way so as not to further arouse his suspicions. I had to stay strong and not reveal anything. My life would end if I did. She would surely kill me this time. She promised me she would if I ever dared to even give the slightest hint of anything that went on at home. After the severity of her beating following my meeting with Officer Mike, I had zero reason to doubt that she would keep her word and that I would have a home in the cold ground with a stone marker above it for eternity.

"No. There's nothing else to tell. Eggy and his friends are just mean all the time to me. That's all."

Mr. Quage looked me over, scrutinizing me as I tried to keep my own gaze locked with his so he would think what I said was true. Was it enough? I didn't know.

"Ok, get back to class."

Mr. Quage instructed.

I did as he asked.

Later, As I finished lunch in the cafeteria, I was approached by Mr. Shedruff. He walked over to the table where I sat with John and Juan.

"Hello, boys; I am going to borrow David for a few minutes, but he will be back to play with you at recess. Come on, David. Let's go have a talk."

My heart was acting like I had run a marathon race and had come in first once again. When we arrived at Mr. Shedruff's office, Mr. Quage was there, sitting in one of the chairs across from his desk.

"Sit down, please," Mr. Shedruff said, waving his hand over the other empty chair and then rounding the corner of his desk and sitting down. He had a look of concern matching that of Mr. Quage's.

"David, Mr. Quage tells me that you've been having some trouble with some of the boys in your class. Is that true?"

Technically, it was a true statement; I was always having trouble with Eggy and his friends; I had just used that as an excuse to lie about my injuries this time. Usually, my body was littered with the results of violent confrontations between my mother as well as the bullies, so it was the truth.

"Y-y-yes," I nervously said.

"What is it they are doing to you?"

"T-t-they beat me up. All the time. They say mean things and call me names."

Tears were welling up in my eyes. I tried to will them not to fall, but one got away, gliding down my cheek and ending up on my shirt.

"Can you please stand up and lift your shirt?"

I did as he asked, slowly raising my shirt up to reveal my chest and stomach, which had deep welts in multiple directions as well as bruises.

"Now, can you please turn around so I can see your back?"

Mr. Shedruff asked with an edge of something I couldn't define in his voice. It was a vocal intonation I had never heard from him as if he was trying to stifle his emotions.

When I turned, I heard him whisper

"Oh, dear god!"

"On his buttocks and legs, too," Mr. Quage said. Mr. Shedruff rested his forehead against his hand and said

"Ok, lower your shirt and get back to the cafeteria," Mr. Shedruff ordered.

I went back to John and Juan, who were lined up and about to go to recess.

"What'd he want?" John asked.

"He was asking me some questions about Eggy and his friends and what they do to me after school," I told him

"Oh boy. Now he's gonna get into trouble and come after you again."

"Yeah, what else is new?" I said.

Later, back in the classroom, Mr. Shedruff called John, Juan, and me to his office over the intercom.

We all went to his office, wondering what was going on this time.

Mr. Shedruff's door was closed as we arrived, and when we sat down on the chairs outside his office, one of the office secretaries called him on the phone to tell him we were there. He emerged and asked for John to come into his office.

John was inside for a few minutes, and then he returned to sit with me, and Juan was called next. He, too, was inside only for a few moments before he too returned. David I want you to go with Nurse Booth into her office. I will meet you there in a moment. John, Juan, get back to class, please.

I looked at my friends with a quizzical look, and John said, "We'll talk about it later."

I did as Mr. Shedruff said, retreating to Nurse Booth's office. Moments later Mr. Shedruff came into Nurse Booth's office with a clipboard and a sheet of paper that had illustrations of a person on it. What was going on, I wondered. Mr. Quage was sitting in another chair across from where I was standing.

"David, I have to ask you to take off your clothes, please. All of them." Mr. Shedruff said.

"Why?" I asked.

"Because we have to see where your injuries are, and I am going to mark where they are on this piece of paper. That's all."

"But, then Eggy and his friends are going to get in trouble and then it will be even worse for me. Please forget about it. Please. I will be ok."

What I said was accurate; if this did somehow get back to them, I would be in deeper trouble than usual with them, and they would have their revenge for getting them into trouble. I was also afraid that maybe Mother was going to find out about this, and no matter how that turned out, it wouldn't be a good time for me.

"No, I'm afraid we can't do that. We are going to have to see the injuries. Please. We are going to help you now. Please take off your clothes."

"O-o-ok," I said. I took off my sneakers first so I could get my pants off. Then I took off my shirt. All that remained was my fruit of the loom briefs.

"The underwear, too, please."

I did as he asked. Nurse Booth, who had been busy writing something with her head turned away, now looked in my direction.

"Oh, NO!"

She exclaimed. Mr. Shedruff, who had a similar reaction earlier when he asked me to lift my shirt in his office, gave her a look that said, 'Calm down,' and she did.

Mr. Shedruff circled me again and again and made marks on his paper where he saw the many welts and bruises, being sure to document every one. Satisfied with his work, he told me, "Ok, get dressed." He asked Mr. Quage to join him in his office as I finished getting my shoes tied after putting on the rest of my clothes.

I was so incredibly nervous.

"What do I do now?" I asked Nurse Booth.

"You just stay here for now. Mr Shedruff will be back."

About 15 minutes later, he returned and invited me back to his office.

"David, I am going to need you to tell me everything about how this happened. We have to make sure that no one hurts you again like this, you understand?"

I nodded.

"Ok, in your words, tell me what happened. I will write it down here on this paper, ok?"

"Just pick a day, any day. They're all the same! All of them! Every day, they hurt me! Every DAY! They punch me and kick me, and hit me with sticks and branches and throw rocks and other things at me! Every day! Every DAYYYY!"

And now I leaned forward and huge tears dropped from my eyes dropped onto my jeans. Jeans that had patches in multiple locations because of them getting wrecked during beatings from Eggy and his friends.

"Look at my pants! LOOK AT THEM!!"

Grandma has to fix them all the time, and my shirts, too, because of them. They hurt me all the time! All the TIIIIME!

Now, I was full-on bawling, hyperventilating. Someone knocked on Mr. Shedruff's door, and he asked, "Who is it?"

And Nurse Booth opened the door and peeked in.

"Oh, come on in."

She sat down next to me and tried to put her hand across my shoulder to comfort me and I flinched and tried to back away from her in the chair.

"I want g-g-g-grandma!!!!" I said through the tears, barely able to get the words out from the hyperventilation.

"It's ok, David, calm down, calm down," Mr. Shedruff and Nurse Booth both took turns saying to me while avoiding touching me.

I repeated it again and again. After a while, they were able to calm me down, and Mr. Shedruff gave up on his attempt to get me to tell him about how the injuries occurred.

Later that day, Mr. Shedruff returned me to class, and I finished the day. At dismissal, John and Juan both wanted to know why I was gone so long at Mr. Shedruff's office

"Just more stuff about Eggy and his friends," I said. Eggy and his friends were standing beside Mr. Shedruff at dismissal instead of their usual location by the brick wall entrance to the schoolyard.

"I have to get home. "

I said as I took off running up the street before they made their way toward me. One thing was certain: I wasn't going to be able to escape their wrath in this way forever. At some point, they would have their revenge on me.

When I arrived home, now it was grandma who looked concerned.

"Mr. Shedruff, the principal called. He said your mother has to have a meeting with him tomorrow at 2:00 PM."

My knees went weak, and I fell to the floor and started crying harder than I had in Mr. Shedruff's office.

"NOOOOOOOO! I'm gonna DIE!!!! I'm gonna DIIIIIIE! She'll kill me, no, please, please don't tell her he called. PLEASE! Please! Don't TELLLL HERRRRRR!" I begged Grandma.

She came over to me, picked me up, and tried to hug me, but I didn't even want a hug from her at that moment; all I wanted was to run away and hide.

"It's ok, it's ok. I don't know what's going on, but he said he is trying to help you."

"NOOOOOO! NOOOOOO!!! Mom will kill me, Eggy will kill me! PLEEEESASE don't tell her. I can't take it anymore!!! I can't! PLEEEEEEASE!!!"

And I tried to break free of her comforting grip. She put me down, and I ran out the front door and up the street as fast as I could. I didn't stop until I got to John's house.

John was outside, throwing out a bag of garbage into one of the garbage cans, one of his household chores.

"Hey! Thought you had to go home." He saw that I had been crying and was still crying, and he said

"Come on, let's go in the house." We went through the back screen door and the inner door to the kitchen. He poured some lemonade from a pitcher for himself and for me and said

"What the hell is going on? Today's been so weird. Mr. Shedruff asking Juan and me about a beating from Eggy, and now this."

"What did you tell him? I asked with a note of panic in my voice.

"I told him that Eggy and his friends pick on you and beat you up all the time and that they pick on other kids too, like me and Juan."

"Ok. Good. Good. "

"Good? What do you mean?! It's not good. Getting beat up is not good. What's going on?"

John begged to know again. I wanted to tell him, wanted it with all my might. I wanted so much to be courageous and share what my mother did to me all the time at home, but I couldn't. I just couldn't, and it drove me insane that I couldn't tell him, couldn't explain that if he knew, I'd be dead.

"Please, can I just stay here with you for a while? Please? Let's play with Legos or something," I suggested, trying to will my tears to stop, and my breathing to return to normal.

"Alright," John said, confusion still imprinted on his face.

We played until dinnertime when I got up from the carpet in his room and said

"OK, I better go now."

"You sure? You know you can stay for dinner."

"I know. No, I better not. I'll see you in school tomorrow."

"Yeah, see you in school. Hey, call me if you need to, Ok?" he said, concern enveloping him.

"I will. Thanks. I wish you were my brother. Just wanted to tell you that."

"Same here. Wish you were my brother too," John said. Tears were welling up in my eyes again. I forced them back by taking a deep breath a couple of times and said

"See ya."

When I walked in the door to my house once more, Mother was home. She sat in the living room chair with a dull look of boredom that showed also in the rest of her body's posture. That was a good sign, at least. It was clear that she hadn't been informed of the call from Mr. Shedruff.

To be sure, I went to the kitchen to find Grandma. She was at the stove stirring a pot of peas and carrots we would have with our meatloaf tonight.

When she saw me, she put her finger to her lips and whispered

"I didn't tell her."

I breathed a sigh of relief and sat down at the kitchen table. Maybe things would be ok after all, at least at home. I could deal with Eggy and his friends if the situation arose, and it surely would.

We sat down at dinner without incident until the phone rang.

Mother got up to answer it. After a few moments of talking, Mother hung up.

"That was John. He wanted to know if you got home ok. Said you were upset. What happened now?" mother asked. I didn't have a chance to answer as the phone rang again.

"What the fuck?! Can't people leave me alone so I can eat?!" Mother angrily said to the air as she angrily stomped back to the living room to pick up the phone receiver

This conversation was a bit longer, and it sounded as if it was getting heated. Mother was angry. I reached out for Grandma's hand. She moved it closer to me, and I grasped it.

Mother returned to the kitchen, now flaring up with her usual anger, and said, "THAT was your PRINCIPAL. He wanted to make sure that I got the message from when he called earlier that he wanted to see me in his office tomorrow at 2:00 PM."

She moved toward me and reached out for me, yanking me off the chair and throwing me to the floor.

"What is it THIS time, huh, troublemaker? Why does he want to SEE me?" she screamed as she punched me in the ribs, trying to do it a second time and meeting with my forearm that was trying to block the punch instead, and then the other forearm when I tried to block a punch to my legs.

"It's Eggy and his friends! They want to talk to you about what they do to me all the time."

Oh yeah?! Is that so? It was strange that they had never wanted to talk to me about it before. You better be telling me the truth. You hear me?"

"I am! I AM! I swear!"

2:00 PM the next day arrived, and Mr. Shedruff had me brought to the office where my mother, Mr. Quage, and Nurse Booth were waiting. I had never been more so scared since the Officer Mike incident. I dared not try and speak, the words would come out all gibberish. My mind was a mess of confusion and fear.

"David, actually, for right now, you can wait outside while the adults talk." Mr. Shedruff said.

"Why? If this involves him and what the brats here do to him, he should be able to be here in the room."

Mr. Shedruff looked at my mother with disdain for her description of Eggy and his friends and relented.

"Alright, he can stay."

Mr. Quage shut the door.

"We asked you to come here today because, in gym class, Mr. Quage noticed that David had some pretty serious-looking welts and bruises in multiple locations on his body. "

"Yeah, he told me that was why I was coming today. Because of what Eggy and the other assholes do to him all the time."

"Well, you see, I'm afraid it's a bit more complicated than that. We are not sure that the injuries he has sustained could be explained by a beating from his peers."

"What do you mean? What are you talking about?" Mother asked, eyebrows furrowing and anger causing her cheeks to redden.

"Well, you see, some of the injuries just aren't consistent with what you tend to see with a typical schoolyard-level fight with peers of his own age."

"These other kids are much bigger than he is, you know that, right?"

"Yes, Ma'am. We are aware. Still, the patterns don't suggest that they came from boys hitting with fists or feet. Is his father present in his life?"

"No, he is not. That loser took off when he found out I was pregnant, and just as well since he was abusive to me."

"Ok, is there another male figure in the home? A stepfather or a boyfriend?"

"No. It's just me and his grandma, and no, there isn't anyone else special in my pathetic life, and his grandmother loves him to pieces and would never, ever do anything to hurt him."

"Well, you see, it just raises questions…"

"Questions? Do you want to talk about questions? Why, after all these years, is this the first time I am in your office when these kids pick on him and beat him up constantly?

"Ma'am, please try and calm down."

"May I ask something?" Mr. Quage piped up.

"Yes, certainly, go ahead."

"David, I want you to tell me the truth now, did Eggy and his friends do something to you again after school yesterday?"

"No. They were with Mr. Shedruff outside when I left."

"So they never had a chance to do anything to you yesterday after school. You're sure."

"Yeah, I'm sure."

"Why did you ask him THAT?" Mother sneered at Mr. Quage.

"Look at his arms. Both of them."

And mother looked at them.

"Yeah, He's got bruises there. So WHAT?"

"He didn't have bruises there yesterday. We know that for a fact. We documented all of his bruises and welts."

Mr. Shedruff showed Mother the sheet where he had marked where every welt and bruise was seen and indicated with a 'w' for welt or 'b' for bruise.

"How do you account for these bruises? If there is no one else in the home and it's not grandma that leaves just one person."

Mother didn't respond, only shook her head.

"I would tend to agree that it isn't grandma; she has shown her support of him at the spelling bees and the school Christmas show last year, and when he was upset about this situation as we questioned him yesterday, he called out for grandma. He didn't call for Mom. Why do you think he did that?"

Mr. Quage asked pointedly.

"Well, isn't this NICE?" Mother said mockingly

"You think you've got it all worked out, huh? Let me tell you something about the motherfuckers who pick on him. Years ago, he had a bad fall from the rocket on the playground because these precious children you are trying to protect wouldn't stop bothering him until they basically threw and kicked him off the structure. That was the way he described it to me.

Then, last year, one of the bastards pushed him, and he fell face first right out in the hallway here outside, and his teeth penetrated his lip, and he had to get stitches. His teeth are still pushed in from that.

Next, he was pushed by that same fucking bastard last year, and he had a deep enough wound from when his knee hit the sharp edge of the curb where you could see the bone in his knee and a fractured kneecap. You did NOTHING to punish the bastard. He got away with it because it didn't happen on school grounds. He didn't even get TALKED TO because of it, I checked, remember. You basically just washed your hands of the incident and wrote it off. He had to ride in an ambulance and have his knee drained, get stitches again, and had to wear a knee brace for a MONTH, and NOTHING was done about it. The fuckers STILL kept picking on him. He was on crutches for the first two weeks, and they knocked him off his crutches one day, took the crutch, and beat him with it.

But oh, no, they couldn't have done something that was consistent or as serious as the injuries he has right now on his body, right? These bastards don't just use their fists and feet; they are cruel and use whatever they have available to them.

"And YOU can't even properly watch them in the locker room."

She said while looking disgustedly at Mr. Quage

"These asshole kids PISSED on his SHIRT the day of the district spelling bee when he was in 3rd grade. PISSED on his SHIRT!"

Mother then paused as Mr. Shedruff and Mr. Quage both looked down at their laps, unable to come up with any words; then she continued

"David comes home every day with the evidence of what they do to him: torn and ripped clothes that his grandmother sews, cuts, bruises, bloody lips, black eyes, bruises and cuts all over his body.

Go ahead, try and do something to me, try and press charges against me. I will sue you, and I will have every single one of your jobs. I'll get this fucking worthless school shut the fuck DOWN forever. Do you think I can't do it? Do you want to talk about questions? All my lawyer would have to ask is why the school turned a blind eye to all the abuse my son suffered while he was here. Why wasn't he kept safe? Why weren't there adequate consequences against the kids who hurt him? The district itself will shut you DOWN to avoid the bad publicity.

For Christ's sake, the kid who pushed him so that he had to get stitches in his lip shouldn't have even still BEEN in this school after he did that; he should have been EXPELLED. Instead, he got no punishment at all and was allowed to stay in the school so he could keep right on hurting my son. You think you're gonna be able to convince anyone that what you're saying about THESE wounds is valid with your pathetic record of keeping kids safe in this fucking shithole of a school?"

And with that, mother got up and took me by the hand, saying

"Come on, we're leaving."

And nothing about the incident was ever said again. No action was taken. In spite of the overwhelming evidence, she got away with it. She got away with abusing me because the school was inept and wouldn't look credible in a case of child abuse due to their history of negligence in keeping me safe.

The system that was supposed to protect children had failed me again.

November, 1978, fifth grade

"Please don't!!!"

I screamed at Mother. I have been trying to get her to stop ever since we arrived home following our meeting with Mr. Shedruff, Mr. Quage, and Nurse Booth.

Crash! Crash! Crash! Pieces of plastic flew through the air.

AAnother toy was destroyed. Using a hammer, Mother destroyed the few toys I had. She was convinced I didn't deserve them since I couldn't follow instructions. No one was supposed to know what went on at home.

"You SHUT UP! Do you HEAR ME?!!! YOU made them suspicious of ME! What did you say to them?"

"Shirley, you said it yourself; you just told me that his gym teacher saw him as he got out of the shower. "

Grandma said while trying to maintain her distance from her mother, who had a hammer in her hand to help her smash my toys.

"You shut up. Just shut the fuck up. How am I supposed to believe that these motherfuckers who never seemed to know that he was being beaten by the other kids suddenly became observant and saw something on his body? Why couldn't these blind and stupid fuckers see anything all these fucking YEARS when the shithead kids kept beating him up? Huh!"

Crash! Crash! And another toy is broken, this time a semi-truck that grandma had bought me from the S & A store recently.

"You! Come here!" Mother yelled at me, hammer held high as if ready to hit anything in her way.

I just shook my head and stood in place. Then she started moving toward me.

I booked it as quickly as I could, making a beeline toward the kitchen back door. Mother was like a cheetah with her speed, though, and she threw the hammer to the floor and pounced on me before I could get any further than slightly the kitchen doorway, grabbing me by the back of the shirt as she was mid-stride in her run and tearing the shirt as she yanked me backward. My head struck the doorway hard, and I went down to the floor. Stars were in my eyes.

Mother started punching me in the face.

"Stop it! STOP IT!"

Grandma screamed as she came closer, trying to grab Mother's arm from behind. Mother used her elbow to strike Grandma in the face, sending her backward to the floor. Now, her attention was back on me. She punched me again and again in the ribs and stomach. I desperately tried escaping again and again with no success. She was just too quick for me.

Grandma was able to get herself back upright and was again trying to stop her, but every attempt she made was met with the same level of success that I had exhibited in trying to get away. Now writhing in pain on the floor and finding it difficult to move without extreme pain, Mother left the room and went to the porch to get the wood 2X4. I saw her coming with it, and I somehow managed to hoist myself up to run, and I made it to my bedroom door. As I got there, Mother reached out with her free hand, pulling my door shut on my leg and slamming it in the door jamb.

I yowled in agony. The door slammed hard on my shin, and I fell to the floor. I tried to get to my feet, but the pain was just too strong, and I collapsed back to the floor like a sack of potatoes.

Grandma was now on the phone, calling the police. Mother saw her and went toward her, wrenching the phone receiver out of her hand and throwing it aside and then lifting her up by the throat, carrying her over to the front door, slamming her into it and holding her there, choking her.

I hobbled on my good leg to Grandma and kicked Mother in the leg, unable to maintain my balance and falling back down as I did so. Mother wouldn't stop choking grandma, and I saw her face turning blue. I grabbed the receiver and started calling the operator so she could get me to the police.

Mother, hearing the phone dial turning, let go of Grandma and spun back toward me, pulling the receiver from me and slamming it down on the phone base. Then she held me by the shoulder and punched me repeatedly in the head.

She kicked at Grandma to get her out of the path of the front door, opened the front door, went through it, and slammed it.

In my mother's absence, Grandma was able to eventually right herself, and she tended to my leg, which was so swollen that it was nearly impossible to get my pants off. She had to roll and peel them off where the knot on my shin had swelled to epic proportions.

I was unable to stand on that leg.

My head was covered in knots as well, and my ribs ached.

There was no way I was going to be able to attend school again for a few days, and that was at least good news, as I would be able to escape Eggy and his friends' scheme of revenge on me that they had most likely already concocted for getting them into trouble with Mr. Shedruff.

Grandma got ice for me as usual and cleaned up the remains of several of my toys that Mother had destroyed.

Three days passed with Grandma at home, and no school for me, and Mother finally returned at around 10 AM. Immediately, upon seeing me on the living room couch watching TV, she yelled

"What the fuck are you doing here? Get the fuck to school!"

I got off the couch slowly, and when I wasn't moving fast enough for Mother, she approached me, put her foot out, and kicked me in my bad leg right on the shin. I cried out in pain.

"Aw, shut the fuck up before I REALLY give you something to cry about. Get the fuck out of my sight!"

Grandma came from the kitchen to see what was happening, and when she saw Mother, she just shook her head and went back to the kitchen

I got myself dressed as quickly as I could and didn't go to school; I just walked around the neighborhood. I had a quarter in my pocket for milk, and I decided to spend it on some wacky package cards, so I went to the Dairy Mart to get them. I grabbed a pack of cards from the display box on the counter and placed my quarter in front of the cashier.

I put the cards in my pocket and walked around some more. I watched people going here and there, walking or in cars, not paying attention to anything around them, just intent on getting wherever they were going. I started asking myself if this was to be my future, where I became so uninterested in the rest of the world that I just became a part of the machine that made up the world. Was that what made Mother the way she was? It was not being able to find a way to be part of it that shaped her. I didn't know.

I finally decided to go to school. I didn't go inside, however. Instead, I went to the side entrance where the concrete steep staircase was. Next to the staircase, there was a short brick wall on the hill. Kids weren't allowed near that wall, either. I slid some flat shale rocks from nearby, remnants of an old wall that was there before the brick one, and I stacked them on top of each other. The wall may have been short, but it was still high enough that it was difficult for someone short like me to climb on.

Using the rocks, I stepped up high enough to be able to grab the top of the brick wall, lift myself up and sit on top. At first, I straddled the wall, but eventually, I had pulled both legs over to meet each other so I was facing the very high and steep hill that went straight down to the concrete sidewalk below.

I just sat there for the rest of the morning. Recess time came, and I turned my head back when I heard swarms of kids coming outside to control the happenings of the playground during this cherished time of play for most kids. I wasn't in the mood to play, however. I didn't know what I was in the mood for other than dying.

After some time had passed, John and Juan saw me sitting on top of the wall.

"Hey! When did you get here?"

John asked, looking to make sure no teachers were following them. If a teacher saw me sitting on that wall, I'd be in big trouble.

When I didn't respond, John came closer and said

"Hey, you ok?"

I just shook my head 'no'.

Juan moved the shale rocks and John grabbed some more of them, and they stood on them to get themselves up to my level.

"You better not fall. I don't want to go to that hospital again. I hate hospitals," Juan said. I still didn't respond verbally.

"Hey, let's go do something. You wanna play tag?" John inquired, even though he probably figured out the answer before he even asked the question.

"Guess what?" Juan asked, "Eggy and his friends haven't been here for the past 3 days."

I remained quiet.

"Here, take my hand, and I'll help you get down," John said as he held out his hand to support me. I didn't take it. Instead, I stood up on top of the wall. I looked down at the sidewalk below, ready to jump down head first to meet it. If John and Juan had been wondering what was going through my mind, now they had their answer.

John immediately said, "NO! Don't!"

Juan followed with, "Please get down. Please. Please don't jump."

John was looking behind himself to see where a teacher was if he should need to call them, and the need had definitely made itself known, now.

"Please get down so I can show you my new Wacky Packages cards I got from the store after school yesterday. I got one that you've been looking for. I'll trade. Please get down. Please," John begged, tears forming in his eyes from the fear of what I might do.

I thought about it for a moment, looking down at the sidewalk, beckoning me to fall into it and end my misery. Ultimately, I couldn't do it.

I turned to face my friends. Juan grabbed my legs to steady them so I wouldn't fall toward the sidewalk, and John said, "Hold your hands out and fall toward me." I did as he said and fell against him. He grabbed me as I did and we all jumped down off the shale rocks. I started crying, the tears falling onto John's shirt as he held me.

"It's Ok, I've got you. Come on." And we fell to our knees on the ground below us. Juan joined us, putting his arm around one of my shoulders, and John put his arm across the other.

We just sat there for a few minutes while I cried hard, getting all the emotions I was feeling out of my body. The sadness, anger, and fear all escaped through the tears that soaked my shirt below.

John reached into his pocket and got out his Wacky Packages cards.

"Look, I got the Tied card you've been looking for. "

I remembered the Wacky Packages cards I had just bought and pulled them from my pocket. I handed them to John to open. That was a big honor. One of the most amazing things for a kid was the experience of opening your cards, whether it was Wacky Packages or baseball or Star Trek cards; opening a brand new pack was one of the biggest deals of anything we had done as children. To allow your friend to open your new cards meant that they were pretty special to you, and John was indeed very special to me, and so was Juan. There was no way I could have jumped off that wall and hurt them so much if I had died from the fall.

John opened the cards, and he rifled through them for all three of us to see. I saw that there was a Spit and Spill card, which I already had, so I said, "Here, you can have this spit and spill card for your Tied card."

"Deal!" John said.

Juan had wacky package cards, too, and we all swapped cards. Before long, recess was over. I went with John and Juan to the line as we were called and had a newfound respect for them. They had really proven they were the highest level of true friends today. Maybe my life wasn't perfect, but at least I had true friends who would always be there for me no matter what. They didn't question why I wanted to end my life; they were simply there for me because they cared. Not everyone could say that they had such true friends. I gazed at my new Tied card and the cards I had traded with Juan, and then I looked at John and Juan, happier than I had been in a very long time.

March, 1980, fifth grade

Art was always one of my favorite things, so every chance I had, I would draw or paint. I had a set of colored pencils that I had just received from grandma. It was art day, and Mr. Difiore addressed the class as we sat down to get started on whatever project he had in mind for the day.

"There is an art contest coming up regarding making our planet cleaner and reducing pollution. You will need to have your entry completed by this Friday so that I can send it to be judged. If you win, you will receive $100 for first place, $75 for second place, and $50 for third place. All winners' posters will be used to make more posters, billboards, and ads that will appear in different areas of the city as part of a clean-up campaign, and you will be honored at an event with the mayor. You can get started on the posters today."

I already had an idea that I was sure would win. I could show what a dirty, polluted, littered city looked like on one side of the poster and a clean, beautiful city on the other side. The slogan would read 'It's your choice'.

I went to work on it. At the end of art class, I had the basic outline of everything in place.

"That is a really great start! Mr. Difiore said as he collected my poster at the end of class. "You can finish it up next art class."

"What are you gonna do with the $100 if you win?" John asked me as we lined up to go back to our homeroom.

"I'm gonna get some perfume for my grandma. Then, if any money is left, I'll get that Tyco race set with the track that goes up the wall," I said excitedly

"I'll get my dad some new tools," Juan said. "He needs some new tools for his job. He's always talking about buying them but never has the money to buy them." Juan said in reply.

"I will get my mom some new pans. She told Dad she wants a new casserole dish because the one we have is too small, and the pan she uses to make brownies is really old."

The next art day came, and I colored my poster very carefully, making sure to stay in the lines and get every area colored, leaving no white behind.

Mr. Difiore passed out comments to all of us in the class, saying

"I sure wouldn't want to be judged because it would be too hard to pick a winner. These are all really great!"

Two weeks later, we were in art class, and Mr. Difiore made an announcement.

"I have great news! We have a winner in the art contest from a couple of weeks back! Congratulations, David, you won second place!"

John and Juan cheered and whistled, encouraging the rest of the class to do the same. After a few moments of applause and cheers, Mr. Difiore called the class back to order.

"David is the only winner from our school. The other two winners are from other schools. David, you and your parents and your brothers or sisters, if you have any, are invited to have lunch with the other two winners with the mayor in two weeks from today! You'll need to wear your best clothes to the event as in a collared dress shirt and tie."

"Does it have to be parents? Can it be anyone else?"

"Sure, it can be someone else. Who do you want to bring?"

"I want to bring my grandma and my two best friends, John and Juan."

Mr. Difiore seemed surprised that I had not wanted to bring my mother and to have my friends there in her place. He paused a moment to consider it and ultimately replied

"I don't see a problem with that. May I also say that this is very, very kind of you to invite your best friends to the event? What a great act of friendship."

I wasn't sure, but I thought I saw a tear in Mr. Difiore's eye. After he made his statement, he wiped his forehead with his shirt sleeve, bringing it down to his eyes as it came down.

John and Juan came over to my table where I was sitting, and both high-fived me.

When it was time to go home for the day, I had to get home quickly to tell Grandma the news.

I knocked so hard on the apartment door that I thought my fist would go through it.

Grandma opened the door, and I bolted past her and into the apartment.

"I WON! I WON!!! I won, won, won, won WOOOOONNNNN!!!"

I shouted as I jumped up and down

"Wait a minute, calm down, calm down; what did you win? What is it?"

"The art contest to clean up the city! I WON! I got $75, and I have to go eat lunch with the mayor in TWO WEEKS, and YOU'RE going with me, grandma!!!"

Now grandma was jumping up and down.

"This is SO great! You won?! You really won?! WOWWW!! Congratulations!"

And she picked me up and hugged me, spinning me around so my legs sailed around the middle of the living room.

"Yes, I REALLY< REALLY WON, and we have to GO right now! We have to go to Bradlees to get a dress shirt and tie because I don't have one. Come ON!!! Get your shoes on so we can   GOOO!"

"Well, wait a minute… I have to see if I have enough money in my purse…"

Grandma went to her bedroom to get her purse off the dresser. She came back and said

"Not enough, I'm afraid. But I can get the rest from the emergency fund if your mother didn't take it to use for something else. "

She went to a drawer in the kitchen, pulled a small wooden box out of it, and found ten dollars inside. She took all of it and added it to hers, saying

"Ok, Mr. super important boy who's having lunch with the mayor, we now have enough money. Let me get my shoes on."

"YAAAYYYYY!" I shouted.

We slowly made our way to Bradlees, and Grandma was tired when we got there, so she suggested that we go to the café to sit down and have something to drink. We both got cokes and grandma pretended to play a song by sliding the straw up and down in the hole in the plastic lid. I imitated her, much to the annoyance of others in the café. Grandma didn't care. When they stared at us she just glared at them and did it some more.

"This is a celebration. If anyone doesn't like it, too bad," she said intentionally loud enough for them to hear.

When we finished our cokes, we headed to the boy's department, where she picked out a white dress shirt and a blue clip-on tie for me. The shirt was in cellophane packaging, pinned to a piece of cardboard with plastic in the collar. Grandma removed all the plastic, cardboard, and pins and handed me the shirt.

"Go try on the shirt."

She told me, pointing to the dressing room. I stopped at the attendant's desk, and he gave me a plastic card with the number '1' on it. I took off my striped shirt, put on the dress shirt, and tucked it in. It seemed perfect as far as the fit was concerned, but I walked out of the dressing room to show Grandma.

"What do you think?" I asked her

"I think you won't find a better shirt than that. You shouldn't need shoes because you have the ones you wore for the glee club celebrations. Those were big on you when you got them, so they ought to still fit ok. Go put your other shirt back on so we can get home, and I can make you a special dinner."

"Anything I want?"

"You bet. Anything at all."

I darted back into the fitting room and changed as quickly as I could.

"Do you need to get a new dress, grandma?" No, I have a nice blue dress that's for special occasions. I think I only wore it once, the day you were born, and I was with your mother in the hospital. That was a really special occasion for me…"

We went to the register, paid for the shirt and tie, and walked out of the store.

On our walk back home, we saw someone walking in our direction. As she drew closer, we recognized the person. It was Mother.

"What are you two doing?" she inquired. I looked down at my holey sneakers, not wanting to make eye contact with her in case she got mad.

"David won the art contest. We had to go buy him a shirt and tie. He got second place, and he's having lunch with the mayor! Isn't that nice?!"

Grandma said with enthusiasm, hoping some of it would rub off on Mom and she would react the same way.

"Where did you get the money to pay for the shirt and tie?" Mother asked, ignoring the fact that I had won the contest and my lunch date with the mayor.

"The emergency fund and what I had in my purse. I still have about three dollars left…"

Mother turned and started walking in the direction in which she came.

"Where are you going?"

Grandma asked.

'Fuck you. Fuck the both of you."

Was all that mother said as she picked up speed walking and crossed the street? There was a bar about a block away that she had probably already come from, and it looked like she was headed back there.

We watched her go and then continued on our own path home. We cut across the park to get there faster.

"So, what are you going to have for dinner tonight, my favorite art contest winner?"

"Spaghetti!"

"Spaghetti it is. "

Grandma got a pot of water boiling immediately as we got home and started working on the sauce. When she finished, we ate most of the spaghetti she had made, leaving some for Mother in case she wanted it.

Mother came home late after I went to bed, but before I was asleep. I had heard her come through the front door, shut it hard, stomp off to her room, and slam the door.

In the middle of the night, at about 3:30 am, she came into the room and beat me in the dark. She punched me again and again in the stomach and back. I screamed in terror into the pillow she held against my head to muffle the sound. I fell off the bed, and she kicked me in the abdomen repeatedly. As stealthily as she came, she left the same way. As usual when this happened, I couldn't sleep the rest of the night. At 5:30 am, I went to the bathroom to pee.

I screamed when I was a red stream instead of yellow. In addition to urine, blood was pouring out with it. Grandma came running when she heard the scream.

"What is it?! What?"

"Look!" I told her, pointing to the toilet bowl.

"Oh NOOO! Go get dressed right now!" and she went to mother's room, telling her

"You've got to get up and take David to the hospital. He's pissing blood."

But Mother was too far drunk to wake up. Grandma went to Mother's purse to take a couple of dollars off to go with the three dollars she had left from the shirt run earlier. Next, she called a cab.

"What is it? What happened to me?" I asked pleadingly

"There is something wrong with your kidneys. You're pissing blood. Did your mother do something to you when she came home? I didn't hear anything this time."

"Yeah. She punched and kicked me in the ribs and my back."

"Ok. It's ok, you'll be alright."

I cried from the fear of what was happening inside me.

"Will I die? Am I gonna keep bleeding and die?"

"No, no, you will be ok. We are going to get you to the hospital so the doctor can help you. You'll be fine."

Grandma seemed to be trying to reassure me as well as herself. She was clearly worried, as anyone would be when a loved one was bleeding from the inside.

I had a sensation that I had to pee again, probably from the nervousness of the situation.

"I have to pee again," I said

"Go. Do it. The cab will be here to take us to the hospital soon."

I arrived at the bowl and peed a little bit, but as before, it was red with blood. I tried to ignore it and flushed the toilet. I returned to the living room when the cab honked its horn out front.

We walked as quickly as we could to the cab and got inside.

"Where to?"

The driver asked.

"We need to get to the hospital quickly, please."

And grandma's urgency in her voice started me crying.

"No, its ok, you're going to be alright. I just want to get you there fast so the doctor can make you ok again." Grandma said, picking me up so I could hug her as the driver took us to the hospital. I cried and cried.

"I have to pee again," I told Grandma through my tears.
"You're going to have to hold it until we get to the hospital, ok?"

"Ok"

I tried to put the feeling of needing to pee out of my mind. I didn't have to do so long; the driver had gone top speed, and since it was so early, there wasn't much traffic on the way to the hospital. We arrived at the door to the emergency department.

"$1.75, please," the driver said. Grandma handed him $2.00, then told him

"Keep the change. Thank you" and she whisked me out of the cab and into the emergency room door quickly.

"Good morning. What's the issue? The desk attendant asked.

"It's my grandson. He's bleeding when he pees."

"Oh wow. Ok." Is there any pain when he urinates?"

"No," I said. Then, Grandma shared my information with the attendant and handed her our state medical card. The nurse took down the information and then said

"Ok, go have a seat, and you'll be called soon."

"Can I go pee?" I said to Grandma.

"Yes, of course…" and then she turned and asked the attendant

Where's the bathroom?

"Oh, that may not be a good idea for him to pee. Not yet. The doctor may want a urine sample. Can you hold it, buddy/" the nurse asked me

"I can try."

I said.

"It won't be long, I promise." The nurse said.

A few moments later, another attendant came out, calling my name.

We went to an exam room in the back, where a kind-faced young doctor was waiting for us.

"I heard you needed to pee, so I figured I better get you back here quickly and see you before you made a mess on my clean floors." He joked

"Why are you peeing red? What happened to you? Did you drink too much strawberry quick?"

I smiled and shook my head

"He fell down some stairs earlier, and when he woke up to go to the bathroom this morning at around 5:30, he saw that he was peeing blood."

It was a lie, but it was par for the course with Mother. Grandma had to lie, or else it would be another night like the one with Officer Mike.

"Ok, well, why don't you head down the hall to the bathroom and pee in this cup for me, and then we'll talk about the next steps."

He handed me a plastic cup that had my name on it, and I did as he asked, walking past other exam rooms and nurses and doctors on their way to destinations in both directions. I found the bathroom and went inside and closed the door.

I stood by the toilet, unzipped my fly, and took out my penis, but I couldn't hold it or the cup straight. I was shaking too much. I didn't want to make a mess, so I took some deep breaths and tried to steady my hands. I aimed and finally was able to pee in the cup without shaking. The pee was red again. I tried not to let out the tears that I knew were coming. I breathed in and out, trying to keep my crying in check. I finished peeing, zipped my fly, and left the cup with the nurse at the desk, as the sign on the bathroom wall had said to do.

I walked back to the exam room, and immediately upon entry, I saw that the doctor wasn't there, so I asked grandma

"Where did the doctor go? What did he say/"

"Well, he doesn't know anything yet. You're going to have to get something known as a cat scan. It won't hurt. It's a machine that sees inside your body. He will look at the pictures the machine makes, and then he'll know what's wrong and how to make you better. He wants you to take off your clothes and put this on."

Grandma handed me a hospital gown. I disrobed and put on the gown. It was huge on me, but I didn't care; I just wanted all of this to be over.

A nurse was next to join us in the room.

"Well, hello there, I'm here to put your IV line in."

"What's it for?"

Well, it's going to be so they can put something in your body so that the pictures the CAT scan machine takes are better, ok? Alright, I want you to lie back, and you don't have to look if you don't want to. It's just a little needle. It won't hurt."

Before I had any chance to ask any more questions or tell her I didn't want the IV, she had already cleaned my arm and inserted it, placing a piece of tape over it to secure it in place.

About 15 minutes later, an attendant arrived with a gurney to take me for my cat scan.

He wheeled me through some hallways and we finally got to the room after a dizzying amount of twists and turns through the hospital corridors.
"Well hello, we are going to be doing a scan of your tummy today. It's going to be very important that you don't move. I will tell you to breathe and then remain still. The scan will only take a few minutes. Before we do that, however, we have to give you some medicine."

"Will it taste bad?"

I asked.

'Actually, you won't taste it. It's going in the IV the nurse put in earlier. It's going to feel warm, though, and that's normal. You'll feel hot for a couple of minutes after it goes in."

He had me lie back on the table and went into the other room. In a couple of minutes, he had started the machine, and it was making a bunch of sounds. My body suddenly felt as if it were on fire briefly. The table slowly moved me into it a small amount at a time. When the test was complete, the attendant came back and said

"Ok, you can get back on the gurney, and they will be wheeling you back to the exam room to see the doctor."

That was exactly what had happened, except that the doctor wasn't there when we returned, only Grandma, sitting in a chair waiting for me to get back. We waited for almost an hour and a half before the doctor came back with the news.

"Well, the good news is that he doesn't seem to be badly injured, just a tear in his left kidney. He will probably see some more blood in his urine today, but that should be all. The kidneys usually heal quickly. I will prescribe a pain medication for him, or he can take children's aspirin in the normal dosage for pain."

"What about how he has to pee more often?"

"Well, that is probably because he got worked up so much, and the nervousness made it so he needed to pee more often. That also happens when the kidney is injured. The signals for when to pee are increased to happen more frequently. That will get back to normal quickly, too. I'm giving you a referral for a urologist, too. He should see him within the week. I will be back with the discharge papers in a few minutes, and you can take him home. Oh, and by the way…"

The doctor bent down and looked at me.

"No school for you today. I want you to rest. Lots of laying around watching TV and eating ice cream. Think you can do that for me?"

"No school? Alright! Yeah, I can do that."

"No running around too much today, or the next couple of days, k?"

"Ok!"

"Alright, get dressed. Be right back."

A few minutes later, after Grandma got my discharge papers and I went to the bathroom to pee again, we were on our way out of the hospital.

"Buses should be running now. We can go home on the bus. "Grandma said, walking over to a bus stop near the hospital.

We made our way home on the bus with Grandma, alternating between brushing my hair back and forth with her hand and hugging me. She had been very scared, and now she felt relieved. I could feel it in her touch. Now I had to deal with the prospect of mother, and suddenly, staying home from school didn't feel quite like the blessing the doctor thought it was for me.

Luckily, after arriving home, she didn't bother me at all, beyond mentioning me in her heated conversation with Grandma about how she shouldn't have brought me to the hospital and her usual threats of throwing us both out of the house and not allowing us to return.

The day of the lunch with the mayor came, and we were to be at a very expensive restaurant in the city to meet him there at 12 noon. John and his mom arrived at my house at 11:15, and John was almost as excited as I was. He had on a light blue dress shirt and a matching navy blue tie.

"Come on! We have to pick up Juan, too!!"

John said with more excitement than I had ever seen him show, other than when I won the spelling bees.

We got to Juan's house and rang the bell for him since the outside door to his apartment building was locked. He came to the door with his mother, who was still fixing the collar of his yellow dress shirt, tucking his tie underneath it. Unlike John and I, Juan's tie was the real thing; we just had clip-on.

Juan's mother told him something in Spanish, then came out onto the porch to give me a hug and say congratulations and that we should all behave ourselves while dining with the mayor. She said that she couldn't go because she had to work in the school cafeteria, like always, but that Juan's father was working nearby on a new building, but he would join us for lunch. We all assured her we would behave and then ran to John's Mom's car and got inside.

At the restaurant, they had set up the tables banquet style for us so that we all were sitting at what appeared to be one long table, but in reality, there were many tables put together.

The mayor came a few minutes before 12 and greeted all of us, shaking our hands and complimenting us on our artistic ability.

At 12:15, the mayor stood and started the official ceremony.

"Good afternoon, everyone, and thank you all for coming," He said into a microphone that was attached to a podium at the head of the table.

"The problem of pollution has been steadily growing in recent years, and cleaning up our city has been a pet project of mine for some time now. I grew up in this city, and I have pride in where I live, as I know everyone here at this table does. Therefore, it is with great pride that I can honor these highly talented and artistic young people who have designed our new posters that will be posted in various locations throughout the city, reminding people about the importance of cleaning up our city and keeping it that way. I would now like to call each of the contest winners to join me here. "

We followed his instructions, standing in a row next to him on the stage. He presented us with framed certificates congratulating us on our winning contest entries, along with checks in the amounts of $100, $75, and $50. The other two winners were a boy and a girl from two different schools. I recognized the boy from the district spelling bee. We received thunderous applause and were about to go back to our seats when the mayor said

"Please stay right here. We have some other prizes for you as well."

And a man came to the podium

"On behalf of Aaron Brothers Art Marts, we would like to present each one of you with these special gift baskets" and he made an arm gesture, pointing out a table beside him which featured three huge baskets filled with art materials. There were drawing and painting pads, professional artist-grade markers and watercolors, drawing pencils, and more inside of them.

"We are also donating $1,000 to each school so that they can purchase art supplies for their art programs."

More applause, and then another gentleman took his place at the podium to tell us

"On behalf of Child World, I am proud to present each of you with a $150 gift certificate for toys that you can buy at any of our stores. Thank you for your dedication to the cleanliness of our city."

The mayor came back to the front and center of the podium and said

You can put your gift certificates in the baskets while we eat lunch. And speaking of lunch, it is coming out now and is being placed on the tables on the other side of the room. Please eat all you want, or I will be forced to take it home and then gain too much weight. Thank you again for your talent and your dedication to cleaning up our city. Let's hear it for them one more time, everyone."

And more applause commenced. People who introduced themselves as working for the mayor had joined our luncheon and the adults all talked amongst each other while the kids all lined up first in line for the lunch.

Grandma, now beaming with pride, got up and hugged me and kissed me on the cheek as I passed her on my way to the tables containing the food.

"I can't believe it! $150 to spend on toys! I don't know what I'm going to buy!" I said with excitement and genuine bewilderment. How was I going to be able to choose $150 worth of toys in a giant toy store filled with everything a kid could ever possibly want? I didn't know, but I was going to try.

"You both have to come with me and grandma to help me pick stuff."

I told John and Juan.

"Oh yeah! You know I will be there," John said

"I'm coming too, you know that," Juan added

We filled our plates up with lasagna, chicken, rice, and ribs and went back for seconds, and then dessert was brought out. We had chocolate pudding, vanilla cake, eclairs and cookies. I ate so much I was stuffed, we all were.

At the end of the event, the Mayor shook our hands and thanked us again, joking

"You are all gonna take my job someday, and I couldn't be happier; you all already would make great mayors. Thank you so much. Take care of your moms and dads and grandmas."

We all went on our way, and while John's mom put the gift basket into the hatch area of the wagon, I asked

"Can we go to Child World RIGHT NOW?!!"

"I thought you'd never ask. Of course, you can, as long as it's ok with your grandma."

"Oh, of course, it's fine with me."

Grandma said, leaning over to hug me again.

About 25 minutes later, we arrived at the Child World parking lot. John, Juan, and I all ran at the fastest speed we had run since our gym class 100-meter dash.

Grandma and John's mom caught up eventually, after I had already entered the store and seen how big it was, exclaimed

"OH MY GOSH! This place is HUGE! And it's ALL TOYS!"

"Well, mostly," Juan said

"Yeah, they have kids' clothes and cribs and stuff too. " John added.

I grabbed a cart and started walking down the aisles. I grabbed two buckets of Legos when I saw those: a Hot Wheels race set and a whole bunch of Tonka, Matchbox, and Buddy L cars. I got an Incredible Hulk and Spiderman action figure, too, of course.

When we got to the register, I had figured pretty well, even though I had no idea what anything cost. I only had to put back one truck.

John's mom drove me home first. Everyone joined me to help me carry my loot inside. I got my toys and art supply gift basket out of the car's hatch area.

"Don't forget the Hot Wheels set and this second tub of Lego bricks," John's mom said when she saw I hadn't grabbed them.

Well, those aren't for me. I want John to have the Legos and Juan to have the Hot Wheels."

"Well, that's very kind of you, but…"

"Please don't say no. I really want John to have the Legos. For all the times I came to your house and played with John after school and all the starships we built together."

"Ok," John's mom said, tears in her eyes threatening to fall.

"And Juan, you stuck up for me so much when Eggy hurt me. Please take the Hot Wheels set"

Juan, whose dad never made it to the event, probably as a result of being too busy on the construction job, said

"They mess with you; they gotta mess with me. Thank you," Juan said. We all high-fived each other and then brought my loot inside.

I felt better than I had after the spelling bees because I was able to do something for the people who were the truest friends I could ever hope for, and Grandma got to feel important, having lunch with the mayor. My heart was running over with happiness.

As my friends pulled away from the curb in John's mom's car, I waved out the window, and they waved back. I spent the rest of the day overjoyed, playing with all my new toys and making a drawing for Grandma.

September, 1980, sixth grade

Sixth grade was upon us, and so was a new teacher, like always. Mr. Mosely, though I didn't know it yet, was actually a better teacher than most of the ones I had experienced so far. He, at least, would try and help me to do better at math, social studies, and history, whereas previous teachers just basically left me to fend for myself. He was kind but firm and he wouldn't tolerate a lot of the behavior that my previous teachers allowed Eggy and his gang to get away with while in class.

Today, being the first day, Mr. Mosely played lots of 'get to know you' type games with the class. Technically, they were icebreaker activities but not as cheesy as icebreakers I had done before. I particularly enjoyed Two Truths and One Lie, one of my all-time favorite icebreakers to this day.

It got to be John's turn,, and he looked deep in thought for a moment, then said

"I like Legos, I like chocolate, and I have a dog named Spike."

It was easy for me, having spent so much time at John's house.

"The dog named Spike is a lie. You don't have a dog."

"That's right," John replied.

Now it was Eggy's turn

"I like chicken, I hate candy, I go to church."

"Well, you told two lies because you don't go to church," Carlos said.

"What do you mean? " Juan asked Carlos, confused

"God would strike you dead with lightning if you walked into church 'cuz you're such an asshole."

Laughter rang out in the classroom, and Eggy walked over to Carlos's desk and playfully punched Carlos in the arm.

"He's just mad because he knows it's true," Juan added, resulting in applause and cheers.

""Hey, FUCK you!" Eggy said, this time actually angry as he stared Juan down.

"Enough with the language! Let's keep the game clean, or we will end it. Got it?" Mr. Mosely informed the class.

Now, it was Rosalinda's turn.

"I like Kites, I have a boat, and I like strawberry ice cream."

"You don't have a boat. If you've got a boat, what do you like to DO on the boat?" Eggy asked, standing up and making a repetitive thrusting motion with his hips and getting applause and laughter from the rest of Eggy's gang.

"HEY! That is not ok! Apologize RIGHT NOW!" Mr. Mosely demanded of Eggy.

"Sorry." He said

Now, a new kid stood up

"Hi, my name is Danny, and I like baseball, I hate football, and I like AC/DC."

YDo you hate football? Is it a lie? I guessed.

"No, I hate football AND baseball. I like baseball is the lie."

Danny was going to be alright with me, hating baseball and football.

After the game was complete and everyone had a turn, it was time to go to gym class. Gym for me would be different this year. I handed Mr. Quage a note upon arrival. It read

'You will excuse David from gym class any time this school year when he says he doesn't want to do the activity. No exceptions."

Mother wrote this note so that she would be able to continue beating me. She would have me say I didn't want to do the activity if it was a day that followed a particularly brutal beating that left evidence behind that Mr. Quage would potentially see when I showered.

"Ok, are you participating today? We are playing kickball." Mr. Quage said, looking perturbed by the note.

"I will play today."

Mother had stayed out all night drinking the night before, just getting home when I was getting ready for school, so I didn't have any new injuries that would betray what was going on at home.

Besides that, kickball was an ok game. It was harder for the other team to kick the ball accurately to the correct base to get me out, so I did better at the game, being able to score points. Neither team picked me unless John or Juan were captains, but at least I wasn't as bad at kickball as other team sports.

At the end of gym class, Mr. Quage had us all sit on the benches before taking showers.

"Look, it's a new school year and you are the oldest kids in the school now. That means I expect you to be better behaved and set a good example for the rest of the school. Understand?"

"Yes, Mr. Quage," all the boys responded.

"That means being respectful to ALL teachers and your friends. Is that clear?"

"Yes, Mr. Quage."

"Just because someone doesn't like something, or likes different things than you, doesn't give you the right to hurt them? Got it?"

"Yes, Mr. Quage."

"The money for your new gym uniform shirt and shorts is due next gym class. Don't forget to bring it, or you won't get a new uniform this year because I am placing the order on the day of your next class. Alright, hit the showers."

And with that, Mr. Quage took up his usual post next to the doorway to the shower room. I didn't know why he hadn't made such an effort to get the kids to behave respectfully before, but I was still happy that he finally had got around to doing it. It wasn't much, but at least it was something.

While we were in the shower, however, there was evidence that his speech fell on deaf ears of the kids he had targeted in the short talk., as Eggy and his friends were at it again, throwing their soap bars at me every time Mr. Quage's attention wasn't focused on the shower room, which was most of the time we were in it.

Before they got out of the shower, Eggy and his friends all peed toward the shower drains, taking turns also waving their pee stream my way, as they stood at different showers surrounding me.

I pushed Luis Matos, who said, "Hey! Are you a faggot?! Only faggot would touch another guy in the shower. "

This elicited laughs that echoed off the tiled walls in the shower.

"HEY! What did I say?!" Mr. Quage yelled, hands on hips and staring at Luis.

After retreating from the shower, all the boys except John Juan and the new kid, Danny, came to my locker to snap towels at me while I finished drying off, leaving red marks everywhere the towels hit.

Danny saw what the boys were doing and went back to the shower, wet a corner of the towel, came out of the shower, twisted it, and started cracking and snapping the towel at Eggy and his friends.

"How do you like it? Huh?" He asked them. As they started to close in on him, Eggy and his friend dropped the towels and said

"Come on, let's go," as if to say 'let's fight.'

"What the hell is going on with you boys? Stop snapping towels and get dressed NOW before you're late back to class."

Mr. Quage insisted.

The crowd of boys dispersed. Danny wasn't as muscular as Eggy or as tall as Luis Matos, but he was taller than John and Juan, and he had a certain presence. He clearly wasn't going to just stand by and take whatever Eggy and his gang dished out. He had stood strong when they closed in on him, showing he was more than willing to fight them if Mr. Quage hadn't been there to prevent it.

"Thank you."

I said to Danny as I put on my underwear.

"No problem. If he thinks it's ok to pick on someone smaller than he is, he's gonna have to think again. Fuck him. "

Danny said with an accent I didn't immediately recognize.

"Where you from?" John asked, clearly curious about the accent too.

"Brooklyn, New York. Moved here this summer."

"You wanna play tag with us later at recess?" Juan asked

"Sure."

Danny said. Just like that, we had a new friend to add to our trio, making us a quartet. Danny would turn out to be the best thing about an otherwise lousy sixth-grade experience.

April 1981, Sixth Grade

I was on my way home after winning the district spelling bee again, on my usual high after winning yet another dictionary and trophy. In previous years, I could attend the regional spelling championship because it was held near enough to where I lived. This time, we were informed that, like the nationals of previous years, the regionals were slated to be several states away; not quite as far as the nationals, but far enough to be somewhat of a big deal for me. That meant I would have to take a bus or train to the event since I didn't have anyone in my family who drove.

I told Mr. Mosely that I wasn't sure if I could attend. I had won the regionals the past two years, and Mr. Mosely said

"It would be too bad if you couldn't attend. You were missed at the Nationals when you couldn't go. You probably would've won the whole thing."

"I know. I don't think I will have the money to buy a bus or train ticket. Or else I would go."

"I will see what I can do about getting the money some other way." Mr. Mosely told me.

"Ok. Thank you."

Now, as I arrived home with John and Juan, and they were celebrating with me as usual, I thought it might be a good time to ask Mother if I could go to the regionals on the bus. My hopes were dashed, however, as she wasn't home.

We tuned in to the CBS news as Grandma poured all of us Kool-Aid. Soon, it was time for my segment for the third year in a row, and that's what I was: a three-time district champion, a record for my district. It had never been done before. They focused on that aspect during the interview.

"How does it feel to know you're a record holder, the first three-time spelling bee district winner?"

I felt like one of the players on a sports team when the reporter asked them a similar question after winning a game.

"It feels great. Great. I can't believe it." I told the reporter.

"Well, you're still spelling words much more advanced than you'd expect for your age level. How is it that you're able to spell high school-level words now?"

"I don't know, nothing has changed. I still picture the word in my mind based on the sounds and the rules of the English language, and I'm just right every time. "

"Do you study the words a lot before the competitions?"

"No, not really, Hardly at all, actually."

"Well, there you have it. A three-time spelling bee champ who doesn't need to study. Incredible. Back to you in the studio."

The anchor desk was featured next, and the anchor said to the co-anchor

"Can you believe what we just heard? Winning all these spelling bees and doesn't study?"

"No," said the co-anchor, "That is one remarkably smart boy."

"Sure is. You know there's a lot of proud people in his family tonight," the anchor finished.

Now Grandma walked in.

"Did I miss you on the news?"

"Yeah, on one channel. Don't know about the other two." And I switched to ABC."

A knock at the door interrupted the festivities. I ran to the front door and said

"Who is it?"

"It's Danny."

I unlocked the door and let Danny in. And now, the TV showed that I was on the ABC local news.

"Look at you! Hey! And there we are, next to you on stage! I hope my mom is watching the news," Danny said.

"How do you do it? You know how to spell so many freakin' words. I can barely spell at all."

Danny said.

"I'm not much better," Juan added.

"John, you really went far in the district bee a few weeks ago, though. It looked like it might have been YOU who won it this year." Grandma told John

"Yeah, they got me on the word 'necessary.' I missed an 's'.

"Hey, I have to start making dinner. Are you all staying?
"

"I can't," Danny said. "Gotta go to my big brother's football game."

"I can," John said, followed by Juan

"Me too."

"Ok, see you tomorrow," Danny said as he tackled me to the floor, tickled my ribs, and made me laugh out loud.

"Looks more like you're gonna PLAY football rather than watch it." Grandma joked about Danny.

"Naw. It will never happen. I hate football. Only going to watch my brother play because my parents said I have to. See you tomorrow in school, Dave."

"Ok. Bye,"

Halfway through dinner, Mother came through the door, doing her best not to stagger and, as usual, failing miserably at the task. She acted as if we weren't at the table eating, walking straight to the pantry to get a cup to fill with gin.

Gulping a large portion of what she had poured, she asked

"So, will you two boys be staying the night since you seem to have no problem eating up our food?"

"Shirley!" Grandma blurted, surprised at how impolite Mother was to my guests.

"Just asking a question," she slurred

"Actually, I have to get home. I'll see you tomorrow." John said

Juan got up from the table and said

"I have to go, too. Thanks for the dinner. I hope you have a good night. "

Juan said to Mother mockingly, hitting her with good manners when she had none. It was the best insult without being an insult. Juan was always doing things like that.

"See you in school," Juan said, giving me a high five as he left. As soon as the door closed, Grandma reared up on Mother.

"He won the district spelling bee again, and that's how you treat people who are happy for him?!"

"Oh, shut up. Just shut the fuck up," Mother sneered at grandma.

'I am gonna have to go on the bus or the train this time because the regional spelling bee is a lot farther away this year."

I said since we were already on the subject.

"Yeah, so?"

"So I'm gonna need money for the ticket."

"Well, good fucking luck getting it. YOU sure ain't gonna get it here."

"What do you mean?"

"I mean, there isn't any extra money for a bus ticket, so you can waste it going somewhere to spell words. That's just fucking ridiculous."

"You always have the money for that booze, though, don't you?" Grandma said, which is exactly what I was thinking and wishing I had the courage to say.

"You get lost. Just get out of my face with the smart remarks before you don't have a face!!"

"I'll get the money somehow."

"Yeah, good; why don't you ask your friends for the money since, for some unknown reason, they like you so fucking much? Ask Juan first. His family's got enough money I'm sure, having an air conditioner in the summertime, paying those high electric bills. The fuckers must be rolling in dough."

"Don't talk about my friends like that. You don't know anything about my friends. You don't know anything at ALL!"

I yelled at Mother. Immediately, I wished I hadn't let the words fall from my lips, but in life, there are no takebacks. I was going to have to suffer for that outburst, no doubt. Mother came toward me, dropping her half-full cup of gin onto the rug.

"What did you just say to me?" and she grabbed me by the hair and kicked me in the ribs.

"You know what?! You can just get out of my house. If your friends think so much of you, you can just get the FUCK out of my house. GET OUT!"

And she opened the front door, dragging me by my arm all the way down the hall. When she got to the porch, she flung me down the stairs and retreated back into the house, locking the door.

I willed myself not to cry as a neighbor walked past me up the stairs and into the building. I stood up and walked to John's house. I knocked on his front door, and his dad answered.

"Oh, hello David, I saw you on the news again tonight. Congratulations on winning the spelling bee again. "

"Thank you, sir. I was wondering if John and I could celebrate my win by having a sleepover. Can I stay with John tonight? I know it's a school day tomorrow, but I promise I will get up and to school with John, ok?"

"Well, sure, it is a special occasion after all. "And John's dad stepped aside so I could enter.

"You don't seem to be well prepared. You didn't bring anything for the sleepover. I will have to get you a toothbrush. I think there's a new one in the bathroom sink top drawer. Will you need some clothes for school?"

"Yeah. I think so.'

Well, John's still a little taller than you, so his pants might be a bit long, but you can roll them up. I think you wear the same size shirt, though."

"Yeah," I replied.

"Hey, what are you doing here?" John asked as he walked into the living room

"We were supposed to have a sleepover, remember?"

I said to him, raising my eyebrows so as to tell him to just go along with the story. He took the hint and said

"Oh yeah, I forgot to ask you, Dad, is it ok for Dave to stay the night?"

"We just settled all that. Yes he can stay the night, but no staying up late because you've got school, understand?"

"Yes. I understand. Thanks, Dad. Come on, let's go build. Your ship from the last time you were here is still put together on my dresser. You can add to it."

We padded off to John's room, and John, looking puzzled, shut the door and said

"What the hell is going on? Are you ok? I just left you a little while ago at your house when your mom came home."

"I'm fine," I said, trying to steel my face so John wouldn't realize I was lying. I hoped it was enough

"I just wanted to have a sleepover to celebrate."

"Yeah, ok," John said in a tone that suggested he knew that wasn't the reason I was there.

A knock on John's bedroom door

"Yeah"

"It's mom."

She opened the door, saying

"John, make sure you put out an extra shirt, underwear, and pair of pants for Dave tomorrow, and he can wear your extra coat from last year. It's in the closet by the front door. The toothbrush is in the top drawer in the bathroom. There are paper bags in the kitchen so you can carry your dirty clothes. Do you like French toast? I am gonna make some for breakfast tomorrow."

"Yeah, I LOVE French toast. My grandma makes it for me. It's SO good."

"Ok, French toast it is. "

"Thank you, Mom.

John said, knowing that French toast is a time-consuming breakfast to make that was usually reserved for weekends.

I hadn't even realized that I didn't have a coat on. How crazy must this have looked to John's parents, me showing up unannounced for a sleepover without even a coat representative of the season? I hoped they didn't suspect something was wrong.

After John's mom left the room, we went to work on our Lego starships. We worked quietly except for prompting each other about whether the other person had seen a certain size or color of the piece that we were looking to add to our structures.

When bedtime came around, John's mom called to us to put on our pajamas, turn off the lights, and get to bed. John had an extra bed for when other members of his family came to visit. I pulled the covers down and changed into an extra set of John's pajamas. John set the alarm clock on the night table next to his bed and went to his drawers and closet to get me the clothes I would need in the morning. He put them next to his on the chair by his desk.

I looked over at the two sets of clothes and thought about how his parents were so great, not only tonight but every time I came over. Even all these years later, I still wondered whether it was this way all the time. John shut off the light, and the glow of the moon cast blue moonlight through the drapes that were slightly open on one of the two windows in John's room.

"John, can I ask you something?"

"Sure"

"Are your parents like this all the time?"

"What do you mean? Like what?"

"You know, nice, doing things for you, stuff like that."

"Yeah, of course. That's what parents do. We argue sometimes, like about bedtime, something I want them to buy me or whatever, but it never lasts. Why are you asking me that?"

"I dunno. No reason. They are just so cool."

"Yeah, I guess. They really like you too. You're like a big celebrity around here. Always talking about how great it is that you won the spelling bees and that art contest with the mayor."

"My grandma always tells me I am lucky to have a true friend like you, too. I don't need a reminder, though. Already know it. Thank you."

"Thank you for what?"

"For everything."

"You're welcome. 'Night."

I lay there for the better part of an hour, unable to drift off to sleep, wondering what it would be like if I could have been born as John's brother, with loving, kind parents and not the useless nothing that had no mother who loved him and was more than willing to throw out of the house with nowhere to go.

John's mother opened the door to check and make sure we were sleeping. She went over to John's bed first, saw he was asleep, brushed his hair back, and kissed him on the forehead. She came over to my bed and did the same.

I wondered some more about what it would be like to be John's brother. I really didn't have to wonder, though; I just got my answer from John's mom.

I finally did fall off to sleep, having nice dreams about the spelling bee and John, my brother from an actual mother.

May, 1981 - Sixth Grade

The alarm clock on John's night table started ringing. John stopped it from ringing and got up, stretching his arms toward the ceiling and standing on his tiptoes.

I smelled something wonderful wafting through the house. The air was thick with the delicious scent of French toast.

"You boys, get up and get to the shower." John's dad said as he walked by John's doorway, going back to the master bedroom to get dressed after his shower.

"Oh, I see you're already up. David, there's a dry blue towel on the rack for you. John, let him use your brush if he needs to brush his hair after the shower. And don't forget to brush your teeth I don't think either one of you did before you went to bed last night." John's dad said.

John went to shower first and after he finished up, I followed him, getting in the shower while he brushed his teeth at the sink.

John was already dressed except for socks when I walked into his bedroom wrapped in the blue towel. John pulled at the towel, and it almost came off completely.

"I saw Dave's butt!!" John shouted.

I pulled the towel back tight and sat down on top of him while he tried to put on his socks.

"Ha ha ha ha! Cut it out."

"You boys, stop playing and get yourselves dressed. You've got French toast waiting for you at the kitchen table, and if you don't hurry up and get dressed, you aren't gonna have enough time to eat all of it!" John's dad called out.

I put on the clothes he had laid out the night before, and he had forgotten the socks, so when he got a pair from himself, he tossed some on the bed for me. I swung the socks around John's head, and he pulled me to the bed.

John's dad came into the room and yelled

"SUUUUPLEX!!!" And pretended to come down on top of us, elbow hitting the bed between us.

"Come on, or I'm gonna eat all my French toast and all your French toast too."

John yelled, "NOOOOOOO! That French toast is ALLLLLL MINE!"

And ran out of the room toward the kitchen. John's dad stopped him mid-stride, picking him up and throwing him over his shoulder, tickling his ribs and belly.

"Wait for me!" I shouted after them, trying to get my pants pulled up and shirt on.

John's dad helped me finish buttoning the plaid button-down shirt and then scooped me up and tickled me the same way as he had done to John, Dropping me in place in a chair at the table.

I had always thought my grandma's French toast was one of the most delicious things I had ever eaten, but John's mom's was every bit as lip-smacking delicious. I had poured a generous amount of syrup over it, and I polished off one piece of toast and asked

"May I please have another?"

"You don't have to be so formal here. You're family. Just take another piece if you want it."

John's mom told me.

"Really?"

"Really, what? Really, you can have another piece of toast? Of course. I made more than enough for seconds for everybody. "

"No, I meant, really, I'm family?"

"Of course you are; you've known John since you were both in kindergarten together. You've spent a lot of hours in this house with us. You're more like a brother to John. You're family. Don't ever forget that. If you ever need anything, we're here for you. Understand?"

"Yes, ma'am."

I wiped my mouth with a napkin to be sure there was no syrup on my face, got up and hugged John's Mom and gave her a kiss on the cheek. Then I said

"Thank you."

She laughed and asked, "What was that for?'

Like I had said to John last night, I replied, "Everything."

She kissed me on the head and said

"Look, you won't be thanking me soon if you don't eat that French toast all up because you're gonna run out of time, and I'll have to boot you out to go to school. Now EAT!"

I sat back down and ate as quickly as I could, getting all of the second slice finished. I drank all the apple juice from the glass on the table that John's mom put by my place, put my plate, glass, fork, and knife into the dishwasher, and said.

"I'm gonna go brush my teeth. "

"Brush your hair too. It's a mess." John's dad said

"Yes, sir," I called out as I entered the bathroom.

I found the new toothbrush in the drawer and opened the package, squeezed some toothpaste on the brush, and started brushing my teeth when John joined me at the sink, doing the same.

We took turns brushing our hair and went to the door, putting on our shoes.

Dad handed John a quarter for milk and asked me.

"Do you need a quarter for milk too, David?"

"Yes, please," I responded.

Ok, you two listen to the teacher and do good in school and he bent down to hug both of us at the same time.

"Remember, anything you need. Ever. We are here for you," he said to me, tapping me on the nose with his finger.

"Ok. I won't forget. Thank you again."

I picked up my paper bag with my dirty clothes from the day before and we both bolted out the door and ran up the street toward school.

The school looked different, coming from this direction in the morning like I was going to a new school.

I ran past Mr. Shedruff at one point, and he said

"You look nice today, David."

"Thank you"

I replied. He was right, I did look nice in John's clothes. My shoes were the only part of the outfit that didn't belong to John. Even with the pants rolled up at the bottom, I looked a sight better than usual, not wearing the patched-up, thread-bare clothes I usually had no choice but to wear.

After spending some time outside on the playground, it was time to line up. When we made it to our desks, Mr. Mosely pulled me aside.

"Will you be going to the regional finals of the spelling bee? We have to know so that we can send a substitute in your place."

"I think I am going. I'll know for sure tomorrow."

"Ok, but tomorrow, you have to let me know."

"Alright"

At the day's end, John and I decided to go to Dairy Mart to get some wacky package cards with our milk money that we didn't use. After we came out of the store, I told John

"Come on!"

"Where are we going?"

"The Spanish Grocery Store"

I replied.

"Why are we going there?"

"So I can get a job. "

"A JOB?! What? You can't. You're not old enough."

"Yes, I am. Remember that sixth grader Jose last year? He worked there last year, bagging groceries and making deliveries."

We walked up the street one block and entered the store.

"Hello, sir; I wanted to know if you are looking for help. I can work after school and on weekends."

"WHY are you DOING this?" John asked

"So I can get money to go to the spelling bee regionals. I need money for a bus ticket and I can't get it from my mother or grandma. They don't have it."

"Yeah, we could use a boy to bag groceries and deliver them."

The man behind the front counter said.

"How much does it pay?"

"$5.00 a week plus tips."

"Ok. I can start tomorrow."

"Sounds good. See you then."

"Are you NUTS?! You don't even know how much the bus ticket is gonna be."

"No problem, we can find that out right now. Let's go!" and we ran in the direction of John's house, paper bag with my dirty clothes crinkling away with every stride.

When we got to John's house, I went straight to the green phone mounted on his kitchen wall. I dialed the Operator and said

"Greyhound bus company, please."

She gave me the number, and I dialed it. After a few moments of giving the greyhound operator the destination and when I would need to travel, I had my information.

"It's a short trip, so it will be $38 round trip," I said to John.

"Can you make enough before then?"

"Oh sure, with tips, it will be easy."

After playing for a while with Legos in John's room, his mom came home.

"John, I'm home." She called out while hanging up her coat.

"Hi, Mom, Dave's here."

"Oh, good. Hi David," His mom called out. "Will you be staying for dinner? You can. We're having chicken casserole.

"Yes, please!"

"Ok, just remember to call home."

"I will." I went to the living room to use the phone on the table. I dialed the number. Grandma answered.

"Hello!"

"Hi, grandma."

"Oh, thank god! Are you ok?"

"Yeah, I was here at John's house all night last night. They asked if I could stay for dinner. Can I?"

"You know it's ok with me, but your mother..." and before she could say any more, I said

"OK, Bye," and hung up.

"I'm staying!"

I said to John's mom, who was putting the casserole she had prepared last night into the oven to heat it up.

"Good. John always has better manners when you are here."

"Come on, Mom, you're embarrassing me," John said, opening the refrigerator door to get some Kool-Aid.

"You want some?" John asked

"Yeah....I mean... yes please"

And he poured me a glass alongside his own.

John's dad walked into the kitchen from the back door with   a   box   in   his   hand.

"What's in there," John asked

"Cannolis from the bakery, and YOU can't have any until after you eat your dinner, all of it"

"Hi, Dave," John's dad said, giving me a half hug around the shoulders.

We went back to John's room to build some more starships before dinner. While we were building, John suggested

"Why don't you ask my parents for the money for the bus ticket?"

"Oh no, I can't do that. They have always done so much for me. That would be too much to ask." I said

"It's not that big of a deal. They would do it for you. You know they think of you as a family; they told you so today."

"No, I can't do that. I will work at the store for the money." I told John, hoping he would drop the subject. He did.

A half-hour later, John's mom called us all to the table by saying

"Come and get it while it's hot! Wash your hands before you come to the table."

We did as she asked and sat down at the table. I started spooning forkfuls of noodles and chicken into my mouth so quickly; John's mom said

"Hey, slow down; you know you have to chew before you swallow. "

"I'm sorry, ma'am. The casserole is just too delicious."

Under the table, John kicked my leg. I looked up at John, and he silently mouthed the words

'Ask them'

'No,'   I   silently   mouthed   back.

"Ask."

'NO.'

"What's going on with you two?" John's dad asked.

"Dave has something to ask you," John said. I rolled my eyes and shook my head.

"Yeah... do you want John's clothes back, or can I bring them back after grandma washes them?

"Well, that's a silly question. Of course. What do you think? We're gonna send you home naked?"

John's dad said and laughed.

"No, I guess not. Thank you, sir!"

"You're welcome. Now, eat up your pasta so you can have a cannoli for dessert."

I didn't need any urging. John's dad had opened the box of cannolis and they looked like they were going to be the most delicious dessert ever.

After I finished my first plate, I scooped out seconds onto my plate and ate that in record time, too. The cannoli was next. It was even more delicious than I imagined.

After dinner, John's mom asked

"Do you want to stay with us tonight again, David?"

"No, ma'am, I need to get home. I told Grandma I would be home after dinner."

That was a lie, but Grandma did sound very worried after what had happened the night before. I wanted to be sure she was ok. Without me around, Mom would target her instead, for sure.

"Well ok, but listen, we are going away this weekend to John's aunt's house. She has a really nice house with a big backyard. If you want to come, you and John will find a lot to do."

I thought about it for a minute, considered it, but remembered the new job. I needed to work the weekend so I could get enough money to go to the spelling bee.

"No, but thank you for asking. Maybe next time."

"Ok, John's mom said. You know we are so proud of you for winning the spelling bee again" and she bent down and hugged me really tight like grandma did.

I cried a little inside, but I tried not to show it outside.

"Thank you, ma'am. " I said, and I ran up the street and all the way home, crying and wishing somehow that grandma and I could live with John's family forever.

The next day I told Mr. Mosely that I would be at the regionals and started the new job after school. I agreed to work until 5:30 each day and all day on Saturday and Sunday. It was a hard week of work. For some of the bigger orders, I had a grocery cart to push a person's groceries to their door for delivery. Most of the time though, I had to carry the groceries myself in my arms, and often they were heavy for me. My arm muscles ached, and my leg muscles did, too, from all the walking. After a whole week of work, I had earned $15.00, thanks to tips.

After the second week, I was only up to $32, and there was just one more day before I would have to leave on the bus to go to the regionals. I was becoming worried. My muscles were exhausted from all the work but I decided that I would skip school the next day so I could work all day to try and get enough money for the trip in time. I knew it was the only way I'd get to the spelling bee.

It was a very slow day at the store, however, and staying there all day had proven to be useless. I was only up to $34. I looked for bottles and cans in trash cans to return them for the five-cent deposit, but that still only brought me up to $34.55. The store was about to close in an hour.

I bagged a lady's groceries and asked her if I could help her bring them home. Every person who had asked me to walk them home after bagging their groceries had always tipped me quite a bit. She said no and handed me fifty cents. She was the last customer in the store for the day, and I waited until they lowered the metal doors over the front of the store before giving up and going home. The owner of the store paid me the wages for that day, and I was still only up to $36.05, and he was generous, paying me more than he owed me for the day.

The bus would be leaving in the morning, and I didn't make enough money for the trip. I didn't know what to do. I went to John's house to tell him the news. After a long, slow, and tired walk, I rang the bell, and his mother came to the door.

"Hi David, we weren't expecting you. Come in"

I walked in and sat down on the couch. John came in from the kitchen.

"Hey, Dave. What's going on?"

"I don't know how to start."

I said, a single tear welling up in my eye.

"I think the beginning is the best place," John's dad said as he, too, joined us in the living room.

"I can't go to the spelling bee regionals."

I said, the tear dripping from my eye to my lap

"Of course you can. You won the last one, remember."

"NO, I can't go because my mom and grandma don't have the money. I told Mr. Mosely I would be going, promised him, and now I can't go. I got a job at the Spanish grocery store, but I didn't make enough money for the ticket, and the bus is leaving tomorrow morning. I can't get any more money."

"You don't need to, David." John's mom said

"Of course I do. I just told you I don't have the whole $38 for the trip."

"No, David," said his dad. "John told us about what happened. I know you didn't want him to. Please don't be mad. "

Now, John's mom sat down with me on the couch, took my hands in hers, and looked into my eyes.

"After John told us, we waited to see if you were going to remember what we told you about being family and come to us for help. We wanted it to be you who brought it up. We didn't want you to be embarrassed about not having the money. We wanted you to feel in your heart that it was ok to ask us. "

"So, you mean... you're going to give me the rest of the money so I can go?! Oh, thank you!"

"No, Dave," John's dad said, "you still don't understand. We are going to bring you to the regionals. We will all go together in the car. Tell your grandma we want her along too if she'll come."

"B-b-but we will have to leave tomorrow morning to be there in time!" My head was spinning with excitement

'Well, then, you just better get home and pack. You can sleep here tonight, too, if you want."

"And it's like 2 and a half states away!"

"What's a couple of states when you've got a spelling bee to get to?"

"OMIGOD! This is so great! THANK YOU! THANK YOU! THANK YOU!!!" I yelled as John's mom hugged me tight again.

"You forgot that we are family. You have to promise not to do that ever again, ok, young man? I told you, you're like a brother to John, and don't think we don't appreciate it. We all love you, David. Please don't ever forget it again. We are family, and we have to be at the spelling bee to cheer you on. Got it?"

Now I was full-on crying tears of joy.

"Alright, get home and pack. Remember to bring enough clothes for a few days. And your toothbrush and hairbrush or comb. And a nice shirt for the day of the regionals. Tell your grandma we will pick her up at 7:30 tomorrow morning," John's dad said.

"I will!! Thank you again! THANK YOU!!" and I ran out the door to my house.

When I got there, I banged on the apartment door furiously until Grandma opened it.

"I have to pack right away!"

"Well, you have the night to pack if you're going to the spelling bee tomorrow morning; why are you rushing?"

"Because I am sleeping over John's house. We are leaving tomorrow morning."

"Wait, no, you don't understand. The bus ticket is only for you, and you can't bring anyone else..."

Grandma said, unaware of the events that just took place at John's house.

"No, No, I'm not going on the bus. I'm going with John and his parents they are driving me there. They want YOU to come too. You'll come, right?! Please come."

"What about your mother? What will she say?"

Grandma asked.

"Is she even home?"

"No."

"Well, she will probably get home late and will still be asleep when you leave in the morning. She won't even know you're gone until we are already on the way to the spelling bee. And who cares what she'll do to me? She'll just beat me no matter what I do anyway."

Grandma looked at me and nodded in agreement. Then she smiled a bit and said

"Ok, ok. I'll come. I'll go pack right now. How long is the trip?"

"It's gonna be a few days. John's parents told me to pack enough   clothes   for   a   few   days.

"Ok, I'll pack for a 5-day trip."

I got the blue suitcase out of the living room closet and started stuffing shirts, pants, underwear, and socks into it. I threw my hairbrush in it and my comb, too. Then I tossed in my toothbrush. I got my dress shirt out of the closet and my clip-on tie and put those in the suitcase too. I tucked my shoes against the nylon elasticized pocket and shut the case, yelling to grandma

"I'm going to John's. 7:30 tomorrow morning, remember! I love you! Bye!"

"Love you too. Bye." Grandma said as I booked it through the front door.

I got back to John's house in record time.

"Welcome back, Dave. Now you can get John busy with packing his stuff. If you're hungry, dinner is on the stove," John's dad said upon opening the door for me.

"Ok, thank you again!"

"David, we are going to have to get something straight."

John's dad said, putting his hand on my shoulder to slow me down so he could talk to me.

"You don't have to say thank you all the time to us. Family doesn't do that."

"Ok. It's just that I'm not used to people doing nice things for me. Well, except for grandma…and you guys, and Juan… You know what I mean?"

"Yes, I think I do, son. Alright, go kick John's butt into gear. Tell him I said to start packing right now."

"Ok!"

I went to John's room, and he was already starting to pack his brown suitcase.

"Want help?" I asked him.

"Yeah. Can you get some shirts for me out of the second drawer in that dresser?"

"Sure, how many?"

"4 or 5."

"I'll get your toothbrush and hairbrush out of the bathroom."

"No, better not; I'll need 'em tomorrow morning before we leave."

"Oh yeah. I forgot. I was thinking about how I just had to pack."

John took his dress shirt out of the closet, too, and I reminded him, "Hey, you don't need that. You're not in the spelling bee."

"I know. I'm gonna wear it anyway. I'm not gonna let you look better than me when we are on TV or in the paper again."

"Ha HA! Very funny!"

"Besides, we might stop somewhere to eat at a nice restaurant or something. Gotta look nice."

We spent the rest of the night playing electronic battleship and building with Legos. When it was getting close to the time to turn off the light, I realized I had forgotten my pajamas, but John let me borrow some of his again. We brushed our teeth and got under the covers in bed. John didn't turn off the light the right way. He asked me

"Wanna read a comic? Dad brought the new Superman comic home yesterday."

"Nah. Can I read one of your Mad magazines?"

"Sure, here."

And he reached up to the shelf above the bed headboard and tossed two over to me.

We read for about a half hour, and John's mom came in and said

"Ok, lights out."

She pulled the covers up over John up to his neck, kissed his forehead, and did the same to me. Grandma was the only one who had ever done that for me.

"I'd tell you two to get some sleep, but I know you're excited about the trip. It's ok anyway, you'll be able to sleep in the car. Goodnight"

"Night," we both said simultaneously.

In the moonlight casting a wave of light through the drapes, I saw that John was still awake.

"What are you thinking about?" I asked.

"I dunno. Just that it's so unfair, I guess. You won the spelling bee and you couldn't even get to the next one to defend your title. I didn't even win, but I can go. It's really not fair."

"Yeah, but like my grandma says, there are other people here on earth because we are supposed to be kind and help each other."

"Yeah. She's right. Your grandma's really smart. Well, Goodnight."

"Night....and John?"

"What?"

"Nothing…"

"Love you too, bro," John said, as if he knew what I wanted to say.

May 1981, Sixth Grade

Spelling Bee morning was here. John's mother came to the room before the alarm went off, stroking our heads and softly telling us.

"Wake up. Time to get up."

John did his morning stretch and got into the shower first. When he finished, I got ready, taking out the clothes I needed to change into when I was done.

John was almost wholly dressed when his dad poked his head in the door.

"You boys, make sure you get dressed quickly. No play fighting or fooling around today. We have to hit the road soon."

"Ok," John replied. "What are we having for breakfast?'

"Not sure. We'll get something on the road." John's dad told him.

After we were showered and dressed, we made sure everything we needed was in the suitcases and walked with John's parents out to the car, putting our suitcases in the back hatch of the Datsun wagon. John returned to the house to get something and returned with a bag of stuff that he brought into the car's back seat.

"I brought some mad magazines and comics and some paper and pencils to draw."

We all jumped in and went to my house and parked in front. Grandma was looking out the front drapes when we arrived at 7:28

Grandma came out with her suitcase, and John's dad asked her where she preferred to sit.

John and I were in the back seat, so Grandma said, "I'll sit in the back with the boys."

She got in, and Dad said

"Alright, first stop, McDonalds!"

"YAAAAAYYYYY! John and I cheered simultaneously.

When we arrived, it was a location that had a play place, and John and I took off our sneakers and went into the ball pit. Since it was a school day, we had the pit and the whole play place to ourselves. We didn't care that we were almost too old for this now. We whooped it up, throwing handfuls of balls up into the air and showering each other with the balls over and over again until, after a few minutes, John's mom said

"Ok, you two, get your shoes on and come eat. We must stay on schedule because we must get to the spelling bee on time."

We did as we were told and went to a table big enough for us to sit.

"We got Egg Mcmuffins all around because your grandma said you like them, David. If you want something else instead, let us know.

"No, Ma'am. The egg McMuffin is great!"

It was. I didn't get to have one very often, but I loved every one of the few I had ever eaten.

"Thank you so much for your kindness to David. This means the world to him."

Grandma said after swallowing a bite of her breakfast.

"Oh, believe me, it's no problem. As we have told David, He's been John's best friend since kindergarten. He's more like a brother than a friend. That makes us family, and family helps each other."

randma, probably thinking about our home situation, looked sad and said, "If only everyone in this world could be like that and help each other when they need it."

"Yeah." John's mom said, "It would be such a better place to live."

"I just believe in doing what's right because it's right, you know because you get what you give in this life," Grandma said

"Yeah, but so many people forget such a basic thing like that." John's dad said

"Exactly," Grandma responded, taking another bite.

"Well, look at you two! You ate all your breakfast already, even the hash browns," John's mom said, surveying the empty boxes and cups on our trays.

"Yeah, can we return to the ball pit until you're done eating? We'll leave right away when you tell us," I asked John's mom

"Yes, as long as it's ok with your grandma. "

"Oh, don't ask me; as far as I'm concerned, this is your trip. I'm on vacation, ha ha!"

"Ok, go play, but we are leaving soon," John's mom told us

We took off running for the play place, tossed our shoes again, and jumped in the pit, burying ourselves in balls of every color of the rainbow, which darted about in every direction.

After a few minutes, John's parents finished eating their meal, and after reminding us to go to the bathroom, we all piled back into the car to get on the road again.

We started playing games of I Spy and Punch Buggy on the trip and then read some mad magazines. Eventually, the car ride made us sleepy, and John and I took turns using each other's shoulders as a pillow. Hours passed, and it was time for lunch.

"Boys, wake up!" John's dad said.

He rubbed our sleepy eyes, and John said, "Are we there?"

"No, we are going to stop for lunch. How does Friendly's sound?"

"Great."

"Yeah, great."

We pulled into the parking lot and went inside to get a booth.

He put in our orders, and John asked his dad, "Can we please have quarters for the claw machine at the front?"

John's mother reached into her pocketbook, pulled some quarters from a change purse, and handed them to John.

"Now share with David."

And John handed me half the quarters. We took off for the claw machine and plotted our strategy. We saw some stuffed animals that we thought we could get. We tried again and again, getting close but having no luck. Once, I had picked up a stuffed dog, and it fell back as the claw neared the home position, but it nearly rolled its way down a mountain of other stuffies to the drop zone. We returned to the table to look at the menu and see what ice cream we would have for dessert.

After the waitress came and took our orders, Grandma started talking to John's parents again.

"I really can't thank you enough. Seeing David able to be a boy is such a gift."

"What do you mean?" John's dad asked

"Well, it's just been so tough for us. We are so poor. I have tried to make sure David has been able to have some things to have a childhood beyond the necessities."

"Oh, believe me, we know what you mean. Things are so hard for us, too. It's really hard to save any money at all. We've had to be creative to be able to give John the life he has. We both had some paid vacation time and John, senior here, just FINALLY got a big pay raise; otherwise, we might not have been able to make this trip happen," John's mom said reassuringly.

"Yeah. We have to count the meals. It's so hard to be a boy when you know that the adults in your life are counting the meals and every cent to be able to pay the bills, and we can't even do that sometimes—always starting from behind. It makes a boy grow up too soon. "

"Yeah, it's tough for sure. But David's always been a boy when he's been at our house, right?"

John's dad said, putting me into a headlock and messing up my hair.

"John's always been so selective of his friends. He didn't talk to anyone else in kindergarten except for David, and it's been pretty much like that ever since. It's just Dave and Juan and now this new kid Danny all these years that he's sought out to be friends with, not that he has much choice with the other kids there at school who are so mean and cruel." John's mom shared.

"Tell me about it." Grandma agreed, "I've had to patch up more than the knees of David's pants because of those awful boys more than my fair share, lemme tell you. They're vicious!"

Our food arrived a few minutes later, and John and I ate every last crumb on our plates. It was the fastest any two burgers and onion rings had been eaten, if there was a record for that sort of thing.

A few minutes later, our waitress reappeared.

"Ok, what's for dessert? Anything you want." John's mom stated

"I want a sundae with three scoops, please, and can I get it with chocolate sauce, whipped cream, and sprinkles?"

John said, "Me too. Same thing."

Grandma said, "Only coffee for me. I'm already stuffed from the meal."

That wasn't surprising; grandma was used to eating tiny portions even when she did eat so that there would be more for me if I wanted it. Even when we went to the diner near the house, she never had large portions of anything.

"Coffee for us, too." John's dad said.

We ate our sundaes faster than our meal and finished, and John asked.

"Dad, can I please have more quarters for the claw machine?"

"No, your mother already gave you a whole bunch of quarters."

"PLEEEASE! We got this one stuffed dog so close. We can get it. PLEEEASE! You always have quarters in your pocket. "

"No, no more quarters. "

"GET HIM!" John shouted, "He's ticklish under his armpits," John started tickling his dad. I was on the other side of his dad, so I took that side, and after a couple of minutes of us not giving up and making him laugh uncontrollably, he finally relented.

"Alright, alright, alright! I give up. You can have the quarters. Lemme go into my pockets." He pulled his old and tattered wallet out of his pocket to get it out of the way so he could dig deep into his pocket where the quarters were. He found some nickels, dimes, and pennies, but he handed those to John's mom, who tossed them into her change purse.

"There's no more quarters after this, ok?"

"Ok," we called out together.

John was right; after one try, he could manipulate the dog into an even better position on the mountain in the machine. I plugged my quarter in, and I didn't need the claw to pick it up; it came down, hitting the dog just right, and the dog tumbled down the chute. John and I celebrated and ran back to the table to tell the adults how we got the dog so quickly.

"It's for you," I said, and I handed it to Grandma. "Thank you for coming on the trip, Grandma."

Grandma looked like she wanted to cry but was working hard to hold the tears back

"Thank you," she said, stretching out her arms for a hug. "You too, John, get over here. If we are supposed to be family, I'm your Grandma, too."

John's dad paid the bill a few minutes later, and after another bathroom trip, we were back in the car for some more games, reading, and sleeping.

Every now and then, we'd stop along the way at a tourist stop where there was a great view, and we'd take it in and then get in the car and keep going. At a rest stop, we stopped for snacks, and on our way out, we saw a rack with brochures showing great things to do in the area. There was one brochure for a place that had go-kart racing.

"Can we go do THAT?!!" John exclaimed.

"Not on our way down, but maybe on our way back. " John's dad said, grabbing some other brochures on miniature golf and a lakeside lodge showing boys swinging on a rope over the lake on the cover.

On the road again, we decided to count certain colors of cars before getting tired and falling asleep again. John fell asleep with his head on Grandma's lap, and I drifted off to dreamland, laying across John's stomach.

Before too long, we arrived at our destination, a Holiday Inn hotel where the spelling bee would be held in their large conference hall.

We brought our stuff inside and checked in for the night. The spelling bee was scheduled to start at 10 am tomorrow morning. If I had taken the bus, I would still be on the road trying to get there and wouldn't have arrived until just before the bee started.

We had another nice meal for dinner and slept deeply that night.

The next morning, after eating breakfast in the hotel restaurant, John and I went back up to the room to change into our nice clothes.

The spelling bee was great, and it did go down to the wire between myself and a boy from a different school, but I misspelled the word 'anomaly' by adding an extra 'l.'

If this had happened in one of my previous spelling bees, I might have been sad, but in recent days, things have changed so much for the better for me, spending more time with John and his family and being on this adventurous trip with them. Now, I couldn't care less about the spelling bee.

We checked out of the hotel because John's dad said he had a surprise for us.

We drove not too far away and went down some narrow asphalt roads that turned into roads made of gravel and then just plain dirt. We pulled into the parking lot for the lodge that John's dad had seen on the brochure earlier.

"Well, boys, here we are. This is where we are going to stay for the next couple of days."

"Are you SERIOUS?!" I blurted out.

"I-I mean WOW! Thank you!" I corrected myself.

John and I couldn't believe it. There were kayaks and canoes crisscrossing the lake and kids swimming at various locations near the shore and beside long docks that stretched far out into deeper water.

"We didn't bring our swimsuits."

John said.

"Yes, you did. I packed one for you and one for David in our suitcase when I was packing your dad and my suitcases. You never know what adventure is going to come up when this big fool is driving," John's mom said while pointing at John's dad.

"You CAN swim, right David?" John's dad asked

"Yes, sir. I learned at the park pool years ago." I confidently told him

"Good, "John's mom continued, "I also packed suntan lotion, scuba masks, and towels. I brought two pairs of extra sneakers for you and David in case you messed up the ones you're wearing. You're welcome."

"Thank you, Mom," John said and gave her a hug. We all went inside to the concierge desk. The place lodge was HUGE. There was one wall where there was nothing but old canoes and kayaks strapped to it. Another wall had several sets of snowshoes attached to it. A large fireplace accessible from all sides was in the middle of an area flanked by numerous overstuffed chairs and couches off to the right of the entrance. The whole place was made up of a mix of wood slats and logs. Native American-style rugs adorned the floor in various locations.

After a few minutes at the front desk, John's dad said

"Ok, let's go up to our room."

We went up two flights of stairs carrying our stuff and arrived at a door that John's dad said was ours.

We opened the door to see a large suite. There were two queen-sized beds in the main room and another queen-sized bed in an adjoining room. There also was the most breathtaking view of the wilderness I had ever seen. The windows went from floor to ceiling, and there were a lot of them. Nearly the whole wall on one side of the room was taken up with windows that displayed the most beautiful lake and trees imaginable. I was mesmerized looking out at it.

"Complete kitchen, and they said there's lots of barbecue grills and picnic tables down at the lake."

John's dad said

"This is incredible! I should go to the store to get food for a picnic and barbecue. Gimme the car keys."

John's dad handed her the keys, and off she went.

"Can we go swimming? PLEEEASE?!" John said.

"Of COURSE! Why do you think we are here? Get into your swimsuits, and let's go!"

He didn't have to tell John and me twice. We went into the second room, closed the door, and changed.

We were ready almost immediately. John's dad gave each of us a towel, and Grandma followed along behind with a folded-up extra blanket she had found by the closet at the front of the suite.

When we got outside, John and I ran as fast as we could down the short path ending at the waterfront. There were indeed lots of tables. We tossed our towels onto one of them, removed our sneakers and socks, and ran down to the water, jumping in immediately. The water was cold, but it felt great.

John's dad was holding the snorkels and said

'If you want the snorkels, they'll be up here."

"Ok!" We both shouted.

After a few minutes of swimming and playing, I asked, "Can we please go try the ropes over there?" and I pointed to where some kids were in line and taking turns swinging themselves on the rope into the lake.

"Yes, but be careful," Grandma said.

The first time I tried the rope swing, I swung myself way out and up in the air when I let go and hit the water with a huge splash. It was invigorating. John went next and almost landed on top of me. We swam back and did it again and then again, and we ended up spending the better part of an hour doing it. After a while, my muscles were getting sore, and so were John's, so we went back to the table, where John's mom had just returned from the grocery store trip.

John's mom and dad pulled hot dogs, hamburger meat, and buns out of the bags, along with several bottles of Coke and Sprite. There also were 2 bags of potato chips, a bucket of potato salad, and 3 packages of different types of cookies. One thing was for sure: we weren't going to be hungry on this trip.

"We were talking to some of the other boys at the rope swing. They said there's lots of fish further out past the big dock. Can we go swimming there with our snorkels?" John asked

"Yeah, the water's deeper there, so you should use the snorkels. Perfect place for them."

And off we ran again, sailing down the long dock with our masks and snorkels and ending our run with a giant cannonball jump to the water.

The boys were right. We swam around deep under the water and saw several fish of all sizes. Each time we got close enough to almost touch them, they darted away. We surfaced and went back down again and again, looking for other things of interest. All we kept finding was more fish. We had gone pretty far out and were in some pretty deep water, and when we surfaced, we found that we were right by the blue and white buoyed rope that indicated we were not to go any further. We swam back to the dock and got out, taking off our masks and snorkels. The other boys we had talked to earlier now joined us

"We saw a lot of fish over there," We told them as we pointed over to the left. They jumped in to check. One of the boys had flippers. When he came back to the dock, I asked if I could use them. He said

'Sure." I put them on and realized the flippers really helped you swim better under the water. Once I got the hang of how they work, I was swimming around under the water like a member of Jaques Cousteau's team of professional divers, or at least that's what I thought in my mind.

I surfaced and came back to the dock, and John asked if he could borrow the flippers.

Again, he said, 'Sure.'

soSo I took them off and handed them to John.

He came back a few minutes later and gave the flippers back to the rightful owner.

"Boys!" John's dad called, "Come on up and get something to eat!"

"Hey, what's your name?" John said to the boy with the flippers

"Matt. What's yours?"

"John and this is Dave."

"I'm Thomas." Said another boy

"I'm Mark," the third boy said.

"Wanna have some hot dogs and burgers?"

"Sure," One boy said

"Come on," I called out while leading the way to our table. When we got back, I realized we were gone a long time because John's mom and dad had already made a lot of hot dogs and hamburgers. They were sitting in piles on paper plates, waiting to be put onto a bun.

"Mom, this is Matt, Thomas, and Mark. Can they stay to eat some hot dogs and burgers?"

"Only if their parents say its ok."

"We'll go ask" one of the boys said as they all ran back to their blanket on the ground.

"You having fun, grandma?" I asked her as I used a towel to dry off.

"Are you kidding? I love it here. It's so beautiful. I haven't been anywhere like this in a lot of years. Your grandpa used to love places like this. We'd go in the summer so he could relax in the sun by the water."

Now, the boys returned with a couple of parents in tow.

"Hello, thank you for inviting the boys to have a barbecue with you. It's ok with us as long as you're ok with it." The dad said

"Absolutely. We are going to have a lot leftover if they don't join us."

"Ok, if they make pests of themselves or you get tired of them hanging around, send them back down to us. We are on the blankets down there" and the dad pointed. "You can have your boys come to visit with us, too, if you want. We've got a cooler full of soda and sandwiches."

"Sounds good. Ok, we are going to need another picnic table to have enough room," John's dad said, and instantly, our new friends went off to the right, where there was an empty table, and carried it over to meet with ours.

Everyone sat down and Grandma asked

"So, are you boys, brothers?"

"I and Thomas are," Matt said. "Mark's our cousin."

"Are you staying at the lodge?" John's mom asked

"No, not inside the lodge. There's a campground down the dirt road over there. We drove here in our trailer. We usually wait till summer, but Dad said the weather was gonna be so great this week he decided to get the camper ready early."

"Oh, is that fun? Sleeping under the stars?"

"Yeah, especially when we really do it. We have tents, too, and we sleep outside sometimes. It's great. I love sleeping in a sleeping bag," Thomas said

"Yeah, NOW you like it. You didn't like it when you were little, and you peed in the sleeping bag," Mark over-shared

John's dad almost spit out a mouthful of food, laughing when Mark finished the sentence.

"Shut up, Mark! You pissed in your sleeping bag too!"

Now everyone was laughing.

After a meal full of barbecue food, chips, and cookies, I asked John's dad

"Can we go look around in the woods?"

"Yes, but you have to stay by the lodge and on the trails. If you can't see the lodge, you went too far and need to get closer, understand?"

"Aw, we've been all over the trails here. We'll show 'em around, and we won't get lost." Thomas said with confidence.

"You boys, check with your parents to be sure it's ok."

"It is. They always let us go off alone. We've been coming here for the past 6 years." Matt said

Just to be sure it was ok, John's dad went to talk to the other boys' parents. They confirmed that the boys knew their way around and would be fine.

As the sun started going down, we all headed back to the picnic tables and ate a few more snacks, then joined the other boys to help their parents clean up and we all walked down the path to the campground to see their trailer.

It was large and had more room than you'd imagine looking at it. With the setting sun making things even darker, we said goodnight to our new friends and told them we would see them at the lake again tomorrow if they were staying. They said they were.

We talked about all the adventures we had and told John's parents about how much better it was swimming with Matt's flippers, and all the fish we saw deep under the water. When we got back to our suite, we put away the excess food in the fridge and cupboards in the kitchen and then all changed into our pajamas

"You and John can have one bed, Grandma can have another, and we'll take the other one." John's dad said.

We sat up for a while watching TV and started to drift off to sleep before even getting under the covers. John's mom got us under the covers before we were completely asleep and gave us her usual kiss on the forehead.

Before I fell completely asleep, I heard John's mom talking to Grandma.

"Did you see how John just made new friends with those boys like that, like it was nothing?"

"Yeah, I did."

"Well, that's because of David. If he weren't here, John wouldn't have tried to make new friends. David is a good influence on him. John sees David up there on the stage in front of those auditoriums full of people at those spelling bees, and it gives him the confidence to be more outgoing. That's why he joined the glee club. If not for David, I know he wouldn't have done it."

"Well, thank you. This has been an amazing gift you've given David, coming here."

"It's an amazing gift that David has given John all these years. He really loves David. It's so great that they could be together to do this. John talks about David and worries about him all the time, Eggy and those boys doing all those terrible things, and the trouble he has with some of his schoolwork…"

"Yeah, Dave really loves John, too. He can't ever stop talking about him and all the fun they have together. I can't remember when I have ever seen him happier than he was today. I've wanted to give him a trip like this all his life but this is even better than I imagined because he gets to do this trip with such special people. "

"Speaking of fun together, we better get to bed because we've got a lot more fun to have together tomorrow. Goodnight.
"

"Goodnight," and John's mom joined Dad in the other room, leaving the door open.

Grandma got up and kissed John and me on the cheek and went to her own bed to go to sleep.

I reached out my arm to hug John, and he reached out his arm to hug me back, and we both fell asleep that way. Grandma was right. I had never been happier.

May, 1981 - Sixth Grade

It was another beautiful day, and after breakfast at the lodge, we all returned to the lake. John's dad said he wanted to stop at the lodge store to get something, and he'd meet us at our table. He got to our table a few minutes later. He had a bag from the store.

"Here you go," he said as he pulled two sets of flippers out of the bag.

"WOW! Thank you!" I said, hugging John's dad.

"Thank you, Dad. What else is in the bag?"

"A new swimsuit for me. Mom remembered to pack suits for you but forgot to remind me to pack mine. I'm gonna go change and swim with you boys today."

"YAY!" John and I both yelled simultaneously.

John's dad went to the nearby restrooms on the side of the lodge changed into his suit, and came to join John and me. We were already in the water.

"Can I jump off your back, Dad?"

"Oh, I don't know. You're getting so big... I might not have a back left.

"PLEEEASE?!"

"Ok, go ahead.

And John's dad bent forward so John could get his feet onto dad's back. Dad held John's hands steady as he inched his way up Dad's shoulders in the crouched position, and then John stood up and let go of Dad's hands as Dad stood up straight, and John flipped off his back and into the water.

"WHOA! Can I try?" I asked

"Sure, hop on"

I did as I saw John had, and his dad said

"Now, as I stand up, you're gonna get pushed into the air. It's like a moving diving board. Just go with the motion and let your body go the way it wants to go. Got it?"

"Yup. Got it."

Ok, we'll go on three. One, two, three, and he stood up and let go of my hands. I flew off his back, high in the air, and hit the water with a huge splash.

"That was INCREDIBLE!!! I wanna do that again!"

"Me, first," John said, mounting Dad's back one more time.

We did the back launches again and again until John's dad said he had enough.

"I've got another idea." He said, childlike glee in his eyes.

"What?" I asked

"Come on over to the dock."

We got out of the water, walked over to the dock, and followed John's dad.

"John, grab onto my waist with your legs and grab my hands and hold tight."

"What's he gonna do?"

"You'll see."

John did as he said, and Dad spun in a circle fast a couple of times. John's legs flew away from Dad's waist, and when he was aimed over the water, Dad let go of John's hands, and he flew over the water and into it.

"Ok, now you."

John's dad said as John swam back to the dock and got out of the water. I did as I saw John do, and like him, I went sailing over the water and into it. It was so much fun!

About a half hour after we had first set up at our table, Matt, Thomas, and Mark came over to see us. "

"Hey John, Hey Dave!"

Matt called out to us as they set their stuff down at our table. Thomas and Mark joined him in waving and running toward us to the dock.

"Hey! We got new flippers, so now we have more to share!" I told them and ran past them to the picnic table to get them. I ran back and showed them the new flippers.

"Cool! "Can I try a pair, please?"

"Sure, here you go."

And I handed him a pair. He put them on and dove off the dock into the water below. I handed the other pair to John. He put them on and dove in, too.

"You can use my pair."

Matt said and handed them to me. I wasted no time putting them on and jumping in the water. I emerged and submerged so many times I felt like a submarine. There were even more fish than yesterday. Many allowed us to swim with them, too, instead of trying to avoid us.

One time, as I emerged, I saw Matt's dad swinging Matt into the water like John's dad did for us.

We stayed at the lakefront for over an hour before we realized we had forgotten to put on suntan lotion. John's mom called us over.

"You need to get some lotion on. You're gonna burn red and be sore tomorrow if you don't." she squirted it on our chest, face, arms, and legs and told us to rub it in while she rubbed some into our backs.

"Hey, there's a path on the other side of the lake over there and it takes you to that small dock. There are some really cool rocks that sparkle when the sun shines on them. You gotta see it. Come on!" Mark said

"Can we?"

I asked John's parents.

"Sure. We can see you from here, but be careful over there. That area doesn't look like it's part of the lodge."

"We'll be careful. Come on, John!"

And we all took off for the other dock.

When we got there, we saw that it wasn't as open an area with a lot of overgrowth and only a narrow path to walk on.

"Whoa! Look at these ROCKS! They're beautiful!" I exclaimed.

"Told you!"

"The last one in is a rotten egg!"

Thomas shouted, jumping into the lake.

We all followed so quickly it was hard to determine who was the last to jump in. We all swam around for a while, taking turns with the flippers, though the water wasn't as deep as the water over by the long dock.

Matt got out and said, "Hey, let's get something to eat! I'm starved!"

We all agreed. As I started to take a step on the old wood dock, a large splinter went into my foot.

"OWWW!" I exclaimed.

"What happened?" Thomas asked with alarm.

"I got a splinter, and it's a bad one."

I sat down on the dock and showed the rest of the boys.

"Wow, yeah, that's a big one," Mark said while John tried to get a grip on the end of it with his fingernail.

"I can't do it. My fingers are too slippery from the water. Come on. Mom can get it. Or grandma. They haven't been in the water. "

We all ran back to the table. I tried not to run on the ball of my right foot where the splinter was lodged.

"Dave got a splinter!" Thomas called out as we got to the table.

"Ok, have a seat," John's mom said. I sat longways on the bench seat so she could see it. She fiddled with it a bit but made no progress.

"We are going to have to get some tweezers. The front desk should have a first aid kit. I'll go get it," John's mom said.

"Grandma got up to look at it and said yeah, that's not close enough to the surface, so you can get it with fingernails. Definitely need tweezers."

John's mom returned a few minutes later and started to go to work on getting the splinter out. The tweezers made it easier, and in no time, the splinter was free from my foot.

"Ok, now go and swim some more, but stay off that dock." And she went to bring the tweezers back to the front desk.

We played some more, got hungry again and this time we ate some of our new friends' sandwiches and drank some of their orange Crush soda.

After finishing that second lunch, John's dad said to Matt and Thomas's parents

"Hey, if you wanna join us today, we have a surprise for the boys. We are going to leave the lake to go do something else today. You could follow us over. I think your boys will like it, too."

"What is it? Where are you going?" Thomas asked, curious as the Cheshire cat.

"It wouldn't be a surprise if we told you. Why don't you boys   go   swing   on   the   rope   for   a   while?

"Yeah, come on, let's go do that!" Matt said. Thomas looked like he wanted to stay behind to listen to the adults' conversation.

"Scoot or we won't go," his dad told him.

Eventually, Thomas took off after us to the rope swing and got in line for his turn with the rest of us.

Later, after some trips to the bathroom and a change of clothes, we all met in the parking lot. We got into our respective vehicles, us in the Datsun, them in the camper and we were on the road and on our way to some mystery destination.

When we slowed down to turn into a driveway, John and I erupted with joy.

"No WAY!!! A go-kart racing track!"

I yelled, remembering the other brochure we had picked up at the rest stop.

John was jumping up and down in his seat. He was beyond the happiest I had ever seen him.

We parked in the parking lot and so did Matt and his brother and cousin.

We all jumped out of the vehicles, practically walking on air.

This is gonna be amazing! Mark said with glee.

And we all hooted and hollered all the way inside to the desk where you pay.

John's dad listened to the attendant as he explained the way the cars work and had him sign some forms before paying. There was an area outside where the parents could sit and watch the kids go around the track. We all went to a rack where there were many different sizes of helmets. After a couple of tries, I found one that felt perfect after tightening the chin strap.

"Ok, an attendant said, pick a car."

I picked a navy blue one. John picked a red one. Matt and Thomas both picked green, and Mark chose yellow.

Before we got in, the attendant told us

"When you use the brake, remember that it doesn't engage fully right away. It's better to plan ahead and slow down before you break so that you can stop in time. Try not to bump each other. You have to keep the safety belt on and over both shoulders at all times. If you didn't hear the belt, double click, press the release, and click it again, listening for the two clicks. You get to race as long you still have fuel. Any questions? Ok, let's race."

The air was heavy with the scent of gas, oil, and rubber. We all got into our cars and eased our way to the starting line, feathering the gas. I was a bit of a lead foot at first, pressing a bit too hard and lurching forward.

The attendant waved the flag, and we slammed our feet on the accelerator. John was ahead quickly, but it didn't last as Matt took the lead after the first curve in the track. I slipped out of third with John right beside me, and then Thomas somehow passed us all on the inside of the track's third turn. We all kept inching forward and falling back for the entire race. The cacophony of engines and plumes of gray and blue smoke pouring out of the go-karts and enveloping the track was enthralling.

When we finished the race, we begged for another turn and then another, and then, before you knew it, we had spent the rest of the afternoon at the track.

Arriving back at the lodge, John and I told our new friends we'd see them again the next morning for a little while at the lake before heading back home.

"You boys need a shower. You stink from the track."

John's mother informed us as we entered the room again.

John and I and then all the adults took turns in the shower before going to dinner at the lodge restaurant. I felt like I hadn't eaten all day, so I decided I better get something that had big portions. I had the lasagna with beef. It was delicious. We all splurged and had all kinds of amazing desserts.

As everyone else sat in chairs and on the beds in the room watching TV, I moved the dining table so I could be closer to the window to draw the view I saw out the window. I used the colored pencils and paper John brought.

His mother moved one of the chairs and sat with me.

"How do you do it?"

"Do what?" I asked

"How do you draw? How do you know where to begin when you look at such a breathtaking view like this one?"

"I don't know. I just start on the thing that's the most important in the picture, and then I do the rest all around it."

"It's beautiful, what you are able to do. That's a special talent that you need to always keep working on."

"I know. Grandma always tells me that, too."

Now Grandma pulled up a chair, too.

"I love to watch him draw. Makes me feel at peace. Lord knows I need it."

"Yes. We all do."

I kept working on the drawing until the sun had caused the trees to look black, like silhouettes.

I got under the covers in bed with John, and we talked for some time while watching TV before sleep called both of us, and we were drowsy. John's mom saw sleep taking us over, and she came to tuck us in and hug and kiss us goodnight.

John's dad made the rounds to our bed too tonight, and before we were completely under the influence of the sandman, he came to tell us

"I'm so glad you had so much fun at the track today. It was so fun for us watching you go around the track. Love you."

"Love you too," we both said

He said, giving us hugs and kissing us on the head.

We fell asleep not long after that.

The morning came with bright sunshine pouring in all the windows. I was first up, so I brushed my teeth and got out of my pajamas and into my swimsuit, and sat at the table by the window to finish working on my drawing.

I was nearly finished by the time everyone else got up. After John's mom finished brushing her teeth, she came to the window to see my drawing.

"Oh my goodness! You've shown me some of your work before, but David, this is really the best drawing you have ever done. The trees are so REAL looking!"

"Really?"

Yes, really. This is so advanced for a child your age. Even for an adult. You should be so proud," Grandma came over and said.

"She's right. I don't think you've ever done anything to top this."

The morning started with some pancakes for breakfast downstairs at the restaurant. We then went back upstairs and packed up all our stuff so we'd be ready to go after we finished another stint at the lake later that morning.

Our table was still set up as a double table, and our new friends were there.

"Hey! Come on! Let's go swim on the other side with the old dock!"

Matt said when we got close enough to the table. After John and I kicked off our sneakers and took off our socks, we ran after them.

"Why are we going back to the old dock?" I asked.

"So we can skinny dip," Thomas said.

"No, we can't," John said. "Our parents can see across the lake to the dock."

"Yeah, but they can't see whether we've got our suits on. It's too far away to see. We swim naked every year when we come, and they never catch us."

We got to the old dock, and all took off our swimsuits, left them in front of the dock, and ran into the water. It was great being able to swim without the suit. It felt like you really were one with nature one hundred percent. We got out and went onto the dock, being careful not to drag our feet and get more splinters, and we cannonballed into the water again and again.

When we got tired, we got out of the water for a last time and then we realized we didn't bring towels. It didn't seem like a big deal at first, but we were so wet we couldn't get the swimsuits up our wet legs. No matter how we tried, they just wouldn't slide up our thighs. The dry nylon kept sticking against the water and froze a little ways up.

"What are we gonna do?" John said, worried about Mom and Dad finding out. We can't go get the towels.

"We'll lie in the sun, and it will dry us off," Matt suggested.

"Good idea!" I said.

We all went onto the dock to lie down on our backs. The sun was bright, so it was hard to see. We closed our eyes as the sun's rays warmed us and slowly dried the water from our bodies. We stayed in the sun for what felt like about 15 minutes, and then...

"If you boys are done skinny dipping, you can put your suits back on. You should be dry enough."

A voice boomed suddenly from the end of the dock. It was John's dad's voice. Hearing his voice made us all sit upright immediately.

"We forgot our towels and couldn't get our suits on because we were too wet from swimming."

Matt said.

"Next time, soak the suits in the water, then you can put them on over your wet legs," boomed Matt and Thomas's dad's voice, and then both dads laughed hard.

"How do you know?" Thomas asked.

"Come on, like your dads weren't kids once, too!"

And the two dads threw us towels and walked back to the picnic tables to wait for us to be done getting our suits back on. Laughing the whole way back.

When we got back, John's mom and my grandma were smiling and grinning like they knew something they shouldn't.

"Have a nice swim?"

John's mom said, and all the adults erupted in laughter. We were all so red in the face with embarrassment; it looked like we had spent a week in the blazing sun without sunblock.

"Why did you come to the old dock anyway?" Mark asked.

"Well, we knew that when you suggested that you start the day swimming where we couldn't as easily see you all, we knew something was up. Then, when we saw you forgot your towels, we decided to bring them to you so you wouldn't be too cold when you got out of the water." John's dad said

"...and since you didn't have your suits on, you didn't have the same goal of staying warm." Matt and Thomas's dad said, causing laughter from the adults again, and this time we all joined in.

"We know you boys have been doing it every year when we come here. I saw your suits on the ground a couple of years ago. You all wanted matching suits that year. Never leave red suits on the ground in the bright summer sun. Gives you away every time." Matt and Thomas's dad continued.

Everyone kept laughing for a while, and then it was time for us to go. We said our goodbyes to Matt, Thomas, and Mark and asked them to keep in touch, and we promised we would do the same.

"This summer you can come camping with us. We will be back here!" Matt said

"You're more than welcome to join us. It's really beautiful here in the early summer. We will be back here at the end of June or early July." Matt and Thomas's mom said.

"Ok, we'll stay in touch. If we can make it happen on the weekend, we will take you up on your offer."

"YAAAYYYYY!" John and I yelled.

"Ok, you two get changed into some street clothes and do it in the BATHROOM on the side of the lodge, not on the old dock." John's dad said jokingly. More laughter.

"See you soon." We said

After we changed, we got into the car and underway. John sat in the middle seat this time, and I had the window in the back seat, so when John fell asleep, he put his head down on Grandma's lap. She brushed and twirled his hair as he fell asleep. Grandma loved John, too.

After driving on a different route for a few miles, we were pulling into a driveway.

"Wake up, boys. Got another surprise for you."

We opened our eyes and saw we were at a miniature golf course and arcade.

"Oh, WOW!" I said

We all exited the car and went inside. There were walls lined up with space invaders, Galaxian and pong games, and another wall with 5 brand-new Pac-Man games. There were 10 skeeball games, too. I was about to spend as much time as I could here. This was too amazing for words.

John's dad cashed a twenty-dollar bill and came back to us with two rolls of quarters, one for each of us.

"Have fun!"

The adults sat in the snack bar area while we played. I had amassed a lot of tickets in a short time playing skeeball, and I decided to see what the prizes at the redemption counter were and how many tickets I would need for each prize.

I saw lots of small toys in the glass display case, but on an upper shelf behind the counter where the big and medium prizes were, I zeroed in on one medium prize. I counted my tickets and found out I only needed about 50 more tickets. I went to work on the skeeball machines with my remaining quarters. By the time I had enough tickets, I was down to three-quarters.

I tried to fold my strips of tickets neatly to tuck in my pocket for now while I used the remaining quarters to play Galaxian and Pac man. John and I were trying to outdo each other's scores. He had more quarters left because he didn't play skeeball, so he kept loaning me more quarters to keep playing more video games after I ran out of my own quarters.

"Ok, boys, we need to eat and get back on the road." John's dad said from the snack bar booth.

"OK, as soon as we finish this game. Can you order something for us?" John said while still trying to pay attention to his Pac-Man eating the dots and avoiding the ghosts.

"Sure, what do you want?"

"Burger good for you? " John said to me

"Yeah."

"Burgers and fries and maybe some onion rings, please."

"Ok." John's dad said

"OMIGOD! I shouted as John's dad was on his way to the counter.

What? What happened?" John's dad asked, concerned.

"John's up to level 9. That's really HARD!" I said.

"Way to go, John! Keep going!" John's dad told him while going on his original errand to the snack bar counter to order our food.

A few minutes later, the food was ready.

"Ok, boys. Food's here; let's eat," John's mom said.

The food smelled delicious, so we gave our game in progress to two high school-aged kids, probably skipping school for the day.

After finishing our meal, John's dad said

"Ok, back on the road we go."

"Wait, I have to get something for my tickets."

"Ok, we will be in the car. Don't be long."

"I won't"

The attendant at the ticket counter counted my tickets and asked what I wanted. I pointed to the item on the middle shelf of the back wall.

"Can I have a bag for it, please I asked?"

"Sure," and the attendant put it in a bag and handed me my prize.

I ran to the car, got in, and we were off again.

We were at a light and saw a mall ahead.

"Can we please go to the mall?" I asked John's dad.

"The MALL? Why?"

"Please. I have to get something. It's important. I promise it won't take long. PLEASE?!"

We pulled into the parking lot, and John's dad said

"JC Penny, ok?"

"Yeah. Perfect."

We all went inside, and I ran toward the escalator to go downstairs to the men's section.

"We'll all be right here in the women's department when you're done."

"Ok," I shouted, not slowing my stride across the store to the escalator.

A few moments later, I was back upstairs and dashing past everyone to get to the gift-wrapping department.

Then the clerk saw me, she asked, "May I help you?"

"Yes, please, can you please wrap this item I just bought here? I also have this second item that I didn't buy here. I will pay extra if you need me to because I didn't get it here."

"No, that's not necessary. I'd be happy to wrap it for you for free."

A few minutes later, my two items wrapped, I headed back over to everyone in the women's department. John's mom was buying a new blouse when I showed up next to her at the register.

When we got back out to the car, I took the two wrapped items out of the bag. I handed one to John's dad and one to John's mom.

"What's this all about? It's not Christmas or our birthday…" John's mom said, confused

"Open them." I insisted.

"Ok. " John's dad said.

They both tore open their packages.

Tears were streaming down John's mom's face. It was a miniature diorama of the woods and a lake in the background, almost exactly like the view we saw from our window at the lodge.

"David! This is beautiful! But how…"

"I got it with my tickets from skee ball. It was just so perfect. Like it was waiting for me to get it"

"Thank you," she said, putting it down on the car seat and hugging me tight and finishing with a kiss on the cheek and then on top of my head.

We're family, remember. We don't say thank you…right?"

Now, she cried even harder. And said, "That's right, David."

John's dad had his head down, too, trying not to cry as he looked at his gift. I got him an English Leather cologne gift set with a new leather wallet

"I saw that you needed a wallet when you took it out to pay for something. Do you like it?"

"David, I love it. How did you pay for it?" John's dad asked, still fighting back tears.

"With the money I made working at the store, so I could pay for the bus trip to the spelling bee. I didn't use it, remember?"

Now, all the adults were crying.

I got more bear hugs than I had gotten in a long time.

"You didn't have to do this."

"Yes, I did. You didn't have to do all you've done for me. I have been having more fun with all of you than I have ever had in my life. I love you so much."

"He always does things like that. You should see the perfume he gave me." Grandma said.

"Yeah, and remember the art contest, giving John and Juan those toys from the money he won?" John's mom added.

Now, I was crying. John's dad scooped me up and gave me another bear hug and then flung me onto my stomach up to his shoulder with one hand while he tickled my stomach and ribs with the other.

"Now you stop that crying, or I'm gonna tickle you till you do. John started trying to tickle Dad, and then Mom got in on the action. Grandma, not wanting to feel left out, joined the fun and tickled John. We all must have looked ridiculous, play fighting and tickling each other in the mall parking lot but we didn't care. It took some time, but we finally got back on the road.

We stopped at many other places on the way back home. Two car museums, an underground cavern tour, a national park and many great places to eat.

When we finally got back home, I was exhausted, but I was happier than I had ever been. The one thing I wanted was a family that loved me, not just Grandma; I actually had it all along in John's family. I was so grateful to them; words would never be enough. In their eyes, it wasn't just words; it was reality.

I was family.

May 1981 - Sixth Grade

We had arrived back home on Saturday afternoon, and Grandma and I were both still on a natural high from our wonderful trip. We walked into the house to find Mother gone, probably on one of her drunken binges again. As more of the day wore on and the light of afternoon turned into the faded light of dusk, we began to feel the tug of the reality that was our lives begin to weigh heavily upon us again.

Grandma put our clothes from the trip into the washer, and we sat in the living room, Grandma in one of the living room chairs and me on the hassock, facing her, recounting the adventures we had experienced on the trip again and again.

"Good people, John's parents. They are really good people." Grandma repeatedly said over the course of the late afternoon and evening.

"Great people." I corrected her.

"Yes. They are. It was so incredibly kind of them to take you to the spelling bee and do all those other things. In a world of people to choose to be friends with, you chose well."

"I know."

"You were so kind to them, too, giving them those presents. I was so proud of you."

"I was just doing what I knew was right like you always tell me. Listen to your heart."

"Not enough people do in this world. They do, John's parents, and you do, but not enough people do."

"What did you and John's mom and dad talk about when we went swimming and driving the go-karts and played games?"

"Oh, we just swapped stories about you kids. They showed me baby pictures of John and other pics of him through the years that they had in their wallets, and I showed them pictures of you. God, looking at the two of you as babies, you almost couldn't tell the both of you apart. You really looked like brothers. We talked about life and how hard it can be; we talked about the things that make it the wonder that it is and the things that hurt us and break our hearts."

"Did you tell them about Grandpa?"

"Yes. About how he worked for that aircraft place as an artist how much he loved you when you were born, and how he died when you were just about two in that car accident. He would have loved to see that you're becoming an artist like him. How he loved his art. It was his life."

"What about mother?"

"What about her?"

"Did you talk about her?"

"No, not really. Only briefly, talking about how hard our lives are because we are so poor, that kind of thing."

Now grandma looked sad, like some of the magic of our trip was fading.

"If only I could do the things for you that they do for John, she said.'

"But you do. What made this week so great wasn't the lodge or the cars on the racetrack or the games or the food or anything else. It was that they loved John, and they loved me so much that they wanted to do all those things to make us happy because seeing us happy brings them joy and makes even more love in their hearts. Like when you buy me something or take me to the diner with the little bit of money you have in your pocketbook. "

"Boy, you are really growing up, aren't you, to understand all that," Grandma said observantly, and she took off her glasses to wipe tears from her eyes before they fell.

"You're absolutely right." Grandma continued, "They shared that they barely make ends meet, that they are only very slightly better off than we are, but that they always try to find any way they can to show John how much they love him and each other. They've had desperately hard times trying to make it in the past, too."

"Yeah, I see John's dad bring him things home when it isn't his birthday or Christmas and think about how lucky he is but then I remember you doing that for me too. I guess that's why we're friends, John and me; we have a lot in common. "

"Yes, you do. More than you know. The most important thing you have in common is the love you feel in your heart and doing the right thing, no matter what it costs."

"Yeah"

"John's parents said their door is always open to you. Don't ever forget that. They meant what they said. You're family. Whenever you need to go there, you go there, understand?"

"Yeah, I know I'm family to them. They sure did a lot this week to prove it."

"Yes, they did, and I love them for it more than words can say, and I know you do, too. Good people. "

"No, great people, remember?"

"Yes, great people, I remember."

A few hours later, I was on the couch watching TV and falling asleep, and Grandma had fallen completely asleep in the chair as the lock on the front door clicked and the door opened. The sounds alerted us and made us sit bolt-upright.

It was Mother in her usual drunken stupor.

Looking surprised to see us, she said

"Well, look who decided to come back. You're back. Too bad," she slurred, even more drunk than usual.

"The fuck are you still doing up? Shouldn't you be in bed… somewhere else?" Mother said, looking at me, laughing after she did so.

"Thanks for all the fucking help at the store today. I had to go by myself and get the groceries home."

"Too bad," Grandma said mockingly, using Mother's words against her.

"You shut the fuck up! It's bad enough the brat's gone with no word, but you, what the fuck is your excuse? Where'd the two of you go for so long?"

"None of your business."

"Everything in this house is my business. Now answer the motherfucking question. Where the FUCK were you?"

Grandma stood from the chair and walked past Mother to the kitchen.

"Don't you walk away from me, bitch! I said where the fuck did you go?"

Grandma looked back at me from the kitchen, and her expression said, 'Get out. Get to John's house.' I stayed put as if glued to my spot. I didn't want mother to hurt grandma.

"Most irresponsible fucking thing I have ever seen. You just leave. No note, no phone calls, nothing. You're just GONE. Now answer the fucking question. Where in the FUCK did you GO?!" she yelled directly into Grandma's face. I called upon every ounce of courage I had and no longer riveted to my spot, I approached her, and now standing right in front of her, I belted out

"You know where we were? We were with people who really CARED about us, unlike YOU."

Whap!

A backhand across my head. Then, as I crumpled to the floor, she grabbed me by the shirt to hoist me back up. I fought it. I kicked at her and tried to punch her, but she was too strong and quick, and she finally got ahold of me and swung me by my arm, causing me to hit my ribs against the kitchen doorway. She wasted no time in picking me up by my left arm and punching me in the stomach and ribs. I used my body weight to swing my feet toward her hips and kicked at her. Because she was so drunk, she lost her balance and fell. I immediately seized the opportunity to scramble away. I picked up an ashtray from the coffee table and hit her in the head with it and ran to my room to get my sneakers. I didn't stop to put them on; I just carried them until I had opened the door, ran out of the building, and partway up the street before putting my sneakers on while sitting on the curb. I then took off at top speed to get to John's house, my ribcage protesting with pain from every breath I took.

When I was a couple of houses away from John's, I slowed down to catch my breath and for my heart to stop pounding. I didn't want to give away the real reason I was now at John's house so soon again. What would my story be? I got an idea and walked the rest of the way to John's house.

I rang the bell, and soon after, John's dad answered.

"David. Hi! What's up?"

"I figured since it's still the weekend, maybe I could stay with John tonight 'cause it's not a school night."

John's dad looked perplexed for a moment, considered it, and said

"Well, you know you are welcome here at any time, school night or weekend. Come on in. I think John already fell asleep, though, so change into your pajamas quietly. They are in the bottom drawer of John's dresser." John's dad said while going back to watching the late show on TV in the living room like this was just business as usual. In truth, it kind of was, since this sort of situation where I showed up to sleep over was becoming the norm.

I tried to be quieter than a mouse as I walked into John's room and changed out of my clothes and into my pajamas. John still woke up anyway when one of the bedsprings on the guest bed squeaked and gave away my presence.

"Hey. Welcome back, bro. Unpacked and decided to come back and spend the rest of the weekend here, huh?" John astutely said.

"Yeah, how did you know?"

"That's what I would have done." I tossed my pillow at him, and he tossed it back to me.

"Go to sleep, or Dad's gonna come in here and whoop our butts."

I knew he meant it figuratively, though. There was no way his dad even spanked him, let alone did the violent things mother had done to me. I did as he said and pulled the covers so I could get under them, and I thought about Grandma and how awful it was that she had to stay there in that house with Mother. I started to cry. A little at first, but it grew. John heard me and said

"Hey, what's wrong? You ok?"

"Yes," I lied. When my crying continued, John got up from his bed and came over to mine, sitting on the edge of the bed and telling me

"Sit up, come on. Let's talk."

"I don't want to talk. I can't. I'm sorry. I can't." I said each word between tears and whimpering, and John encircled me with his arms and held me. He held me as long as it took for me to get all the tears out. He never asked me any more questions. He just held me, and we eventually fell asleep while he was still holding me.

The next thing I remember was John's mother waking us up just enough so that we could position ourselves lying down on the bed instead of sitting up. She slid us down so we were both lying with our heads on the pillow, pulled up the covers over both of us and then kissed our foreheads as she always did. I think I started crying again toward daylight breaking, and John calmed me, telling me

"It's alright. You're ok."

So that I could get back to sleep.

The next morning, we woke up to the smell of fresh bacon and scrambled eggs being cooked. Dad's coffee was percolating, too, and the air was heavy with the scent of it.

Since it was Sunday, we didn't change out of our pajamas; we just headed to the kitchen, where the food was already being scooped onto our plates by John's mom.

"Hey, sleepy heads she said. David I'm so happy you decided to finish the weekend out with us. Oh, by the way, I will be doing a wash today, so you can put your clothes you wore yesterday in with the load, and you can wear some of John's clothes today, k?" she instructed

"Ok," I said, shoveling a forkful of eggs into my mouth.

"You're going to get some space in John's dresser too, so you can put some clothes for when you stay over, so you'll always have some handy, ok? Speaking of which, we really have to get to the store to get summer clothes. We really should have done that already. John needs some new shorts and shirts for summer."

"Will I have to go home then when you go to the store?" I asked, worried that the rest of my weekend with John would be cut short.

"No, of course not. You are coming with us, as long as it's ok."

I smiled and responded, "It's ok. I spend so much time here now; if I'm not home, Grandma just knows I'm here."

"That's good. We told her that any time you wanted to come to our house, you'd always be welcome, and we meant that. Any time."

I never ceased to be astounded by the polar opposite that John's household was compared to mine.

After we finished breakfast, John and I retreated to John's room to read mad magazines and play electronic battleship, as usual.

A little while later, John's mother came to the room to collect my clothes from the day before. She looked at the tags before putting them into the laundry basket she was carrying.

"You two need to get to the shower. We are gonna be leaving soon to go to the store."

I asked John if he wanted to go first to shower and he said no, so I went. As I was unbuttoning my pajama shirt, I looked in the bathroom mirror and saw that my ribs were very badly bruised. They were sore, too, but from so many years of my mother's abuse, I had gotten used to it. The times when I WASN'T in pain from something she had done to me were the rare times, not the reverse.

A knock at the door, and I flinched and pulled the shirt back over me, buttoning one button before opening it.

"Towel for you. Forgot to put fresh towels in the bathroom last night when we got home."

John's mom said, handing me a blue towel. I said

"Thank you," and shut the door. Midway through my shower, John opened the door and came in to brush his teeth. When I finished my shower, we swapped places, and I brushed my teeth with the toothbrush they had assigned to me.

I got dressed in a pair of John's rustler jeans and a striped t-shirt when John's mom came in to tell me

"Get that dirty underwear and those pajamas into the washing machine. I just started it. "

"Ok," I said and did as she asked. Before too long, we were all ready to head to the store.

We all jumped in the Datsun and took off.

"What store are we going to?" I asked.

"Sears. And if you boys behave, we'll go to Friendly's for lunch. You know what I mean by 'behave,' John, right?"

John, looking embarrassed and blushing, said, "Come on, don't, you're gonna embarrass me."

"He just hates going clothes shopping and trying them on and he always gives us a hard time about it."

"Ma, stop!" John said, hitting her seat with his foot.

I just looked at him and laughed.

"What's so funny he asked?"

"Nothing. I just didn't know you were a bad kid, that's all."

"Stop it! I'm not! He cried out, making me laugh even more.

John reached over and put me into a headlock, and started giving me a noogie.

"John, stop messing with you brother!" John's dad blurted out loudly, and the whole car got quiet.

"I'm sorry, it's just... well, you know... like we told you, you are brothers... so that just slipped out. "

"It's ok," I said and thought about how really ok it was. If only they know. Maybe they did know.

"I'm sorry John," I said and gave him a half hug.

"It's alright," John said as he smiled and hugged me back.

We got inside Sears, and John's mom and dad started picking out shorts, shirts, and even a couple of pairs of pants for him. John's mom gathered a separate stack and handed it to me.

"Go try on all that stuff. We'll be there in a minute," John's mom said, and John walked toward the fitting room. When I stayed beside her, she said

"What are you waiting for? You too. Go!"

I looked at her with confusion and said, "Wait…but…"

"Don't stand here wasting time asking questions; go and try on those clothes, or we won't be going to Friendly's."

I looked at her, confusion still overtaking me, and started walking away slowly. And she smiled at me and said

"Move it."

By the time I had arrived, John was already showing one of the outfits to Dad. He checked the fit and said

"Ok, now put on another outfit."

John and I both came out wearing some of the new clothes and now Mom joined in the checking for fit before telling us to try on the next set of clothes.

We finished trying on everything and then went to the shoe section, where John and I tried on new pairs of shoes. After checking the fit of each choice, John's dad asked us

"Which ones do you like?" I pointed to a navy blue pair of Asics runners, and John pointed to a khaki-colored pair in the same style. The shoes joined the clothes in the cart and after tossing in some socks and underwear, we went to the checkout to pay. Then, we loaded the car's hatch with our clothing haul and got in the car to head to Friendly's.

I had decided to get a cheeseburger with the works, like usual and saw that John's dad had ordered the same thing.

"Great minds think alike," John's dad said, taking a big bite of his burger

"I just love burgers," I told him.

"Yeah?" He replied, "You better prove it. If you don't hurry up and eat all of it, I'm gonna eat it."

I took the biggest bite I could, not able to even get it all in my mouth, and John's mom said

"Oh, come on, don't be gross."

Then John and his dad did the same thing, and we all started laughing.

"I swear," John's mom said, "You are just as bad as the kids."

John's dad just smiled at her, and sauce, bits of lettuce, and tomato from the burger tumbled from his smile to his plate, and now the laughter from all of us got louder.

We finished with ice cream sundaes again and headed back to John's house.

Back in John's room, Mom had emptied the bottom drawer of his dresser and told me

"Put your t-shirts, shorts, pants, socks and underwear here. Your new button down shirts, put those on the empty hangers in John's closet. He's got room. "

I did as she said, putting away some of the clothes in the drawer while looking up at her and trying to find the words to tell her how grateful I was or to ask why they bought me new clothes, and apparently, my look was enough. She knelt down next to me and hugged me. "I love you so much. Don't you ever forget it. We all do. That's all the reason we need, got it?"

"Yes," I said, tears streaming down.

"Besides, we can't count on you to remember to bring some spare clothes over. You always forget to bring them when you show up at our door, wanting to stay the night."

She said amusingly, gently wiping my tears away with her hand.

I hugged her again with so much force; it was like one of Grandma's bear hugs.

When I finished, she said, "YOU are gonna squeeze the stuffing out of me, and then Dad's gonna get SO mad at you, and he'll do THIS!"

And she wrestled me to the floor and tickled my belly and then my ribs right where I had hit the doorway at my house the night before. The thing is, I didn't even feel the pain anymore. John joined us, trying to save me from his mother's tickling spree by tickling her too, and then Dad, hearing the ruckus and laughter, came in and joined us, bringing a pillow to the fray.

When we were done, we had totally messed up John's room. We had a good old-fashioned pillow fight, and we were all exhausted. We all helped to put John's room back in order, returned all the pillows back to other locations in the house, and had a quiet rest of our Sunday together.

At the end of the night, before bedtime, I fell asleep lying against John's mom on the couch in front of the TV, and John fell asleep lying across his dad's stomach. When it was time for bed, they both tucked us in and kissed us goodnight, when they saw that we had forgotten, they set out our clothes for tomorrow before they left the room and gently closed the door.

May 1981 - Sixth Grade

Mother flung me across the room and into the coffee table. I struck it hard, the knick-knacks flying in all directions. She picked up the yardstick like a ninja warrior and brought it down again and again. Somewhere that I couldn't see, there was a light of some kind. I was nearly blind as Mother went toward that light and brought back the 2 X4 from the back porch. She came back into the living room, and as I tried to get to my feet, she used all her strength to thrust the piece of wood into my abdomen and ribs again and again. When I went down for the final time, I was on my back with her looking over me, punching me with all her might in my stomach and face. I screamed and screamed.

"NOOOOOO!!!! NOOOOOOOOOOOOI!!!!! Please STOOOPPPPPPP !!!! NO MOOORE! Please STOOOOP." And I saw her fists coming at me again.

"David, it's ok, it's ok, calm down, you're having a nightmare. I heard the words, but I wasn't awake yet, the silhouette of my mother still looming over me, punching me again and again

"NOOOO! NO PLEEEASE! PLEEASSE! Leave me ALOOOONE! DON'T HURT MEEEEEE!"

John's mother stood over me in the bed and tried desperately to wake me up fully and calm me down. John's dad was in the room now, too.

They both tried to get their arms around me to calm me down, but I pushed against them and hit at their hands and arms

"GET AWAYYYY! No MOOOORE!"

"What's wrong with him?" John asked, looking scared.

"It's a really bad nightmare. John's mom said, and then she grabbed me and shook me."

"WAKE UP DAVID!! Come back to us, do you HEAR me? COME ON! WAKE UP!!!"

She shook me some more, and finally, it was over, and I was back in the real world of John's bedroom. I shook uncontrollably all over, cold and hot waves flowing over me and pain crying out from every point in my body. I was covered in sweat, and my pajamas were completely stuck to my body. Continuous rivulets of tears blasted from my eyes.

"Where am I?" I said through the tears.

"You're here with us," John said, taking my hand.

Sweat ran down my face and onto the already-soaked pillow. The sheets were soaked with my sweat too, almost as If I had wet the bed, only it took up the whole bed where my body had been since the night terror began. I was on fire and shivering at the same time. Waves of pain shot through me again and again. My heart was pounding and skipping beats alternatively.

The night terrors had been going on for a while now, and this one was one of the worst yet. It was as if I was there all over again for one of my mother's most vicious attacks. I felt it in every fiber of my being. I could smell the wood of the 2X4, smell the alcohol on Mother's breath, and feel every strike as though it were really happening.

John's mother held me tight and tried to calm me down. I still couldn't stop shaking.

"Somebody get me the thermometer?"

"I will" John said and ran to the bathroom medicine cabinet. Seconds passed, and he was back. John's mom let go of her grip. And I tried to hold on, then let go, and then hold on again. I didn't know what to do. All I wanted was for the pain to stop. The terrible pain.

"Ok, sit down on the bed." John's mother said, and John's dad steadied me when it looked like I was not going to be able to sit without falling over.

"I'm going to take your temperature, David. Please try and stay still for a moment, ok?"

I nodded as best I could, and I opened my mouth so she could put the thermometer under my tongue.

"A couple minutes later, she pulled it out of my mouth and said, "Omigod! It's 103.3"

John's dad immediately said

"John, get the bags of ice and all the ice out of the ice cube trays in the freezer. Get all the ice into the tub, plug up the drain in the tub, and start pouring the cold water; open the faucet all the way, only the cold water, got it?"

"Got it. Is he gonna be ok? I'm scared" and now John was crying.

"He's gonna be fine. We just have to get the fever down. Now go do what I said."

John ran to the kitchen and did as Dad said. After he was done, he went back to the bedroom

"The water's pouring."

"Good. Now go and knock on all the neighbors' doors and tell them you need all the ice they have. Tell them it's for a temperature over 103 degrees. That it's an emergency."

"Ok," and he was off again.

Meanwhile, John's dad said

"We need to get these wet pajamas off of you."

John's mom started to strip the shirt off my torso. Dad went to work on the pants and underwear. When they were done, John's dad scooped me up from the bed and brought me to the bathtub.

"It's gonna be very cold, but we have to do it." And he plunged me into the water. The shock of the cold surprised me and started me crying again. I was still wracked with pain.

John returned with ice, and neighbors were in the hall with more. He kept making more trips back and forth until he had collected all the ice from the neighbors.

John's family took turns adding more ice as I shivered and screamed with pain. Eventually, the cold calmed the pain, and I started to feel better.

One of John's neighbors asked if we had enough ice or whether he should get more from the 24-hour gas station down the street.

"No, I think with the cold water, this is enough. He's gonna be ok now. Thank you so much, though; thank you, all of you." John's dad told them

As I started to return to normal, John's mom said

"In a few more minutes, you can get out of the tub, k?" while stroking my wet hair.

"O-o-o-k-k-k-k," I said, shivering more from the cold water than the fever now.

John's mom came back with some fresh underwear and a towel for me.

Ok, come on out now. And she held the towel open for me.

I stepped out of the tub and into the waiting towel. She wrapped me in it, and I started shivering more profoundly again. Tears streamed down my face again.

"It's ok. You're safe. You hear me. You're safe." And she gently held me, wrapped in the towel. John was crying again, too. He came and held me gently, too.

We stayed that way for a while until I stopped shaking. "Ok, let's get your temperature again, young man." John's dad said as I opened my mouth for the thermometer to go back under my tongue. A couple of minutes later, he took the thermometer from my mouth and read it out loud, "100.5. Good. It's coming down."

"Ok, get some new underwear on and come to John's bed." I sat down on the toilet, slid the new underwear on, and stood so I could pull them up the rest of the way. I walked into John's bedroom, where Mother was stripping the wet sheets off the bed.

"There's fresh pajamas on John's bed. They are his flannels, so they might be too hot for you, but they're the only clean pajamas left. You don't have to wear them if you want.

"It's ok, I want to wear them," I said and walked to John's bed and put them on.

John's mom finished making the bed with new sheets and said

"Ok, bed's ready for you if you want it. Or you can sleep with John if you want to. Or us. It's up to you.

"Can I sleep with you, John?"

"Yeah, of course. Come on, get in."

And he held the covers up for me so I could get under them.

Wait a minute, not yet, John's dad said, and he bent down with his arms open so he could hug me.

"I ran to him and started crying again. He hugged me gently and stroked my head. Love you, buddy."

"Love you too."

He kissed my head and then I went back to John's bed and got in.

John's mom pulled the covers up while John's dad told John

"You let us know right away if he starts getting hot or he has another nightmare."

"I will. "

I tried to get to sleep when I heard John crying. I said

"What's wrong?

"Dude, you scared me. You really scared me."

"I'm sorry, I said. "

"When your temperature went up like that and the way you looked... I thought you were gonna die."

"I know. I'm sorry. I was scared, too. You saved me, though. You all did."

"I have nightmares sometimes, but not like that. Mom was trying to wake you up for over 5 minutes and she couldn't get you back. It's like you were stuck in that nightmare and couldn't wake up."

"I guess I couldn't. I'm ok now because of you. Thank you."

"You don't say…" He said

"…thank you to family…I know…I know. Love you, bro."

"Love you too. 'Night!"

Then John hugged me, and a few minutes later, sleep overtook us.

When we woke up, John's mom was opening the blinds on John's window to let more of the morning light in.

"Boys, you don't have to go to school today. We are gonna keep you home for one more day. Dave, later, I'll call the school and tell them you stayed over here last night and that you'll be back in school tomorrow.

"Thank you. Why are we waking up now, then?"

"Because I'm gonna make you some breakfast before I have to go to work. John's dad will be gone all day, but I will be coming home at lunchtime. Ok, up out of bed. Stop pretending to be asleep, John."

"Aw, mom! How did you know?"

"Mom's always know."

Then John's alarm started ringing. John reached over to the night table and turned it off.

John and I got out of bed, and I helped him make the bed. He grabbed his dirty clothes, and I grabbed mine, and I followed him toward the bathroom, dropping the clothes in the basket in the hall as we went.

We brushed our teeth and went to breakfast.

John's dad was sitting there looking at a story in the newspaper. When we sat down, he stopped paying attention to the paper.

"Well, good morning. Hope you had some better dreams the rest of the night."

He said to me.

"I did."

"That's good. You wanna talk about it?"

"Let him eat his breakfast. He can talk about it later." John's mom said.

She served us some scrambled eggs and toast, poured orange juice, and sat down with us after kissing John and me on the cheek.

"What you did last night was a remarkable, young man," she said to John

"How you stayed calm and got the tub ready and got ice from the neighbors."

"Yeah, you may not realize, but you worked so quickly that it was what really helped David's temperature come down."

"I was so scared." John said, "If his temperature had gone up too high, what would've happened?"

"It's over now, John; you don't have to think about that."

"No, I want to know what would've happened. Tell me."

Nobody said anything

"Would he have died if his temperature stayed too high?" John asked

"Yes," John's dad said

Now John started crying hard.

"But your quick work getting the water and ice, you saved him, John. You saved his life."

"From a DREAM?! He could have died from a nightmare. WHY?" John said through his tears.

"John, it was more than a nightmare. It was a night terror. Those are far worse. They can do what you saw David go through last night. The body is a fragile thing in some ways and those night terrors upset the body's balance in many ways."

"So yes, it was a big deal what you did. You are a hero." John's mom said.

John got up from his chair and hugged me.

"I love you too," I said as if the hug was enough to tell me what he wanted to say.

We ate our breakfast and got out of our pajamas and into some shorts and tees for around the house while Mom went to the door and said

"Ok, boys, get over here."

We did as she asked.

"Dad's about to leave for the day But I will be back at lunch around noon, like I told you earlier. John, if David's temperature returns, you call my job and let me know and I will be home earlier, ok? It shouldn't be back now that the episode is over, but you can't be too careful. That was one awful night terror."

"Ok, Mom, you can go to work now," John said impatiently. She gave him a big hug, a kiss on the cheek, and then another on his nose and said

"I have never been more proud of you than I was last night. I love you so much."

And then she turned to me and said, "You mind your brother. You listen to him if something happens and he tells you to lay down and rest, got it?"

"Yes, ma'am."

And she hugged me gently and said.

"I love you so much, too."

"Love you too."

"Ok, Bye," Mom said as she went to the car to get to work.

"I gotta go too."

And John's dad gave us both a hug simultaneously, one of us for each arm and he kissed us on the forehead.

"You two behave. Don't burn the house down."

"Dad!" John said and laughed

"Well, you'd think that's what mom thinks, the way she carries on…Ok, Bye, guys."

"Bye," we both said together as he walked out the door and got into the car with Mom.

John turned on the TV and watched it for a while from the couch while I read a Mad magazine.

I decided to do something else. I went to the kitchen and unloaded the dishwasher, put the new dirty dishes in it, and poured some Cascade powder into the reservoir on the door like I had seen John do lots of times. Then I took the trash out and threw it in one of the barrels outside.

Next, I washed out the kitchen sink and turned my attention to the laundry. I put all of the clothes and the sweat-soaked sheets in the basket into the washer, poured in some Cheer detergent, and started the washer.

John came out to the kitchen to see what was going on.

"What are you doing?"

"Chores," I said.

"Why? Some of what you're doing was supposed to be MY chores."

"I just want to, that's all. Is that ok?"

"No…"

"Look, John, I was scared too. It was the worst one I ever had. Can't I do something nice for you to say thank you?"

"When are you gonna understand? You don't HAVE to thank someone that's like family…"

"Well, maybe YOU don't think so, but I do. Nobody ever does anything for me except you, your family, and grandma."

"By nobody, you mean your mother. I've seen how she is. She never even comes to see you in the spelling bee, or the glee club shows."

"I didn't say my mother…"

"Don't you get it? You don't HAVE to say it. Everybody knows because of what you DON'T say."

I looked down at the floor and said, "I just mean that things are hard for me…"

"I was in the hallway getting a drink of water at the fountain at school when I heard your mother yelling at Mr. Shedruff and telling him she was gonna get him fired if he said anything to the police about what she does to you."

"But the door was closed…"

"Doesn't matter she was so loud, everybody heard her."

Now I understood, or at least I thought I did.

"So you told your mom and dad? That's why they have been so nice to me."

"Is that what you think? No, I didn't tell them. But they know. They know something bad is going on at your house. They know because they aren't stupid."

And John stomped off to his room.

"John!"

I called, but he ignored me and slammed his bedroom door.

I opened it and went to his bed where he was crying into his pillow.

"Look, it's hard, you know, I could die. I almost died when I was out of school for so long a couple of years ago."

John sat up on his bed and said

"When are you gonna do it? When are you gonna say it? When are you gonna let people help you?"

"I TRIED, don't you understand?! I TRIED. A cop didn't even help me. I almost DIED after that time. And nothing happened after what you heard when you were getting a drink of water."

Tears were rolling down my cheeks.

"Please don't be mad at me. Please. I can't lose you. I love you like a brother. You know that. Please, John. If I lose you, all I'll have left is grandma."

"You're not gonna LOSE me, dummy, can't you get it through your head? You never LOSE family. I love you, Mom loves you, Dad loves you, we all love you."

Frustrated, I yelled

"Why are some people so willing to care in this world? Why?"

"You don't wanna know why some people are good. You already know the answer to that. Love. I can't answer the question you really wanna know: why there are so many bad people who should care but don't. Who are mean? Can't it just be enough that there are people who care and love you? Not for a reason. Not because we feel bad for you. We loved you before we knew anything about what happened at your house. You know it's true."

"Well, yeah, it's all I ever wanted. Only grandma loved me, I thought."

"You remember when you were gonna jump off the wall at school?"

"Yeah."

"You remember how me and Juan got you down before you jumped?"

"Yeah, I figured you did it because it was the right thing to do or pity."

"Well, it was the right thing to do, but we also did it because we CARE about you and what happens to you. It's not pity. You have been our friend for a long time, since kindergarten. How do you feel about us?"

"What do you mean? I love you guys, you know that."

"Well, don't you think we could feel that way, too, about you? Without any reason other than the fact that we do?"

I bawled. I didn't know why; I just had to get the tears out. John had simply told me the truth. I had such a bad situation that I wasn't able to understand that others could care about me as I did about them. For ten years, I had lived a life feeling no one could possibly love me, that my grandmother was the only one who loved me for some unknown reason. That people, especially family members, love each other simply because they do, and they don't require someone to give anything back except love as well. The floodgates kept flowing, and John held me as I let it all out.

At ten years old, John was able to make more sense of things than any adult in my life ever could hope to.

John and his family were indeed great people.

After I got all the crying out of my system, John felt my head for fever.

"I'm ok, I said."

"Aw, shut up. I have to check because mom told me I had to."

"That the only reason?" I said with a smile.

"You know it's not, asshole." And he gave me a hug again. When he let go, he said. I'm not gonna let you die on me. It'd be like if mom or dad died. Get it?"

"I do. Let's do something."

"What you wanna do?"

"I don't care."

"Let's build ships."

"Ok."

When John's mom got home at lunch and saw all the chores that had been done, she said

"Wow, you boys have been busy this morning, getting so much work done for me. Thank you!"

"Welcome," we both said.

"David, want to help me make some lunch?

John's mom asked

"Sure," I replied

John's mom pulled some cans of canned chicken from the cupboard and opened them with the can opener.

"Can you get me the big bowl in the cabinet over there?"

And she pointed to her left.

After I brought it over and she finished opening the chicken, she said, "I need the mayonnaise from the fridge too."

I got it out and she scooped it into the bowl and went to the spice rack for some spices and sprinkled them into the mix.

Returning to the spice rack, she got a wooden spoon from a holder by the sink. She handed it to me.

I started stirring as she said, "That was quite a bad dream last night, wasn't it? What was it about? Do you remember?"

"Yeah. I always remember. Someone was chasing me, hurting me."

"Do you have these night terrors a lot?"

"Yeah, sometimes. Sometimes, they don't happen for a long time."

"Do you know who it is? Who is chasing you and hurting you in your dream?"

"No," I lied.

"You gave us a bad scare. You know how special you are to us."

She reached out her hand and stroked my chin.

"Why are some people so awful?" I asked.

"I wish I knew. I think if we could figure that out, we'd solve one of the biggest secrets of nature. I don't know if even the experts who know a lot about how the mind works can answer that question and solve that riddle regarding every nasty or awful person. I think it makes us appreciate the people who are kind and loving even more, don't you?"

"Yeah. Me and John were talking about that earlier. About mean people and about why people who love each other don't need a reason to love each other; they just do. And how when a person is loved, they don't have to do anything back for them, just love them back."

"John   said   all   that?"

"Yeah, he did."

"Well, he's right. About all of it."

"I'm sorry." I didn't understand before. I didn't understand what you meant, not saying thank you to the family because you don't have to. I didn't know. I didn't know." Tears were falling heavily again.

John's mom told me, "Put the spoon down and stop stirring."

There is something else you should know. You don't EVER need to be sorry about anything that you don't know. That's the other reason there are other people on this earth. To help us learn about what we don't know. Come here."

And she picked me up and hugged me and put me back down gently on the chair.

"John, get out here, young man!"

He came running.

"Yes, Mom?"

"David just told me what you said to him earlier. You are one smart boy. Get over here."

And she bent down and hugged him hard and kissed him on the head.

"Shoes on, both of you. No chicken salad for lunch today. Today, we are going to Chuck E Cheese."

"YAAAYYY!" we both shouted.

When John came back with his sneakers on, he said.

"I get shotgun seat in the car on the way there."

"Yes, today you are a two-time hero, and you earned it." John's mom proclaimed as she pulled the plastic wrap from one of the kitchen drawers and put a piece of it over the bowl of chicken salad, handing it to me to put back in the refrigerator.

We spent the rest of the day at Chuck E Cheese, eating pizza and playing in the ball pit, crawling through all the tubes, and playing skeeball all afternoon. We all won enough tickets to get John a new telescope to look at the stars at night. We didn't have to give him our tickets except for the reason we wanted to because we loved him. That and he saved my life.

Twice.

June 1981 - Sixth Grade

John's alarm sounded its bell, signaling another new day, and it was going to be a tough one. Going back to school after a week away was sure to be a big adjustment. We both just stayed motionless for a few minutes after John had silenced the alarm clock.

"Hustle up, boys! School day!" John's mom called out when she didn't hear us getting out of bed.

The smell of coffee and cinnamon toast permeated the air. I loved cinnamon toast almost as much as chocolate. I raced to that shower and got clean as fast as I could, put on the new school clothes, and ran to the table.

"Breath check," John's dad said, stopping me from getting to the table until I breathed out so he could smell it.

"Just as I thought. Go brush your teeth."

"Aw, man! I want that cinnamon toast while it's still warm."

"Mom will pop more in the toaster if it's cold when you get here. I love it whether it's hot or cold, so it'll get eaten," Dad said.

John loved cinnamon toast, too. He was brushing his teeth at the sink without a towel, even around his waist; he hadn't even taken the time to dry off when he got out of the shower.

I finished brushing my teeth at the same time as John finished, but because I had already gotten dressed, I got to my kitchen chair first. I had already eaten a whole piece by the time John made it to the table.

"You boys are going to have a lot of schoolwork to get caught up on. I expect to see you doing it when I get home today, John. You too, David, if you come over after school. No playing until you get your work done, no excuses. Understand?" John's dad told us.

"Yes sir." We both said. John had caught up to me and was on his second piece of toast now too.

We gulped down some orange juice and ran to the door to put on our new sneakers. John's mother was filling the dishwasher when we completed tying our laces, and we both ran to her, kissed her on the cheek, and hugged Dad, sitting at the table.

"Do well in school. Bye," Dad said.

'Bye."

As we arrived at the school and went to the playground, we met up with Juan, who was playing tag with Danny.

"Hey, where have you assholes been?!" He said jokingly.

"We went to the spelling bee regionals and then to this lodge in the woods. They had ropes and docks and boats…" I told him.

"Nice!" Juan replied.

"Yeah, we went and drove on a race track, too," John said.

"Wait a minute… WHAT?!!!" Danny exclaimed.

"It's true. We did. We played Pac-Man and Galaxian and skee ball, too," I continued. "John got to level 10 on Pac-Man."

"You're kidding! I played it, and I can't get past level 5 before losing all my guys."

"It was incredible! You guys gotta come with us this summer. We made some new friends, and we are gonna camp outside in tents!"

"I'm in," Juan said.

"Me too," Danny said without even thinking.

"Hey John, Hey Dave! Welcome back from vacation! Nice new clothes!" Mr. Shedruff said as he walked by.

"Thank you!" we said.

"You never told us what happened with the spelling bee." Danny inquired

"Oh yeah. I lost. It was me and another kid. I added a letter to the word."

"That sucks," Juan said, somewhat surprised

"Nah, not really. The rest of the vacation made it so I didn't care."

"Yeah. So you wanna come over to my house today?" Juan said to us.

"Can't gotta get caught up on all the work we missed," John said

"Same here I added."

"Well, maybe tomorrow."

"Yeah. You should come to my house tomorrow. I have a new telescope," John said proudly while looking over at me after he said it."

"Geez, man, what the hell, and what didn't you guys do or get?"

"Well, we left SOME stuff to get another time, ha ha!"

Someone pushed me from behind, lurching me forward toward Danny. I turned to see it was Eggy and friends.

"Welcome back, faggots." He jeered.

I'm not sure what got into me, but I pushed Eggy back with all my strength, and he fell back against Carlos, causing both of them to tumble to the ground.

"HEY! What the fuck?" Carlos said, getting up and coming toward me.

"Fuck off, Carlos!"

Danny yelled, pushing him to the ground. Eggy got right in my face with his fist pulled back, and Juan grabbed it and flung him backward, and this time, he fell against Luis Matos, nearly taking him with him as he fell again.

"Who's the real faggots? You were all standing close enough to each other to be up each other's asses."

Danny said in his thick Brooklyn accent. John, Juan, and I all high-fived him and laughed as the bell rang. Mr. Shedruff, upon seeing Eggy and his friends, said, "Get up and get in line."

Upon entering the classroom, Mr. Mosely said, "Hi John, Hi Dave. Whoa, ho, ho! I am diggin' the new threads! You look SHARP today, gentlemen!" and he high-fived us. "When everybody else gets started on their math, you two come see me so I can get you caught up on what we've been doing."

"Yes, sir," I said.

Mr. Mosely spent most of the first-period class explaining how to do the math we missed and what we needed to do in history, geography, reading, and spelling.

It was a lot, but he said, "Look, no rush. If you can't get to it all along with this week's work until the weekend, It's ok. I understand. Any questions, just lemme know. I'm canceling history and geography today and tomorrow so you can have some more time to catch up with everything, but you gotta work during that time, understand? And SHH! Don't tell anybody why I canceled history and geography."

"Our lips are sealed. Thank you, Mr. Mosely." John said.

"Thank you so much," I added

"Ok, that's enough jibber-jabbering with me. Go get started on all that work."

"On our way!"

I said as we both darted back to our desks.

At the end of the day, we had completed a lot of the work, but there was still plenty to go. We were bogged down with books, but I had convinced John that we should go see my grandmother and let her know I was ok and tell her I missed her before we went back to his house.

"What if your mother is there, though?"

"Then we'll just leave."

"Sounds good to me. I sure don't wanna see her," John said matter-of-factly with his tone

"Me either"

When we got there, Grandma opened the door, and I wasn't sure if she was happier to see John or me. She hugged each of us equally.

"Just LOOK at you! New clothes and shoes and everything! Oh, John, your parents are just too much! You have to thank them for me."

"Here we go again," John said, rolling his eyes. I kicked him lightly in the calf muscle.

"David!" Grandma said

"It's ok, I'm just playing"

"You be a good boy, you hear?" Grandma said, "And I mean all the time when you're there. Are you going back there tonight?"

"Yeah. We've got a ton of work to catch up on. We're gonna do it together at his place, and I'm gonna sleep over again."

"Ok. I miss you, and I love you both. Oh! Wait! Don't leave yet!" and she moved quickly to her bedroom, pulled two new Hot Wheel cars from her purse, and gave one to each of us.

I got them today at the store for you. You have a Hot Wheels race track, don't you, John?

"Yeah, I DO! This car is gonna go SO fast on it! Thank you, Grandma!" And he gave her a hug.

"Ok, you two get going and do all that homework. Love you!"

"Love you too."

We both said back. When we got to the porch, we tore our cars out of the packaging and spun the wheels. We threw the packaging in the empty barrels in front of the house from when they collected the trash earlier and went on our way back to John's house.

When John's dad got home, he did indeed see us working: John at his desk and me on the living room rug, lying on my belly with books strewn about.

"Hey, handsome! " John's dad said as he came through the door with a very large brown bag, the size of at least three grocery store bags. He put it in the living room closet, shut the door, and said, "None of your business. It's a surprise for this weekend if you boys are good. And NO peeking. Got it?"

"Yes, sir, "and I reached out my hands for a hug. Instead, he picked me up and swung me around. John came to the living room.

"Hi, handsome number two," he said, picking John up and swinging him the same way."
Why are you two still in your school clothes and not your play clothes?

"You said to get right to work when we got home, so we did."

"Well, you're on the right track for that weekend surprise, I'll tell you that. After dinner, I want you to bring all your work to me so I can check it over. Both of you. If you need help, let me know. Now get back to work 'til mom calls you to the table.
"I got the you know what. Two of them, actually."

"TWO?! Wow."

"Well, I had to get one for David too. It wouldn't be fair if he had to watch John use his."

"You are so crazy."

" Me? Look at you, getting all those clothes…"

"ME?! You told me to do it!" John's mom said, laughing.

"You know I can hear you, right?" I said into the doorway to the kitchen where they were talking."

"You get to that schoolwork, or you're grounded, and no surprise this weekend. Move it."

"Leaving!"

I said as I ran back to my work on the living room floor. I wasn't about to be stuck with doing schoolwork on the weekend and miss out on the surprise. My hand was getting writer's cramp, but I pushed onward.

More laughing from the kitchen.

After dinner, John showed Dad how much he had done. He checked it over, gave a couple of suggestions, and said.

"Alright, keep going. How about you?" I showed him mine, and he said some of the same things about a couple of my answers. Then he continued with, "How about your math?

"I didn't do it yet. Was saving it for last. I hate math."

Ok, get your book and some paper and let's go to the kitchen table. Numbers are my life. They have to be.

"Why? I asked?'

"I'm in insurance. Insurance is a whole lot of numbers."

A lot of the work I had to do was fractions. John's dad was patient and explained the rules of multiplying and dividing fractions again and again as we went through the problems, no matter how many times I got frustrated and wanted to quit. When I started getting really tired, he said

"Ok, that's enough for tonight."

And I took my books back to the living room and put them on the chair our new sneakers were parked in front of.

We walked to John's room to see how he was doing and found him asleep at the desk.

"John, wake up and put your books by the door. You boys can have a second dessert."

"A second dessert?" I asked, puzzled

"Are you going to stand there arguing with a father's good nature, or are you going to stuff another cupcake into your face?"

"And he made a silly cross-eyed face." We both laughed, grabbed a cupcake, and brought it to the living room.

"No, No, No, not in here; you know better, John. Get yourself and Dave a plate and eat them at the table like a civilized human being. "

"But I'm not civilized!" John said while making monkey noises.

"We know. Act like it anyway. Pretend." Mom said.

"Ha ha! " John sarcastically laughed while getting us plates from the cabinet.

We ate our cupcakes, cleaned up the crumbs, and put the dishes in the dishwasher.

I got the cascade detergent out and poured some in the reservoir and started the dishwasher.

"Dad, Dave did my chore, the dishwasher again."

"You're gonna complain that your brother did your chore? Are you sick?"

"No," he said sarcastically again," It just means if we're gonna be fair about the chores, what will I have to do since he did mine?" You can vacuum the living room on Thursday."

"Ok."

"Alright, go get into your pajamas and come watch some TV. You still have a little while before bed."

"Did my mother call you?"

I asked, thinking about the diametrically opposed environments of John's house with people who care and my house where only grandma does.

"No, why? Was she supposed to?"

"No, I was just wondering."

And I retreated to the bedroom with John to put on our pajamas. We got them on and went to the bathroom to brush our teeth.

We came out and crashed against Mom and Dad on the couch as usual. After watching some shows, we started to conk out and before we got too far asleep, John's parents got us up off them and our feet onto the floor so we could walk to the bedroom. John's mom tucked him in, and his dad tucked me in.

"You did very well with your homework tonight, math included. You can do it; you proved it."

"I did it because you had to keep repeating the directions."

"Maybe so, but it was more than that. And you didn't need my help with the rest of your homework. I'm proud of you."

"What did you say?"

"You heard what I said."

"Yeah, I did. It's just no one ever says that about my work unless it's spelling, reading or art."

Well, you worked hard, and that's something to be proud of, right?"

"I guess…"

"Then shut up and go to sleep" he joked, crossing his eyes and then smiling and kissing me on the head. "Night, buddy."

"Wait!" I said as he started to get up, holding my hands out for a hug. I got it. And then he got up and turned off the light, and left along with Mom, saying, "Remember, no peeking in the closet."

And closing the door as they went. A few minutes after he left, I asked John

"You asleep?"

"No, why?"

"Can I come to your bed to talk to you?"

"Yeah."

I pulled the covers down, ran over to John's bed, and sat down on the side of it.

June 1981 - Sixth Grade

The next day was gym day. I realized I didn't have my gym shirt and shorts with me; they were still at my house.

"It's ok. John's kit from last year should fit you. Third drawer in the dresser. And take a towel from the hall closet." John's mom said when I told her about it.

We showered and ate breakfast as usual, and we went to the table to get some breakfast. English muffins and jam, along with a bowl of cocoa puffs cereal, waited for us.

We sat down and devoured the breakfast.

"You boys need to get home right away again after school today to keep working on getting caught up. Hear me?" Dad said.

"Yes, sir," we both said through mouthfuls of cocoa puffs.

After getting our last bites in, we got into our sneakers and dad said

"Remember what I said." as a reminder

"But Dad, we are gonna have a lot of time to finish catching up in school today. What if we only have a little bit to do, and it won't take long to do it?"

"Then you'll still come home right after school. No exceptions, and that's my final word. Got it?"

John put his head down and said

"Yes, sir,"

"Now get to school. Both of you."

We walked slowly, and I asked John

"Why were you trying to make him say it was ok to come home later?"

"We promised Juan we'd go over to his house after school today, remember?"

"Oh, yeah."

"Well, maybe we can go over tomorrow when we're all done catching up."

"Wouldn't be fair to him after we promised."

"You're right, but still…"

"Dad will be ok with it. He always talks about how important it is to keep your word." John said, closing the subject.

The morning was filled with all of the usual schoolwork plus a little more catchup work for us anytime we finished the day's lessons early. Then came gym time.

Gym, today meant we were to wait on the benches while Mr. Quage said a few words before we did anything. He had a box with him.

"Today, boys, we are going to be changing some things around here. From now on, you're not just going to come in here and pick just any locker to put your stuff into. You'll be assigned a locker, and you will use that locker every time. You will also lock up your stuff not only when you leave but when you shower as well.

He started passing out combination locks to every boy, then continued talking.

"If you forget your combination, you can come to me; I have the combination for each lock I am giving you. The way to unlock it is like this: One full turn to the left and then around to your number, two full turns to the right and then around to your number and around to the left to your number, and the lock clicks open. You will take the lockers that are directly behind you. You will not skip any lockers. Take them one after the other in line. Yes, Mr. Quage, if you understand. "

"Alright, suit up so we can play some basketball."

"Should have done that a long time ago, using the locks, so Eggy wouldn't be able to mess with people's stuff."

John said as he, Juan, Danny and I all picked lockers next to each other

"Yeah, that's right," I agreed.

The basketball game went the way they usually did. Danny was the captain of one team, and Luis Matos was the captain of the other, so I was on Danny's team, the skins, so our team took off our shirts and left them on the bleachers outside the boundary line of the gym basketball court. Eggy and his friends made fun of my miserable attempts to dribble and all my missed shots the few times I did get the ball passed to me at the right moment where I could take a shot.

After the game, a lot of boys had forgotten their combinations already, but Mr. Quage was ready with his clipboard in hand with the list of combinations to help the boys who forgot theirs, as promised.

After we showered, Eggy and his friends were up to their usual tricks, snapping towels at us as we were trying to open our locks.

"Quit it!" John said.

"OWWW!" I said as one snap hit particularly hard against my thigh.

"What's wrong? Can't open your lock because you're too busy playing with each other's butts, faggots?"

Eggy said while laughing and getting another snap in with the towel, this time right near John's crotch.

"You shouldn't be talking about faggots, remember yesterday, so close to each other, up each other's asses." Juan said, and the entire locker room erupted in laughter, including John and I.

'It's ok, he won't be able to fuck anything with that tiny dick," Danny said, pointing at Eggy's crotch. Now, there was so much loud, echoing laughter that before Eggy could have his revenge on Danny, the noise brought Mr. Quage over.

"AY!!! He yelled. You boys stop fooling around and get dressed. Do you want detention? MOVE IT!!!"

The clinking and clanking of combination locks being unlocked and locker doors opening was the only sound in the locker room.

At dismissal, Mr. Shedruff kept Eggy and his friends by him while the rest of our class were able to go first and get out of the school's view before he would let them have their turn to go. He had been doing this on many days after school recently. Like Mr. Quage and his locks, he should have been doing it all along.

When we got to the school gate, John started walking in the opposite direction to his house.

"Hey, where you going?"

"To see Juan. He's got a hot wheels set too, remember, the one you gave him."

"I'm gonna go do my work. I don't wanna get in trouble. Gimme the house key."

He reached into his pocket, retrieved the key, and tossed it to me.

At 5:30, John finally walked into the house and past me on the living room rug, doing my catch-up work. He went straight to his room without a word. Mom and Dad were both home.

Dad called.

"John, get to the kitchen. Front and center."

John came out of his room and walked past me with a worried look on his face. I just kept doing my work.

"You were supposed to be home right after school today to do your homework. Where have you been?"

"Juan's house."

"You are grounded. You'll come home directly after school tomorrow. No dessert tonight or tomorrow night and no TV. If you don't come home right after school tomorrow, you'll be grounded for a week."

"But dad, we promised Juan, honest, we did. You always tell me how important it is to keep my word."

"Who is we when you say 'WE' promised him?"

"Dave. He was there."

"David, come here."

"Yes, sir," I said.

"What did you or John say to Juan yesterday about coming over."

"Well… he wanted us to come over yesterday, but we both told him we couldn't and that we had to do our catch-up work for the time we were gone on vacation."

"Is that all you said?"

"No, then we told him maybe tomorrow."

"Ok, thank you, David. Go back to your homework."

"Yes, sir," I said and went right back to it as he asked.

"So you said 'maybe' you would come over. That is not a promise because you didn't say you definitely would be there. And David came home right away to do his work like he was supposed to."

"But DAD!"

'No buts. You broke your word to me, saying you would come straight home after school to keep your word that you didn't really make to your friend. You are grounded. Now go to your room and do your work. I will be checking it later. Go on now."

"Dad, I didn't have that much left; I can get it done tonight and tomorrow; why does it matter so much that I get home right away after school to do it?"

"Because it's not about the work itself, it's about the importance of doing the things that are important before the things that are not as important, a lesson everyone needs to learn about life, young man. That's why. That's MY reason, and it might not be the same as your teacher's reason or reasons, but you WILL do as I say, even if you don't like the reason. Got it?"

"No, I don't 'got it', but whatever."

"Now you are grounded Saturday, too. It is no surprise for you, either. Only David will be able to get his surprise."

"I don't care. You can throw it away; I don't care," John said, tears on his cheeks. He stomped to his room and slammed the door.

"Slam your door like that again, and it will be Sunday, too, young man!"

A few minutes after John went to his room and dad came to the living room to sit and read the paper, I said, "Can I please talk to you?"

"Of course. Come here." I got up from the carpet and stood in front of him

"I want to tell you about something that happened yesterday. We didn't come home straight after school yesterday."

"Oh, really. Where did you go?"

"To my house so we could see my Grandma."

"Did you stay long?" John's dad asked, his eyebrows furrowing.

"No, sir. We only stayed a few minutes, I swear."

"OK. You are grounded, too. No dessert or TV tonight, and come straight home after tomorrow. Understand?"

"Yes, sir." I understand. It's just that…"

"What?"

"Well, see, grandma gave John and me Hot Wheels cars and remember what you said about parents doing nice things like that just because they know it brings joy to them to see how happy it makes the kids?"

"Yeah."

"Well, John wanted Juan to be happy 'cuz he knows Juan likes Hot Wheels. He wanted us to play with the new cars on Juan's set."

"Yes, ok, but John still broke his word to me. I can't just him do that and get away with it, right?"

"Right, sir."

"Ok, I will reduce his grounding down so it ends tomorrow night, but only if he apologizes for the way he talked to me. Sound good?"

"Yes, sir. There is something else too."

"There's more? Ok, spill it."

"Yesterday, Eggy and his friends were picking on John and me again."

"Oh, were they? What did they do?"

"They called us faggots, and they pushed us. I pushed Eggy back, and he fell down and knocked Carlos down, and Juan pushed someone who knocked another kid down when he fell."

"Is that all?"

"No, Danny said that we weren't the ones who were faggots because they were close enough to be up each other's asses."

"What did you do when he said that?"

"Laughed. Everybody on the playground did. There's more."

'Ok, go on."

"Today in gym class, after our shower, when we were trying to open our new combination locks we have to use on the lockers now, Eggy and his friends were snapping towels at us. He said we were too busy being faggots and touching each other's butts, and that's why we couldn't open our locks. Then Juan said he should remember about yesterday, when they were so close to each other they were up each other's asses. Then Danny said it didn't matter because he wasn't gonna be able to, um... you know... that word... anything with his tiny dick."

"Ok, and what happened then?"

"Everybody laughed, and that was it because Mr. Quage came over and told everybody to get dressed."

"Did you laugh?"

"Yes, sir, I did."

"Did you call them names or say anything else like Danny or Juan did?"

"No, sir."

"Well, yesterday, when you were defending yourself and John when they pushed you, that's understandable, especially after all you've been through with those bullies for so many years. And I know he started it with his terrible comments, but how do you think Eggy felt after what Danny and Juan said both days?"

"Bad."

"Because you've been through so much with them when they do it to you, right?

"Yeah. It hurts so much."

"Think about how much it must have hurt Eggy in the locker room when he was naked. How much he hurt inside because everybody was looking and pointing and laughing."

A tear rolled down my cheek.

"Yeah. It must have hurt a lot."

"You know it did."

"I'm so sorry for laughing. I won't do it again."

"I know you won't. You told me that you didn't join the others and say anything bad to them even though you probably wanted to. You're still you. "

"Huh? What do you mean?"

"You're still you in here" and he put his hand on my chest over my heart.

"You know how much it hurts when others say and do mean things to you, and you didn't say things to hurt Eggy like your friends did.

But, you're still grounded with John until tomorrow night for laughing at Eggy when others were picking on him."

"Ok, sir."

"And you'll apologize to Eggy?"

"Wait, what? NO! He will hurt us even more if we apologize."

"Wait, you don't understand. You'll apologize by telling your friends not to say or do mean things back to Eggy because you know it doesn't help anything. It will only make things worse and keep the cycle going. Defend yourself if they try to hurt you, but don't say or do things like they do to make things worse because it doesn't help you or them. Understand?"

"Yes, sir. Can I please ask you something?"

"Sure."

"What would happen if I went home to my house instead of coming here?"

"You mean, what would happen with your grounding?"

"Yes, sir."

"Well, then I would have to call your grandma and tell her about it, and it would make her feel bad that you weren't behaving and being your best self while you were here at our house, and she would ground you at your house. You can't escape consequences when you do something wrong, son. You have to pay for what you've done one way or another. Got it?"

"Yes, sir."

"Now let me ask you something. Why did you tell me everything you did?"

"Well, I told you about going to see grandma because it wasn't fair for John to get punished for not coming straight home when I didn't yesterday. I didn't want him to be grounded on Saturday because then I wouldn't enjoy whatever the surprise was if he wasn't there with me."

"What about the situation with Eggy? Why did you feel you had to tell me about that?"

"Because I knew it wasn't right to hurt him even though he hurt me so much so many times."

"And now you're both grounded together."

"Yeah, I felt bad because he really loves Hot Wheels, and he wanted to share his new one with Juan. Now he doesn't have to be all alone and sad while he's grounded because I can be with him."

"What are we gonna do with you two? Brothers till the end. Go tell your brother I want to see him right now so I can tell him he's only grounded till tomorrow night as long as he apologizes to me, or do you want to talk about something else and get that grounding reduced some more?"

'No sir. I'll get him."

John's mom was in the doorway, listening to most of what was said.

"Can you believe those two?" she asked.

"No, I can't, but I'm really proud of them, especially David. So mature for his age and being so brave and standing up for John and doing what was right?"

"Yeah, there's so much to be proud of there."

When I went into John's room, he had his head down on the desk. It was wet with his tears.

"John, Dad wants to talk to you."

"Get out. Leave me alone."

"He wants to talk to you about the grounding. You're not grounded till Saturday anymore."

He lifted his head off the desk and looked at me.

"What?"

"Yeah, it's only till tomorrow. Go apologize to him."

"What did you say to him?"

"It doesn't matter. Just go apologize to him, and your grounding will be over tomorrow night. Go now before he changes his mind. Oh, and I'm grounded with you."

"Wait, what?"

"I'll tell you about it later. Go apologize, PLEASE, so we can have our surprise on Saturday, or I'm gonna kick your ass."

John got up from his desk and left the room confused and shaking his head.

After dinner, we worked on our homework and showed it to Dad, and he helped me finish the catch-up work on math.

I respected John's dad even more now because I saw the reason that John was such a great friend and brother to me was because of what his dad and mom had taught him and expected of him. They helped make him the wonderful person he had always been to me, and I was very grateful for that. It wasn't all sunshine and apple pies at John's house; it was downs as well as ups and learning how to cope with whatever happened.

That night, when John's mom and dad came to tuck me in, my heart felt warmer than it had in a long time. I gave Dad an extra-long hug, too. After they left, I went over to John's bed to tell him what Dad and I had talked about.

We spent our grounding, missing dessert, reading mad magazines, and just enjoying being together.

I got all A's on my makeup work in every subject. Even math, which was the main factor in helping me cross the line with passing grades in everything for sixth grade.

We spent Friday after school going to see Grandma again and then ended the day at Juan's house, sharing our new Hot Wheels and using them on Juan's racetrack.

Saturday, John's dad presented us with our surprise: two model rockets. We learned about fuel, where to launch, trajectories, safety, and the most important thing of all:

Love.

June, 1981, Sixth Grade

The time that I spent at John's house had consumed most days. I only went home and stayed there one or two days a week, and usually only until Mother got home and started her usual behavior towards me, causing me to flee back to John's house.

John and I had decided to spend the afternoon on one particular day with Grandma at my house before heading to his.

I looked to see if Mr. Shedruff had Eggy and his friends with him, waiting for us to leave. Today, however, not only were they not there, but even Mr. Shedruff himself wasn't present. We tried to be careful, looking to see if they were off to the right side next to the gate as they usually were, and of course, that's where we found them. Eggy saw us and started moving toward us

"Come on," he said to the others.

Instead of going through the gate, we turned and ran toward the side entrance concrete staircase where children weren't allowed. We found it to be gone. They had removed the old, deteriorating concrete staircase and now it was just a steep grade, far too steep to go down by foot. We would tumble to the sidewalk below and be hurt for sure if we tried it. Now, with no teachers paying attention to this area because they were on the front side of the school participating in dismissal, we were trapped.

Eggy said, "Where you goin' baby fags?" and kicked me in the chest.

Luis Matos punched John in the face, landing a hit to his mouth, while the other Luis kicked at me on the ground.

I was somehow able to get to my feet, and Carlos ran at me to punch me in the face, but I was quicker, and I grabbed his wrist and swung him around toward the hill where the staircase used to be. He landed just past the top and slid all the way down to the street.

Eggy was going to town on John, punching him hard again and again, and I tried to get between them, but Luis Matos was able to get a kick to my stomach and knock me down before I could try and help John. They punched and kicked us again and again, yelling, "Who's got the tiny dick NOW faggots?" And Eggy stomped on John's ribcage three times as he lay on his side clutching his stomach in extreme agony.

When they felt like they had hurt us, they quit and ran off toward the front entrance.

We worked at getting ourselves to our feet, and I looked over the hill, and Carlos was gone, so I guessed he didn't get too badly hurt on the fall.

John was a mess, tears flowing from his eyes, one of them swollen shut, his nose looking broken, his mouth bleeding. He was clutching his side and flinching and crying out in pain with every breath he took.

John looked just as surprised to see my condition as I was looking at his.

"We have to get to my house," I insisted. "Grandma can help us."

John nodded his head, trying not to speak because of the pain.

When we got there, Grandma said, "OH NO! Not again! John! Oh, look at you! Both of you come on," and she took us to the bathroom where she started pouring water over two cloths and wiping John and my wounds, me with her right hand, John with her left.

She retreated to the kitchen to get ice for our many swollen facial areas, bruises already becoming prominent.

After that, she said, "John, put the ice pack down and take off your shirt. You too, David." We both unbuttoned our shirts and removed them.

John's ribs on his right side were turning a scary shade of purplish red, but my ribs weren't much better. She felt them very gently, and John screamed in pain.

"Ok, you boys, get some ice on those faces. John, I'm gonna call your dad at work and let him know what happened. He gave me his work number when we were on the trip in case I ever needed to reach him there. Your mom, too."

She went to the address book on the table by the phone.

After a few minutes of explaining, Grandma hung up the phone.

"He's coming to pick you up in a few minutes," Grandma said, telling us.

"Go sit on the couch. We did, and she came to sit between us, rubbing our backs and comforting us."

John's father arrived quickly, knocking furiously on the door.

Grandma opened it. He saw us on the couch and exclaimed

"OMIGOD!! I can't believe this… Boys, are you alright?! Are there more injuries? Are your legs ok?"

"My legs are ok." John said.

"My right thigh hurts. One of them kicked me hard there," I said

John's dad, a mess of emotions from sadness to anger, said, "Grab your shirts. Don't put them on. Let's go."

Grandma said "Boys, call me later to let me know you're ok. I love you!" we just nodded back and left after John's dad, his stride very fast down the hallway and out to the car.

"Get in."

dad said. We both got into the back seat.

A few moments later, we were in the school parking lot. John's dad got out and opened the back door on his side of the car.

"Let's go."

He made his way to the main entrance and rang the bell. A buzzer sounded, and we marched our way down the hallway, trying to keep up with John's dad with the pain of our injuries trying to slow us down. He led us into the main office and straight to Mr. Shedruff's door, who sat at his desk doing paperwork.

"Excuse me Mr. Shedruff, we need to have a talk, and we need to have it right now.

Mr. Shedruff, surprised at our sudden entrance, got up to shake John's dad's hand, and then, seeing the state John and I were in, he exclaimed, "My God! Get to Nurse Booth's office!"

'No boys, stay right here. Mr. Shedruff I want you to look at them because you HAVE to right now. You can't just turn your head like you and the teachers do when the kids get even one step outside the school ground boundary, ignoring what Eggy and the other bullies do, seeing them hurt other kids, and doing nothing. John told me that's what you do. Well, not this time, Mr. Look at them.

Mr. Shedruff only kept his head down, looking at his desk.

"I SAID LOOK AT THEM!" John's dad yelled, his voice vibrating the wall.

He looked up.

"Look at this!" dad said, gently turning John and me so he could see not only our bruised, swollen, and bleeding faces but also our deeply bruised ribcages.

"Do you condone THIS?"

"No, of course not, but I…"

"Safety of the kids is your job, do you DENY IT?!"

"No, of course not, it's one of my many jobs as principal…"

"You'd do best to remember it's the most IMPORTANT job you do, Mr. Principal! Do you HEAR me?!"

"Yes, sir, I do. Please calm down. "

"I will NOT calm down when my son and another boy I care about, like my own son, have had THIS happen to them on YOUR watch. No, I won't."

Mr. Shedruff lowered his head again.

"Now, from now on, you or another teacher will stand guard at that gate every day at arrival and dismissal and make sure this doesn't happen again and don't you dare give me any high and mighty regulations about what's outside the school grounds. If you can see anyone within your field of vision doing something they shouldn't, you will make yourself into the educator who cares about children you claim to be, and you will stop them."

"And what about when they are out of eyesight, up the street."

"You and I had an understanding a few months back after John came home with a busted lip, and you said you were going to keep the troublemakers with you until John or Dave or any other kids they target have had the chance to leave safely. That obviously didn't happen this time."

"No, I was in a meeting today at that time."

"Well, from now on, you are to see to it that you or someone else does it from now on, and you will have a guard on that front gate. If you don't, I will be contacting the school district and my lawyer, I promise you. The boys will tell me if you have done as I've asked and if you skip even one day, I will be back, and believe me, you won't like it if I do return. You are goddamn lucky I don't beat you until you look like they do, but I'm a peaceful man. If these boys or any of their friends look like this when they get home after school ever again, god help you because I assure you I will no longer be a peaceful man. What the boys look like right now will be just the start of what I do to you. We are going to the hospital now, and the bill will not be going on my medical insurance; I will be having the bill forwarded to the school. Have a nice day, Mr. Principal. Remember your number one job. Let's get you to the hospital, boys."

And John's Dad stomped his way down the hall and outside, opening the car door for us once we got there.

Now we understood why Mr. Shedruff suddenly took an interest in keeping Eggy and his friends next to him at the end of the day so frequently lately. We didn't utter a word for some time. The air was heavy with silence, only the sound of the engine and the bumps in the road cutting through the silence.

Then John's dad finally spoke.

"I am sorry you had to see me like that, boys. It's just that this has gone on for far too long, just too many years, and I gave him a chance to do something productive about it, and he failed.

I'm sorry I lost my temper, but the one thing I cannot abide is a child needlessly hurt when it can be prevented. Are you feeling more pain?

"Yes, Dad. My ribs are really bad. And my stomach," he said, tears silently falling."

"I'm hurting, but I've been worse," I said.

"We'll get you patched up soon. We're almost to the hospital."

We were at the hospital for a long time that night, getting X-rays and CAT scans. While we were waiting for the results, John paced the room again and again, still red faced with fury over what Eggy and his friends had done to us.

The doctor arrived with X-rays and pictures from the CAT scans and said, "Dave's nose is broken, and so is the orbit of his left eye, the bone that surrounds it, and he's got a cracked rib on his right side. John's nose is fractured, too, and he has four cracked ribs and an inflamed spleen. Now you're going to have to keep a close eye on him, and if the pain in his abdomen gets worse or he looks flushed or pale or has cold sweats, get him back to the hospital right away. It's gonna be a rough next few days for them. Those boys you told me about, you need to press charges against their parents to stop them from doing this ever again."

"Oh, believe me, they won't do it again. I already took care of that with the principal. He's gonna look a lot worse than they do if they ever look like this again."

After receiving the discharge papers, we went to the hospital parking lot, and John's dad said

"You want to stay with us again tonight, David?"

"Yes, sir. Please."

'Of course."

We parked on the street near John's house, and John's mom, seeing us as we walked in, said, "Oh dear GOD! No! No! No! Are they alright?"

"Sure, for almost having a ruptured spleen and four cracked ribs, that's what John's got. David's got a broken nose and his eye socket bone.

"Oh, NO! Get to the couch and sit."

"I'm gonna call Grandma," I said.

"Good idea. She must be worried something fierce after seeing what you two looked like earlier."

While I called Grandma and told her about our injuries and that we were ok, John's dad told Mom what had happened at the school when he went to talk to Mr. Shedruff. After I got off the phone, I sat back down on the couch with John, who was crying silently. Rivulets dripped onto his shirt.

"There's macaroni and cheese casserole in the oven. I can warm it up again if you're hungry."
Mom said, looking us over with concern.

"No, thank you," I said

John just kept silently crying.

Mom sat down next to John on the couch and gently put his head on her chest, and he started bawling like I had never seen him do before.

"It hurts soooo m-m-much, Mom. Make it stop, Mom, please! Make it stop!"

She stroked his head gently.

"John, let's get you to bed. Come on."

"No, Mom, NOOO. I'm scared, Mom!"

"You're safe. It's over."

"But what if something happens to my spleen?"

"We will get you to the hospital as fast as we can go. We'll call an ambulance if we have to. Don't think negatively, though, John; you're going to be ok. We are all going to make sure you are."

Mom helped John take off his shirt, pants, and socks and, seeing the ace bandage wrap around his ribs, didn't even bother to get him into his pajamas. She just pulled the covers down and had him get into bed. She gently pulled the covers over him and stayed with him. Lying next to him in the bed and stroking his face and hair.

'My beautiful boy. Why did they have to hurt you so badly? It's ok. Mom's here. I love you."

"I love you too, Mom."

He started crying hard but had to stop because of the pain.

In the living room, John's dad said, "David, you're going to have to help him through this. He's gonna have a tough time. Eggy and his friends haven't done nearly as much to John as they did to you over the years, but every time they have hurt him before, it hasn't been like this, not this bad, but he always has a really hard time with it emotionally every time. Things affect him deeply and change him. He gets distant and doesn't really want us to be with him. He's not going to be the same for a while, and he's gonna need you to be strong and help him."

"I know," I said. "I know what he's going through."

"Yes, if anyone knows, you do. You need to keep an eye on him tonight, too. If it looks like he's running a fever or he's in more pain, you need to tell us right away."

"Yes, sir, I promise I will.

"And you are to tell us if YOU have any unusual pain or other symptoms too. Got It?"

"Yes, sir."

"I love you. I'm sorry that so many things like this happen. I wish I could just wave a wand and make it all go away, but I can't. I get so frustrated that I can't. That's why I lost it in Mr. Shedruff's office, I guess. I know it's impossible to prevent every instance of bullying like this, but when it IS preventable, and it isn't prevented, that just sends my blood boiling."

"Yeah, I know what you mean."

"Ok, go be with your brother."

"Yes, sir."

And he gave me the gentlest half hug around the shoulders he could and sent me on my way to John's room.

"Hey, John," I said.

"Hey," he weakly replied. Mother was silently crying, her tears running off the side of her face and onto the bed.

"Dad said I should be with him," I told mom.

"Ok. Let me know if he needs me." She said and left us to be alone.

"Can I sit with you?"

"Sure. Are you ok?" he asked.

"Yeah. Not as bad as you this time."

"I…I was really scared. Scared for you. I was trying to get to you so many times to help you, but I couldn't," John told me.

"It was the same for me. I couldn't get to you. I'm so, so sorry. I tried so hard. I threw Carlos down that hill, though, where the stairs used to be."

"I know. If he was still up there for the whole thing, we would've been hurt so much more."

"I don't know where the strength came from, but all of a sudden, I had it, and I used it."

"Like the Incredible Hulk, huh?'

"Yeah," and I pretended to tear my shirt, flexing my muscles and growling like the Hulk.

John laughed a little but he had to stifle it because it sent a jolt of pain.

"Hey want me to read Charlie and the Chocolate Factory out loud to you?"

"I'm not THAT bad off. I can still read, you know."

"I know. I just felt like reading out loud."

"Ok, go ahead."

I grabbed his copy of the book from the bookshelf over his bed's headboard and started reading through my one good eye until I got halfway through the book. John's dad came to the door and gave me a thumbs-up, and I gave him one back.

Later, he tried to get up to go to the bathroom, but he was having a lot of trouble moving to get into a proper sitting position without pain flaring and stopping him.

"I'll help you stand" and I put my shoulder under his and helped him get to the bathroom. He almost keeled over from the pain when we got to the bathroom, but I held him steady by the shoulders while he peed. He lost his balance a bit and peed on his underwear. He leaned on me the same way for the walk back. When we got back to his bedroom, helped him to the chair by the desk. Before he sat, I said

"Don't sit." And I got clean underwear out of his dresser. Then I pulled his pee-stained underwear down to his ankles and said, "Sit."

He did, and I pulled the wet underwear off his feet, put the clean pair over his feet, and told him to stand again.

I pulled his underwear up to his waist and guided him back to bed, gently placing the covers back over him.

John's dad was back in the doorway.

"That was really something to see."

"What's that?" I asked

"You helping him to the bathroom and back and changing his underwear."

"No big deal. Grandma did it for me a lot, so that's how I know what to do," and I walked past Dad to toss the dirty underwear in the laundry basket.

"He never would allow us to help him like that. He's so damn independent. I swear, you two really are brothers."

John's dad said, a tear falling from his eye

"He's gonna be ok," I said. "I'm going to make sure he is. He saved my life twice. I owe him."

"Twice? I know about the one time with the fever… but… twice?"

"Maybe I'll tell you about it sometime," I assured him.

"Ok, yeah, I'd like to hear that story."

I went back to reading Charlie and the Chocolate Factory until John fell asleep, and then I got up to turn the light off. I stayed with John all night in his bed and calmed him down every time he woke up whimpering from the pain when he moved around. I checked him for a temperature every half hour or so by placing my hand on his forehead. I did the same thing the next night, not getting a wink of sleep either night. I was determined that he was going to be ok, and I wasn't missing a moment to make sure. John's mom and dad kept coming in to check on him too.

Danny and Juan both called John to tell him that Eggy, the two Luises, and Carlos had all been expelled from the school for good. It was the last straw for each of them, so we would never see any of them again. I couldn't help but wonder if Dad's speech to Mr. Shedruff might have been part of the reason. It could have been that the school year was ending soon anyway, so they kicked them out for all of us to have some peace for the close of the school year.

Other kids who followed Eggy and his gang were watched closely by Mr. Shedruff, and there was a teacher or Mr. Shedruff guarding the gate in the morning and at dismissal every day without fail.

Over the next few days, I nursed John back to health, steadying him when he walked and helping him to the bathroom.

After a couple days in bed, John's mom came to his room, asking

"Do you want to try and take a shower today?"

"John winced and said "No"

"Your dad can help you to shower if you need it"

"The pain is just so bad still It hurts so much to stand for more than a couple minutes.

"Ok. David, talk to him and maybe you can get him to change his mind."

"I will" I promised

A little while later, I said

"Look, I've been helping you to get to the bathroom and back. I didn't let you get hurt worse, right?"

"Right"

"Ok, so I can help you with the shower, k? I will be careful so you don't get hurt, k?"

John thought about it for a couple seconds and said "Ok, but if it hurts too much I need you to help me get back to bed, k?"

"Of course" I replied.

I walked John to the shower, and took off his ace bandage from his ribs. He wailed in pain when the bandage was completely removed.

"It's ok, I've got you."
And I helped him lean on me after helping him take his underwear off. He got into the tub, and I Held him by the thighs while turning on the water. I tried to hole him steady from outside

the tub, but it wasn't working> He kept wincing in pain and losing his balance.

"I can't do it. I need to get out."

"Wait, no, I have an idea." I stripped and joined him in the tub so I could have him put more of his weight on me. I held him steady with one arm, while gently scrubbing his back and chestwith a soapy washcloth. I handed him the washcloth so he could wash his privates and butt. I put some pert shampoo on his head and srcubbed his hair so he wouldn't have to raise his arms and make his rib and abdomen pain worse.

We both got out of the tub and John's mom came to the door and knocked. I wrapped my towel around my waist and opened the door.

"Everything ok?"

"Yeah, he's ok."

"I don't know how you got him to do it but I'm grateful you did."

"I had to get in the shower with him to hold him steady enough so it wouldn't hurt so bad."

"True brother and a great son. I love you." And she kissed me on my wet hair.

"I love you too"

"How are you, baby? You ok?"

"Yes mom. I'm ok."

And she kissed John on his wet head too as we made our way back to John's room to change into some fresh underwear.

John's belly was ok again after a couple more days of rest, but as always, after altercations with Eggy and his friends, the full healing of his injuries took longer. It takes some serious time to heal from broken or cracked ribs and a broken nose, and this time was no exception.

I never did tell John's dad the story of how John saved my life the first time, pulling me down from the wall at school when I was about to jump. It was ok enough that dad knew John cared enough to do it.

Before long, we were preparing for upcoming summer adventures, and John was back to his energetic self, and so was I.

John and I didn't know it yet, but this was about to be the greatest summer of our lives.

June 1981, Summer Break

It was nearing the end of our time in elementary school, and that meant new school choices for middle school. Mother decided that I would not be going to either of the two public middle schools in the area and that instead, I would be going to a Catholic school for seventh and eighth grade. Since she didn't have the money to pay, she claimed hardship as the school accepted a select few kids on a reduced tuition basis each year. That meant she would still have to shell out money for tuition that she didn't have, and, as usual, she tapped our family friend Frank for the money.

She promised him that this time she was really serious about possibly taking him up on his offer for us to come and live with him even though, as usual, she had no intention of following through on her promise and, of course, never did.

Mother and I received a tour of the school, and it looked nice enough for a school in a very old building. You could smell the history in the building materials the school was constructed from. The principal and vice principal were both nuns, but the 7th-grade teacher was just a civilian teacher who seemed really nice while we were on tour.

John had said he wasn't sure which school he would be going to, but we never really pursued the thought of it much, past casual conversation a couple of times, and we didn't really give it a second thought when there were far more important things to think about, like what we were going to be doing for summer.

One afternoon, when John's dad came home, he walked into the house and said

"Boys, come out to the car; I need you to help unload some stuff."

We didn't even bother to put sneakers on; we just followed Dad out to the car like puppy dogs in our socks. Dad opened the hatch and we saw that it was packed full of all kinds of things.

"Wow! What IS all this stuff?" John asked

"Well, remember Matt, Thomas, and Mark? Their parents said we should go join them camping this summer, and I talked to them on the phone a few days ago and we are going camping with them this weekend."

"YAAAAYYY!" John and I both cheered.

We unloaded bags of stuff and other things not in bags, like a camp stove in a box and some tents. There also was a new large cooler and some rolled-up sleeping bags.

We helped Dad bring all the stuff inside and found that Dad had bought us new swimsuits and swim goggles. There were also two sets of flippers.

"Why did you buy flippers? You got us flippers last time we were there?"

"Oh, they're not for you. Remember, they only had one set of flippers of their own last time. I figured I'd get some extra fins so you can all have them and not have to share."

"Always being kind thinking of others." Mom said, giving Dad a kiss on the cheek as he passed her with the jumbo cooler in his hands.

The next morning arrived, and it was the last day of school in our old school, forever.

We didn't do much except clean out our desks and help Mr. Mosely pack boxes of things to put away in storage for summer. With it being the last day, there was to be no school lunch, so we brought our lunch boxes. I had to borrow one of John's old Peanuts lunch boxes used on days like this when no school lunch was served. He rocked a Star Wars lunch box, as he was a serious Star Wars fan. I liked it too, but I was always more of a Star Trek fan, so we, of course, always argued about which was better.

We said our goodbyes to Juan and Danny, who both were going to the public middle school next year. We would see each other soon, we assured each other and went on our way.

When we got home, we packed enough clothes and supplies for a week, and we stayed up late planning and talking about all the things we were going to do on our camping trip.

"Where are we going to go to the bathroom when we're camping?" I asked John's dad

'Well, we're not going THAT far into the wilderness. Remember, there were bathrooms on the side of the lodge, and we're gonna be off to the left dirt road further down, in the campsite, so there are probably bathrooms there. You won't be poopin' in the woods, don't worry."

Saturday morning came, and John's alarm went off early. It was 5:00 am, and we were both still too tired to wake up.

"Up and at 'em, boys! We need to shower, eat breakfast, and be on the road in an hour. Let's go!" John's mom yelled

We ignored her. A few minutes later, John's dad came in, pulled the covers down, and picked me up, throwing me over his shoulder as he did so, tickling my ribs and belly while he walked to the bathroom and put me in the tub. I giggled like a boy half my age as he found every ticklish spot on my ribs and abdomen. He turned the shower water on and got me soaking wet while I was still wearing my pajamas. John got up to see what was happening and went to the bathroom door, laughing and pointing at me getting socked from the shower. Mom was laughing so hard at the door as well.

"It's gonna be THAT kind of trip; I can see it now…" she said, giggling along with John.

"You two get a move on, or you're next!" John ran out to the living room to escape, but he was no match for Dad. Dad picked him up and threw him over his shoulder, too, tickled him, and dropped him in the tub with me. Now, Mom was back at the bathroom door and laughing even harder.

"You wanna be next?"

Dad said to Mom, moving toward her

"Don't you DARE!" she said, moving backwards slowly

"Then come on, let's go make breakfast."

And they retreated to the kitchen while we took off our wet pajamas and underwear, leaving them in a heap on the floor. John got in the shower, and I brushed my teeth at the sink, and then we switched places as usual.

"Put those wet pajamas into the dryer when you're done!"

John's mom yelled from the kitchen

"Ok," I said with a mouthful of toothpaste.

After we got dressed and had breakfast, we packed the car, and we were on our way at 7:15.

Upon arrival at the campsite, we saw our friends, and we all high-fived each other.

"We reserved a spot for you right here with us," Matt and Thomas's dad said. "We'll help you get set up. It'll go faster that way. Come on, boys, let's get to it."

By the time we had set up, it was very late in the day, so we all went to the lodge restaurant for a late dinner and then came back to sit at some nearby picnic tables to talk, drink soda and beer, and watch the night sky get darker and darker so we could see the bright stars. It was beautiful. We listened to the crickets chirping away as we talked about what was to come tomorrow. Later, we found the camp bathrooms and showers and made our final pit stop for the day. We went back to our tents, took off our clothes, put on pajamas, and got into our sleeping bags.

I had a tent with John, John's parents had one, our 3 friends had their own tent, and Matt and Thomas's parents had theirs.

"This is so cool," John said.

Then, in the quiet, we started hearing sounds that made both of us a little scared. Each time, Thomas would pipe up and tell us what the noise was.

We heard a hoot.

"That was an owl."

He said

We heard something scamper up a tree.

"That's a squirrel."

We heard a flutter

"That's a bird."

We heard what sounded like footsteps coming toward our tent.

Mark didn't say anything.

My pulse started to race as the footsteps were slowly inching closer.

"What's that?!" John said nervously, too afraid to move.

Thomas still remained quiet.

'Thomas! What IS that?!" I said.

Suddenly, our tent was falling down all around us, and we started screaming in terror.

"That's my brother making your tent fall down." Thomas said before laughing hysterically.

We crawled out from under and everyone was up out of their sleeping bags and laughing.

"Camping initiation!" John's dad said while laughing

"Yup, every kid's gotta go through it!"

Matt and Thomas's dad added, laughing and high-fiving our dad and the boys.

"Alright, help them get their tent set back up so we can all get some shuteye."

Matt and Thomas's dad told the boys.

We finished a little while later and eventually got to sleep under the stars, listening to the sounds around us and not afraid of them anymore.

The next morning, the moms were busy at work making breakfast on the camp stoves.

At the table, the dads were talking. We all joined them in our pajamas.

"Boys, we're gonna go fishing today," John's dad said while pointing at Matt and Thomas's dad. "Do you wanna join us?

"Naw, fishing's boring. We're gonna go hiking," Matt replied.

"Ok, make sure you bring your canteens and a roll of masking tape to mark trees in case you go off the trail. Matt, you brought your watch and compass, right?"

Matt and Thomas's dad said, "Yes, Dad."

"You look at the time on your watch and the position of the sun in the sky before you go. Take a towel in case you go swimming. You drink water every half hour. If you run out, you get more water within a half hour before you keep going. Before you leave, go in the cooler and put two sandwiches in each of your knapsacks' front pockets with some ice. Back here to check in and 12:30. Got all that?"

"Yes, dad."

"Ok, go on over to the camp bathroom and brush your teeth." John's dad said.

We all rummaged around in our knapsacks, pulled out our toothbrushes and toothpaste, and took off toward the bathroom.

When we got back to the table, breakfast was ready. The moms made us scrambled eggs, serving them on our metal camp plates. We ate as quickly as we could so we could get started on our hike.

We changed into tee shirts and our swimsuits and then filled up our canteens, took a trail map from a holder at the trail entrance, shoved sandwiches into the front pocket of our knapsacks, threw them on our backs, and started on our way.

"We gotta find some good small sticks on the trail for a school project. " Matt said.

"School project? School is done for summer."

"It's for next year. They want us to do a project about something we did during the summer. We're gonna make small rafts from sticks and twigs we found here." Thomas said.

We were on the trail awhile and we found some nice sticks. Every time John and I saw a good one, we handed it to Matt or Thomas.

"Ok, we're gonna detour off the path here," Matt said while he took his knapsack off and pulled out the masking tape. He tore off three pieces and placed them on a tree, making an arrow pointing in the direction of the way back.

As we walked off this beaten path, eventually, we came upon a stream. Matt marked another tree, and we kept going.

"We're going to see a waterfall soon." He informed us.

"Yeah, it's SO cool! Thomas said.

"Yeah, we can skinny dip there, and our parents won't catch us," Matt said

"That's right. They don't know about THIS place. We found it years ago," Mark added

After about 15 more minutes of walking, we got to the waterfall. It was a breathtaking sight, seeing the water tumbling down from up high and blasting the water below.

In seconds, our clothes were on the ground and we were climbing up a steep hill to some rocks close to the waterfall. The sound of it was so loud we could barely hear each other shout and cheer as we leaped off the rocks to the cold water below. We got out of the water and jumped again and again, sometimes getting close to where the waterfall was hitting the water.

When we got tired, we got out of the water, dried off, and laid out towels on the ground to sit on.

We let the sun warm us up, and we drank some water; then Matt and Thomas got the sticks out of their knapsacks along with some twine and scissors. They handed John and me some twine and then showed us how to twist the twine around and between the sticks to fasten them together.

"Our dad taught us how to do this. He learned it from some really old Indian who used to live near where he did when he was a kid."

"Let's play truth or dare," Matt said.

"Ok," we all said.

"Ok, I'll go first. Mark, truth or dare?"

"Can I know what the dare is gonna be before I decide?"

"Nope. You know the rules. Gotta decide without knowing."

"Shit. Ok, truth."

"Did you touch Katie's boob, and if you did, what did it feel like." Everybody stopped winding twine around the sticks so they could listen to Mark's answer."

"Yes, I did. It felt squishy, like when you hug mom."

"You're a LIAR," Thomas said

"Am not. How do YOU know?"

"Because Katie's chest is flatter than a piece of paper, so how would it be squishy?!"

We all laughed.

"Ok, Matt said, you know you have to do the dare because you lied."

"No way, I am not lying, and you can't prove it, so I'm not doing the dare."

"Alright, alright, somebody else take a turn."

"Ok, I got one," I said. "John, truth or dare?"

"Truth."

"Juan said you have a crush on Rosalinda. Is that true, and what would you do on a first date?"

John got red in the face and said, "Yes, I like Rosalinda, and if I went on a date, I would eat pizza with her."

"…And…?" Matt said, urging him to go on.

"…and we'd drink some coke…"

"…AND?!..." Thomas said

"…and I'd kiss her…"

Everyone giggled, and I said "OOOOOH, John's in LOOOOVE, and he wants to KISS her!!!" and then started laughing, which got everybody else laughing. John got up to come toward me but I was too quick, and I ran to the water and jumped in again. He quit chasing when he got to the water's edge and turned around, going back and sitting down, so I got out of the water and came back.

"Ok, My turn," Thomas said

"Matt, Truth or dare?"

"Truth."

"Did you really kiss Dana, and if you did, what was it like?"

"Yes, I really kissed Dana, and… she had this lip gloss on, so it tasted like bubblegum."

"…AND"

Mark said, "…and she liked it, and she kissed back…"

"…AND…" I said.

"…what, that's it…"

"Sean at school said he saw you do it, and he thinks you slipped her the tongue. Did you?"

"Well, yeah, a little."

"OHHHHHH!!!!" Everyone shouted in unison while clapping their hands.

"What was it like?" John asked.

"It was weird. Our tongues touched, and I felt funny."

"Where?" Thomas asked.

"None of your business where!" Matt said, and he grabbed Thomas by the hands.

"Somebody get his feet!" Matt called out for help.

I scrambled to grab Thomas's feet.

"NOOOO! What are you DOOOOOING?!!!" Thomas yelled, and with Matt leading the way, he said.

"Ok, on three, swing him way back and then forward into the water... One.... Two.... Two and a half.... two and three quarters... THREEEEE!" and we flung Thomas through the air and into the water. Everyone Joined in, jumping in and getting out before deciding to go up to the high rocks and jump in that way some more."

After some time in the water, we got out and we played one more round of truth or dare.

"Ok, one more." Thomas said, "Mark,"

"Hey, not fair! I already went."

"Doesn't matter. If someone calls your name, you have to do it. Besides, you lied earlier and didn't do the dare."

'I did NOT lie, but ok, whatever. Dare."

"Ok, you know that girls camp off to the left side of the lake across from the lodge?"

"You have to get their flag off the flagpole, and you can't use the rope to do it. You have to climb the ladder that's attached to the pole."

"WHAT?!!" Mark exclaimed.

"And you have to do it naked," Matt said.

"Oh, HELL NO! I'm not doing THAT, Fuck no, uh-uh!"

"Ok, ok, you can use the rope to bring it down, but you still have to do it naked. You can keep your sneakers on in case you need to run, but nothing else. Deal? Matt bargained, and he spit into his hand, holding it out in front of Mark to shake.

"Deal." Mark agreed, spitting into his own hand and shaking Matt's hand.

"Alright, you made the spit promise. That means you can't back out. If you do, it's 50 punches in the arm from all of us. We'll wait till the girls there are at lunch, and nobody is around outside.

We played in the water for another hour and then, getting hungry, decided to tear into some lunch. We all ate up both our sandwiches and then finished tying our small rafts. When they were complete, we packed our stuff, got dressed, and moved on to hike some more.

We hiked back to the spot where we went off the trail, taking our arrows off the trees as we went.

"Dad says it's important to respect nature and leave nature as we found it," Thomas said, tearing off one of the masking tape arrows from a very old tree and putting the tape pieces into his knapsack alongside our empty plastic sandwich bags.

A little while later we returned to where we diverted and got back on the trail. We headed back to our area at the campground. We saw the dads out in the water on a canoe with their fishing rods in the water, and we waved and shouted out to them. They waved back.

John's mom came over to us and said, "You boys, ok? You all drinking enough water?"

A crescendo of yes's filled the air.

"Did you eat?" Matt and Thomas's mom asked.

More yes's.

"John, how are your ribs?"

"They're ok. No pain"

John's ribcage wasn't bruised anymore, but his ribs still were hurting from time to time because ribs take a long time to heal.

We reloaded our canteens filled our knapsacks with more sandwiches and ice, and said, "Ok, we're gonna go hike some more."

"Alright," John's mom said. "Be careful out there."

This time, our walk took us over to the left side of the camp, where we could see some of the girls at the camp playing in and by the water. We kept going past the campgrounds to a bridge across the water to a small island in the middle of the lake. Then, a second bridge connected the island to the lakefront on the other side.

Getting onto the lakefront, we continued left a way to a path into the woods. A short way in, we diverted off the path and came to the edge of a clearing. There were just enough trees and shrubbery to hide us. We had a perfect view of the girl's camp.

"Alright, Mark, get ready," Matt said.

Mark took off his knapsack and put it on the ground and opened it up. He took his shoes off to get the swimsuit off and then put them back on once the swimsuit was in the knapsack. The shirt soon joined the swimsuit and he closed the pack up.

We sat there and waited for a few minutes while the girls all slowly piled inside the mess hall for lunch.

"I'll go take a look and make sure they're all gone. If they are, I'll wave you over. If someone sees us and chases us, go up the trail that we just came off of. Keep going in the direction we were headed. We'll run up that for a while and then cut off and go into the woods. That trail leads to the boy's camp. They'll think it was them who did it." Matt said, prompting us to say

"YEAH!" and give him high fives

Now Matt stepped out of the bushes to peek around. He gave the all-clear sign.

Mark stepped out of the bushes and ran over to the flag pole, lowering the flag.

When he got it all the way to the bottom, one of the clips that held the flag was stuck. He called Matt over

"It's stuck. Help me get it."

Matt and Mark worked at it but it wasn't budging. John called out to them.

"Someone's coming!"

"Oh NO!" Mark said, panicking.

"Hey, what are you doing?" a girl about our age said, coming toward us. As she got closer, she looked down at Mark's waist and screamed, running in the other direction and exclaiming

"There's BOYS here, and one of them's NAKED!!!!"

More screams erupted as the clip finally came loose, and Mark got the flag. As we ran towards the trail, John and I joined them and followed Matt and Mark up the trail and then off the trail into the woods. We found a good spot with lots of covers and heard swarms of girls hitting the trail in search of us. Mark put his clothes back on, tucked the flag into his knapsack and we made our way through the woods to the side of the camp to the left of the trail in.

We went back across the bridge and acted as if nothing had happened.

When we got back to our campsite, we all high-fived and took out our sandwiches. We conquered the girl's camp and took their flag, and now it was time for a victory lunch.

"Oh, boys, don't eat any more sandwiches. We're gonna barbecue some hot dogs." Matt and Thomas's mom told us.

"Even better," John said.

Lunch was hot dogs, potato salad, and Coke, and we ate till we were stuffed.

The dads hadn't caught any fish, nor did they care if they did.

"It's just nice to be out on the boat." John's dad said.

"Don't drink too much beer. If you fall out of the boat and drown, I ain't comin' to save your ass." Matt and Thomas's mom said jovially, eliciting giggles from the adults.

"You boys been behaving?" John's dad asked. John put on a mischievous grin and said

"Yes, Dad."

"You better be," John's mom said."

"Oh, we are, Ma'am. We are behaving... yes, we are," Mark said, and all of us boys laughed out loud.

"Yep, they're up to something." Matt and Thomas's dad said.

"Should we make them talk? " John's Dad asked.

"Let's."

And John's dad picked me up and threw me over one shoulder, and then John over the other, and Matt and Thomas's dad picked them up and did the same and ran with us down to the lake, throwing us in. Matt and Thomas's dad ran back to get Mark, and he ran top speed to get away and stepped on a rock, slowing him down enough for Dad to catch him, scoop him up, and throw him in the lake, too. The moms laughed hysterically.

When the dads were done throwing us around in the water, we all came back to sit at our picnic tables and get dry. We took off our wet shirts, placed them on some bushes t, and set our wet shoes in the hot sun to dry. We all got our second pairs of sneakers and socks out and put them on. We didn't bother with shirts because it was getting so hot anyway.

"You men are as bad as the boys," John's mom said with a smile. "If they start barfing because you thew them in the water and wrestled with them after they just ate all that food, you're cleaning it up."

The afternoon was filled with swinging on the rope at the lodge and more exploring in the woods. We also dug for worms for the dads so they'd have some fresh bait for the next day. We put them in a plastic bag and left them in the soda cooler, and every time one of the moms went to get a can of soda, they got grossed out, saying, "EEEWWWW!"

As the day drew to a close, John's dad said, "You boys are filthy, and you stink of sweat. Go and take a shower." We agreed and got all our stuff for the shower. When we arrived, there were other boys who were campground guests in the showers using all of them, so we had to wait for them to finish. Once they did, we disrobed, put our stuff in the cubbies on the wall outside the shower room, and went inside.

The showers were like the ones at my school, open community style, with six showers on one side and six on the other. We turned on the water and used the time to talk about the day while we soaped and scrubbed.

"That was so cool, then you know what. Thomas said.

"Yeah, did you hear her yell when she saw Mark?!"

"AAAHHHHHH!!! We all mocked the screaming girl and then laughed."

"Yeah, it doesn't even matter whether you even touched a tit or ever even saw one after what you did," Matt stated

"What do you mean?" Mark asked

"Dude, a girl saw your dick; that's way better than the fact that you never even saw a tit."

"Screw you, Matt; I DID see a tit. But YOU'VE never seen a pussy"

"Oh yes, I have."

"You have not!" chimed Thomas

"Yes, I have, and I'll prove it. I'll show you tonight. We'll all meet in our tent"

"Show us? What?" John asked quizzically.

"Just wait. You'll see."

We finished our shower, put our underwear on, and wrapped the towels around our waists for the walk back. We passed the moms on the way, and Matt and Thomas's mom said

"You better have underwear on under those towels."

"We do," Thomas said.

When we got back to the camp, the dads were sitting at the table playing poker, and I asked them

"Can John and I please go to Matt Thomas and Mark's tent?"

"Sure," John's dad said, barely looking up from the card hand he was holding. We took off for their tent taking off the towels and laying them across another bush next to our drying shirts from earlier.

We got inside the tent, and Matt pulled 3 Playboy magazines out of the bottom of his knapsack

'An ocean of waves of "WHOOOOAA."

They came upon the tent as Matt got out a flashlight from the knapsack, too, and turned it on, opening one of the magazines to the centerfold and unfurling it like a flag.

"I got them out of a box in the garage," Matt said.

"HOLY SHIT!" Mark said looking at the page, eyes wide with wonder.

"Now you've seen a tit. Two of them, actually. Wanna touch them? Go ahead," Thomas said, and we all giggled, trying to stay quiet.

"Yeah, and a pussy too," I said, and more giggles followed.

Then Matt closed it and said, "You think THAT was amazing? Look at May."

And he opened it for all of us to see.

"DAAAAAMMMMN!" was all we could say

He opened the third one up, and then we heard a booming voice outside the tent say

"IF YOU BOYS ARE DONE WITH MY PLAYBOYS, I WANT THEM BACK NOW!!"

We all simultaneously tried to poke our heads out of the tent and saw Matt and Thomas's dad laughing. John's dad was still at the table, and he, too, was laughing hard.

"Dammit, Dad, How did you know?"

"Like I told you last time we were here, and you boys were on the dock with your peckers and nuts to the sky, parents ALWAYS know." Now we were all outside the tent and Matt handed the Playboys to his dad, and then dad went on.

"You made it OBVIOUS. Do you want to ALLLLL go in one tent together with a FLASHLIGHT on?! I mean, seriously, come on. I KNOW you weren't reading BOOKS in there, you didn't BRING any! Wait till your moms hear about this."

"NOOOO! Dad," Both Matt and Thomas said simultaneously

"PLEASE" don't tell mom Matt begged

"Are you kidding? I HAVE to see the look on her face when I tell her THIS!!!"

"NOOOO dad PLEEEEASSE DON'T TELL her!! It was repeated again and again by Matt and Thomas's dad as he just kept on laughing while playing cards with John's dad.

"Dad, if you tell Mom, you'll be in trouble too for having Playboys."

'What do you mean? She doesn't care. She knows I have them in the garage. Besides, she looks like Miss May."

"OH, GROSS, Dad! Now, when we look at mom, we are gonna think of Miss May!"

"Who said you were gonna ever look at Miss May again? Those are MY Playboys."

Now the moms were returning from their shower, and Matt and Thomas's dad got up and said

"You are never going to guess what these wonderful boys were doing while you were in the shower

"No, Dad! LALALALALALALALALALA!! Matt and Thomas yelled to try and drown out dad

"Cut that, or you're grounded when we get home." Matt and Thomas's dad said, "Go sit." He paused and then continued

"Anyway, these boys, the five of them, like this, in their underwear, were all in one tent with a flashlight looking at Playboy magazines."

The moms looked at each other and then at us, sat down at the table, and put their heads in their hands

John's mom said

"You're kidding, right?" Matt and Thomas's dad dropped the playboys on the table in front of her. Both moms started giggling.

"Nope, it's the truth. They were in there lookin' at the centerfolds, so close to knowing what their peckers were for" Now everyone roared with laughter

When the laughter died down, Mark said

"I know what a penis is for. We learned about it in school."

"Ok, professor, what is a penis for?"

"It's to put inside a lady, and when you do, a baby comes out in nine months."

"That's it? That's all of it?" John's dad said, stifling a laugh, trying to escape.

"Yeah, that's it."

"Well, how do you put the floppy penis inside the lady?" Matt and Thomas's dad asked.

"I don't know," Mark said.

"Well, I'll give you a hint… what happened to your penis when you were lookin' at the playboys?"

"It started to get hard."

"Ok, so what does that tell you?"

"OHHHHHHHHH… so the man looks at the Playboy to get his penis hard so he can put it in the lady?!"

Laughter beyond all imagining erupted from everyone. The moms had tears rolling from their eyes.

"What? Why are you laughing?" Mark asked, confused

"Out of the mouths of BABES!!" Matt and Thomas's mom said as the laughter continued.

"SO FAR from knowing what their peckers are for!" Matt and Thomas's dad said, causing more raucous hysterics.

"I think the lady might have something not so nice to say to you if you bring a Playboy to bed," John's mom said between laughs.

When the laughter died down. Mark's dad said, "Come here. All you boys, get closer and listen. It's ok to look at those magazines but you have to realize that not all women look like that. The women in those magazines are some of the most beautiful women in the world, appearance-wise, but there are other kinds of beauty in women other than looks; if looking at the women in those magazines makes you appreciate any women you find attractive for any reason, then the women in the magazines have done their job. Got it?"

A flurry of 'Yes sir's to tell him we understood.

"I think these boys need some man talk. Maybe you and I can double-team them while we're here?" Matt and Thomas's dad said, looking at John's dad across the table."

John's dad said, "Oh yeah. The way they are acting, they are old enough."

"I'm gonna put some dinner on. Chef Boyardee beefaroni, everybody?" John's mom said

Lots of yes's and yes please's from the group.

"Boys, go put on some clean shorts before dinner, please. You were so eager to look at those playboys after your shower that you forgot to put them on." John's dad said as a reminder.

We all darted back to our tents and found some shorts to put on. And came back to the table.

"How old are your boys?" John's dad asked.

"Thomas is 10, Matt just turned 12 going on 20, and Mark just turned 10." Mark is my sister's kid. Dad left them when he was a baby, and she's been struggling ever since. I try to help her as much as I can. Take him with us any time for trips, out seeing the country in the camper, all that kinda stuff. He spends more time with us than he does at home. How 'bout you?"

"Your situation sounds like ours. They're both 10, but David isn't ours. He's been John's best friend since kindergarten, and they are more like brothers. He's been going through some stuff at home, so I've been doing things like you, trying to give him more of a childhood. I love him like my own. SO smart, and he's so damn mature, aren't you?"

"Yes, sir," I said.

And he reached out and picked me up from my spot at the table and sat to the side so he could put me on his lap, hugging me as he did.

'They both are really, both super smart and mature, but David's more adventurous, going out for the spelling bee, on stage in front of so many people, and singing in the glee club, they both do that."

"Yeah, they are both wonderful kids. Matt's the adventurous one in our group, and whatever he does, the other two have to follow. They all do great in school, almost all straight A's, so I hear you on yours being smart, but they gotta have time to be kids, you know?"

"Yeah, I love seeing them so happy, like when we are here."

"Tell me about it. My boys can't stop talking about that trip to the racetrack. They keep bugging me to go again."

"We should. What do you think, troops? The go-kart track this week?"

"YEEEEEEAAAAAHHHHH!" from all of us.

"Ok, we'll do it."

After dinner, we all played blackjack for a while, and then all my friends and I went to the dock by the lodge to lay on it while watching the night sky and trying to see all the constellations and call them out loud. We fell asleep there eventually, and the parents had to come and pick us up and carry us back.

They removed our shoes and socks and tucked us into our sleeping bags, zipped us in and we fell asleep.

The morning sun was particularly beautiful, shining through the trees when we woke up. The moms were making bacon and scrambled eggs on the camp stoves, and the scent made us hungry, so we unzipped our sleeping bags and got up quickly to brush our teeth at the camp bathroom. After our delicious breakfast, we thanked the moms, packed the knapsacks, and filled the canteens.

"Back by 12:30; remember we are going to the Go-kart track today." Matt and Thomas's dad reminded them.

A flood of 'yes sirs' filled the air.

We walked at a quick pace using the same route as we had the day before, wanting to get to the waterfall so we could skinny dip again. As soon as it was within view, we started to strip, and by the time we reached the edge of the water, we were ready to jump in.

We stayed until noon and started back the way we came and arrived at camp in time for lunch.

The moms were quiet and didn't give their usual enthusiastic welcome back. The dads hadn't gone fishing and were at the picnic table playing poker again. They said nothing to any of us.

We sat down, and I asked, "What's for lunch?"

"Beef stew," John's mom said.

"Oh good. I love that," John replied.

It was a silent lunch, and my friends and I couldn't figure out what was going on. After everybody had finished lunch, we got our answer, and it wasn't good.

John's dad said, "There was a woman from the girl's camp here while you were off on your hike."

My heart started pounding, and Matt and Mark looked at each other across the table, fear seeping into their facial expression.

"She said five boys were at their camp yesterday and that one of them was naked. The naked boy and another boy stole their camp flag. She checked the nearby boys' camp, but they found nothing there, so they came to the campgrounds here to ask around if anybody knew anything about it. She said the fact that one boy was naked caused one girl to scream, and it made a lot of the girls at the camp run. It was almost a stampede. Three girls got hurt, and one twisted her ankle.

Now Matt and Thomas's dad got up from the table and said, "If we look in your knapsacks, will we find a flag in one of them?"

All of us were sweating bullets and didn't say a word.

"Look, we're not saying you did it, but you have to see it from our side. Look at the evidence. Five of you, five boys there taking their flag, us in the boat seeing you five boys walking on the bridge from that direction right while the screams of the girls were happening. This is your last chance to come clean or the punishment will be double.

Mark got up from the table and said, "It's in my knapsack."

The moms tilted their heads down.

Matt's dad went to his knapsack and pulled it out, walking over to him, looking very angry.

A single tear came from his left eye, and he said, "It was a dare. We were playing truth or dare, and that was the dare." He blurted out, tears flowing heavily now.

"Are you gonna hit me he asked, looking even more scared."

"Have I ever hit you or Matt or Thomas?"

"No, sir. But you look like you're gonna right now." Dad ignored him and continued.

"It's one thing to go skinny dipping, but this is something else. What the HELL were you thinking?"

"I'm sorry. I'm so sorry that somebody twisted their ankle and that other people got hurt." Mark said, whimpering.

"If you had THOUGHT about the possible consequences before you did this, all of you, then you wouldn't have something to be sorry about right now because you wouldn't have done this."

"We were sitting here yesterday at this table talking about how mature and smart you boys are," John's dad said while looking at John and I

"And the whole time, you're sitting here knowing that you pulled this stunt. I am very disappointed right now."

Matt and Thomas's dad started again

"You'll help your mothers prepare the meals tomorrow, and you'll wash and dry all our dirty clothes in the camp laundromat. Today, you five are marching over to the girls' camp, and you are going to apologize to the camp director and the girls who got hurt, and we are NOT going to the Go Kart track today. Is that understood?"

By now, all of us had tears falling from our eyes and onto our shirts.

"Get your canteens and fill them and come back here." We walked to fill our canteens at the water fountains and came back to stand in front of the dads.

"Ok, come on," John's dad said. We followed them over the bridge and to the reception office, where the Camp Director's office was located.

We walked up to the desk, and the director stood.

"Hello," she said, surveying the five of us, our faces still wet with tears.

"Hello, Ma'am. Here's your flag. I took it, and I'm sorry I scared the girls, and some got hurt." Mark said, trembling. The director said, "Thank you." taking the flag from his hands.

Matt and Thomas's dad spoke sternly next, saying, "You have the free labor of five boys today. I would appreciate it if you would please give them work to do around the camp, any odd jobs or cleaning you need to be done."

We looked at him in awe, unable to believe we were going to have to spend the day working at the girls camp.

"Keep them as long as you need them today and send them back when they're done with all the work you assign them, not before." John's dad added.

"We can do that. We have some stairs that need fixing at the main hall and some window frames that need painting and some weeds to pull up." The camp director said.

"You better behave while you're here THIS time." Matt and Thomas's dad warned them.

"Ok, let's go see Jim from maintenance and get you boys going on your work."

They walked to the main hall, and Jim was there cutting some wood next to a partially disassembled staircase leading to its front door.

"Oh, ok." He said, looking at how young we were, clearly confused.

"They are the boys who were here yesterday."

"OHHHHH, I see." He looked at Matt and said

"Make a muscle." Matt flexed his bicep.

"Ok, you'll do well with helping me with these stairs."

"Yes, sir."

"Who is the one who stole the flag?"

"Me, sir." Mark sheepishly replied while raising his hand.

"Ok, you'll be with Mr. Gerome doing trash and general cleaning around the grounds. Go see him in the mess hall right over there," and he pointed to his right where a large building stood sheltered by some trees in the short distance. "The girls you need to apologize to are there right now as well"

"You, sir, will pull weeds around this main hall and the reception office," he said, pointing at Thomas

"And you two will paint the window frames. Over here on the ground. Be careful not to get any on the screens or windows," He said to John and me.

By close to dinnertime, Jim called us all back together. We were all worn out. Thomas had blisters on his hands, Matt was rubbing his arms, which were tired from all the hammering of boards on the main hall porch and staircase, and Mark could barely walk because he had to walk every bag of garbage from every location to the dumpster instead of putting them in Mr. Gerome's EZ-go golf cart to drive them over.

"Ok, you can go see the director, Miss Standley. You all did great work today."

We entered the office, and Miss Standley looked up from the paperwork she was doing and asked

"Ok, work all done?"

"Yes Ma'am" Mark said.

"Ok, Thomas, you go to the infirmary to get the nurse to fix up your blisters, and then you can all go back to your camp. Oh, and Mark, you can raise the camp flag before you go, too. Here you go," and she handed the flag back to him.

"Thank you, ma'am," Matt replied.

And we all filed out to go to the infirmary on the other side of the mess hall, following Mark because he knew where it was thanks to his trash detail work.

After the nurse put some ointment and Band-Aids on Thomas's blisters, we all made our way to the flagpole, and Mark ran the camp flag up the pole. We then hauled our exhausted bodies back to camp. The dads were helping the moms make dinner, sloppy joes. We walked over to face them.

"I trust you all finished the work." Matt's dad said.

Many 'yes, sir's

"Ok, then go shower."

Before we left, Mark called Matt and Thomas's dad.

"Uncle Steve"

"What is it?"

"I'm so sorry." And a dam of tears broke under his eyes. He bent and picked up Mark, hugged him, and put him down.

John and I held out our arms, and both said we were sorry too, and he hugged us both."

I started crying hard

"I'm so sorry for disappointing you." I stammered through the tears, "Me too, Dad."

"It's ok, boys, it's ok,"

"Remember, we're disappointed by what you did; we're not disappointed in you. We will never be disappointed in you. I felt bad that you didn't think before you acted, but everyone is guilty of that from time to time. We all make mistakes and in this case, you all made a big one. Ok?"

"Ok" we said

"You all learned another lesson from this, too. That when you play truth or dare, just go for the truth, because it's often much less embarrassing or likely to get you into trouble than the dare. Go shower."

"Yes, sir."

And we all picked up our gear and clean underwear and went to wash off the remnants of all the work we had to

Summer Break, 198, continued

The next morning, we ate breakfast, and the moms went to town to get more food supplies. John's dad."

"Boys, come to the table. We need to have a talk with you."

The dads explained the mechanics of how sex actually works and how it makes a baby, showed us a condom, and talked about how they are used. The more important part of the conversation was about the importance of responsibility and what it takes to be a real man:

"It's important to respect a girl and make sure that you are both ready to have sex. If you feel like you are, but she doesn't feel like she is, then you aren't ready either, and you accept that because it takes the both of you equally to make that decision."

Matt and Thomas's dad interjected

"Yeah, bringing a kid into the world is a huge responsibility. You have to be ready in every way because having a child is the most important decision you will ever make in your life. If you are not able to afford to have a baby, then you never have unprotected sex. Not ever. Not even once, because once is all it takes, and you have no way of knowing if this is going to be the time that the sperm and egg meet and make a baby. Once you and the girl have both decided that you are ready to have sex, you wear a condom every time until you both talk about having children, and you are both ready to have children, then you can stop wearing the condom each time you have sex."

"Think about having a baby like what you went through with the girl's camp and the flag," John's dad said. What did you find out after you thought you got away with stealing the flag?"

John replied

"Some girls got hurt."

"Right. That's the consequence; in this case, a girl got hurt; in the case of having sex without a condom, the consequence is the girl gets pregnant. What else happened?"

Thomas, looking down at his blistered hands, said, "We had to do a lot of work."

"Right, to pay for what you did. You can't escape the fact that you always are going to have to pay for your actions no matter what the situation. In the case of having a baby, you end up literally having to pay. It costs a lot of money to raise a child. That's why it's so important for you to talk about it before you decide to have sex without protection. You also have to be ready to be a father. Being a father is more than just having sex and bringing a child into the world. You have to be mature enough to raise that child."

Thomas said, "Dad, can I ask a question?"

"Of course. I want you to"

"Well, you took a condom out of your wallet and showed it to us. You and Mom had sex without a condom because you were ready, and Mom got pregnant with us, right?"

"Yes"

"Ok, how come you still have a condom?"

"Well, remember, people who love each other don't just have sex to bring a baby into the world; they do it to show each other their love. After your mom had you, we both talked about it, and we weren't going to be able to afford to have more kids and still be able to give you boys the life you have, so we decided that I should wear a condom when we have sex because the birth control pills mom was taking so she wouldn't get pregnant were doing bad things to her."

John's dad continued, "It's the same way for your mother and me, John. We feel like you are the most precious gift we have both ever had and we wanted to give you the best life we could, so we didn't want to have more kids of our own. But it allowed us to be able to put money away in the bank to help another child, David here, whom we love like our own and have since the first day of kindergarten, and you and John started behaving like real brothers.

Matt and Thomas's dad added, "And the same is true for you, Mark; you know I think of you as my boy even though you're my sister's boy."

Matt said, "I need to ask; you told us about being ready to have a baby; when do you know for sure you're ready to have sex?"

"Well, you have to both talk about it and agree, as we said before, but your body has a way of telling you that it's ready or getting ready to be able to have sex and bring a new life into the world, and that usually comes before any conversation you can have with a girl."

"I French kissed a girl, and I felt funny, and my penis got hard. " Matt said

"Well, that's a little bit of a sign for sure, but not proof."

"I had a dream about her, too, and my underwear and pajamas were all sticky when I woke up. Actually, it happened more than once."

'Now that IS proof because that sticky stuff was the semen we talked about; that's what comes out of your penis when you have sex. Sometimes it happens, and it's part of growing up, and you are ok if it happens. You're 12 now, and that's when it can start, or sometimes later, like 13, 14, or 15. This is a perfect example of what I was talking about with your body being ready before you're really ready in other ways to have a child. Matt, you are going to have to listen to your body because that semen coming out when you sleep is telling you that if you have sex without a condom, you could get the girl pregnant."

"Wow! Really?" Matt said with surprise

"Yes, really. But you're probably not going to have to worry about it for a while because most girls aren't going to let you have sex with them until they are mentally ready anyway, but if you DO get to the point where you both can't contain your feelings anymore and you are ready to have sex, you put the condom on first. Understand?

"Yes, sir. "

Now John's father started talking again

"I want you to know that when you are ready to have a baby, it is the most incredible feeling ever to know that you and the girl you love more than anything in the world have brought a new life into the world that you will love just as much as the girl. John, when I held you in my arms for the first time, I knew that I wouldn't ever be able to do anything else in my life that would be able to top bringing you into the world, and I have loved you and been proud of you ever since, and that's why parents REALLY love their kids' birthdays. Not to give you presents, but to celebrate the day that we saw you come into the world and know that we made that decision and that it was the best decision we ever made. Seeing and helping you growing up has been the best thing that has ever happened to me in my life."

"Same with me for you guys. After Matt was born, we decided that it was such an awesome experience we decided to have one more child, and Thomas, you were born. I couldn't love you boys more than I do." Matt and Thomas's dad said while looking at them. "Any other questions?"

John said to Matt and Thomas's dad

"Can we call you Uncle Steve?"

"Yes, of course you can. That makes us family. Come here, you two." And he gave us both a big bear hug.

Now Mark asked John's dad

"Sir, what's your name?"

"John. I'm John Senior, and he's John Junior."

"Can we call you Uncle John?"

"You know you can. I think it's great. I've got three new nephews. Come here!" and he hugged Matt, Thomas, and Mark.

"Ok, you boys go skinny dipping." Uncle Steve said.

"Wait, WHAT? Again? You KNOW?"

"Well, lemme ask you this: when you hiked the east trail, you went for a while, and then you went off the trail even further to the east, and you walked about 15 minutes and saw a waterfall, right?"

"Yeah, how did you know?" Thomas asked.

"Well, I was a kid once, too, and I went to camp at the boy's camp, and that was before the lodge and this campground were here. It was my first time away from home, and I was scared. But I made new friends, and when we were out exploring, we found that waterfall, and we went skinny dipping there every chance we had that summer and three summers after it. That was the special secret place that we were sure that WE were the first to discover, but I'll bet a bunch of other kids discovered it before we did. We've talked about those summers through the years and how they were the best years of our lives, and you will, too."

"So it's ok to go skinny dipping?" I asked

"It's ok there, right?" Uncle Steve said while looking at John's dad.

He said, "Absolutely."

"What about if our moms find out? Thomas said"

"Oh, like your dads, I don't think there's too much you boys get up to that your moms don't already know about," John's dad said reassuringly

Then Uncle Steve added, "That waterfall used to be my special place, but now it's yours. We won't talk about it with your moms, and we won't bother you while you're there. We talked about what it means to be a man just now. Go be boys a little longer while it lasts. Now go on."

Hugs all around, and when I hugged John's dad, I gave him a kiss on the cheek and said, "Thanks, dad."

And he started crying and hugged me again and kissed me on the head three times."

"You're welcome, son. I love you."

"Love you too." I said, then to my friends, "Ok, let's get our suits on."

"What for?" Matt said. "We're just gonna take them off when we get there. We can just go with what we've got on."

"Oh yeah," I replied

"Back by 12:30 so we can eat lunch and go to the go-kart track," Uncle Steve reminded us

"YAAAAAYYYYY!" From all of us. We packed our knapsacks and set off on our way.

When we got to the waterfall, we didn't go skinny dipping right away; we sat and went over what our dads had just talked about with us for a few minutes while we drank some water from our canteens. After a few minutes of that, our clothes were off, and we felt even freer than we had before, climbing to the rockface and jumping off. For me, the time we spent there at that moment and the rest of the time during the remainder of the week was better than the two times we had been there before.

That time in your life is very awkward for any boy, not fully a boy anymore, but not yet ready to be a man either. It was even more awkward for me since I hadn't really been the kind of boy I should have been allowed to be until this time in my life. I had to learn what being a boy AND a man were all about at the same time. That talk we just had with the dads, however, made everything clear to me. Uncle Steve was right, too. I would indeed look back on that time in my life as the best and the most precious, and that's why I'm sharing it with you here. To this day, I am so grateful to John's Dad and Uncle Steve for that talk and the respect they showed us in understanding that difficult moment in our lives.

After going to the Go-kart track, we all stopped at the store for some soda and snacks on our way back to camp. Uncle Steve had a separate purchase that he said he had to make and that we should go to the car and wait for him.

The next morning, when we were packing our knapsacks for another trip to the waterfall, Matt found a box inside his pack with a note on it. He showed it to us. It was a package of condoms. The note said

'You're not ready for these yet, but now you'll be prepared when you are. Love you. Dad'

July, 1981 - Summer Break-The Amusement Park

Each weekend that summer after that week's vacation at the campground, John and I took some sort of a trip with Mom and Dad, and this weekend would be a truly exciting one. We were going to the amusement park I had gone to a couple of years earlier with Frank. This time, however, I would be going with Uncle Steve, Aunt Anne, and the boys. We had arranged it so we would meet there and we were going to spend the weekend together at a nearby motel.

"Come on, boys, get in here for breakfast. We need to get on the road in the next half hour."

I was still in the shower and John was only just getting dressed due to us sleeping almost a half hour past when the alarm sounded.

After a few minutes we finally had put ourselves together and were sitting at the table eating our eggs and toast.

"Wonderful park, where we are going today. We've gone many times in the past when John was younger," Mom said.

"Yeah, I know. It's a great park. I went there a couple of years ago. They have this one rollercoaster that's SO fun. I went on it 5 times!"

"Yeah, there's a bigger coaster there that I love. We are going on that one a lot, I guarantee it."

Dad said.

Breakfast finished a few minutes later; we turned our attention to getting the suitcases into the car. A last check to be sure the door was locked, and we were off for our weekend of riding rollercoasters and eating more junk food than we knew what to do with.

When we pulled into the amusement park lot and drove to the right, we saw cousins Matt, Thomas, and Mark standing by their car with Uncle Steve and Aunt Anne. The boys didn't even wait till we had completely parked before coming over to the car and waving. We got out, gave each other high fives and hugs, and we were on our way inside.

"I'm gonna ride that big coaster first!" Mark proclaimed.

"Me too!" I said.

"Me three!" John said.

Then Dad interrupted our upcoming roller coaster participation survey by saying, "I think it's safe to bet that we are ALL going on it."

The attendant at the front booth stamped our hands, and we made our way over to the big coaster. Then I had a sudden terrible thought: what if I was still too short to ride it? That would be so embarrassing in front of my brother and cousins. Then I thought about it some more.
It was two years since I had last been there, and I had to have grown SOME by now. But that coaster had the tallest height requirement out of all the rides. I would have had to grow a lot to be able to ride. Would it be enough? I didn't know.

"Hey, you listening?" I heard Thomas say.

"What?"

"We've been asking if you wanna take a bathroom run before we get on the rollercoaster."

"Oh, sure. Sorry, I must have been daydreaming." I said as an excuse to cover up my fear about still looking like a baby here at the park.

We all went to the bathroom, and as always, the parents took longer. It gave me a chance to look around at other rides that didn't seem as much like baby rides I could recommend that I could ride so we would all ride them. I didn't have long to wait as the parents all returned to meet us outside the bathrooms.

"Ok, on we go, entrance to the rollercoaster is right around the corner."

The rest of the boys all bolted ahead to get in the line. I stayed back with my parents, who were still just walking.

"Son, you ok?" Dad said.

"Yeah, you've been acting weird since we walked in. You sick?" Uncle Steve asked.

"Naw, I'm fine," I responded, trying to cover up my anxiety. "Just didn't wanna run, that's all."

"You afraid? This is a big rollercoaster and we'll understand if you are." John's mom inquired

"Naw, I'm not scared. I WANT to ride it." I said.

"Ok, as long as you're sure. Yes, I'm sure. We went through the lanes where you line up when the line is much longer than usual, and we came to the attendant standing where the yellow mark on the wall was painted, indicating the minimum height requirement. My heart was pounding as I stepped with my back against the wall.

"All set. Go on in."

"Really? I'm tall enough."

"Yep, you are. Over an inch and a half over the line."

'YEEEEAAAHHH!" I yelled and ran to meet the other boys in the line. That was all I needed to see. If I could ride this, I could ride EVERYTHING in the park, and I intended to do just that."

"Your mood sure changed, Dad said."

"Yeah, I guess."

"Were you worried that you weren't tall enough?"

"Yeah, I was."

"Well, we could have told you that you probably were tall enough; your old pants were almost 2 inches too short when we went and got those new shorts and pants for you at the end of the year."

I was beaming now, and from what I remembered about the smaller coaster, this was going to be even more fun than that, and that was one of the most amazing things I had ever experienced so far.

When it was our turn, we boarded and pulled the lap bar down. My heart was beginning to play a tune on my ribs again and I was starting to sweat with anticipation.

Soon, we were in motion, and a similar sound of the anti-rollback chain dog was clanking away, bringing us to the top of the lift hill. We approached the hilltop, and I looked out over the distance and realized how much higher I was compared to the other coaster from last time. Cresting the hill now and looking down at the steep drop, I gripped the bar with all my strength, and we were suddenly going as fast as a car, and I screamed with more joy than I had felt the last time. There were so many different elements, all stacked on top of each other. The twists, curves, and hills were outstanding, and as we pulled into the station, we all looked at each other, unable to speak because we had all blown out our vocal cords. I don't even remember screaming, but I obviously had done it a lot.

"Again! Again! Please! Again!" I hoarsely exclaimed as we all exited the station. My pleas were met with similar requests from all the boys, and the parents all laughed and said, of course, we are going again."

"YAAAAYYYYY!" all around, and we got back in line. This time, we knew what was coming, and we got brave and raised our arms a few times. As we floated out of our seats, we grabbed the bar again quickly before we were swept up out of our seats completely.

After a full five consecutive rides on the coaster, it was determined that we should take a break, get something to drink, and ride other rides.

We all decided to get some lunch. We got a giant pizza so that multiple people could all take from it instead of buying individual slices and, of course, lots of cokes.

When we finished, we all went on the pirate, the zipper, and the hurricane, and then it was time for more junk food. The swinger called us next, and this time, I was able to ride the big version.

The family rollercoaster I had ridden the last time I had been there was fun but mild by comparison to the other rides we had been riding this time. A couple of turns on the slingshot garnered a special surprise for Matt. There were two girls riding the Slingshot in the seats in front of us. They had been in line and giving Matt the eye. They looked slightly older than us, and they weren't with their parents. When we got off the ride, one of the girls started talking to Matt, saying

"I just love all the rides. The scrambler's my favorite. What's your name?"

"Matt."

"I'm Elizabeth, but everybody calls me Beth. Wanna ride the scrambler together?"

Matt looked at his dad, who said

"Why are you looking at me? You know you can walk around the park by yourself."

They had never made that bargain, but Uncle Steve was trying to give him some distance from us and make him appear older than he was. He didn't want to make Matt out to be too young when there was an interested girl who suddenly wanted to get to know him better.

Matt whispered, "Thanks, dad."

"No problem. Got your wallet?"

"Yes, sir."

That wallet question was meant to make sure he had protection with him, just in case.

"Meet us at the arcade at 3:00," Dad said, leaving him free to explore the park with his new friend without family around to cramp his style. "And take some money. Here's $20. Have fun!"

"Yes, sir!" Matt said excitedly.

We didn't see Matt until 3:00 at the arcade, and he was holding his hand when he got there. She handed him something and walked off so Matt could rejoin us.

"So, what happened, bro?" Thomas asked, curiosity making him practically explode.

"Later, I'll tell you later," Matt said, trying to keep what happened to himself until he could talk without the adults around.

Uncle Steve smiled and said

"Get her phone number?"

"DAAAAAD!

"Ok, ok, ok. I'll take that as a yes." We all laughed, and Matt playfully punched Uncle Steve in the arm a bunch of times.

That night, we checked into our rooms at the motel, two adjoining rooms. Two double beds in each room. And an extra portable bed in one. The boys would all have one room, and the adults would be in the other.

After we got unpacked and settled, Matt said

"We're gonna play some Blackjack."

John's dad said

"Ok, Casanova!"

"Uncle Joooooohn! Come on!"

And everyone laughed again. Matt shut the door between the two rooms and we all gathered around the table at the far corner of the room by the window.

"Dude, that girl was smokin' hot! How old was she?" Thomas asked, prompting Matt to tell us everything.

"She's 13"

"Cool! John said."

"We rode the scrambler, and you know how that is when it gets going. Makes you slam into the other person. We were pushed against each other the whole time."

"Ok, then what?"

"We went on the Ferris wheel, and while she was talking to me, she put her hand on my leg."

"Cool!" Mark said

"So we went and got some cotton candy. I asked her if she wanted me to buy her some. She said no, she'd just eat mine when she wanted a bit, and every time she took a bite, she waited till I was taking a bite too, so she could kiss me."

"No fucking way!" I blurted out.

"Unreal!" Thomas said.

"I swear."

"What happened next?"

"We played some of the midway games, and I didn't win anything at darts or the ball toss, but I played basketball, and I won her a little doll."

"Is that when you went back to the arcade?"

"No, then we went and got some fried dough, and she said, let's go in the funhouse. So we did, and when we got in there, she said she thought I was hot, and she started brushing my hair with her hand, and she asked me if I wanted to REALLY kiss her. I said yeah.

"Nice!" John said.

"But she didn't want to just kiss on the lips. She stuck her tongue in my mouth, I mean WAY in, and I did the same to her."

"OHHHHHH" We all yelled out

"SHHHH! Quiet. Our parents will wonder what's going on and come in."

"So, is there more?" I eagerly asked

"Yeah. So we were kissing, and I put my hand on her shirt and touched her boob.

"You're lying. You're making this up." Thomas said disbelievingly while the rest of our jaws were on the floor.

Matt spit into his hand and said, "I promise I am telling the truth."

Thomas spat into his hand and shook Matt's hand, saying, "Holy shit, dude! It's all TRUE?!"

"Oh my god, dude, you are so lucky!" Mark blurted out.

"So that's it?"

"Nope. Look, she gave me her phone number."

"OMIGOD!! WHAT! So you can see her again. DAAAAMN!!!!" Thomas said.

A knock at the door to the adjoining rooms, and we all said, "Who is it?"

"It's your parents. Who else would it be? We're in the next room." Uncle Steve said through the door.

"Oh, ok," Matt said, "What do you want?"

"We're gonna go across the street to the IHOP to get some dinner. If you're done telling your adventures at the park today, come on, let's go."

"Coming!" We all said

While we were at dinner, Matt said to his dad

"Dad, can I hang out with Beth again tomorrow at the park?"

"That's gonna be hard to do if you don't know if she's gonna be there."

"But I will know. I got her phone number. And he took it out of his pocket to show Dad."

"Can you believe this one?" Uncle Steve said, "I knew she gave you her phone number, you sly devil."

"DAAAADD!"

"I'm just playing. Yes, you can hang out with her if she wants you to. We'll leave you be. Remind me to give you some money to put in your wallet later so you can just meet her without us around."

"I think it's so cute. First big crush," his mom said.

"MOOOMMM! Stop"

"Well, it IS cute!" she said, with a few giggles from the other adults.

Back at the motel, Matt called her. We all gathered around Matt, and he kept the receiver away from his ear so we could hear. It rang 4 times, and then she answered

"Hey Beth, it's Matt."

"Oh hey, Matt."

"I'm gonna be at the park again tomorrow if you wanna hang out."

"Matt, I gotta be honest with you; I was playing truth or dare with my friend I was with, and she dared me to find a boy in the park and French kiss him. She was with me and following us around to see if I'd do it. She was behind us on the fun house ride."

"Oh...I know how it goes with truth or dare.... so..."

"Yeah, but you are a really great kisser, and I really do think you're cute, so.... Yeah, why not? What time will you be there?

"I should be there when they open."

"Ok, wanna meet somewhere?"

"Sure, how about the arcade?"

"Ok, I'll see you there."

"Ok, Bye."

"Bye, cutie."

Matt hung up the phone, and we all started cheering and clapping.

"Dude! This is SOOOO cool!" John said

A knock at the door between rooms. Thomas opened the door.
"What's goin' on? Aunt Anne asked.

Thomas, excited from the moment, without thinking blurted out

"Beth is gonna be at the park tomorrow, and she said Matt's a great kisser."

Thomas, realizing what he just did, put his head down as Matt's face blushed with embarrassment.

"I'm sorry, Matt," Thomas said.

"Get him!" Matt said, and we all moved toward him and trapped him. We held him while Matt punched him in the arm continuously.

"How many times are you gonna punch me," Thomas said

"50," Matt said

"50?! But I didn't even make a spit promise that I wouldn't tell. STOOOOPPPPP!"

"DAAAAAAD! Make him stop!"

"Why? I think it sounds fair… It's fair, right?" he asked the moms, and they agreed, and all the adults started laughing."

"DAAAAAD! Come on; my arm hurts so much!"

"Alright, alright, Matt, enough," Dad said, grabbing Matt's fist as it came back for another punch.

"It's ok; I'll get the other 20 punches in later. Matt promised Thomas.

"If you do, you'll be grounded. Now stop"

"Alright, alright…"

"If you're not too tired, maybe you all wanna join us at the motel pool. We're gonna change and get over there.

'YEEEEAAHHH's all around.

"Ok, suits on, and let's go," and he closed the door.

We all changed as quickly as a wink and were ready to go. And we went next door to the parents' room to wait for the moms to finish getting into their suits.

"Why aren't they ready yet?"

Thomas said after a few minutes.

"Mom's ALWAYS take forever to get ready; you should know that by now," Uncle Steve said

"Yeah, unless they are ready and YOU'RE not, then there's hell to pay if you dare to even ask if you can go to the bathroom before leaving." John's dad added.

The moms finally came out, and we all grabbed some motel towels from the stacks on a shelf above the closet rod by the door, and we were on our way.

It was late in the day, and the temperature was going down, but the water wasn't quite as cold as I expected, probably due to retaining all the heat from the sun blasting on it earlier.

The dads did their usual play-fighting with us, picking us up and throwing us around in the pool, and we felt less tired than we had when we got back from the park.

By the time we all had felt like we'd had enough, we headed back to our rooms.

"Shower up tonight so we can sleep in a little in the morning. We need to get out by 8 so we can have breakfast and get to the park when they open." John's dad informed us.

"Ok" from all of us.

Each of us finished showering and got into our beds.

Mark was last to get under the covers. As soon as he pulled up the covers a bit, he leaned over onto his right arm to talk to Matt, who shared his double bed with Thomas.

"What are you gonna do if Beth wants to kiss you again?"

"Are you stupid? What do you think I'm gonna do?! I'm gonna let her."

"What if she wants to touch you down there?" John asked

"I dunno. I might let her because she let me touch her tit."

A knock at the door between the rooms.

"WHAT?!" we all yelled

"Are you all decent?"

John's mom asked

"Yes, Mom," John said.

The door opened, and both moms came in for their nightly routine of tucking us in properly and kissing us goodnight.

"Get to sleep now, boys"

We heard Uncle Steve say from the doorway.

As the moms left the room, one turned off the light before shutting the door.

As if the conversation never stopped, Mark asked Matt

"Yeah, but are you gonna let her touch you down there outside your pants, or are you gonna let her go inside?"

A pillow flew across the room from Matt's bed and hit Mark in the head

"None of your business. Now gimme my pillow back and go to sleep."

"Nope. Mine now. I've got two pillows."

"You won't if I come over there and give you the 10 punches I owe you, and I won't punch you in the arm this time; I'll punch you in the balls."

"Fine, here," Mark said, defeated, and he tossed the pillow back

We all drifted off to sleep, and I dreamed about my rides on the rollercoasters

Morning light seemed to come quicker, and we all got up and were ready to go in a flash. Everyone except the moms and Matt, who had changed his clothes twice before finally deciding on an outfit and now was in the bathroom trying to make sure his hair looked just so.

"Dad, do I look ok?" he asked after finally coming away from the bathroom mirror.

"You looked fine to her yesterday after riding rollercoasters, and you look a lot more put together now, so yeah, you look ok."

"Thanks."

"Besides, she's not interested in your hair; she's interested in your lips, remember?"

Laughter erupted throughout the whole room.

"DAAAAAAAAAD!" Matt yelled while chasing his dad around the room.

"Want some chapstick?" Thomas chided.

"Punches!" Matt warned Thomas

"Ok, enough, enough. Seriously, now. Matt. Come sit."

Matt did as he asked.

"Gimme your wallet."

He put another 20-dollar bill in it to add to the leftover dollars from the day before.

"Your mom and I are letting you go off on your own because we trust that you'll make good decisions. You treat Beth nice, if she wants something or is hungry or thirsty, you buy it for her."

"I will dad, I did all that yesterday without you telling me."

"Good boy. Look, she likes you a lot, that's obvious, and she's older than you, and girls mature faster than boys, so you always need to remember to be the kindest, best version of yourself you can be and make good decisions. All of them. Get me?"

"Yes, Dad."

"Uncle Steve hugged Matt and ruffled up his hair."

"UGGGH! DAD! Come ON!!"

"Go fix your hair," and Dad and everyone else laughed as Matt stomped back to the bathroom

"And YOU boys be good." Uncle Steve said, looking at all of us. "Don't tease him if you see him in the park when we're walking around. You give him privacy."

"How can he have privacy in an amusement park with all those people," Thomas asked

"You KNOW what I mean, and if you need a reminder, I'll let Matt give you the 20 punches he owes you. "

"Yes, Dad."

The moms came out of the bathroom, and Matt was still fixing his hair in our bathroom next door.

"Come on, Matt," his mom said, now impatient since she was ready to go.

After breakfast at Denny's, we arrived at the park, and after a reminder from Dad that he should meet us back at the arcade at 3, Matt went straight to the arcade, where he saw Beth waiting for him. We went off in the opposite direction and started our tour of the rollercoasters once again before the crowds got too big.

My friends and I all had 6 scoop ice cream cones that melted way too fast in the sun, and Mark nearly lost half his scoops to the ground below several times as the structural integrity of the ice cream tower was compromised by the blazing sun again and again.

We ate caramel apples, hot dogs, cheeseburgers, and seemingly everything else that the park offered between rides. We rode the Trabant, the Tilt-a-Whirl, the bumper cars, the spider, and all the other rides we rode the day before. By the time 3 o'clock rolled around, we were ready to play some arcade games.

Matt got there with Beth at 3:00 on the dot with Beth, who was carrying a giant stuffed bear.

She put the bear down to hug Matt and kiss him on the cheek before picking up the bear and telling him to call her as she walked off.

"Where did she win that big bear?" Mark asked.

"She didn't win it, I did, at basketball. You have to win three times to get the big prize."

"Nice!" I said.

We played our games at the arcade, including a lot of skeeball as usual, and we chose to get a whole bunch of candy from the prize shelves with our ticket winnings and promised to share with each other when the parents said we had to in order to be able to get all that sugar for a prize.

Matt wasn't quite himself but we didn't pay any mind to it because our focus was on having fun at the arcade at the moment.

When we got back to the motel, now Matt was really feeling down.

"What's wrong, Matt," I asked him

"Nothin'."

"Come on, out with it. Do you and Beth have a fight or somethin'?

"I don't wanna talk about it." He said, lying down on his bed." The dads were in the doorway and heard what he said.

"You afraid that you're not gonna get to see Beth again since we live far away."

Matt rolled over to look at Dad.

"How do you ALWAYS know?!"

"I'm the dad. Why do you always forget?"

"Dad, she's the most beautiful girl I've ever seen. I just wanna be with her all the time, and I won't be able to."

"Summer love, buddy," John's dad said. "Sometimes you meet someone, and it's just for that short time. When you meet other girls, the feelings you have about being sad that you can't be with Beth will pass."

"Were you a gentleman?" Uncle Steve asked

"Yes, of course, Dad."

"Did you have fun together and make memories?"

"Yes"

"Then you'll hold those memories in your heart, and if you don't get to see her again, you'll think about the special moments you shared, and you'll be happy that you had that little bit of time together. Don't be sad, son, be happy that a girl thought enough about you that they wanted to be with you, and were happy when they were. You let a girl love you, and you loved her back. That was one of those good decisions, ok."

"Yes, sir."

"Ok, why don't you all put your suits on and we'll all go swim."

"I don't want to. Can I stay here in the room when you go?"

"Ok,… but we'll miss you," Matt's mom said.

"Why don't you come? You'll feel better. We're all here for you."

Matt started to cry. Uncle Steve hugged him and said, "It's ok. We're here. We love you."

And then we all took turns hugging Matt. When he got all the tears out, we changed into our swimsuits and went to the pool. The dads threw us around the pool like usual while Matt sat on the edge of the pool, dangling his feet in the water. With some splashing and verbal taunts from us, before long, Matt started coming around and behaving more like his old self and was right in the middle of the fun with us.

Out of respect for Matt and the way he was feeling about Beth, we never asked him anything about what else he and Beth did together that day besides playing basketball and winning a giant stuffed bear. That was his business and his memories that he should be able to have to himself, and that was exactly the way we left it.

August, 1981, summer break, the end

There were more trips that went on the rest of that summer each weekend, but all good things have to come to an end. After another trip go-karting with Uncle Steve and his family, we returned back to John's house, and John's dad told me

"David, we need to talk to you about something."

"Sure, what's up?" I said as I sat down on the living room floor with John

"The new school year is going to start, and you're going to be in a new school, and so is John."

"Yeah, I know. We'll still be able to see each other after school and on weekends. Where is John going to 7th grade? Do you know yet?"

"Yes, we know. It will not be in a school here. We are moving out of this city and over to the next town."

"Wait… what?"

"You won't be able to just walk to his house and be there in a few minutes. We're going to be pretty far away compared to the way it's been for you now."

Tears welled up in my eyes

"I can't come and stay with you?"

"Well, no," John's mom took over. "Not like you've been able to here. You'll be able to see each other from time to time. Nothing changes the way we feel about you, David."

Now, the tears were silently pouring off my cheeks.

"I'm so sorry, David. My job made an offer for me to work in their office there, and we'd have a nice house if I took the job. Believe me, I didn't even say yes to the offer until the other day. I just couldn't bear to take it knowing how you feel about us, and we feel about you."

John was crying harder than I had ever seen him cry. Mom said, "John, come here." And he went to her waiting arms so she could hold him. John's dad did the same for me.'

He stopped hugging me and then pulled me back from his chest so I could sit on his knee.

"David, knowing you, loving you has been the best thing for our family, and we meant what we always said; we really do think of you as a son."

"Yes, David. Seeing you and John having fun, watching you sleep, it's all I can do but hug the stuffing out of you every time I look at you. Come here. "

And John and I switched places, both of us bawling.

We spent the rest of that night back and forth between Mom and Dad. Until bedtime when they tucked us in like usual.

"Night, buddy." Dad said to me, hugging me and kissing me on the forehead, "I love you so much, son."

"Wait!" I called to him as he got up to leave "When are you moving?"

"The day after tomorrow, we start packing, and we will be gone by the end of the week." And tears started welling up in his eyes as he looked at me

"Goodnight."

"Goodnight. I love you."

Dad came back and hugged me again, kissing me on the head and cheek before getting up to go again.

"Come on, you, let's get these covers up."

I pulled my arms up out of the covers and held them out so she'd hug me. She did and said

"Life can be so hard, but no matter what, we all love you."

"Please take me with you. PLEASE?!" I cried. "

"We can't. For so many reasons. It's going to be much more expensive going to live where we're going with our new house and what about grandma? You're going to have to take care of her."

"I love you so much, please."

"I know. I love you, too. We are going to still see each other, I promise."

She kissed me on my forehead and cheek and said.

"I love you more than words can say. More than my heart can show, just like I feel about John. Don't you ever forget it, son."

"I won't," I said, tears soaking my face and pillow.

"Goodnight"

"'Night"

After she turned out the light, I got out of bed, ran across to John's bed, and got in. We held each other and cried ourselves to sleep.

The next day, we woke up early and took our showers, going to the kitchen table and sitting down to be greeted by a plate of French toast stacked high.

We barely ate. John went to lie down on the couch after breakfast, looking sadder than I had ever seen him look.

I sat down on the floor in front of the couch. I didn't want to do anything.

"Boys, we had one more trip to take today if you want to go," Dad said

"Where?" I said.

"Chuck E Cheese. Before lunch. What do you say?"

"I don't wanna go. John said, rolling over on the couch so his face was to the back of it.

"Me either," I said.

Mom and Dad sat down on the carpet. Mom took me in her arms, and Dad picked up John from the couch and brought him down to meet us.

"Look, you two, we are family no matter what. Goodbyes are always hard, but let's spend the last day here together having fun. Don't let our last memory together be of such sadness." Dad said.

"Ok, I'll go." I said, "But only if John goes too."

"I'll go" John said through tears.

"Ok, we'll leave at 11:30."

John and I tried to put the situation out of our minds by doing the usual things, playing battleship, Legos, and Hot Wheels, but nothing felt right.

11:30 rolled around, and we took off for Chuck E Cheese. We spent the afternoon there playing games and like always, more skeeball than anything else. Our mood improved more and more as the day went on, the excitement of the high scores in skeeball causing big celebrations where we would jump up and down and point at the ticket dispenser as it kept pushing out loads of tickets. It was like continuously winning jackpots on a slot machine.

I had won a lot of tickets, and so did John. I told him to tell the girl behind the ticket counter what he wanted. He said a small semi-truck. I paid for it with my tickets. He used his tickets for three Hot Wheels cars and some different types of candy for me. I gave him half the candy, too.

We went home and watched some TV before bed before changing into our pajamas and getting into bed.

Mom came to me and said

"Thank you for always being such a wonderful brother and son. I love you."

"Thanks, Mom, I love you too," I said as bullets of tears started again.

A big hug and kiss on the head from mom.

"'Night."

"'Night."

Now Dad came to me.

"Aside from John you're the best son I ever had. I love you."

'I love you too, Dad. So much. You're the best dad ever," I assured him.

He picked me up so that the covers completely fell away from me and hugged me almost as hard as a bear hug before gently putting me back in bed and pulling the covers up.

"'Night."

"'Night, dad."

And he turned off the light and slowly closed the door.

I saw John crying into his pillow and went to his bed, bringing the Lego bucket with me. I went to his nightstand drawer and opened it to get his flashlight out and didn't have to say anything. Silently, under the covers, we built Lego starships, helping to make each other's ships even better as we built them. We didn't sleep a wink, and by the time dawn had arrived, we didn't have any more Legos to add, so we put the ships down on the floor and got into bed to finally get some sleep.

At 8 am, John's mom stepped over our many starships to get closer to the bed to kiss us good morning on our heads and tell us

"Pancakes and eggs for breakfast when you're ready, angels."

We showered and got to breakfast, and it was quiet except for the sound of clinking forks on plates.

After breakfast. Mom gave me a box.

"Use this for your clothes and other things, k? Don't forget your extra toothbrush."

"Oh no, I can't pack that."

"Why not?" Mom asked

"I have to leave it for your new house. I'll need it when I come visit."

"Oh, that's right." She said, "Yeah, leave your toothbrush."

"I want to leave my rocket too, so I can set it off with John at the new house. Is that ok? "

"Of course." She said.

After I packed everything up, Dad said.

"Bring it to the car. We'll drive you home."

"Ok," I agreed.

We drove to my house, and everyone got out of the car.

"Ok, well, I guess this is it, Mom said. Come here, young man."

Mom hugged and squeezed me so hard she nearly squeezed the stuffing out of me. She cried hard for a minute while she held me, then, getting herself together, said, "As soon as we get unpacked you are coming over for a big party. Promise."

Dad was next.

Biggest bear hug ever and then turned me upside down, holding me by my ankle and tickling my belly. I giggled uncontrollably, and then he set me back upright and hugged me again.

"I meant what I said. Aside from your brother, you're the best son ever. I love you so much. You are smart, and kind and I can't ever thank you enough for what you did for John after that last incident with Eggy and his friends."

"I love you too, Dad, and I meant what I said too. You're the best."

John, already crying gave me a huge hug and kissed my cheek, then hugged me some more before saying.

"I'll see you at the new house."

"Spit promise?" I said

"Yeah," He said, and he spit in his hand. I spit in mine, and we shook hands."

"What's that all about?" John's dad asked

"Spit promise. We learned it from Matt, Thomas, and Mark. I promised that we'd see each other at the new house and now I can't break my word. It's the truth, and it will happen."

"Oh," Dad said, tears falling as he walked back around to the driver's door of the car. Mom was next to get in. John gave me one last kiss goodbye. I kissed his cheek and high-fived him, saying

"Love you, bro."

"Love you too," John replied. "You're the best brother anyone could ever have."

"No, that's you," I responded.

"We're going to call you with our new number when we have our phone set up," Mom promised, hanging out the open car window."

"Ok, Bye."

John got in the back seat and shut the car door.

We all waved to each other as they pulled away from the curb and down the street.

I picked up my box of stuff and went up the rickety old stairs of the porch, down the hall, and knocked on the apartment door. Grandma opened it, and immediately, I started bawling when I saw her. I dropped the box and reached out my arms for a hug. She reached out, too. She held me there in the doorway of the house until I got it all out.

"I know it's hard. They called me the other day to tell me. You have so much to be thankful for that someone so special like John and his wonderful family were and always will be a part of your life. And they're not gone forever. You will still be able to talk on the phone and see each other sometimes. Even when the family goes away, they are still family, and they're in here," and she touched my chest over my heart."

"I know, it's just so hard," I said through tears still coming down.
"Come on, let's go inside."

I picked up my box and brought it inside.

As I unpacked the clothes that they had bought me, I thought about Matt and Beth. He had to say goodbye to that girl, Beth, but even though it was for a short time, he loved and was loved by someone, and that was what mattered. It was the same for me and John's family.

During that short time over the past few months, I learned so much about family and life. I learned that a true family was more than just the one you were born into; about dedication and loyalty, doing the right thing, taking responsibility for your actions, being the best that you can be, not resorting to copying others' bad behavior, and so much more. In short, I learned what being a boy was all about and what being a great man would be all about. I had an entire childhood jammed into just a few months and now I would be prepared for whatever changes would come next in my life, and there would be many.

Knowing all this didn't make it any easier, though. Effectively, even though they were still going to be in my life, I lost my family because they wouldn't be the safety blanket they had become when I needed them most. Knowing that I wouldn't be able to walk up the street to their house anymore broke my heart and my shredded my soul.

I stayed in my room for the rest of that day and I didn't eat anything. Grandma tried again and again to convince me to try and eat, but I just couldn't. I fell asleep on top of my bed, and at around 11 o'clock that night, my Mother came home in her expected intoxicated condition.

She looked at me on my bed and said

"Oh great, the shithead is back," and she stumbled to her room. At around 4 am, she came to my room and, as usual, just started punching me for no reason. Again and again, she hit me. I didn't fight her; why bother, I figured. I just let it go on. I didn't yell, I didn't even cry. I felt nothing. When she was through, she went back to her room and shut the door.

I was home.

September, 1981, seventh grade

We moved from the tenement that I had so far lived in my entire life and moved to a different tenement a few blocks away. We weren't even fully unpacked yet when the first day of school had arrived. I was having difficulty with the tie, which was not a clip-on. I had gotten it along with new dress shirts and blue uniform pants, necessary to go to school there the week before. Nervous, I didn't know anyone except one of my former classmates who DIDN'T pick on me but also didn't hang out with my friends and me.

Paulo was quiet and didn't really make friends with anyone, or at least he hadn't in the old school. I walked into the schoolyard with my new clothes on, and not knowing where I should be one of the teachers on the playground instructed that I should go to the left side of the playground with the boys, and the right side was reserved for the girls.

A bell loudly clanged on the wall above the playground entrance to the school, and the teachers all clapped their hands, signifying lineup time. We were expected to not make a sound, a teacher reminded and we all shuffled into class steadily. We were to put our lunches in the coatroom and hang up our jackets if we had   them.

Our teacher was at the front of the room, writing her name on the chalkboard. As we took our seats, the teacher said

"Alright now, let's do this without talking. Everyone get to your seats and face forward with your hands on top of the desk."

"My name is Miss Levesque, and I will be your teacher this year, except for English, which you'll go to Miss Spaulding's class next door each day for one period, and religion, which you will go to see her for one period three days of the week. When I am standing and instructing the class, or if we are reading, I will expect complete and total silence from every single one of you. If you are not quiet or you disrupt my class in any way, I will make a checkmark next to your name in my book. If you receive three checkmarks, you will have one day of detention. If you have 5 or more checkmarks, you will receive two days of detention."

It was already becoming clear the kind of teacher Miss Levesque was.

"You will not speak to answer a question if I have not called on you. You will not make a comment on another student's answer unless I have called on you. If you fail to meet these expectations, you will receive one check for each time you forget the rules. You get three bathroom passes each week. To go outside of the normally scheduled times. You are expected to go to the bathroom when we all go together as a class. Have I made myself clear?"

"Yes, Ma'am," resounded off the walls, echoing hollowly in the high-ceilinged classroom.

"You will stay on topic, and there will be no silliness while you are supposed to be learning. You will not laugh at other people's answers. You will not have conversations with your classmates in the classroom unless it is part of a discussion for a lesson or you are eating your lunch, at which time you may talk to the students on either side of you. Is this clear?"

Another "Yes, Ma'am" from everyone.
"Now, we are going to start with names so that I can make my seating chart. When I call your name, you will say your complete name and only your complete name. Is that clear?"

"Yes, Ma'am" again.

When she got to the row two over from mine, a girl sitting across from me said her name was Natalie. She was beautiful. Thick red hair tumbling past her shoulders, a few freckles on her cheeks, and beautiful blue eyes, I would discover later. There was no doubt. I was going into crush mode already just looking at her from a distance.

After the seating chart, we went into our first lesson, math. When Miss Levesque turned her back to write on the board, a boy behind me used his sharpened pencil to poke me in the back. It hurt, and, surprised, I called out

'OW!"

"That's a checkmark, David," Miss Levesque said as she turned and made a checkmark next to my name in the book."

"But that's not fair. He poked me with a pencil," I said, pointing to Glen, sitting behind me

"He's LYING!" Glen retorted. The boy next to him in the next row was trying to stifle a giggle

"…and one check for you as well, Glen." back to the book to make a checkmark next to Glen's name.

She went on with the lesson. Another poke in the back from Stephane, sitting next to Glen

Glen stifled a laugh as I jumped and said, "Hey, STOP it."

"Another check for David."

"But he poked me," I said, pointing to Stephane.

"Did you poke David?" she asked Stephane.

"No, Ma'am."

And she turned back to face the board, and Glen poked me again, this time in the butt.

"Would you QUIT IT!" I yelled at him.

"Detention today for David. Not getting off to a good start, are we, David."

I looked at Glenn as he smirked at me and then flipped me the bird when Miss Levesque turned her back to the class again to face the board.

But recess, after lunch, was what I was interested in. I wanted to get a better look at Natalie, and she was indeed gorgeous in every way. Her uniform blouse was tight against her midriff, mice hips were in her uniform plaid skirt; she was truly the epitome of beauty for someone in her grade, as perceived by boys her age.

I was talking to Paulo at lunch.

"Man, is she incredible," I said as I looked across the playground from our side over to hers.

"Yeah, she is," He replied.

A boy next to us, Pete, interjected.

"Forget about her." She doesn't make friends with boys.

"I'm gonna get a better look at her."

"How?" Peter asked

"The only water fountain out here is on their side of the playground. I'll ask Miss Levesque if I can get a drink of water."

"Good luck," Paulo said.

I went over to Miss Levesque, who had a permanent scowl on her face. Her lower lip flopped down, and her face crinkled up like she was smelling a skunk every second of her life.

"Miss Levesque, can I please get a drink of water?"

"The proper way to say it is 'may I get a drink of water.'" She said as if someone had hit her across the stomach and made her upchuck her lunch.

"MAY I PLEASE get a drink of water," I said, emphasizing certain words.

"Don't give me an attitude, or you'll get another check. Yes, you may get a drink of water."

I ran over to the other side of the playground, slowing down to almost a crawl as I got closer to where Natalie was standing across from the water fountain. I turned the knob to start the water flow from the faucet and sipped as I stared at Natalie. I drank for a long time getting in an extended look, taking in her beauty as she talked to two other girls from class.

"That's enough water, David! Return to the boys' side right now." Miss Levesque shouted to me.

Her call caused Glen to look over at what I was doing. He poked Stephane in the arm, who stood right next to him. They both whispered something together and then laughed.

I walked back slowly, keeping my eyes on Natalie as long as I could before looking in front of me again.

"She really is something else," I said to Paulo and Pete.

"Yeah, but if you're a boy, she acts like you don't exist. The only boy she talks to is her brother. He's in 6th grade. He doesn't like anyone talking to her or even looking at her either. He fought a sixth grader last year after school because he just kept looking at her." Pete told us

"Damn!" I said. "Did he win?"

"Yeah, he won. The other kid had a black eye and a bloody nose. Look, that's him over there, playing tag with the other sixth-grade boys." Pete said, pointing directly at him.

"What's his name?" I inquired.

"Michael. Don't call him Mike, he hates it."

"Ok, see you." And I started walking away.

"Where are you going?" Paulo asked.

"I'm gonna go play tag. Come on."

"What are you up to?" Pete asked.

"Nothing, I just wanna play some tag. Come with me."

Pete and Paulo looked at each other and then at me and started walking toward Michael and the sixth-grade boys. I figured that if I became friends with Michael, maybe he would be ok with me talking to Natalie. It wouldn't happen today, but I could start the process at least. There was no way I was ready to even approach Natalie yet. I was far too nervous. Just looking at her when I went to get a drink of water had given me butterflies in my stomach.

I said to one of the other sixth-grade boys

"Hey, can we play?"

"Sure, you're it."

I ran after a couple of other boys and caught them, and then I ran after Michael. He was faster than a jackrabbit, dodging and bobbing and weaving away from me and taking off in a new direction every time I had just about come close enough to catch him. Eventually, getting tired, when I got close to him, I jumped toward him and caught him. We both lost our balance when I caught him, and we fell down.

We both laughed. Paulo and another sixth-grade boy said, "You're it."

Michael and I were exhausted and breathing hard, sitting on the ground.

"I need some water," Michael said. He got up and said to a nearby teacher

"Miss Harris, I need a drink of water. May I please go get some water?"

"Yes, Michael."

"Come on," he said, and I panicked. We were going to have to walk past Natalie again to get a drink of water because she still hadn't moved from the spot where she was talking to her friends. How was I going to be able to not look at her as I walked by? I had to try. As we walked over, Michael said

"You're new here, huh?"

"Yeah," I said as we were getting closer to Natalie, trying to keep my focus only ahead and on Michael, not off to the side where Natalie stood.

"What's your name? I'm Michael."

"David"

And we high-fived each other just as we were approaching Natalie. For no reason, he stuck his tongue out at her as we were about to pass. It gave me a reason to be looking, so I figured I'd be safe. She stuck her tongue out at her, too, and one of Natalie's friends laughed and playfully kicked at Michael as we passed.

"Ha! Missed me!"

"I'll get you later," Natalie said, laughing. Then she smiled....at ME."

"No, you won't," Michael said, sticking out his tongue again.

"That's my sister."

"Oh yeah?" I said, trying to act nonchalant while getting my heart to slow down both from our game of tag and the fact that Natalie had just sent it racing again with her beautiful smile.

"Yeah, she's cool. For a girl."

"That's cool," I said.

We got to the fountain took a long drink, and walked back past Natalie and her friends, who were now giggling as we passed, and Natalie looked at me again and smiled.

I smiled back, and the other girls tittered and giggled some more.

Now, my chest was sore from all the pounding my heart was doing. I tried to keep my gaze to their direction as limited as I could so as not to make Michael mad. I wasn't about to blow all the progress I had just made.

She looked at me and smiled TWICE! I was sure I had an advantage over other boys now. I would be able to talk to her once Michael saw me as his friend and wouldn't kick my ass for talking to her or looking at her. I was sure of it.

After some more tagging, the teachers called us to line up: boys on the right and girls on the left. Natalie smiled at me again as she got in line one person back in the line. This was another reminder that we should all be silent when making our way back to class, and in a minute, we were back at our desks.

The rest of the school day went the same way as the morning. I was up to six checkmarks by the end of the day, and I would have had even more if I hadn't stifled myself for about a dozen more pencil sticks. They were relentless, doing it every time the teacher wasn't looking in their direction. When they started to get no reaction from me, they poked me harder and then harder.

About 5 minutes before the end of the day dismissal bell, Miss Levesque gave me two detention slips that she informed me I would have to bring home and have my mother sign and bring back, and I would serve my detentions starting tomorrow.

My heart sank. Here we go again. Mother would be angry, for sure, with my already having to serve detention on the first day of school.

As the bell rang and we all got up to retrieve our lunchboxes and coats for those who brought one, Pete came over to me and said

"Hey, wanna get a soda at Dairy Mart."

While we didn't have school cafeteria lunches, we did get milk every day that we could buy if we wanted it, but most kids opted not to, so they ended up with pocket money like my old school.

"Yeah." And we walked out of the schoolyard and toward the store. We passed Natalie and her brother with a couple of the other girls in class, and I didn't dare look at them as we passed until Michael said, "Hey!"

And gave me an excuse to look.

"Hey," I said, catching a glimpse of Natalie's red hair glowing in the sun.

"We're gonna play kickball at recess tomorrow if you wanna play."

"Sure," Pete and I both said.

Then to me, Michael said, "I want you on my team 'cuz you run fast."

"Alright," I responded.

"Ok, see you."

"See you," and we kept going toward the store. We bought our sodas and walked off in different directions. Pete lived up the street from where John used to live, and I lived a few blocks away from where I used to live on a different street. I chugged my can of RC and looked around at the neighborhood. It was slightly better than my old one, but not by much. One thing that was different was that I now had my own key because the landlord had issued us three of them.

I unlocked the door, and Grandma was in front of the TV, sewing one of her dresses.

"How'd it go?" she asked between stitches.

"It   was   ok.   I   got   detention."

"What? Not already?!"

"Yeah, two boys poked me with their pencils, and it hurt, so when I made a noise and told them to quit it, Mrs. Levesque gave me checkmarks. You get three checks, and you get a detention. I got detention for two days."

And I took the slips out of my pocket to show her.

She looked at them and said, "This seems so unfair. Your mother doesn't have to know. I'll sign them."

"No, she said it HAS to be signed by my mother."

"Oh. Well, you know she isn't going to be happy."

"Yeah, tell me about it."

"Did you make any friends?"

"A couple. Two in my class and another sixth grader."

"That's good. Ok, go get out of those school clothes and into your play clothes. You don't want your mother to have another reason to be mad."

I did as she said. As I was putting on my play clothes, I had a funny feeling, and everything got weird for a second. I saw sparkling colors in front of my eyes, and I couldn't move for a second. I didn't think anything of it and just went ahead with getting dressed.

Later, Mother came home right about dinnertime and didn't ask me anything; just went to a living room chair and sat down.

After about twenty minutes, seeing me lying on the floor doing my spelling homework, she said

"Well, how was your first day."

"It was ok. But…"

"And I stood up and went to my room to get the detention slips. I returned to the living room and handed them to her.

"What's this?"

"Detentions."

"Detentions?! DETENTIONS?!! On the first goddamn day?"

"It wasn't my fault."

"If it wasn't your fault, then WHY did YOU get DETENTION she sneered, grabbing me by the ear with one hand and slapping me across the face with the other. Next, she started taking off her belt.

"A new school, a Catholic school that's supposed to be better than public school, and you can't even behave on your first day.   Get   your   pants   off.

"No, please just let me explain."

"There is NOTHING to EXPLAIN. You got detention your first day, no explanation is needed. Now, get your pants off!!!

I did as she said and took off my pants and underwear, and the lashings started before my underwear hit the floor. She struck me again and again as hard as she could with the belt, the skin searing with instant pain where she struck.

"Your shirt. Take it off."

"Noooo please!!!!! No MORE!" I pleaded through tears.

"I SAID get the SHIRT OFF!" And she yanked at my tee shirt and tore it around the neck opening while pulling it over my head. Once it was free, she picked up the belt, doubled it up, and hit me again and again across the back."

"Now get the FUCK out of my SIGHT. Can't behave on your first day in a new school? Fine. You don't have to eat dinner."

I picked up my clothes and spelling book and went to my room and dumped myself on the bed. It may have been a new school year with lots of changes, but the things I wished the most would change stayed the same.

September, 1981 - Seventh Grade

A few days had passed, and it was the middle of the second week of school. I was walking home after a day when I DIDN'T have detention due to what Glen and Stephane and now a couple of other boys were doing to me, and I was on my way home after school. I had made a bit of progress with Michael, and he definitely saw me as a friend. Today I had dared to walk with them to their house. I still kept my eyes away from Natalie unless Michael, who was walking next to her, gave me a reason to look in his direction and see her at the same time I was looking at him. She was wearing blue pants today, and she looked even better in pants than a skirt. Her wider hips and narrow waist came together so perfectly that it was as if the maker of the pants made them just for her.

Then we got to their house, I said, "See ya," to Michael.

And Natalie said "Bye" and smiled. Every time she smiled I felt all warm and fuzzy inside. I walked toward my house and passed the Dairy Mart, where Glen and Stephane were just leaving, each with candy bars in their hands. When they saw me walk by, they walked quicker to catch up, and they kicked me hard in the butt every few feet.

"Quit it!" I turned and said to them.

They just laughed and said, "Fuck you."

And they continued doing it.

"STOP!" I said, turning around again.

WHAM! A fist to the nose. Glen punched me hard, and all I could see were stars and then red blood pouring from my nose and onto my school tie and dress shirt. I only had 3 dress shirts and 2 ties to rotate for school.

Glen and Stephane, of course, ran away as soon as Glen had done it.

I continued my walk home, and when I got there, as usual, Grandma fixed me up.

"This dress shirt is probably ruined. You're not going to be able to wear it anymore. I won't be able to get all that blood out of the shirt without scrubbing hard, and if all the blood does come out, scrubbing will ruin the shirt fabric."

After she cleaned me up, she said, "Come on, let's go to Bradlees. I'll use up the emergency fund to get you another shirt."

We went to the boys department of Bradlees and when we went to the register and I saw Eggy in the line with his father, checking out two lanes away. I tried to make it like I hadn't seen him as we were both leaving the store at the same time. His father was stopped by the door, checking the receipt, and we walked past him toward the exit door.

"Faggot baby," he said under his breath as we passed, barely loud enough for us to hear it.

"What did that boy say?" Grandma asked.

"Just keep moving, keep moving."

When we got far enough away, I told her

"That was Eggy."

"Oh, THAT'S him? Looks like trouble, for sure."

"Yeah."

When we got back home, mother was home. She was holding my bloodied dress shirt.

"Where were you, and why was this in the trash?"

She said with fury rising in her, "That can't be cleaned. One of the boys at school punched him in the nose and ruined his shirt."

"How do you KNOW it can't be cleaned when you didn't even try?" Mother inquired, rage getting stronger in her tone of voice.

"It's thin linen material. If I scrub it hard like I'd have to do to get the stain out, the material will be ruined, and I will make a hole, or it will become threadbare," Grandma said.

"YOU!" Mother said, redness washing over her face now and turning it to a scary shade of crimson. She lunged toward me and knocked me down. She grabbed my hair and started slamming my head on the bare floor where the area rug ended

"New school and STILL kids are beating you up? WHY? Huh, WHYYYY?!!"

And she slammed my head again and again. When she got up to go to the closet where the clothes dryer was kept, I staggered to my feet and stumbled my way into my room, closing the door and locking it.

The door was no match for mother in a fit of anger, however, and after several kicks and flying paint chips, the door jamb itself broke around the lock, and she was inside my room. She swung the stick at me again and again, and as I tried to escape her, I kept moving backward. I stood up lost my balance, and went to steady myself against the wall, but my hand went through the window, and the glass cut my hand deeply.

"Stop!" I screamed as a steady flow of blood from the wound made streaks through the air as I tried to deflect her swinging of the stick.

Grandma came and said, "ENOUGH!!! STOP IT! PLEASE STOP!!!"

"Mother And mother turned to Grandma, swinging the yardstick with all her might toward Grandma, striking her across the chest and sending her backward and almost causing her to fall down.

"Grandma! Grandma! Help! I'm bleeding a lot!"

"Blood gushed from the wound on my hand."

Mother just stood there breathing heavily as I passed her, dripping copious amounts of blood on the floor as I went to Grandma. She hurried me to the bathroom to wrap up my hand. Next, she went to the bedroom to get her shoes on, told me to do the same and we quickly left the house toward the bus stop for the bus that would transport us to the hospital.

I had cut into an artery on my hand, and that was why there was so much blood. The doctor, having stitched the wound, sent me home.

That night, just before bed, I had just finished brushing my teeth when I had a funny feeling, a tingling in my mouth and wave after wave of sparkling colors, and I lost control of my body. The last thing I could do was fall to the floor, which I did. Even though I saw Grandma, I couldn't say anything to communicate to her, and I shook violently.

Then the episode ended, I was weak, and all I could do was cry. Grandma held me, saying, "Are you alright? You had some sort of seizure."

"I'm ok now."

Mother had left the house to go drink, so she hadn't been there to see the event, and Grandma told me to sleep in her bed that night so she could keep an eye on me.

A couple of weeks later, the same type of thing happened again, and this time, Mother was there to see it. All 3 of us were in the hospital right after the event occurred. The emergency room doctor gave us a referral to a neurologist, and we went to see him a few days later.

After a series of questions that seemed to go on forever, the neurologist said, "I think we need to get an EEG and some scans of his head. It sounds like there is a possibility he has epilepsy."

In another week, I had a CAT scan and an EEG scheduled on separate days. Since I had already experienced two CAT scans, I was prepared for what would come with another. I did have questions about the EEG and an electroencephalogram.

"It's nothing, really," The attendant assured me as she squirted goo from a tube onto electrodes and placed them on my head in various locations. "You can sleep during the test if you want. At some points there will be colors of light flashed from over your head while you lie there with your eyes closed, but other than that, you really won't know anything is even happening." She said as she placed another electrode against my scalp. The test went according to plan, and the process of taking the electrodes off was a bit more involved, with the goo dry and hardened.

The doctor, upon going over the results, looked at us with concern.

"It appears he does indeed have epilepsy. I am going to prescribe medication, Tegretol, to control the seizures. He may still have them from time to time, even with the medication, but it should control them enough so he has less of them. Some children only have epilepsy for a short time, outgrowing it during or after puberty; others have it for the rest of their lives."

We agreed to a timetable of return visits to see the neurologist on a regular basis and to schedule scans and EEG tests in the future to monitor the condition. The school would have to be contacted and alerted that they have an epileptic student and what to do should I have a seizure at school.

Things were definitely changing with this new school year, but not for the better.

October, 1981, seventh grade

We sat in religion class as Miss Spaulding tried explaining one of Jesus's teachings, reminding us to follow along in our 'good news' book, a mini bible we were required to now keep with us at all times. It contained stories of Jesus's benevolent speeches, acts, and edicts, none of the negative aspects of the bible. It was like bible light, a way to ensnare young people into the Catholic religion.

It didn't make sense to me that god was all-knowing and all-seeing and all-powerful, but he allowed the suffering of children such as myself. It didn't make sense that he would love someone so much but not save them from torment or make it so that it couldn't happen. I would fail religion simply because I thought doing the assignments was ridiculous for someone like me, who god had clearly forsaken my entire 11-year life thus far. No god would allow the suffering and torment that I had gone through, or at least not the one portrayed in the Christian-based faiths.

I questioned Miss Spaulding in her teaching a few times at first but deemed it impossible to get through her strongly held belief. She was perfectly fine with believing in something with no evidence, while I felt that it was our duty to be evidence-bound. I was not a welcome sight in Miss Spaulding's religion class now that I made clear how I felt.

She labeled me as the troublemaker and looked at me with disdain each time I entered her class. She also stopped calling on me when I raised my hand. Nope, I can't have any actual debate or employ the scientific process of how to ascertain or determine evidence in the presence of a blind believer. Staunch believers shut you down and put up the proverbial sixteen-foot walls topped with barbed wire to keep you out.

After today's dull religion session ended, we had a second recess, which was welcome. I needed some air to breathe after sitting in the hall of intolerance.

Natalie was with her usual group of friends, with their mouths going a mile a minute, talking about who knows what. I messed up and forgot myself for a second too long as I stared in her direction, and Michael caught me.

"Hey, why are you looking at my sister like that?" He said, pushing my shoulder.

"Oh, I wasn't; I just was looking out the fence. I thought I saw someone I know drive by," I told him."

"Oh, sorry," he said.

And we got back to playing tag. He was still going to be difficult to get past, even though he was ok with me as a friend, it seemed. Maybe with more time. Maybe.

I went to take a drink of water after asking for permission from my horse-lipped teacher, who hadn't actually taught us anything so far this year, and to my surprise, Natalie asked for a drink at the same moment. We both ended up getting to the fountain at the same time

"You go ahead," she said

"No, you." I insisted.

"Thank you. At least you have manners. My brother doesn't." she said jokingly

I stared at her drinking the water, and I wished I could just go on watching her, being this close to her forever. My stomach was doing somersaults when she said

"Thank you, love."

"Y-You're welcome," stammered.

When I got back to the game of tag, I came down off cloud nine fast as Michael charged at me. I thought it was just the game of tag starting up again, and he was 'it,' but that wasn't the deal.

He saw me staring at Natalie, and now he wanted me dead. He made sure I knew it when he caught up to me, grabbed my shirt, and tore it as he threw me to the ground. He was on top of me in a second, and he punched me in the face, hitting my cheek. I wasn't going to stand for this, and I shifted my weight so he fell off me, and I started punching him back in the ribs and stomach. All the other boys on the playground were cheering at us and encouraging us loudly when Miss Levesque and another teacher came over and split us up.

"Ok, let's go, both of you. March to the principal's office right now!" and Miss Levesque followed us into the school.

Sister Simone was the principal and had been for more than thirty years, from what I heard on the day of the tour. She was a short, rotund but kind nun.

Miss Levesque brought Sister Simone up to date on what had just occurred.

"Michael, I am very surprised at you. This is not like you. What happened? "

"He's a JERK; that's what happened," Michael said, looking at me in the chair beside him in front of Sister Simone's desk.

"I'm the jerk?! You started this, running after me and pulling my shirt and knocking me down."

"Well, you shouldn't have been doing what you were doing."

"BOYS!!! That is ENOUGH," Sister Simone stated sternly."

We both stared at each other a moment longer, still heated.

"Look at me."

We did.

"You know we do not tolerate fighting. I will be calling each of your parents to inform them of what you have done. You will be suspended for one day, and you will have 3 days of detention. Is that clear?"

"Yes, Ma'am." We both said simultaneously.

"Michael, you go on back outside to finish recess, and this time, behave yourself."

"I will, ma'am."

"And do you have anything to say to David?"

"I'm sorry, David."

I looked at him as he said it. He seemed to be genuine.

"Ok, now go on back outside." Sister Simone said while focusing her attention on me as he walked out of her office and down the hall.

"David, you've been having a bit of a hard time adjusting to the school. Do you want to talk about it?"

"It's just that I'm new, and some of the kids have been mean to me, and they get me into trouble on purpose because they think it's funny."

"I'm sorry to hear that. The adjustment period can be hard for someone when they are new, but over time, you'll get into their friend circles and be one of them."

"I don't want to be one of them if they're mean. It's not right to be mean." I said, a tear trickling from the corner of my eye.

"That's right, David. It's not. Remember that, and act on it, and you'll behave as God wants you to, wants all of us to, toward one another. You may go back outside."

"Yes, ma'am."

And I walked down the hall to discover recess to be over. My class was filing back into the classroom. As I got closer to the classroom door, the sixth-grade class was coming back in. As we passed each other, Michael grabbed my hand and said, "Hey, I really am sorry, k."

"K, me too," I replied.

We finished the day in the classroom, and I had a rough night to look forward to. I made my way outside when I heard behind me

"Hey look, it's the seventh grader who thinks it a big deal to beat up a sixth grader, ha ha ha ha!!"

It was Glen talking to Stephane.

"Hey, want us to get some first graders for you to beat the shit out of?" Stephane said mockingly, getting other kids, boys and girls laughing.

They followed me home, taking turns pushing me, kicking me, taking my books, and throwing them into the street.

"Come on, big man, if you're so great, take us on. Come on, we'll even let you take the first punch." Glen said, trying to get me to start a fight. I just ignored them.

When I got home, they went past me and on to wherever they were going.

I walked in, and Grandma saw my torn shirt and a hole in the knee of my pants. She said

"What happened NOW? "

I told her the story, and she said, "What kind of school is that, anyway? More bullies, more problems... Sister Simone called and said you were suspended for a day."

I took off my torn and holey clothes and gave them to Grandma so she could mend them.

Mother came home after I went to bed, so I had to get up to tell her about being suspended.

My clothes were off once again, at her insistence, and she beat me with the yard-stick again. She finished with the belt, this time using the buckled end against my ribs. The beating lasted for more than half an hour. I had no more tears to cry by the time it was over. Every inch of my back and chest was covered in bruises and welts.

October, 1981, seventh grade

When I returned to school after my suspension, I was at the chalkboard in the classroom; I was trying to work out a math problem on the board but was not able to do it because I hadn't understood the directions. No matter how many times I tried to explain that fact to Miss Levesque, she wasn't listening.

"It's not my fault you can't listen in class when I teach. I am NOT going to keep repeating myself just because YOU can't get it. Have fun staying at the board. You'll be there until you get it done."

When I would try and figure it out on my own and was wrong about my method, she would slap my knuckles with the edge of the ruler, saying, "No, no, no, no, no, that's NOT what I said to do" and the class would laugh. She had apparently suspended the rules when I was at the board, failing to be able to do my work as others could because she just let them go right on laughing at me and ridiculing me.

"Tell him, class, YOU understood it, didn't you?" encouraging the class to say 'yes' and to tease me about being stupid.

I stayed at the board all day except at lunch. I endured the rest of the class, except Pete and Paulo, ridiculing me each time a lesson was complete, and Miss Levesque checked on my progress, seeing it hadn't taken place, ridiculing me and allowing the class to laugh at me. I cried several times, and each time I did, she said

"Keep up that crying and interrupting other people's work, and I will give you another check," so I was forced to cry quietly. My knees were sore and exhausted by the day's end from standing at the board in one place all day. I wasn't even allowed to go to the bathroom.

When I left, Glenn and Stephane ran after me and caught up, grabbing the drawstring cords at the neck of my coat and pulling me down. Then they dragged me on my belly across the sidewalk and into and up the street, leaving me in the middle of the street and running off.

Cars honked their horn for me to get out of the middle of the street and drove around me, trying to get where they were going. I got up to discover my jacket was ruined beyond any fixing grandma could do, and so were my pants. My hands were scraped up as well.

"Oh, Lord, not again!"

I took off my coat and the rest of my clothes, got into my play clothes and my old jacket that didn't quite fit me anymore, and left the apartment. I didn't know where I was going, but I didn't care. I just hated my life and needed to get out and do something. I didn't know what I was going to do, but I knew I had to do something. I wanted them dead. All of them. Anyone who hurt me. I got an idea. I went back home and hung up my coat. While Grandma was in the kitchen starting to work on dinner, I sneaked into her room. Grandma had some of Grandpa's things in her top dresser drawer; she had shown them to me before. There were some drawing leads and other artist materials, his glasses, and the thing I was looking for, his pearl-handled buck knife. I brought it back to my room and opened it and checked the sharpness of the blade. It was very sharp. I put the Knife into the pocket of my school pants for tomorrow.

After another beating from my mother regarding the condition of my new jacket and school pants, I went to bed. I didn't sleep, however. This year was full of changes and new starts that really weren't that new at all because it was just a continuation of my previous school and life at home.

Tomorrow, however, would be a truly new start. It was a guarantee if anyone teased or hurt me.

The alarm clock sounded, and I got up from bed right away since I wasn't sleeping. I ate no breakfast, choosing instead to get to school right away.

"Why are you leaving so early?" Grandma called to me as I put on my old coat to go. I didn't respond.

Mother said, "Oh, let the little troublemaking bastard go."

I ignored her comments, thought I did stroke the pearl handle of the buck knife in my pocket.

I continued on my way.

The schoolyard was empty and eerily quiet, a state that was not something I had ever heard there except at the end of the day after everyone left while I was serving detention for things that weren't my fault.

I looked around at the places in the schoolyard where the boys would go down at the edge of my blade if they picked on me, the places in which the girls would meet their fate for laughing or teasing me.

Moments later, the first of the teachers and children started arriving. I saw Natalie. I hoped she wouldn't have to see what I would have to do if I were driven to it today.

Miss Levesque walked past me and into the building without speaking to me, as if I weren't even standing there. A few minutes later, Pete arrived followed by Paulo right after.

"Hey," Pete said.

"Hey."

"Hope Miss Levesque doesn't do what she did to you again yesterday. God, she is such a bitch."

I didn't respond.

"You alright, Dave? You look tired and pale."

"I'm alright, and I'll BE alright," I replied and walked away to be alone. I didn't want my friends to be close and possibly get hurt if I had to take care of business with it.

Stephane and Glen walked into the playground next, attached at the hip, as if they were just one person as usual.

Neither one of them looked in my direction, however, choosing to keep to themselves among some of the other boys in class.

Two of the other boys glanced in my direction and then turned back to Glen and Stephane. My fingers wrapped around the knife in my pocket. They didn't say anything or make any gestures.

The bell rang, and we all lined up. In the classroom, we all sat down after putting our coats and lunches in the coatroom.

The day started with math, and Miss Levesque explained her lesson for the day and then went around the classroom to see how the students were proceeding with the work. She was calmer today and more patient. She didn't ridicule me when I needed more instruction and didn't strike my knuckles with the ruler when I didn't do the number operations as expected. She explained again and stayed with me until I was able to get it.

In English class, we diagrammed sentence structure, and it was a great morning. I made no mistakes when I went to the board to diagram my particular example.

Lunch and recess were going just fine as well and no one looked at me or did anything untoward to me.

I was thinking about John's dad and Uncle Steve and what they would say about what I wanted to do, what I had been pushed to do after so many years of abuse, how it would be lowering myself below their level, and how wrong it was for me to allow myself to be alright with hurting someone else. I thought about what Eggy and his friends did to John, cracking four of his ribs and almost busting his spleen. I didn't ever want to be as low as that, and what I was planning to do to someone that day if they hurt me would definitely make me one of them.

I was sitting on the steps to the building when Michael came over to me.

"Hey. Are you ok? We want to play some tag. Want to join us?"

I looked up at him and said

"Ok, first I have to do something. I'll be right back."

"Miss Levesque, may I please use the bathroom."

"Yes, of course, David."

I went inside the school and to the bathroom, wrapped the knife in some paper towels, threw the knife into the trash, and used some more wadded-up paper towels to cover it.

Inside my mind, I said, "I'm sorry, John, Dad, and Uncle Steve, for wanting to hurt them as they hurt me. I'll defend myself if I can, but I won't ever become like them. Spit promise. I miss you, and I love you."

I got back outside to Michael, who said

"You took long enough. I thought you were taking a dump. Come on before we run out of time to play tag."

"Ok," I said. Pete, Paulo, and I joined most of the sixth-grade boys playing tag, and the rest of the day went just as well as it had started. There was at least SOME hope.

November, 1981, seventh grade

The day had come for parent/teacher conferences, something Mother had refused to go to since I attended first grade. I knew that it wasn't going to be good. I had been subjected to many detentions as a result of Glen and Stephane's antics and intent of getting me into trouble so they could continue to pick on me.

Mrs. Levesque was doing her best job at constructing a false front of being a proper teacher in the most rudimentary definition of the word.

"I have tried to help David all I can because I think he has great potential to be able to excel in other subjects as he does at spelling and reading. He is a wonderful boy that his classmates like very much."

What was she talking about? She was laying it on thicker than molasses. Do my classmates LIKE me? Oh, sure, so I can be the class laughingstock and buffoon, which SHE has encouraged by not actually teaching and allowing them to make fun of me. Aside from that one day where she made a little more effort, she hadn't tried to approach me on my level of need.

My mother, looking confused, said, "He tells me that other kids pick on him, poke him with pencils, pinch and twist his arm, and call him names. Two boys have beaten him after school and dragged him into the street by his coat drawstrings."

"Well, they don't do that in class; I can assure you, I would know about it."

I was aghast at what she was saying. Of COURSE, they did it in class; every second that she had her gaze away from them, they took advantage of it.

"As far as what goes on outside of here, I can't see the students here doing these things to him outside of here."

"But they DO!" I blurted out

"Be quiet. "Mother said. "We are listening to your teacher right now."

I did as I was told and just sat there listening to Mrs. Levesque's fabrications.

"The thing of it is, David just doesn't apply himself. He daydreams, and he just doesn't care about the work."

That was partially true. I could have cared less about the geography and history, but I did try to do the math, and with John's dad's help the previous school year, I was able to do it because he was patient with me and repeated the steps and taught the process to me in ways I could understand. He was 100 times the teacher this pathetic excuse for a liar was. Not once did her two pets, Glen and Stephane, get in trouble, in spite of causing the most trouble for me and the other kids in the class.

I didn't argue the point any further because, as usual, I wouldn't be believed.

I just sat there while she continued to spin a yarn of lies that could knit an extra-large sweater of falsehoods.

When we finished, she displayed her most fake smile, thanked us for coming, and assured Mother that she would continue trying to help me to do better with my learning.

Outside the school. Mother walked briskly as if to intentionally put distance between us. I tried to keep up but found it difficult unless I ran. At one point, she got through the crosswalk light just before it changed, and I was stranded on the sidewalk to wait for the next one for a minute. It allowed her to get a huge head start on getting home. She was able to get inside first, and she put the chain on the door so that I couldn't get in, even though I had used my key to do so.

"Unlock the chain!"

I heard bumping and other noises in the apartment. What was she doing?

"Come on, Let me in. Grandma! Come to the door to take the chain off."

"I can't, your mother won't let me in."

"Goddamn right. Useless fucking BRAT still can't get it together in a new school, one that is supposed to be BETTER and able to HELP more than public school. That's fine. You're not going to do what's necessary; you won't live in this house!" she came to the door to open it and threw my suitcase with some clothes in it out the door into the hallway.

"Where will I GO? I have nowhere to GOOOO!" I pleaded, grabbing her arm. She grabbed my wrist and, with all her strength, much more than necessary, twisted my hand off her arm and then threw me to the hallway floor and kicked me in the face. Her shoe made contact with my cheek, and I went backward to the floor, hitting my head on it. She slammed the door shut."

I picked up my suitcase and walked out of the building and to the closest bus stop.

A few minutes later, the bus arrived. I remembered the time when grandma and I went to the YWCA to try and get a room, I knew there was a YMCA up the street for men, so I asked the driver

"Does this bus go to the YMCA?"

"No. go up the street, make a right, go three blocks, and cross the street. The C-3.

"Ok, thank you sir."

"Welcome," and he shut the doors.

I walked over to where he said to catch the correct bus and waited for almost half an hour because I had just missed the bus before I got there. Once I was aboard, I put the 25 cents into the fare box and hoped the driver wouldn't notice that it wasn't enough. He didn't. Just waved me back.

I sat down, waiting for the bus to go by the Y, and I would get off at the next stop and walk back.

After about 15 minutes of travel, we passed the Y, and I pulled the cord to sound the buzzer.

The bus stopped at the next stop, and I walked back to where I had seen the Y. The streets around it didn't look any better than the area of the city where I lived. Old broken-down tenements and cars that looked long past their proposed period of feasible operation.

I walked into the Y and saw a man behind the counter.

"Excuse me, sir, I need a room."

He looked up and around me to see where the rest of my party was

"Who are you here with, boy?"

"No one, sir. I'm here by myself."

"By yourself!" he said with surprise, looking over the counter and seeing my suitcase.

"On a trip from out of town?"

'What do I do? Do I lie?' I thought. It was looking like I wasn't going to be able to check in without having an adult to accompany me so I went with the story.

"Yeah. They aren't here yet. They won't get here until tomorrow. I got here earlier than I was supposed to."

"Ok, who made the arrangements in advance?"

Now, I panicked. How do I get out of this one?

"I'm not sure. Might have been Uncle Ron," I said, picking what I hoped would be a name they'd have on their list of upcoming guests.

"Oh, ok, Ron Lantis is coming in tomorrow night on the Greyhound; I see it here in the notes. Doesn't say anything about a second person..."

That was because we were coming from different places."

"The man looked at me and said, hmmmm... ok. Very peculiar... he still should have provided that as information for check-in... but since it's for only two nights and we have a lot of vacancies, I will allow it. Now you listen here; this is primarily an adult-man facility. That means not very many boys unless there's a reason for them being here, like swimming or basketball or the Y youth group activities. You will behave yourself like a gentleman. Understand?"

"Yes, sir, I understand."

"Ok, come on, let's go to your room. It will be on the 4th floor. Pool in the basement, and you listen to the lifeguard while you're there. There is no need to bring your own towels to swim; we have our own to provide for you. The recreation room closes at 9 PM. Check-out is at 10 AM. Any questions?" The man said as we were walking to the elevator."

"No, sir. Thank you, sir."

"Ok here we are on the 4th floor. You'll be in 419. The bathroom at the end of the hall. Community showers. Protect your stuff, leave any of it in your room, lock the door, and wear the key around your neck with the lanyard that's attached to the key before showering if you decide to. One last time, questions?"

"No, sir."

"Ok then, if you need anything, there will always be someone at the front desk even after we lock up for the night at 11 PM. Enjoy your stay."

The man left, and I unlocked the door. It wasn't a big room, but it was what I had, so I wasn't going to complain. It was better than being out on the street. I opened my suitcase to see what mother had put in the suitcase and I found two pairs of pants, two shirts, some underwear and socks and that was it. No swimsuit. No pool for me. No matter.

The one thing that I did want was food. I wondered if they had any. I decided to scout around and find out. I locked my door and put the key in my pocket. I boarded the elevator, went to the first floor, and walked by the front desk, where there were some flyers regarding programs offered by the Y or organizations using the Y space for their programs or activities.

I saw that there was an after-school activity room on the first floor, and the room number was listed. I walked around the hallway on the first floor and found the room darting in for a snack. There was a table where a lady sat with sandwiches, bags of chips, and containers of chocolate milk, and behind her were several long conference tables where children worked on homework and were playing games and drawing.

"What can I get you?" the lady asked me.

"May I please have a sandwich and a bag of chips and milk, please?"

"Two 'pleases'... wish all the kids who come here had your manners. I don't remember seeing you here before. Did your parents just sign you up for the after-school program this week?"

"Yes, Ma'am, and thank you. I have to get home now," I lied as I darted back out the door as quickly as I had come in.

I walked past the recreation room and saw teenagers playing pool, foosball, bumper pool, and air hockey

Once the elevator stopped at my floor, I opened the door and sat on the bed to eat my dinner. I looked out the window at the view of the city. From up here, it didn't look so bad. I ate my sandwich and chips and drank my milk, remembering that at least this time, aside from when she kicked me in the face, mother hadn't beaten me again today. Regardless of what else happened, it was a good day.

I needed to go to the bathroom, so I walked down the hall, where I found the men's bathroom with community showers.

After washing my hands, I walked back to my room, saying hello to two guys, one of whom was holding a basketball and either going to the indoor or outdoor basketball courts.

I didn't have any pajamas with me so I just would have to sleep in my underwear that night. I really didn't care as long as I had a bed to sleep in.

I took off my school clothes and hung them on hooks on the back of my door, tucked myself into bed, listened to the sounds of the city, and fell asleep at 11 years old, by myself, at the Y.

November, 1981, seventh grade

After school, for my soda run, instead of going into the Dairy Mart, which was closer to the school, today I went to Pasquale's Market, which was closer to my house, just a block away.

I got my usual RC cola and chugged it while thinking about what was to come for the weekend John and I were talking to each other on the phone on a regular basis 4 or 5 times a week, and we had set up the date of this Saturday as the day I would finally get to see his new house. His parents were busy in their spare time painting rooms and buying furniture to really make it a great place before having company come over. Today was Friday, and they would be arriving soon after school to pick me up and bring me to their house for a weekend sleepover, so I had to get home quickly. As I got closer to my house near the end of the block, I saw John's parents' Datsun wagon, and I dropped my can of soda and ran at top speed.

They were all outside the car, and when John saw me running, he ran toward me, and when we reached each other, we hugged and high-fived each other.

Dad picked me up and gave me the biggest bear hug and kissed me on the cheek and head.

"OHHHH, we've MISSED you, son!" I told him.

"I've missed you too!"

Mom was next picking me up and holding me and saying, "My baby! You're getting so big I'm gonna have trouble picking you up at all anymore let alone hold you. Love you!" and she kissed me on the head three times."

"Love you too."

"Did you pack yet?" Dad asked.

"Yeah, mostly. Just gotta put my hairbrush and shampoo in the bag and some socks and underwear. I had to wait for Grandma to do the wash today. "

'Don't worry about the shampoo, we have plenty of that" John's mom told me

We all went inside, and Grandma gave John a big hug and handed him a new Hot Wheels car

"Look at you! Growing before my very eyes," she said to John, getting even more handsome than ever she said, kissing John's cheek and messing up his hair."

John blushed and said, "AWWW… grandma!" and then when he looked at the Hot Wheels car, he said, "Wow! Thank you for the car!"

"May I get you something to drink?" Grandma asked.

"No, better not; we have to get back to the house because we have a surprise for the boys, and we have to get home soon for the surprise."

"Surprise? What surprise?" John inquired.

"The one you don't know about because it's a surprise Dad said, reaching out and poking John in the belly and tickling him a little.

John giggled and said, "Ok, ok, ok."

I went to the laundry basket of clean clothes and sifted through it to get a couple of pairs of socks and underwear out of the basket to tuck into my suitcase. I packed them inside and changed out of my school clothes and into some play clothes which were some of last school year's clothes that John's parents bought me.

"Ok, I'm ready to go," I said with a suitcase in hand.

"Ok then, let's get going. Mom said."

"Alright, Edith, it was wonderful seeing you again." John's dad said, giving Grandma a hug, followed by a hug from Mom.

"Wonderful seeing you again, too. You be good." Grandma said, pointing to me.

"I will," I assured her.

Once outside I tossed my suitcase in the back hatch and got in the back seat with John.

We traveled over the water and across a major bridge from the city to the next town over, which was a borderline city of its own, and about 12 minutes later, we pulled into a driveway next to a medium-sized house.

It was a good-looking house nestled between some other nice similar-looking houses on a quiet street. Kids were riding by on bikes and playing games on the sidewalk and in their yards. It was a little too 'city' to be suburbia, but it was close.

John took me to see the backyard which had a small deck and a barbecue grill.

"We're gonna barbecue tonight, too. Dogs and burgers."

Then, they took me through the backdoor to see the inside of the house. It had the smell of fresh paint and new furniture. John grabbed my hand to take me to his room so I could see how much bigger it was. There was definitely lots more space for everything, and he had a new bed with a headboard that had a bookcase built into it, and the old second bed I had slept in was gone, and its place was John's old bed.

"Where'd the old bed go?" I asked.

"In here" John said, taking me to the family room where that old bed and one that looked just like it were in the family room, which was separate from the living room. There was a huge couch and three beanbag chairs on the floor.

"Look at this." John excitedly said, pointing at something on top of the console TV in the family room.

"You got an Atari! No WAY!!!"

"Yes, way!"

"How many games you got?"

"Ten so far."

"WOW!!!"

"Can we play?"

"Not yet, son, you need to get unpacked. You can put your stuff away in the same dresser drawer you had before. You've got three days. We are making this a long weekend for you boys," John's dad said.

'Yes, sir! Three days! YAYYYYYYYY!!!" John and I cheered.

As I was unpacking and putting the last of the clothes away, the doorbell rang.

"Boys, would you please get the door John's mom called from the kitchen.

"Yes, Mom," we both replied, running to the door.

"Who is it?" John said.

"Take a guess," a voice that sounded familiar said.

John opened the door, and Matt, Thomas, Mark, and their parents were standing there, all crowded together.

"OMIGOD!!! No WAYYYYYY!" and we jumped around and hugged and high-fived everyone.

"Surprise!" John's mom and dad said to John, and me as Uncle Steve and his family made their way into the living room.

"Dad, can I please show them around?" I asked

"Yes, you can."

"Come on! John's got a new Atari," I excitedly exclaimed as I herded the boys toward the family room."

"Are you SERIOUS?!" Matt said.

"I get to play it first! Thomas said.

"Me too," Mark added.

After seeing the rest of the house, John's dad said to Uncle Steve.

"You can all sleep here in the family room. That couch folds out into a bed and the boys can use these other two beds in here and the couch in the living room."

"Thank you, sounds great, Aunt Anne said."

"Burgers and dogs on the grill tonight if the weather holds up. It might rain later on, hopefully, after we're all done eating. If it does rain earlier, we'll get pizza delivered or something."

"Yeah, that sounds great."

Matt was grabbing his dad's arm, trying to get his attention.

"Yes, son, what is it?"

"Can we PLEEEEASE play Atari now?"

"Yeah, go ahead. Remember to share."

"Yes, sir."

"Their other cousin has an Atari too now, so they know a lot of the games, and they aren't always good about giving someone else a turn."

"Typical boys, possessive," Mom said.

"Yeah, they are."

After an hour of playing video games, Dad called us from the back deck.

"Boys, turn off the Atari for now and come join us out back; the food's almost ready."

"Yes, Sir," everyone said as John turned off the Atari and TV.

There was a large wood slat table with a yellow flower print umbrella overhead. The boys all sat there. The parents were already sitting in folding outdoor chairs nearby, except for John's dad, who was at his station, grilling away, turning burgers and dogs, and making sure that one side didn't cook more than the other.

When he finished, Dad brought plates of dogs and burgers to the table and buns and said

"Make 'em how you want."

After we ate too much, we all sat around talking. Dad said to Uncle Steve.

"Thanks for bringing your boys. Aside from the times John talks to Dave and your boys on the phone, he's been really down. Doesn't want to eat, having trouble fitting in at school, you know how it goes."

"Yeah, it's hard being in a new school, starting all over again. Matt had problems at first, too, but he's finally starting to fit in." Uncle Steve added and then shifted focus to me.

"How's your new school, Dave?"

"Awful. My teacher is so mean, and so are the kids. Made a couple friends but…."

"Yeah, it's tough, buddy, I know."

"It's the same as my old school, really."

"That's a shame," Matt's mom said.

"Well, we're not going to think about any of that THIS weekend. This weekend, we are going to just focus on having fun." John's mom said, trying to turn the mood of the conversation to things more positive.

"Speaking of that, there's a lake and place to have picnics and cookouts not far from here in the next town. Getting too cold to swim, but we're going there tomorrow for a picnic."

John's dad informed us.

"YAAAAAYYY!" came from the mouths of all us boys.

The outdoor festivities had to end due to rain, but that was ok because we were coming inside anyway. All of us, adults included, took turns playing all of John's game cartridges on the Atari until late into the night. Around midnight, John's dad said

"Ok, boys, let's shut it down for now and get some shuteye."

"Yes, Dad," and he got up and turned off the game system and TV, picking up the Atari off the floor and putting it back on top of the TV.

After tucking ourselves in, Mom and Dad did their usual runs of making sure we did it right and giving us our goodnight kisses.

John and I still weren't sleepy, so we talked a bit before the sandman won us over and the next thing we knew, it was morning, with light filtering in between the blinds on John's window.

Mom suggested we all have breakfast outside to enjoy the nice morning sunshine. It only rained briefly the night before when our cookout had ended, so things weren't as soaked and water-logged as they would have been if it had rained longer.

With so many people in the house, showers took a while, but who really cared? Everybody just took turns alternating their time at the Atari while we waited for everyone to be ready.

Showering duties complete, we piled into our respective cars and headed to the lake.

It wasn't as big as the lodge and didn't have nearly as much foliage, and the woods didn't go as far, but it was enough for a nice day enjoying each other's company and for us to be able to be boys for a while, trying to catch grasshoppers and fireflies.

At one point, we all sat around and swapped stories about the new school year. Only Matt had anything interesting to talk about in the fact that he had met a girl he liked and they were talking. That prompted me to talk about Natalie, telling them I, too, was just talking to her now and then so far.

The next day was a trip to Chuck E Cheese, which would be the last time I would ever play in a ball pit. We gathered up large quantities of tickets that we wasted on large quantities of candy we ate while playing video games once we got back to John's house.

On the last day, we just sat around and stuffed ourselves with junk food and played video games until 2 PM when Uncle Steve and his family had to head out to get on the road for their long trip home. Big hugs all around and promises to stay in touch and they were on their way.

That left John and I to finish out the day playing Atari with Mom and Dad, which we did until midnight again.

After lights out, I told John, "It doesn't even matter that your school's not so good. I wish I lived here with you."

"I wish you did, too. I do hate it so much at that school."

"Yeah, same with mine."

It is the same old story: appreciating the good things you do have as a result of experiencing the bad things is a lesson life never stops teaching us.

The next morning, John's mom and dad brought me home. Lots of hugs and I love you's later, and they were on their way back home. I just spent the rest of the day in my room, missing John and Uncle Steve and his family.

When it was time for bed, I took my epilepsy medicine and lay in my bed wondering if things would ever be balanced so that things were more to the positive side of things in my life. I drifted off to sleep, dreaming about John, Matt, Thomas, Mark, and John's parents. At least I had my good dreams and memories of fun times with people I loved.

May, 1981, seventh grade

After it was determined that I would stay back in seventh grade because of my poor performance, Mother started frequenting the bar scene even more, and on one of the jaunts, she had brought him home one night to sleep over.

In the morning, they woke up and came to the table for breakfast.

"Hi, I'm Leo."

he said while holding his hand out to shake mine. Leo was about ten years or maybe older than Mother, and his skin was deeply tanned and leathery like he worked hard for a living out in the sun. Turned out that's exactly what the situation was. Leo worked for a traveling carnival. His ride that he was responsible for was the carousel, and he had a real calliope from before the turn of the 20th century that was the centerpiece of the ride.

After hearing all about it, I got to see the ride in person while he was setting it up at a location near our house.

I had been stamped on my hand as a guest of a carnival employee, so I had free reign to go wherever I pleased, as long as it was safe and I wasn't in the way as they set up. I helped set up the gates around the Scrambler and Himalaya rides, as well as the carousel, of course.

Since Mother had a thing for Leo, I got to see and be part of the setup and teardown of many rides. At one stop, I watched as the men were assembling the Himalaya ride. It has long bars that are called sweeps that extend from the center to the edge of what eventually would be the platform.

In order to secure the pieces at the entry end, someone has to insert a pin, then a secondary pin and chain, and before moving to the next one, they have to step over the next sweep and do the operation all over again. There are many sweeps, and it's one of the most time-consuming parts of setting up the ride, so I suggested

"Wouldn't it be easier if you did it from underneath?"

"Yeah, it would, kid, but none of us can fit under there."

"I can. " I told them.

"Yeah, but what if the sweep falls on you?" Tommy, the ride operator, said with concern

"You've never dropped one, yet all the times I saw you doing it. You just keep holding it and I'll steady it and tell you to move to your left or right so I can get the pin in, and then I'll slide on my back to do the next one."

Tommy looked at Jeff, one of the roustabouts, and Jeff said, "Kid's right. Might work, and it would cut our time in half."

"Alright, we'll try it."

They handed me the box of pins, and I crawled under. After the first couple of, I got a real rhythm of sliding and locking the pins in place and shifting my body to the next one, and we were done with that part of the ride's set up in less than half the time. They thanked me high-fived me, and told me to go see Joey on the scrambler to help him. I did work with pins for him too, and then I went to work helping Leo on the carousel. I had special work there as well. He taught me how to wear a riggers belt where I would be strapped to the camshaft bar, inserting the much larger pins and using a hammer to tap them into place and slide a locking pin through a hole on the other side for the poles that held the horses.

The guys all agreed that my work was so good that I should be a member of the crew. They talked to the operations manager, and he agreed and hired me on the spot. I was given a yellow plastic bracelet, signifying me as a member of the crew.

Pay was great, especially for me, being a kid being paid the same salary the adults received, and because I was crew, food and drinks cost nothing and whenever I had free time, I could ride everything all I wanted, something I took full advantage of.

I then used the same belt apparatus on the traveling rollercoaster as well, except for the highest places; I was suspended by a crane and wore a tool apron around my waist that held the pins. In the other locations, I climbed around and used a carabiner clip on a strap attached to my belt to secure myself to the framework as I darted around, slipping pins in. Basically, I was the pin boy. If your ride needed attaching pins or locking pins, I was your guy to get it done.

I became adept at the carnival games, too, learning all the secrets of each game so I could show players how to win and make it look easy doing it. I filled in for people's breaks and got to run the rides for them when they went to eat or to the bathroom.

The two rides I would most frequently 'break' the operators were the Scrambler and the carousel.

Since the carnival traveled around a lot, in a new place for a week each week, all summer and fall, it became easier for me to stay there at the carnival with the rest of the crew instead of having Leo or someone else drives me home every night after closing. Staying there also meant getting to hang out with all the guys after closing time. I learned about the ride shutdown procedures, powering down the generators, and buttoning up the midway games for the night. Then, everyone would gather in the main food tent that was usually reserved for the patrons of the carnival to have an end-of-day party. The men and women drank beer while I drank coke.

After sharing stories of the night, we talked about what needed to get done the next day before opening so we all had jobs. I was always on the pin inspection team with Tommy, making sure that all the pins on every ride were still in place. I also helped grease chains and gears and ensured the general safe operation of the rides. I checked perimeter fences to be sure they were still in their proper place and ensured that there were no other safety hazards to be worried about, such as broken or worn safety belts or other apparatus used to keep riders safe.

When the carnival isn't yet open for the day, there is a lot of work to do before the first guests are allowed in.

At the end of the night, I stayed in either Tommy's trailer or one that was shared between 4 guys, including Leo.

Mom stopped going out with Leo after that first summer when I was 12 years old, but because I was established as such a valued member of the team, the next year, and the carnival sent me a schedule of stops for the summer and asked if I would be on the crew again that summer. I, of course, said yes.

Some of the guys had nicknames, and they had one for me this year.

And upon seeing me, Tommy said, "Hey, look, Pin is back. Welcome back, man, we need you." And the whole crew high-fived me and welcomed me back.

There was a new ride that year that I became fascinated with, the Gravitron, and I loved watching it being put together. I didn't have much time to watch it, however, as like last summer, I was all over the grounds doing my pin work.

My work was done except for covering breaks one day; I decided to take a break and stood behind a girl at the Zipper line who was by herself.

"Oh good, now I won't have to ride alone," she said.

I asked her, "Why were you gonna ride alone?"

"Aw, my friend's just chicken, that's all."

"It's a great ride. Been on it?"

"No, the first time. You?"

I showed her my bracelet. "I work here."

"Oh, WOW, that is really great. So you get to ride everything free?"

"Yeah, I get free food too. And pay, of course."

"Man, I wish I was that lucky."

"It's not all fun and games, though; it's really hard work setting up and tearing down."

"Yeah, I guess so. That's why you're so sunburned. Look at your arms," she said, rubbing my arm.

A tingle went through my body at her touch.

It was our turn to ride, and we yelled a lot; she did more yelling than I did, however. After we got off the ride, she said

"Hey, wanna come with us and get something to eat?" I said sure. What's your name?"

"Katrina. And this is Elizabeth, Liz for short."

"I'm Dave. So, you're here by yourselves, not with your parents?"

"Yeah, we're both 15, so our parents trust us to go alone."

After we went to the food tent, Liz said.

"I'm really tired; I'm gonna head for home."

"You want me to come with you?" Katrina asked.

"Naw, you stay and have fun. Call me later."

"I will. K, bye."

The lights of the carnival looked especially nice that night in the thick, dark blanket of night in that vacant field where we had set up. Between times when I had to take care of breaks, Katrina stood by and watched me fill in for people in the games and rides.

She was amazed at how easy I made the ball toss look when I was demonstrating it to customers. It hit the rim of the basket just right every time and rolled in and stayed in, as it had to in order to win a prize.

"When people try it, they can't do it. But you do it every time! That's crazy!" Katrina said with surprise

As the night wore on, we walked the whole carnival numerous times, the crew had seen me with Katrina, and some of the guys gave me a thumbs-up from a distance.

"Let's go get something to drink. I'm really hot," she said, putting her hand around my waist as we walked.

After we got some cokes, we went to the funhouse ride. Remembering what had happened to Matt on the funhouse ride when we were at that amusement park, my heart started beating faster. We got on the ride, and inside, she leaned over to kiss me, and I didn't stop her. In seconds, our tongues were going at it, and my hand was under her halter top, and hers was rubbing my crotch from outside.

When we got to the end of the ride, we acted as if nothing had happened, but she wanted more.

Before getting off the ride, she said, "I want you inside me right now." I looked at her, and knowing what she meant, I went to the carousel with her. I told her to wait outside the gate, and I would be right back.

I went inside the carousel gate and pulled Leo aside, saying.

"I need a condom."

"What? Who's getting some ass tonight? Tommy?"

I said

"No, Me."

"You?!" He said, surprised.

I said, "Yeah," and I tilted my head in Katrina's direction.

"Oh, her, yeah everybody when they went on break were coming and telling me about you two walking around, talking about how lucky you are."

"So, do you have one?" I pressed.

"Yeah," and he got his wallet out, pulled one from inside, and handed it to me.

"First time?" Leo asked.

"Yeah," I said.

Leo smiled and said, "Oh boy, it's gonna be a hell of a party at closing tonight. Alright, go on, good luck, kid. I was gonna take my break in the trailer in a few minutes, so hang a sock on the door handle, so I don't walk in on you if you're still there, k?"

"K," I said.

"And remember, you're breaking Tommy in 25 minutes, so you're gonna have to make your push and squirt happen quickly."

"Yup," I said, making my way back to the fence, unlocking the entry chain, and closing it back up.

We went to the trailer, and I did as Leo said, taking off my sneakers and socks and putting the sock on the door handle before going inside.

When we emerged from the trailer 20 minutes later, we walked past the carousel, and Leo said

"Ay," and I looked back, and he mimed a question mark in the air as if to ask if I was successful. I gave a thumbs up, and he pumped his fist in the air a couple of times.

I said goodnight to Katrina a little while later and she gave me her number to call her.

At the close of the day, the whole crew was inside the food tent, waiting for Tommy and I to get there after finishing the work of making sure all the midway games were secure for the night

As we entered, all the guys had shaken their bottles of beer and were holding their thumbs over the top, and as Tommy and I walked in, they showered me in the spray of beer foam and were hugging me and putting their hands on my shoulder and shaking my hand."

"Congrats on losing your virginity, buddy."

"You're a man now."

"That's it, no more wondering what pussy's like anymore."

and similar comments were thrown around by all the guys and even some of the women who worked at the carnival."

"That was the best-looking girl to come here in FOREVER, too! Dude, HOW did you bag that babe?!!"

"I dunno, just happened. Started talking to her in line at the Zipper, and that's it."

Laughter all around.

"That's IT?!" said Tommy. "Bro, let me have some of whatever YOU'VE got, being able to get a girl like that who's MY age."

"How old was she?" Leo asked.

"15," I said.

"And you're, what, 13?"

"Yup. 14 in a few weeks"

"DAAAAAMMMMNNNN!" and "SHIIIIIITTTT!" all the guys said

"Well, it comes as no surprise, him being able to get in tight places with his PIN," Tommy said, starting a wave of uproarious laughter and everyone chanting, "PIN! PIN! PIN! PIN! PIN!"

And spraying me with more beer.

"Wait, wait, I have a question." Ralph from the ice cream booth said, "What's that mark on your neck?

I rubbed my neck where he pointed.

"Oh, I guess she did that there too."

"TOO? What do you MEAN 'too'? You got ANOTHER hickey?"

I said, "Yeah, on my thigh, right by my crotch."

More cheers.

"She MARKED you so other women will know you belong to another girl! Oh man, kid, she's got it BAAAAD for you!" Ralph said.

"Did you get her number?" Tommy asked.

"Yeah."

Still more cheers

"Yeah, go buy some more condoms 'cuz as long as we're set up here, she will be back for more."

"Think so?" I said.

"Dude, she marked you TWICE and gave you her number. Trust me, she will be back for more dick. Wait and see."

I took the guys' advice and bought a six-pack of condoms at the pharmacy. It was a good thing I did because the guys were right; she came back every day we were there, and all six condoms were gone in 4 days. The joke among the crew became that when a sock was on a door, any door, even if it wasn't me, they said it must have been me laying pipe.

It might not have been love in that traditional sense with Katrina, but I loved the way she made me feel and vice versa, and at least I was following dad and uncle Steve's advice and using a condom every time.

Looking back, even though the crew's behavior was kind of nasty and juvenile in regard to women, these people lived a hard life every day. They didn't have the luxury of a girl to go home to every night. Their place of residence was wherever they were set up that day. Traditional relationships just generally don't work for them. The carnival is one of the toughest ways of life, and few women want to live it 24/7. The 3 or 4 women we had working for the carnival were the rare exceptions, being married to one of the crew members.

Not that long ago, I had to learn what it meant to be a boy by being one of the boys, and now I was learning what it meant to be a guy by being one of the guys. There are far worse situations in this life, as I can most certainly attest. Like all the fun I had with Matt, Thomas and Mark, the carnival crew is one of the few great memories I have growing up, and I will cherish the hard work and fun we all had during those summers. These were people who were there for each other no matter what.

At the end of that summer, I still stayed on for weekends throughout September and most of October, so one of the crew would drive me back and forth on those weekends so I could still be part of the crew.

I had sacked away quite a sum of money after those summers and spent little of it, so I was going to open a bank account with the money. I was preparing to leave the house on a Saturday morning to go to the bank to get a new savings account when I went to the drawer where I had hidden the money in a sock at the back, and the sock was gone. I took all the dresser drawers out and looked in the drawers and in the empty dresser itself, and nothing.

I figured maybe somehow the sock with the money had gone into the clothes basket with the dirty clothes to be washed. I checked it. Nothing.

Grandma said, "What are you looking for?"

"I had a sock with money in it in my drawer, and I can't find it," I told her

Mother was sitting at the table nursing a drink and smoking a cigarette, and she said

"Oh, that money is gone."

"WHAT?!" I said

"I needed money to pay the rent and bills. So I took it."

My head was spinning. All that work, all those days setting up and tearing down in the hot sun and drenching rain, all those hours and hours, and all the money was gone.

"You had no FUCKING RIGHT to TAKE my MONEY!" I screamed

She got up and lifted me up by the chin and threw me backward. My head hit the stove

"Don't you try talking to ME like that? And yes, I DID have the right because this is MY house and YOU are living in it and if YOU are making money, then YOU can contribute to the household expenses. Don't like it? Fuck you. Move out."

I was livid beyond all imagining. I wanted so much to hurt her right now, to make her feel what she put me through all these years, to make her understand how wrong she was for stealing my money, but I just couldn't do it. Just as I came to the realization that I wasn't going to allow myself to become anything like my bullies, I wasn't going to allow myself to become like her, either.

I left the room and went to my room to pack some things and then returned to the living room closet, took out a jacket, and went for a walk.

I still had at least a little money in my wallet, so I went to the Y. I just couldn't stand being in that house right now. I got in before without an adult and now I was older, so I figured I would be able to get in again, plus I could pay my way. I didn't care where I was right now, all I knew was I was out of the house for the moment, and that meant everything to me.

March 1983 - Eighth Grade, September 1984 - Ninth Grade

Eighth grade had been proceeding along as the previous two years in seventh had, with my work only slightly improving and Mother's never-ending fits of rage and hatred of me not showing any signs of slowing down, although I did seem to hit a bit of a growth spurt and due to my work at the carnival, had developed some adequate muscles that I could use to free myself and flee more easily when she started in on me. My eighth-grade teacher was a lady by the name of Mrs. Bystrowski, and while she had a good heart and cared about the kids, she wasn't a very good teacher, choosing to focus so heavily on religion that everything else took a backseat and therefore wasn't as highly regarded.

I had graduated eighth grade and couldn't have been more thrilled than to be leaving Catholic school forever. I had taken an entrance exam to a technical trade school and was accepted with adequate scores in mathematics but above-average reading and language skills.

On my first day, I was in the hallway waiting to enter a classroom while rosters were updated by administration and I struck up a conversation with another boy who was standing next to me at the time.

"So much paperwork and waiting. I thought that orientation talk would never end." I said to him.

"Yeah, those things always go on too long. Do you know what your homeroom is gonna be now?" He replied.

"Yeah, I'm D-3. You?"

"I'm in D-1"

"I'm Dave."

"I'm Allen."

With that meeting, we were then instructed over the school PA system where we were to proceed next, as teachers in the hall also helped students along, giving directions and helping the freshman class get where we needed to go.

The first days and months of high school were the usual ups and downs. At home, things were changing, however.

We had moved yet again, just around the corner and up the street, to a much nicer apartment. I had been working in Pasquale's Market, stocking shelves to get some of my own spending money. I wasn't earning what I had at the carnival, but at least it was a little something to make my meager existence better.

Grandma had a smoker's cough for the previous year or so that was steadily getting worse. She hadn't smoked nearly as much as my mother, who was a pack-a-day smoker by this point, but she did still have at least 10 cigarettes a day. Multiply that by the 50 years she had been doing so, and the damage to her body had clearly been done.

Mornings were especially bad, and she was hacking up phlegm for a half hour each day.

Just past the beginning of the year in 1985, Grandma was losing large amounts of weight due to not eating, and she was becoming weak. Her breathing was labored all the time, even when she wasn't doing anything considered stressful. She hated doctors, in spite of her insistence that I see them during my bleeding kidney episode. Still, we insisted that she go to the hospital to get checked out.

It was determined that she had emphysema and stage 4 lung cancer. They also found that it had metastasized and gone to several parts of her body. The prognosis wasn't good. It was deemed that she wouldn't be able to withstand the many treatments and procedures she would need to have in order to fight the disease, and even if she had done so, it was no guarantee that she would be able to survive much more than a year if she was even that lucky. The cancer had simply taken her body over.

Mother and I visited her and watched her get worse with each visit. I called John and Uncle Steve to tell them about it, and they all came to see her as well. In the last week, she had to have fluid removed from her lungs constantly, and she was on a ventilator nonstop. At the beginning of her fourth week in the hospital, we decided to turn the ventilator off and remove her ventilator mask and I held Grandma's hand as she passed away. She couldn't speak, but the last words she mouthed were to me:

"I love you."

And Grandma was gone.

My one beacon of hope, the only source of continuous light and unconditional love in my life was no more.

I was destroyed.

John, his parents, Uncle Steve, and his family all attended the funeral. A distant cousin of hers that I never knew she had was there as well. Some of her coworkers from when she had worked at a bank before retirement were also in attendance, but that was about it. John, Matt, Thomas, and Mark, seeing the state I was in, took turns holding me while I got the tears out. The thing is, I could never have cried enough tears and was crying inside long after I exhausted the tears in my eyes.

Mother looked like her normal self, just going through the motions, saying what needed to be said, entirely unemotional at all.

Mother disposed of Grandma's things immediately following the funeral, and her room in the apartment wasn't used anymore.

My world was turned upside down. I had no desire to go to school and stayed home for over a week.

Mother made no mention of her, no acknowledgment of Grandma's existence, and continued as if this was just life as usual.

I hated Mother before, but now I hated her so intently with every fiber of my being to such a degree that I wished it had been her buried six feet in the ground instead of Grandma.

I felt guilty for spending more of my time away from home in the recent years before her death, was sad that I missed out on more time with her, wanted to have more time to have a proper goodbye, but I came to realize that any amount of time with the loved ones we hold so dear is not enough, and I also realized that my hatred for mother and wishing that she were the one who was dead was useless, because effectively, my whole life, she WAS dead.

April 1984 - Ninth Grade

Back in school, we went through exploratory shops for that first year, and we would spend two weeks in regular classes and then two weeks in one of the classes the school offered until we had experienced all of them before deciding which one to pursue for the remaining 3 years.

I was trying to decide between drafting and carpentry and while I was deciding, I was getting to know Allen better. He had quickly become a best friend to me and was the one saving grace in a very typical and mundane high school experience.

One day, when I came home late because I had spent time with Allen at his house, Mother approached me as usual, with her liquor-stench-ridden breath, and she said

"Why don't you just get the FUCK out for good if you don't want to be here, just GO! Go on, FUCK OFF, you've never been anything but a worthless bastard anyway. She moved to punch me, and I grabbed her fist and flung it away from me. I got right in her face, screaming

If you EVER raise a hand to me again it will be your LAST because I will put you THROUGH THE WALL! Now LEAVE ME ALONE!!! NOW AND FOREVER, LEAVE...ME ....ALONE!!!"

She backed down and slithered away and back into her glass of booze.

I had done it. She never touched me again. I had taken control and said enough was enough, effectively defending myself.

The first step in my life, free of physical abuse, had begun.

That night, alone in my room, in my mind, I thanked grandma, John, for his parents, uncle Steve and their family, my carnival family, and my then-new best friend Allen, who all contributed to making me into the person who could finally do what needed to be done. Thanks to all of them, I was no longer that frail little boy anymore who believed he was nothing because Mother said so. I was a strong person who was ready to take life on, and I didn't hate myself anymore. I was celebrating being me and a REAL new start in my life, more profound than any I had yet encountered.

I was free.

Epilogue

There is nothing worse than betraying the trust of a child. All adults who are a major influence or part of a child's life have a duty to their safety and welfare. People who are sworn to be the guardians of children's well-being have a responsibility to do what they swore to do when they decided to become advocates and educators of children. That wasn't the case with Officer Mike or the school administration years later, who didn't follow through on the warning signs and ample evidence in front of them.

The life I went through as a child with the level of extreme physical and psychological abuse I endured from my mother and the bullies is incomprehensible, but even in today's day and age, where people are quicker to report suspicions and the abundant amount of services available, child abuse still exists.

The people who were part of my life shaped me and who I became: the strong and resolute person who was not going to stand for it any longer. Every experience for a child is a learning one, and sometimes it can take years of work and inner growth to be strong enough to advocate for yourself.

The one piece of advice I can give anyone who is experiencing abuse is to look to yourself and the positive life experiences the people who genuinely care about you have provided as your strength and realize that you are not that person the abuser or abusers tell you that you are. You are a person just like anyone else, and no one deserves to be abused in any way even one time.

I trusted a police officer and school administrators to keep me safe, but they failed. If the system is failing you, then you have to be your own voice, your own power, to make it stop happening. There are listings for support services at the end of this epilogue that can help you to start advocating for yourself. You can make the violence stop. I know because I did.

Also, in today's world of more prevention resources and a greater understanding of the detrimental and highly traumatic effects of bullying, there is no excuse for anyone, most especially educators and those entrusted to the care of children and teens, to turn a blind eye to it or allow it to go on. Are you actively involved with anti-bullying programs or initiatives that your school or child's school offers? Get active right away. Your participation could save children emotional or physical distress or injury, or it could even save their lives.

Regardless of whether it is verbal or physical abuse or the proliferation of online bullying that has made it impossible for a child to escape their tormentors even when they are in their safe spaces, everyone, whether they believe their child or children are being abused or not, regardless of whether their child or children have been labeled as bullies or not, we all need to be part of the process to help stop bullying.

As far as where everyone wound up in my life story, I still talk to John and his parents after all these years. When I told John and his parents that I had planned to write my life story, John's parents told me that it was one of the hardest things they felt they had to do in their lives when they moved to the next town. The alternatives for John at that time were Catholic school, for which they didn't want to waste tuition money that could be saved for college, or public school, where they couldn't take the chance of John going through more experiences such as what happened with his cracked ribs and nearly ruptured spleen.

When John's dad was offered the position in his company in the next town over in a much better school district, they eventually came to the realization that they just had to take it, but it broke their hearts having to leave me behind knowing the reality I faced at home. Over the years, and particularly at the end of that sixth-grade year, they did what they did for me in the best way they thought would be possible, helping me have refuge with the person their son called and treated as his brother. If they had called the authorities, it could have set off a whole chain of events that would have probably made my life even more miserable in the family services and foster care system, and being away from their family and grandma who I loved. I am truly grateful for all that they did for me and how they taught me about life and what a true family is all about. I still love them with all my heart and think of them as family.

I lost touch with Matt, Thomas, Mark, and their parents after a few years, as people tend to do as they get older and meet new people and life gets busier.

Carnival life being what it is, I lost touch with them also. When I moved, just as high school was beginning, I never had their schedule of stops forwarded to the new address. If I had, I probably would have worked for them again for another few summers. Carnival people get a bad reputation as being 'carny trash' but the people at the carnival where I worked were NOT like that. They were extremely hard-working people with great hearts and an incredible sense of duty and purpose, and they were always there for each other in times of need. It takes a special kind of person to work in the traveling carnival industry, and believe me when I tell you, these people who surrounded me at the carnival where I worked were just that: special.

My epilepsy, thankfully, was something I grew out of. By the middle of the first year of high school, I was no longer taking medication for it, and EEG and scans of my head proved I was likely to be free of seizures.

Juan has a family of his own, and his mother worked as a cafeteria lunch lady until she finally retired a few years ago.

Peter became a forest ranger and I can't find anything on Paulo. He had a lot of family in Portugal so he may have moved back there not long after 8th grade.

Eggy and his friends are all either dead or in prison as a result of gang affiliation, which should not surprise you. Stephane is dead as well, and Glen, though still alive, has a long list of run-ins with the law. I've heard that Natalie and her brother Michael are both doing well and have families of their own as well.

Miss Levesque retired the year after I graduated 8th grade, and she lived out the rest of her life doing work with the church. Most of my teachers from elementary school have also passed on, and so has Mr. Shedruff.

Allen became the second person in my life I was proud to call my best friend, but he is second to no one. Like John before him, Allen is one of the finest people with one of the kindest hearts I have ever met. He has 3 kids of his own and a grandson that I am proud to call my great-nephew.

If you want to know more about where my story took me next and learn more about Allen's influence on my life, I will be doing a follow up to this first part of my autobiography soon. I am planning to call it 'Healed Man.' You may not believe this, but I became a teacher and have been one for 25 years now. But that's another story...

I truly hope that you find the strength or help someone else find the strength to end the violence, to end the psychological abuse. Below are services to help you on your quest to become free, as I did, or help someone else who needs it.

Child help abuse services: call or text 800 422 4453

Suicide prevention hotline: 988

Resources for reporting suspected abuse: ChildCare.gov

Physiciansupportline.com 888 409 0141 offers emotional support and services for people experiencing issues related to circumstances leading to PTSD.

Boystown national hotline 800 488 3000 for children and parents dealing with anxiety, depression, bullying, abuse, and suicide intent.

STOMPoutbullying.org and nationalsafeplace.org for bullying online chat support.

Crisistextline.org for confidential support.

Thetrevorproject.org at 866 488 7386 for LGBTQ+ issues.

Teenlineonline.org at 800 852 8336 for all teen-related issues.